Counseling Psychology

Strategies and Services

Counseling Psychology
Strategies and Services

Robert Henley Woody
University of Nebraska at Omaha

James C. Hansen
State University of New York at Buffalo

Robert H. Rossberg
State University of New York at Buffalo

Brooks/Cole Publishing Company
Pacific Grove, California

Brooks/Cole Publishing Company
A Division of Wadsworth, Inc.

© 1989 by Wadsworth, Inc., Belmont, California 94002. All rights reserved. No part of this book may be reproduced, stored in a retrieval system, or transcribed, in any form or by any means—electronic, mechanical, photocopying, recording, or otherwise—without the prior written permission of the publisher, Brooks/Cole Publishing Company, Pacific Grove, California 93950, a division of Wadsworth, Inc.

Printed in the United States of America

10 9 8 7 6 5 4 3 2 1

Library of Congress Cataloging-in-Publication Data

Woody, Robert Henley.
 Counseling psychology : strategies and services / Robert Henley
Woody, James C. Hansen, and Robert H. Rossberg.
  p.   cm.
 Bibliography: p.
 Includes index.
 ISBN 0534100023
 1. Counseling. 2. Psychotherapy.   I. Hansen, James C.
II. Rossberg, Robert H.   III. Title.
BF637.C6W66   1989
158'.3—dc19   88-31705
                                                         CIP

Sponsoring Editor: *Claire Verduin*
Marketing Representative: *Dawn Beke*
Editorial Assistant: *Gay C. Bond*
Production Coordinator: *Fiorella Ljunggren*
Production: *Stacey C. Sawyer*
Manuscript Editor: *William Waller*
Interior and Cover Design: *Vernon T. Boes*
Typesetting: *Straight Creek Company*
Cover Printing: *Phoenix Color Corporation*
Printing and Binding: *Arcata Graphics/Fairfield*

Preface

The origins of counseling psychology go back almost half a century, but its emergence as a mature psychological specialty has taken place over the last 25 years. Despite meeting with an icy reception from some quarters, the discipline continued to grow, drawing its strength from behavioral science, education, and humanistic philosophy. Now it stands proudly as a well-developed human-service specialty, with its taproot reaching the established scientist/practitioner model.

Counseling psychology has always been a specialty in search of an identity. Nevertheless, it is inextricably related to professional psychology, and it maintains its connections to education. Public policy provides a home for counseling psychology in social, health, and other human sevices, as well as in education. Governmental regulations, such as licensing, are devoted to the nurturance of counseling psychology.

In preparing this book, *Counseling Psychology: Strategies and Services,* we have sought to resolve any dissonance that might still be voiced. For example, some university training programs still have difficulty moving from an antiquated orchestration of counseling and the rest of professional psychology to a modern-day harmonization. We have also tried to recognize the future concerns and uncertainties of counseling psychologists.

Foremost, this book is intended to serve as a text for any graduate-level course devoted to introducing students and trainees to the scope of counseling psychology. We stress the uniqueness of counseling psychology and also give attention to clarifying its links to various other educational and psychological specialties. This text is designed for training counselors in various counselor-education and counseling-psychology programs.

Beyond being useful as "basic training" in the classroom, the book has contemporary qualities that make it useful to practitioners already in the field. We have included many practical suggestions and guidelines, as well as the research on which they are predicated. This text can be a guidebook for experienced professionals who wish to improve their services to clients and stay up to date.

Our material is designed to identify strategies that are clearly aligned with the specialty and to prepare the reader to apply them. We have also, however, included ideas, methods, and strategies that deserve further research and refinement. We have given particular attention to ensuring that the reader grasps the evolution of each point, acquires knowledge of both the theoretical and the technical facets, and accepts that the composition of counseling psychology is not final.

In planning this book, we recognized that some of the most useful learning that we and our students and trainees had gained had come from actual services to clients. Thus we were committed to making the material practical and in tune with the reality of practice. We reveal what actually occurs on the job, as opposed to the ivory-tower perspective that often plagues the university classroom. We deem it essential that the early stages of training be tailored to the societal and professional expectations placed on the counseling psychologist emerging from the campus to the world of work.

Chapter 1, "The History and Development of Counseling Psychology," defines the role of the helper in social systems and describes the evolution and emergence of counseling psychology. Chapter 2, "Public Policy Mandates for Counseling Psychology," makes it clear that the stature and nature of counseling psychology are determined by the needs and preferences of society as manifested in legislation and governmental priorities. The professional is not free to be self-determining.

With the foregoing historical and public policy backdrop, important theoretical and technical alternatives are explored in Chapter 3, "Critical Theories of Counseling." and Chapter 4, "Individual Counseling and Therapy."

Service contexts are emphasized in Chapter 5, "Career-Development Strategies," Chapter 6, "Group Counseling and Therapy," and Chapter 7, "Family Therapy." Two primary skill areas are the focus of Chapter 8, "Clinical Assessment," and Chapter 9, "Consultation." Two rapidly expanding subspecialities for counseling psychologists are detailed in Chapter 10, "Forensic Psychology," and Chapter 11, "Health Psychology."

Finally, our initial evolutionary and public policy considerations are given contemporary analysis in Chapter 12, "Ethics and Law." It is crucial that the counseling psychologist adhere to the standard of care required by professional ethics, governmental regulations, and the law. Otherwise, sanctions, penalties, and malpractice judgments can be imposed.

We consistently maintain allegiance to the academic aspects of counseling psychology. Nonetheless, we wish to underscore the importance of cultivating the personal aspects. A postitive self-concept and healthy lifestyle are as essential as academic knowledge to the effective practice of counseling psychology. This quest for the fully functioning person is interlaced throughout the material.

The preparation of this book has renewed our spirit for advancing counseling psychology. We hope that we can afford the reader the same motivation.

Acknowledgments

We are grateful to the following reviewers for their helpful comments and suggestions: Virginia B. Allen of Idaho State University, Sheldon A. Grand of the State University of New York at Albany, Diane McDermott of the University of Kansas, David J. Reynolds of Temple University, and Holly Stadler of the University of Missouri.

Robert Henley Woody
James C. Hansen
Robert H. Rossberg

Contents

Chapter 1

**The History and Development of
   Counseling Psychology**   *1*

Historical Background   2
The Emergence of Counseling Psychology   6
Whiteley's Historical Periods in the Development of
      Counseling Psychology   11
Professional Concerns   16
The Future of Counseling Psychology   16

Chapter 2

**Public Policy Mandates for Counseling
   Psychology**   *19*

The Origin of Helping Services   19
The Origins of Public Policy   20
The Effect of Legislation   21
Public Policy Mandates for the Future   26
Credentialing and Licensure of Counseling Psychologists   27
Summary   29

Chapter 3

Critical Theories of Counseling   *32*

The Two Cultures of Psychology   33
The Science of Behavior and the Image of Humankind   36
The Issue of Determinism and Freedom   38
Value Orientations   39

Critical Counseling Theories   45
Summary   53

Chapter 4

Individual Counseling and Therapy   55

The Therapeutic Relationship   56
Skills Used in the Therapeutic Relationship   60
Social Factors Influencing the Therapeutic Relationship   72
Summary   78

Chapter 5

Career-Development Strategies   84

The Role of Work in Society   84
Vocational Development and Career Patterns   86
Developmental Counseling:
        A Framework for Counseling Psychologists   91
Specific Interventions in Career Development   93
The Settings of Vocational and Educational Counseling   97
Special Concerns in Career Development   100
Summary   103

Chapter 6

Group Counseling and Therapy   107

Types of Groups   107
Group Dynamics   109
Stages of a Group   115
Summary   125

Chapter 7

Family Therapy   128

The Development of Family Therapy   128
The Family as a System   129
Minuchin's Structural Approach   132
Bowen's Family-of-Origin Approach   139
Satir's Communications Approach   143
Summary   147

Chapter 8

Clinical Assessment 150

Historical and Evolution of Clinical Assessment in
  Counseling Psychology 150
Aspects of Clinical Assessment 154
Diagnosis 155
Using the Diagnosis to Guide Treatment 156
Applications of Clinical Assessment to Counseling
  Psychology 159
Assessment Methods for Counseling Psychology 162
Summary 167

Chapter 9

Consultation 171

History of Consultation 171
Definition of Consultation 172
Models of Consultation 173
Consultation Procedures 179
Research on Consultation 183
Summary 183

Chapter 10

Forensic Psychology 186

Entering the Legal System 188
Criminal Justice 194
Institutionalized Mental Patients 201
Family Law 204
Personal-Injury Law 208
Summary 213

Chapter 11

Health Psychology 217

The Goal of Health 220
Dealing with Stress 222
Body/Mind Liberation 227
Beyond the Individual Client 230
Toward Being a Health-Oriented Counseling Psychologist 232
Summary 233

Chapter 12

Ethics and Law

Professional Ethics   237
Distinguishing Ethics and the Law   242
The Law   243
Selected Problem Areas in Ethics and the Law   246
Summary   262

Appendix A: Ethical Principles of Psychologists   267
Appendix B: Ethical Standards   277
Name Index   287
Subject Index   295

1

The History
and Development of
Counseling Psychology

Humans have constantly struggled against the unknown and against the ignorance, fear, and anxiety it induces. One of the most pervasive human emotions is a sense of impotence in dealing with forces that are beyond our understanding and control. Throughout history, however, we have managed to construct moral codes to govern our behavior and social institutions to help us interpret our behavior. As a colleague and I have written elsewhere:

> There is a historical constancy to this search for help by [humankind] that is compelling. It constitutes a kind of imperative that suggests that fear, anxiety, in fact any confrontation with the unknown has created a demand for a mediator, an interlocutor, and intervener between [human beings] and the unknown. Every society has produced some such person [Rossberg & Band, 1978, p. 4].

In some societies the role of helper has been filled by priests. In others this role has been combined with that of the healer In still other societies the political leader or solver of social problems has emerged to perform this function. In modern and seemingly more complex societies, applied psychologists have largely assumed this role.

Indeed, the role of helper has become increasingly specialized as the problems to be addressed have themselves become more complex. According to Halmos (1966), "the loneliness of man in mass society and his increasing concern with personal relationships has encouraged the emergence of a microsociology, a sociology of friendships, acquaintanceships, and face-to-face cooperation" (p. 25). The professionalization of this process in the 20th century has led to the further development of applied psychology in a culture where "the dominant motive seems to be personal unhappiness about concrete human relationships" (p. 26).

Counselors have come to add their insights to this continuing search for meaning in the human condition.

Some contemporary writers are quite cynical about the counselor's efforts. Barzun refers to this modern manifestation of intervention as "philanthropic moralism," which "means to cure or at least to help at any cost" (1959, p. 23). He also questions the motives of at least some who enter this field, speculating

1

that their desire to help may be both generous and selfish and may have implications for personal power and control. With respect to the relationship between helping and power, McClelland asserts that even though it appears the helpers are acting from generous motives, they may in fact be exercising power over the person receiving help:

> One way of looking at giving is to perceive that for help to be given, help must be received. And in accepting a gift, in help, the receiver can be perceived as acknowledging that he is weaker, at least in this respect, than the person who is giving him help. Thus giving and receiving may have a ''zero sum'' quality analogous to winning and losing. To the extent that one person wins or gives, the other must lose or receive. [1975, p. 18].

Another critic, Paul Halmos, has labeled counselors a secular priesthood that identifies its ministry as implementing a ''comprehensive moral purpose, [in] a kind of humanistic Kingdom of God'' (1966, p. 28). He comments further that the professionalization of this process has provided ''excellent camouflage for [counselors'] *'agape'* and the formal technological jargon, the impersonal clinical manners, the social science collaterals and so on have all helped to reassure the counselor that he was doing a job of work and no more'' (p. 31).

These are strong sentiments, perhaps expressed with excessive rancor, but they nevertheless require us to confront their implications. Indeed, it is possible to recognize elements of truth in the observations of Halmos, Barzun, and McClelland while proceeding to examine the historical and social forces that led to the evolution of the applied professional activity known as counseling psychology.

Historical Background

Whiteley (1984) identifies five basic roots of counseling psychology: (1) the vocational-guidance movement, (2) the mental-health movement, (3) the psychometric movement, (4) the development of applied nonmedical counseling and psychotherapy, and (5) certain social and economic forces that contributed to the evolution of the profession.

The Vocational-Guidance Movement

The history of applied psychology has its roots in ''the rise of empirical science and the increasing influence of a commercial-industrial social class'' beginning in the late 18th century (Miller, 1971, p. 38). These two developments led to the need for a more democratically based school system to train qualified workers for the ever-burgeoning industrial complex. Indeed, the demand for workers with special skills and the need for personnel to help channel these prospective workers into increasingly complex jobs made it inevitable that the role of the schools would expand dramatically and that a social mandate for the vocational guidance of youth would emerge. As Miller notes, the division of labor brought about by the industrialization of American society, the growth of technological complexity, the emergence of vocational education, and the extension of opportunity to increasingly large segments of the population made the evolution of a guidance function necessary.

The growth of empirical science, particularly as it applied to the field of mental measurement, naturally created a need for the merger of vocational guidance with the empirical technical knowledge of assessing skills through testing. At first this process was fairly primitive because of the limited knowledge in the field. Super (1942) writes that the increasingly technical developments in individual analysis, particularly refinements in test development, led many of the early psychologists in this field to assume that the process of assessment was congruent with vocational guidance. He cites a 1928 work in which the psychologist Clark Hull "enthusiastically described the prospect of a purely mechanical type of vocational guidance in which the counselee is given a battery of tests which is automatically scored to prescribe the vocation which the counselee should enter" (Super, 1942, p. 4).

Hull's notions were expressed almost two decades after the publication of Frank Parsons' 1909 textbook *Choosing a Vocation.* Parsons established the basic approach to vocational guidance that was to dominate the field for decades. His paradigm included three major tasks for the counselor, namely, individual analysis, occupational study, and "true reasoning" designed to help counselors understand their characteristics and their relationship to the world of work (Super, 1942). In fact, the extension of Parsons' paradigm, the development of technological advances in the psychology of human assessment (particularly the measurement of individual differences), and advances in the sociology of work were all part of the exciting developments in vocational psychology that influenced the specialty of counseling psychology.

Two significant events in the early 20th century marked the expansion of vocational guidance. These were the convening in 1910 of a national conference on vocational guidance by the Boston Chamber of Commerce and the subsequent formation in 1913 of the National Vocational Guidance Association (Whiteley, 1984). The latter organization was in many ways the precursor of professional developments that ultimately led to what we now know as counseling psychology.

The Mental-Health Movement

Our understanding of mental illness evolved in large part from Sigmund Freud's conceptualization of human motivation. He was the first observer to note the continuity between mental illness and mental health, particularly in the relationship between early experiences and later behavior (Rossberg & Band, 1978). These observations led to the development of a psychology of personality and an understanding of human development that contributed to changes in attitudes about the treatment of mental illness. Indeed, before Freud there was widespread doubt that any intervention could be useful in dealing with psychopathology. The notion of the reversibility of mental illness was a direct outgrowth of Freudian discoveries and contributed to research and professional training in human development, clinical psychology, and various subspecialties in educational psychology.

The recognition that the mentally ill had strengths that could be used in their rehabilitation became a major part of Donald E. Super's theories. In a seminal article in 1955 he described the metamorphosis of vocational guidance into counseling psychology and pointed out the unique role of the counseling psychologist in working with the residual competencies of individuals with significant mental-health disabilities (Super, 1955). Concern with the prevention of mental illness became a focus of counseling psychologists as the specialty emerged.

The Psychometric Movement

The evolution of objective methods for assessing people's abilities was critical to the development of counseling psychology, providing a solid empirical base. Individual analysis, part of Parsons' classical paradigm, was transformed from an intuitive, individual effort dependent on the insight of the counselor to a more scientifically based process. The validity of its predictions of success in various educational and occupationally related activities continuously improved.

As Anastasi notes,

> Group testing was launched during World War I with the Army Alpha and Army Beta designed for military selection and classification. Soon many group intelligence tests, modeled after these prototypes, were produced to serve similar purposes in industry and in the educational system, from kindergarten to graduate and professional schools [1984, p. 358].

A testing boom in the post–World War I era led to the development of instruments to measure interests, aptitudes, achievement, and personality. Mass testing was a possibility, and although the industry did not live up to the expectations of the scientific community with respect to Clark Hull's dream of an automatic vocational prescription, the development of the psychometric movement has proceeded across the decades and now provides a broad spectrum of assessment devices. Complete with imperfections, testing is now part of the repertoire of every counseling psychologist.

The Refinement of Nonmedical Counseling

Parsons' original conception of counseling was based on the aspect of his paradigm for guidance that he labeled "true reasoning." It was a rational process that related the data obtained by analyzing the individual with the occupational study. It contained none of the nuances and subtleties that have come to inform more advanced counseling methods. True reasoning was intended to be matter-of-fact and quite prescriptive in its focus. Parsons' original work contained an abundance of gratuitous observations and advice as an appendix to his main theme of "choosing a vocation." For example, he advised his readers to be wary of physicians. In addition, he suggested that each person had an obligation to perspire freely on a daily basis, a graphic example of his advice to exercise.

Nevertheless, counselors were searching for more gentle ways to help people make educational and occupational decisions. The work of E. G. Williamson (1939) and W. H. Cowley (1937) and the tenets of general clinical counseling (Hahn & Maclean, 1950) were all attempts to move in this direction. The vision of clinical counseling shared by many of the aforementioned writers was of an essentially rational, logical, gently guiding system in which the counselor assumed much of the responsibility for the process. Among the principles espoused by Hahn and Maclean as guidelines for general clinical counseling were the following (pp. 38–57):

- Counseling should not be forced on individuals.
- Counselors must strive to develop client understanding of self and environment.
- The counselor should act as a special type of corrective mirror.
- The counselor should help the counselee consider all practical educational-vocational alternatives.
- Counselors must search out all the angles of a counselee problem and use all pertinent tools and techniques in its solution.

Although these principles included an admonition that "final educational-vocational decisions must be made by the counselee," the locus of responsibility, the selection of the tools and techniques, and the analysis of the data remained largely the province of the counselor. Counseling was intended to deal largely with educational and vocational problems. In addition, the unfortunate designation of "directive counseling" was including in this approach, implying that adherents of this viewpoint were imitating the medical model. This model implies that the professional counselor collects information, analyzes the latter, and then comes to a conclusion by virtue of his/her own reasoning. The implication is that the client is a passive participant in the establishment of an intervention strategy.

If this point of view could be said to reflect a rational/empirical view of humankind and the world, Carl Rogers's perception was significantly different. Rogers was influenced by a phenomenological viewpoint that shifted the locus of responsibility from the counselor to the client, on the assumption that the real issue of counseling was clients' experience and their perception of that experience. Changes in behavior would occur not by rational/empirical (directive) intervention but rather by providing a climate in which clients were free to change their self-perceptions. Rogers believed that changes in behavior resulted from these changes in self-perception. This view represented a fundamental shift away from an authoritatively based counseling to a less directive, indeed *nondirective,* approach. (We shall explore these issues in greater depth in Chapter 3, "Critical Theories of Counseling.")

Rogers (1942, 1951) helped shift the focus of attention of counselors away from a strict concern with educational and vocational problems toward increased attention to the affective and emotional domains of human development and behavior. This influence extended the interests of counseling psychologists to the broader issues of human adjustment. It certainly raised the possibility of an alternative style of intervention in the lives of clients. In fact, in equating counseling and psychotherapy, Rogers raised the issue of nonmedical intervention and interaction with clients who presented a variety of life-role problems, including family relationships, adjustment to disability, and general social adjustment.

The Effect of Social Change on the Development of the Profession

The final historical root identified by Whiteley had to do with "the social and economic forces and developments in society which have had an impact on the profession" (1984, p. 5). Schwebel (1984) notes that a number of developments after World War II contributed to the general growth of professional psychology in the United States and to the evolution of counseling psychology in particular. These developments included the public's growing awareness and acceptance of applied professional psychology, returning veterans' increasing demands for personal and career counseling, and an evolution in the scientific underpinnings of professional practice. As a result, counseling services expanded in universities and colleges, professional psychology developed in the Veterans Administration, and training programs for professional psychology expanded.

Whiteley provides a fitting summary of almost half a century of evolution by noting that "by the end of the second world war a largely political reform movement (vocational guidance), the mental hygiene movement, two influences from organized psychology (psychometrics and psychotherapy), and the effects of two world wars merged to produce a field of applied-scientific psychology that had greatly outgrown its vocational guidance roots" (1984, p. 5).

The Emergence of Counseling Psychology

Counseling psychology as a subspecialty emerged from the synthesis of the forces outlined above at about the midpoint of the 20th century. Whiteley traces the evolution of the Division of Counseling Psychology of the American Psychological Association through a series of steps. He notes that with the previous establishment of the Divisions of Clinical Psychology, Counseling Psychology, Educational Psychology, Industrial Psychology, and School Psychology and the impending organization of the Divisions of Psychologists in Public Service and of Military Psychology, the shift toward an applied professional emphasis in the APA was well under way (1984, p. 10). Interest in establishing a Division of Counseling Psychology had a number of origins, including developments within the Veterans Administration and among some of the members of the National Vocational Guidance Association. In addition, a number of independent lines of investigation were synthesized and ultimately culminated in the evolution of comprehensive research activities in the area of vocational development theory. At the same time, the maturation of the field of rehabilitation psychology contributed to the emergence of counseling psychology.

Developments in the Veterans Administration

After World War II the Veterans Administration was given a mandate to help returning veterans in the transition to civilian life by creating two rehabilitation programs, one educational and occupational and the other emotional (Whiteley, 1984). The establishment of the position of counseling psychologist to deal with both vocational problems and the personal conflicts that frequently affect vocational adjustment was a major step in the integration of many of the themes that had run through the history of this subspecialty. Consequently, counseling psychologists were employed at regional offices of the VA and at colleges and universities to help millions of veterans achieve functional and satisfying roles in civilian life. The VA also established counseling psychologists in its medical centers. The function of the counselor was to deal with the vocational and emotional problems of returning veterans with medical difficulties. Moreover, counselors provided services to veterans with problems that developed later in civilian life from service-connected disabilities or other eligible conditions.

The continuing evolution of psychological services in the VA medical centers has had a profound impact. The agency remains one of the major sources of employment for counseling psychologists. In addition, these developments helped form educational, training, and research links between the VA and university settings that remain in effect to this day. The relatively short-term contractual arrangements between the agency and college and university counseling centers often demonstrated to these centers the need for service to students other than returning veterans. These centers are another major source of employment for counseling psychologists.

Developments in the American Psychological Association

Whiteley notes that the original interest in the establishment of a Division of Counseling Psychology in the APA can be traced to 1943 and the efforts of applied psychologists to establish appropriate professional homes for themselves. He writes that

> Division 17 of the American Psychological Association had [several] names during its history, beginning in 1944: the Division of Personnel Psychologists, the Division of Counseling and Guidance Psychologists, the Division of Counseling and Guidance, and after August 29–30, 1951, Counseling Psychology. (This latter designation became official APA policy at the time of the 1953 annual convention.) [1984, p. 10].

Among the founding members of the organization were university professors and researchers, developers of applied tests, and psychologists interested in vocational guidance and occupational adjustment in the broadest application of the term. These leaders represented in their practice, interest, and writing a living embodiment of the various roots of counseling psychology, including vocational guidance, psychometrics, and personal adjustment counseling. They synthesized these roots in a variety of social, educational and rehabilitative settings.

Among the founders of the division were a number who identified the common ground of what came to be known as the discipline of counseling psychology. They were all concerned with serving target populations who were dealing with normal development problems or whose development had been modified by events in their lives such as displacement because of war, rapidly changing social circumstances, and physical illness or injury. In short, all of these psychologists were concerned with dealing with the circumstances of normal development in the personal and vocational area and the factors that interfered with that development. These psychologists included Hugh Bell, Edward Bordin, John J. Darley, Mitchel Dreese, Frank Fletcher, William Gilbert, Milton Hahn, Francis Robinson, Winfield Scott, Dewey Stuit, Donald Super, Edmund Williamson, and Gilbert Wrenn, all university professors and leaders. In addition, George Bennett and Harold Seashore, two well-known test developers, were instrumental in laying the foundations (Whiteley, 1984). To this group one needs to add two other individuals who, although not among the founders, certainly helped give definition to the emerging field—namely, Robert Waldrop and Joseph Samler, both of the Veterans Administration.

This group represented many of the leading institutions of higher education that would continue to provide leadership and trained psychologists to the field of counseling psychology for the next half century, including the University of Minnesota, Columbia University, and Ohio State University. Commercial organizations such as the Psychological Corporation were also represented, in addition to the VA.

The men mentioned above were heavily involved in the leadership of the National Vocational Guidance Association and the American College Personnel Association, which were soon to be involved in a metamorphosis of their own into the American Personnel and Guidance Association in the early 1950s.

The Synthesis of Ideas

Clearly many of the psychologists cited above had become aware of the congruence of their ideas, the commonality of their roots, and the overlapping activities in the various realms of their practice. It is interesting to speculate about the source of this grand synthesis, but to point to a single source is perhaps to run the risk of overlooking some seminal sources and simplifying a rather complex process. Nevertheless, it does appear that there was a single source, the publication in 1942 of Donald C. Super's *The Dynamics of Vocational Adjustment*. Super himself pointed out in an interview in 1978 that "I was interested in economics, history, sociology, psychology and political science" (Pappas, 1978, p. 585). Indeed, those interests and a remarkable degree of synthesizing activity were included in his deceptively thin book. Super pulled together the impact of the Industrial Revolution in North America and its economic and political implications; the findings from the psychometric movement in the area of intelligence, aptitudes, interest, and personality; and the impact of those data on the nature of vocational adjustment. In addition, he presented the rudiments of a theory of vocational development and choice. He included observations about the choice of occupations as a dynamic process evolving through various stages, the impact of a variety of social institutions and social changes on that process, and the potential contributions of the professional counselor. Super also made some cogent observations regarding the impact of potentially catastrophic events such as unemployment on the process and made the connection between work and leisure activities. His prescient observations included the insight that counselors required supplementary knowledge about the nature of their clientele when dealing with special groups like the handicapped. Moreover, he noted that working with these special groups did not relieve the counselor of the responsibility to be knowledgeable in general counseling. While refraining from being prescriptive, Super also suggested a plan for formal course work combined with "apprenticeship" activities. In its formal outlines, it could serve as a model for a contemporary training program in counseling psychology (Super, 1942, p. 274).

Perhaps more than anything else, Super recognized the contribution of sociology to vocational psychology. Later, in a candid self-appraisal, devoid of false modesty, he correctly noted that "I did, sooner than anyone else ever did, bring in the sociological and economic aspects. In fact, I claim, perhaps wrongly, that I was the first among us to say we've much to learn from sociology" (Pappas, 1978, p. 590).

In the final paragraph of *The Dynamics of Vocational Adjustment,* Super points out that

> like medicine in the early days of the medical schools and medical associa-
> tions . . . like every other young profession, the vocational guidance move-
> ment is going through a process of organization, growth, self-scrutiny, and
> slow unification. There is reason for believing that it will in due course take
> its place among the recognized professions [1942, p. 275].

There is little in this book that is not prophetic when read from a retrospective point of view. We are not suggesting that it was the only early statement in this field that provided synthesizing insights. However, we are saying that it is probably the most complete of the early attempts and that a complete histor-ical view of the emergence of counseling psychology demands a rereading of this book so that its contributions to the emergence and coherence of the field will be remembered.

The Development of Vocational Psychology

As a result of the fusion of vocational guidance, psychometrics, and nonmedical counseling, a significant area in psychology emerged that was concerned with the development of a science of vocations. The early and classical concerns of counseling psychologists were in this area of research and practice. Indeed, if there is a substantive concern unique to counseling psychology it is the area of vocational psychology.

Super points out that

> vocational psychology focuses on people thinking about careers, preparing
> for occupations, and leaving the world of work to devote what knowledge
> and energies that they have to leisure activities that may resemble in content
> the work that they did for pay or which may involve quite different types
> of knowledge and skill [1983, p. 6].

He notes that this area has also been called career psychology. The specific concern of the counseling psychologist is a person's career development throughout the life span. This concern involves knowledge of the general area of human development and the particular characteristics of career development as well as knowledge of the nature of occupations over a long period. Super's (1983) historical survey of the evolution of vocational psychology provides a comprehensive summary of the developmental psychology of careers.

Many of the developments cited by Super could easily serve as a substantive history of counseling psychology itself. Some examples include the work of psychologists in the field of measurement, such as the development of tests of intellect (Alfred Binet, Arthur Otis, Lewis Terman, Robert Yerkes, and Douglas Fryer) and the refinement of differential aptitude testing (John Flanagan, Dewey Stuit, and Thomas Harrell in the armed forces). The development of interest measures by E. K. Strong was another significant event in this area.

Super (1983) also cites institutional activities in differential psychology at the Carnegie Institute of Technology, the Minnesota Mechanical Abilities Project at the University of Minnesota, and developments at Teachers' College at Columbia University and at Ohio State University.* In addition, the application of differential psychology to careers was carried forward by the work of Thorndike and Hagen and of John C. Flanagan. There were, of course, many other psychologists involved in the application of differential psychology to the vocational area. Super's own work and the work of Anne Roe, John Holland, and others helped apply the principles of developmental psychology to career issues. Ultimately, "a science of careers" was fashioned and evolved into research programs and applications in vocational development and career pattern development (Super, 1983). Indeed, the fusion of an improved technology in differential psychology with a new understanding of the science of careers led Super to observe that "matching people and jobs is as important as ever, and our methods and instruments are far better than they were 1, 2, 3, or 4 decades ago" (1983, p. 32).

The Development of Rehabilitation Psychology

Overlapping the emergence of vocational psychology was the development of rehabilitation psychology. Practitioners concerned with the social, psychological, and vocational rehabilitation of the physically impaired as well as of those disabled in other ways also became part of the evolving counseling psychology movement.

Jaques and Kauppi (1983) write that people working in vocational rehabilitation maintain "a focus on the assets of the individual rather than on limitations or pathology" (p. 208). In focusing on the strengths of clients to help them develop to their maximum capacity, the specialists in rehabilitation psychology shared a common emphasis with the emerging discipline of counseling psychol-

---

Differential psychology is concerned with the identification of measurable individual differences and their relevance to the behavior of groups and individuals.

ogy. In fact, those drawn to psychology because of an interest in handicapping conditions shared a good deal of common ground with those counselors and psychologists concerned with the vocational development and vocational behavior of the mainstream population. These practitioners found themselves in the same professional organizations, responding to the same social mandates and engaged in overlapping activities in social agencies.

Rehabilitation psychologists, who ultimately formed their own division in the APA, were frequently members of the Division of Counseling Psychology. Rehabilitation psychologists and counseling psychologists combined to form the predecessor of the American Rehabilitation Counselors Association of the American Association for Counseling and Development. The faculty involved in the development of training programs in rehabilitation counseling were frequently counseling psychologists. Indeed, educational training at the master's level for rehabilitation counselors was often found in departments that offered doctoral programs in counseling psychology. The VA, particularly in the post–World War II era, provided both workplaces and training centers for psychologists concerned with the vocational rehabilitation and education of veterans. Indeed, the practical requirements for service to veterans produced a fusion of activities among those psychologists interested in vocational psychology and the practical concerns of vocational rehabilitation. This fusion contributed to the development of counseling psychology. As Jaques and Kauppi note in their excellent summary of the evolution of vocational rehabilitation, "some counseling psychologists saw a need for their profession to be involved in rehabilitation [but] it was recognized that counseling psychology . . . could not fill the rehabilitation personnel needs" (1983, p. 232).

Whiteley's Historical Periods in the Development of Counseling Psychology

Thus far we have identified several historical developments that contributed to the evolution of counseling psychology. John Whiteley (1984), in a fine historical synthesis, has provided a view of the various periods of growth in counseling psychology. We have decided to use his historical model to convey a step-by-step development of the field:

1. First period (1908–1950): formative influences
2. Second period (1951–1956): inaugural definitions of the profession
3. Third period (1957–1962): emerging differences on status and focus
4. Fourth period (1963–1967): positive initiatives by counseling psychology
5. Fifth period (1968–1976): alternative directions for the profession
6. Sixth period (1977–1983): rethinking professional identity
7. Seventh period (1984–present): challenge and opportunity

The First Period (1908–1950)

Whiteley identifies during the first 50 years of this century many of the historical roots that we have considered in this chapter, including industrial changes, great shifts in population from farms to cities, and the accompanying expansion of educational and occupational demands and opportunities. We have also pointed to the influence of catastrophic historical events of that period, including two world wars and the Great Depression of the 1930s; the evolution of the new science of vocational psychology; initiatives in vocational rehabilitation; and an increased awareness of the social and mental-health needs of the society. The professionalization of counseling psychology began during this period as well.

Whiteley identifies the five roots of counseling psychology mentioned earlier in this chapter. In addition, he points out two categories of theories that "pre-eminently influenced counseling psychology, namely theories of personality, counseling and psychotherapy and theories of vocational psychology, occupational choice and career development" (1984, pp. 20–21).

By the close of this first period, it was clear that counseling psychologists had identified vocational development as the major sector of their area of practice and research. Moreover, they were making inroads in preventing and treating mental illness.

The Second Period (1951–1956)

This second period was a time of significant expansion and consolidation for the profession. The growth of graduate education, efforts to develop research germane to the field, and the first of a series of attempts to define the characteristics of counseling psychology were all aspects of this period.

It was an optimistic and expansive period, reflecting responsiveness to what have been called "keystones of consciousness" (Whiteley, 1984, p. 21). These included the expansion of theories of human development and behavior to include the vocational area. Whiteley also notes that social attitudes changed during this period "to embrace an increased acceptability of seeking psychological services and a heightened demand for assistance with personal, educational, and career problems of adjustment" (1984, p. 21).

The APA provided the framework for the emerging identity of counseling psychology. Division 17 changed its name to "Counseling Psychology" and became the second largest division in the association. Major attempts were made to define the nature of training for counseling psychologists. The most important scholarly outlet in the field was founded in 1954: the *Journal of Counseling Psychology.*

Scholars in the field were interested in consolidating the contributions from the literature of personality theory and human development. Counseling psychologists incorporated Freudian notions along with those of the behaviorists like B. F. Skinner and substantial ideas from the client-centered group, especially Rogers.

The relationship of personality theory, differential psychology, sociology, economics, and anthropology to the area of vocational psychology, occupational choice, and career development characterized many of the theoretical advances during the second period. Donald Super continued his insistence that "scholarship and research in the field be informed by the related academic discipline of sociology, cultural anthropology and economics'' (p. 26). Harold Pepinsky, in a review of the status of the field during this period, focused on problems of ''definitions of counseling as a profession, foundations of theory and method, analysis of the counseling process, discussion of therapy in groups and research (especially on the effects of counseling)'' as the major intellectual and professional concerns of counseling psychologists (p. 30).

The challenges posed by adapting material from intact theories, incorporating relevant information from related disciplines, and defining areas of professional practice and research were heady and were consequently attractive options to both established leadership and potential members of the field. The opportunities for expansion of counseling psychology seemed to be limitless, and professional possibilities created an ambience in the profession that was contagious.

The Third Period (1957–1962)

Whiteley describes the third period as one of mixed accomplishments. He points out that it was marked by conflict ''concerning the status and proper focus of the specialty'' (p. 82). In addition, it was marked by missed opportunities, particularly those related to the expansion of the role of the federal government in the area of counseling. During the previous two periods of development, counseling psychology had forged significant relationships with the government in order to provide service to returning World War II veterans. The result, of course, was the evolution of close working relationships with VA installations, an integrated training program, and an enriched professional expansion. Division 17, however, failed to respond to the Vocational Rehabilitation Act of 1954 and the National Defense Education Act of 1958 and left the professional development of subdoctoral counselors in rehabilitation counseling and school counseling outside the domain of organized counseling psychology. The irony of this situation is that the majority of trainers and educators were counseling psychologists. The major professional beneficiary of these significant pieces of legislation was the American Personnel and Guidance Association.

Counseling psychology seemed overly concerned with differentiating itself from clinical psychology and industrial psychology and more generally with maintaining itself as an ''independent'' specialty. Whiteley notes that the APA Education and Training Board initiated studies to determine the status of counseling psychology. Among the concerns of the board were questions addressing the possibility of the ''decline'' of counseling psychology, the ''quality'' of graduate students, and the ''scientific status'' of the field (p. 37). Indeed, counseling psychology was on the defensive as a subspecialty, which may account, in part, for its failure to take a more active stance with respect to federal initiatives during this period.

Growth in the field primarily involved advances in the literature of vocational psychology, occupational choice, and career development. Several contributions were made by researchers such as Super and his associates in the Career Pattern Study, Roe in occupational psychology, and Holland in vocational typology. In addition, a series of studies on work adjustment and employment satisfaction under the leadership of R. U. Davis, G. W. England, and L. H. Lofquist began during this period. The major significance of the studies and other theoretical contributions of this period was that they began promising lines of inquiry that laid the groundwork for significant advances in the field over the past quarter of a century.

The Fourth Period (1963–1967)

As Whiteley notes, the critical half-decade from 1963 to 1967 could be characterized as "counseling psychology at a crossroads" (p. 67). At issue were professional identity, overlapping with other psychological subspecialties and the determining of future directions for the profession. One issue that needed to be addressed concerned the "differentiation between clinical and counseling training in approved university programs" (p. 55). This issue focused on common bases of knowledge, overlaps in clinical techniques and client populations, and changes in both subspecialties that fostered competition for jobs in the marketplace.

Counseling psychology attempted to address some of these issues by convening the Greystone Conference in 1954. The conference came to the conclusion that there were indeed serious issues involving professional identification. Alternatives to the training model and to the professional activities of counseling psychology were suggested, including increased efforts toward professional psychological identity, which involved seeking licensure and American Board of Examiners in Professional Psychology (ABEPP) diploma status (p. 74).

Although the Greystone Conference had a short-term positive effect on counseling psychology, it has been noted that "the issue [of identity] is still not resolved" (p. 26). Almost 25 years after Greystone, the field is still dealing with the same issues.

The Fifth Period (1968–1976)

One of the major efforts of the fifth period of development was a continued focus on the roles and functions of the counseling psychologist. "Three different but complementary roles were identified: the remedial and rehabilitative, the preventive and the educative and developmental" (p. 69). These three overlapping roles encompassed clear functions for counseling psychologists: to aid those with existing problems, to anticipate and move to prevent difficulties, and to help people and groups maximize their potential for growth. These activities can be carried out in educational settings, health-related settings, public policy enclaves, and community mental-health agencies as well as in independent professional practice.

Another major development of the period was the founding of *The Counseling Psychologist,* which provides a professional and research forum for professionals and also encourages communication on social and educational issues. Among the topics covered since 1969 are the theory of vocational development, counseling theory, student unrest, counseling and race, new directions in training, counseling of women, family counseling, and many others. The journal has stimulated professional discussion and has provided excellent text material for graduate education programs.

This was a period of substantive research developments in vocational psychology as well as in personality theory. It was also a period of further advancement in theories of counseling and psychotherapy. Developments in behavior theory and therapy and the evaluation of humanistic and existential theory and therapy gave those in the field a clear choice from among these approaches and also from among modifications in the classical psychodynamic approaches.

The Sixth Period (1977–1983)

The period from 1977 to 1983 might best be characterized as a time of continuity in counseling psychology that further established the substantive theoretical and research base of the field. The transition from vocational psychology and occupational exploration to career development and intervention was clarified. Research in this field began almost two decades earlier and had reached maturity in many areas. In addition, new lines of investigation were stimulated by empirical data and unanswered questions.

There was also increased interest in the settings in which people lived, worked, and were educated. Counseling psychologists examined the interaction among family settings, work settings, and educational settings and the application, remediation, prevention, and developmental functions that had earlier been delineated.

Practitioners also began an effort to project their subspecialty into the future. This led to a variety of initiatives that attempted to reinterpret the historical context of the program and to anticipate developments in the 21st century.

The Seventh Period (1984–Present)

Whiteley entitles the final period ''challenge and opportunity'' (p. 89). He lists the challenges facing counseling psychology as follows:

1. redefining the field's relationship to the rest of the profession
2. increasing counseling psychologists' research productivity and unique contributions
3. increasing communication of the field's goals and functions to a broader constituency
4. responding to economic changes in society and their implications for research and practice
5. becoming active in prevention activities

The present period in counseling psychology is no less challenging than some of the earlier periods in its history. The field needs to address the issues defined by Whiteley. In addition, a shifting of professional concentration toward applied activities and independent practice threatens the theoretical base and research efforts that are crucial to the continued development of counseling psychology and its unique professional identity.

Professional Concerns

Counseling Psychology is in a rather contradictory situation. On the one hand, there has been a significant increase in the number of educational institutions applying for accreditation of their counseling psychology programs (Tipton, 1984, pp. 111–112). On the other hand, Division 17 of the APA seems to be in a period of decline. The division has slipped from second place to seventh place in memberships among all divisions. It has fewer than 3000 members in an organization of well over 40,000 members.

Two writers state that "the division seems to be in a no-win situation" (Huebener and Corzzini, 1984, p. 117). The division does not seem to meet the needs of younger psychologists. Indeed, Ursula Delworth in a presidential address to Division 17 noted that "the young psychologists coming out of our graduate programs today are seeming to see the division and perhaps all of the American Psychological Association as less relevant to their needs and interests" (1984, p. 184).

Delworth cites the overlapping of job functions with clinical and school psychologists as one issue. The trend toward generic training in all applied psychology may lead to a situation that eliminates differentiation by specialty. Each specialty attempts to define itself as broadly as possible to attract a wide constituency and to provide this constituency with the broadest possible latitude with respect to function. The result, as noted by Delworth, is the development of "three sets of almost identical guidelines to describe what is still recognized as three different specialties. When one examines the definition of practice provided by each of the applied areas, it is clear that each area could easily adopt any of the definitions of practice applying to the other" (pp. 183–184).

As Boll (1985) notes, counseling psychology has had relatively few changes in training since the Boulder Conference almost 40 years ago. Some present models of training have been challenged, and the Education and Training Board of the APA is evaluating the accreditation of doctoral programs and analyzing "the content of psychology education and training as well as the methods of providing that education and training" (p. 1030). This may lead to proposals for the development of generic education for applied psychologists with specialization to evolve as a postdoctoral endeavor. Obviously, this issue has implications for the future of psychology as a whole and for the nature of the organization of the APA.

The Future of Counseling Psychology

There have been significant shifts in the field in recent years. Fitzgerald and Osipow (1986) point to the increasingly applied nature of the specialty. They also confirm the point made earlier in this chapter that there seems to be a convergence among the applied specialties in the field. They suggest that the time may have come for consideration of a "proposal for the merger of clinical, counseling, and school psychology with a broader *human services psychology*" (1986, p. 543).

Others are not as supportive of the suggestion to merge. Albert Thompson predicts that "counseling psychologists with their history of dealing with the normal, everyday reality problems of the entire spectrum of age and level of adjustment will have an increasingly important role to play" (1980, p. 22). He goes on to assert that if we do reach the point at which psychology develops a general practitioner, an evolution that he considers likely, "professional training in counseling psychology will be the best preparation for the role" (p. 22). Osipow agrees with this point of view and contends that the counseling psychologist may be the closest thing to a general practitioner that the mental health specialties provide. He points out that "we may not be called counseling psychologists anymore, and I suspect that we will still be looking for our identity" (1980, p. 19). Others such as Tyler (1980) are convinced that the practice, concerns, and education currently labeled as the primary domain of counseling psychology will define the role of the psychological general practitioner of the future.

Our own position is essentially an optimistic one with respect to the general role of the practitioner who, we believe, will function in much the same way that counseling psychologists now function. There will be expanded roles for these practitioners in community mental-health centers, in health maintenance organizations, in organizations such as the VA that treat increasing geriatric populations, and in schools, colleges, and other educational institutions. It is also likely that industry will need counseling psychologists. In short, we believe that the demand for practitioners in this specialty will increase no matter what the label of the area of practice may be.

Our optimism leads us to the conclusion that opportunities will continue to exist, and new directions in business, industry, and health will emerge (Zytowski, 1985, p. 137). Counseling psychology will be a vital force well into the 21st century.

References

Anastasi, A. (1984). The K-ABC in the Historical and Contemporary Perspective. *Journal of Special Education, 18*(3), 357–366.

Barzun, J. (1959). *The House of Intellect.* New York: Harper & Brothers.

Boll, T. J. (1985). Graduate Education in Psychology: Time for a Change? *American Psychologist, 40*(9), 1029–1030.

Brown, S. D., & Lent, R. W. (1984). *Handbook of Counseling Psychology.* New York: Wiley.

Cowley, W. H. (1937). A Preface to the Principles of Student Counseling. *Educational Record, 18,* 217–234.

Delworth, U. (1984). Present Realities and Future Scenarios. *The Counseling Psychologist, 12*(4), 183–185.

Fitzgerald, L.F., & Osipow, S. H. (1986). An Occupational Analysis of Counseling Psychology. *The American Psychologist, 41*(5), 535–544.

Goldman, L. (1980). Research in More Than Technology. *The Counseling Psychologist, 8*(3), 41–44.

Hahn, M. E., & Maclean, M. S. (1950). *General Clinical Counseling.* New York: McGraw-Hill.

Halmos, P. (1966). *The Faith of the Counselors*. New York: Schocken.

Holland, J. L. (1982). Planning for Alternative Futures. *The Counseling Psychologist*, 10(2), 7–14.

Huebener, L. A., & Corzzini, J. G. (1984). Division 17 Membership Nonrenewals: Causes and Complications. *The Counseling Psychologist*, 12(2), 117–118.

Jaques, M. E., & Kauppi, D. (1983). Vocational Rehabilitation and Its Relationship to Vocational Psychology. In W. B. Walsh & S. H. Osipow (Eds.), *Handbook of Vocational Psychology* (Vol. 2), (pp. 207–258). Hillsdale, NJ: Erlbaum.

McClelland, D. C. (1975). *Power: The Inner Experience*. Irvington, NY: Halsted Press.

Miller, C. H. (1971). *Foundations of Guidance* (2nd ed.). New York: Harper & Row.

Osipow, S. H. (1980). Toward Counseling Psychology in the Year 2000. *The Counseling Psychologist*, 8(4), 18–19.

Pappas, J. P. (1978, June). Donald Super. *Personnel and Guidance Journal*, pp. 585–592.

Parsons, F. (1909). *Choosing a Vocation*. Boston: Houghton Mifflin.

Rogers C. R. (1942). *Counseling and Psychotherapy*. Boston: Houghton Mifflin.

Rogers, C. R. (1951). *Client-Centered Therapy: Its Current Practice, Implications and Theory*. Boston: Houghton Mifflin.

Rossberg, R. H., & Band, L. (1978). Historical Antecedents of Counseling: A Revisionist Point of View. In J. Hansen (Ed.), *Counseling Process and Procedures* (pp. 3–20). New York: Macmillan.

Schwebel, M. (1984). From Past to Present: Counseling Psychology's Socially Prescribed Role. In J. M. Whiteley, N. Kagan, L. Harmon, B. R. Fretz, & F. Tanney (Eds.), *The Coming Decade is Counseling Psychology*. Washington, D.C.: Division of Counseling Psychologists, American Psychological Association.

Sprinthall, N. A. (1986). Kudos to Don Blicher. *Newsletter, Division of Counseling Psychology, American Psychological Association*, 7(3).

Super, D. E. (1942). *The Dynamics of Vocational Adjustment*. New York: Harper & Brothers.

Super, D. E. (1955). Transition: From Vocational Guidance to Counseling Psychology. *Journal of Counseling Psychology*. 2, 3–9.

Super, D. E. (1983). The History and Development of Vocational Psychology: A Personal Perspective. In W. B. Walsh and S. H. Osipow (Eds.), *Handbook of Vocational Psychology* (Vol. 1), (pp. 5–37). Hillsdale, NJ: Erlbaum.

Tanney, F. (1982). Counseling Psychology in the Marketplace. *The Counseling Psychologist*, 10(2), 21–30.

Thompson, A. A. (1980). Counseling Psychology in the Year 2000. *The Counseling Psychologist*, 8(4), 21–22.

Tipton, R. M. (1984). Trends and Issues in the Training and Development of Counseling Psychologists. *The Counseling Psychologist*, 12(4), 111–112.

Tyler, L. (1980). The Next Twenty Years. *The Counseling Psychologist*, 8(4), 19–21.

Whiteley, J. M. (1984). A Historical Perspective on the Development of Counseling Psychology as a Profession. In S. D. Brown & R. W. Lent (Eds.), *Handbook of Counseling Psychology*. New York: McGraw-Hill.

Zytowski, D. G. (1985). Frank, Frank! Where Are You Now That We Need You? *The Counseling Psychologist*, 13(1), 129–135.

Public Policy Mandates for Counseling Psychology

In this chapter we analyze the social forces that created the current professional status of counseling psychology. We also follow the evolution of public policy mandates that fostered growth in the professional activities of the field. We discuss the public policy support for the subspecialty of counseling psychology and its relation to public support for guidance and counseling and for vocational psychology. In this context we consider the legislative manifestations and implications of those policies. Finally, we examine the issue of credentialing as a manifestation of public policy and the emerging legislative mandates through certification and licensing.

The Origins of Helping Services

Levine and Levine (1970) were astonished to find that clinical services in psychology from 1896 to the mid-1920s, which they had assumed were primitive manifestations of applied clinical work, were based on goals much like those of current community service. Their findings would certainly suggest that we are struggling to solve the very same social problems that have existed for almost a century. Although the context and substance have changed dramatically, the fundamental issue of the helping professions is unsolved—namely, delivering quality services in a timely fashion and in sufficient quantity to deal with the problems that led Witmer to start his psychological clinic in 1896 or Healy to organize his psychiatric clinic for children in 1909.

Many of the helping services were originated by people with no formal training. The traditional "do-gooder" saw a social need for recreation, relief, or cultural enrichment and organized a structure to meet that need. Later these activities were taken over by socially sanctioned "official" organizations. Frank Parsons, hardly a trained vocational counselor, in an altruistic mood established the Breadwinner's College at Civic Service House in Boston. He went on to develop an organized guidance service, the Vocational Bureau, in 1908. In a report to the Executive Committee of the bureau in that year he suggested that

"vocational guidance" should become a part of the public school system in every community, with experts trained as carefully in the art of vocational guidance as we are trained today for medicine or the law, and supplied with every facility that science can devise for testing the senses and capacities and the wholly physical, intellectual and emotional makeup of the child [Borow, 1964, p. 49].

The evolution of helping and development services begins with a perceived social need. If this need is consistent with the general social climate, it is possible to organize political forces to meet it. Indeed, the forces that are organized may exert an influence on the goals themselves. In addition, the emergence of the professional practitioner creates another force behind the development and maintenance of the service. The Levines argue that the mental-health profession may contribute "to the development of mental illness by providing the doctor role, the necessary complement to the patient role" (1970, p. 19). Thomas Szasz (1961) presents similar arguments.

The social need is real. It is perceived by a rank amateur who attempts to meet that need directly. This attempt is followed by the institutionalization and modification of both the need and the structure created to meet it by a complicated sociological, political, and economic process. The process is further complicated by the emergence of a coterie of professionals who have a vested interest in defining and meeting the perceived needs in very particular ways. It also leads to the maintenance of a power relationship between the providers of the service and the receivers.

The Origins of Public Policy

Herr and Pinson (1982) describe the political process that typically leads to enabling legislation in human development and mental health. Laws that respond to human needs and provide the resources to meet those needs result from a complicated process of compromise among competing groups. Furthermore, the resulting policy is frequently made by creatively interpreting legislation passed for other purposes or even by directing resources into activities somewhat removed from the original intention of the appropriation. In the latter instances, policy may follow perceived opportunity rather than the reverse.

Herr and Pinson outline the major eras during which public policy took shape in the area of guidance and counseling:

the social reforms in the late 1800s
the rise of individualism in the early 1900s
the concern for the handicapped and mentally ill in the 1920s
the economic exigencies and employment concerns in the 1930s
national defense in the 1940s and 1960s
Democratization and broadened access in the 1960s
concern for equity in the context of economic austerity in the 1970s

Public policy on counseling is a reflection of these broad social trends as filtered through politics. It is the result of an interaction between the potential beneficiaries of the policy and those who would provide the service. (Frequently, there is a "third party" to the evolution of policy, namely, so-called qualified observers or experts who are perceived to have nothing to gain personally.) Groups having vested interests in policies that have an impact on the practice of counseling psychologists represent millions of people. For example, one estimate suggests that 32 million Americans need mental-health treatment and that only 7 million actually receive it (Pinson, 1982). If even a part of this population and the professionals who treat it form a lobby, we are talking about a formidable advocacy group.

Many others have a vested interest in career intervention in schools, colleges, continuing-education programs, and other outreach services. To this group we can add those with problems of alcohol, family deterioration, and drug abuse. Think of the members and veterans of the armed services who need services. Add to the potential clients the powerful employee unions and professional associations, and the strength of the advocacy constituency becomes even more pronounced. Indeed, some assert that it was the influence of the Veterans Administration that led to the establishment of the specialty of counseling psychology in the first place (see Chapter 1).

The impact of public policy on counseling psychology is rarely as direct as is in the case of the VA. Frequently the advocacy of groups such as the physically and emotionally handicapped, the mentally retarded, and the delinquent have an indirect impact on practice. Sometimes it is advocacy for broader issues such as the improvement of schools or the expansion of career planning, development, and education that provides opportunities for research and service (Herr, 1982).

Economics frequently plays a role in advocacy. For example, it is argued that rehabilitation of the physically and emotionally handicapped has economic utility in that it leads to reduced costs of treatment and even a net gain to the economy by virtue of the contributions of those who are rehabilitated. A similar argument has been made for prison inmates. As Herr notes,

> If the original appeal of guidance and counseling to decision-makers was philosophical, the more recent appeal has been the demonstrated effects of these processes upon individual behavior related to national, social, economic, and occupational procedures. The appeal of the future is likely to be the cost-benefit effects of guidance and counseling and related processes [1982, p. 168].

We contend that appeals for resources have always had an economic base. The "cult of efficiency" has a long history in American policy-making for health, education, and welfare services. During a period of economic optimism and expanding economies the philosophical arguments can be advanced with some confidence. In times of economic difficulty those arguments tend to be muted in favor of a cost/benefit stance. We do agree with Herr, however, that the emphasis on the social and economic utility of programs is likely to increase in the foreseeable future.

The Effect of Legislation

In this section we consider specific pieces of legislation that have had an impact on the development of counseling psychology. Within the framework of our thesis that counseling psychology shares legislative origins with vocational psychology, counseling and guidance, rehabilitation counseling, and the other mental-health professions, we survey specific legislation in these areas.

Legislation Affecting Counseling and Guidance

In 1910 the first national conference concerned with vocational guidance was convened in Boston, and three years later the National Vocational Guidance Association was established in Grand Rapids, Michigan. In the same year the U.S. Department of Labor was formed. Thus, immediately preceding World War I a national organization of interested professionals and a national agency devoted to the concerns of the work force were organized.

The way was therefore cleared for the historical legislation passed in 1917, the Smith-Hughes Act. Smith-Hughes was "the first major federal legislation to provide government aid for subcollege industrial, agricultural, and home economics education. While the intent of the act was to provide support for vocational education . . . funds furnished under the Smith-Hughes Act and under subsequent [legislation were made] available for vocational guidance work" (Borow, 1964, p. 51). In later years this allocation of federal resources for vocational guidance was confirmed under the terms of the George-Reed Act (1920), the George-Dean Act (1936), and the George-Barden Act (1946). The federal government had declared that the policy of the United States was to reinforce those professional activities that had a direct bearing on vocational education.

The next major series of laws arose out of the Great Depression. The federal government, first in the last years of the Herbert Hoover administration (1928–1932) and then under the terms of the New Deal led by Franklin D. Roosevelt, attempted to deal with the severe unemployment and its dire consequences. In 1931 the Minnesota Employment Stabilization Research Institute was established in Minneapolis to study psychological factors in both employment and unemployment. As a result of its research, much information was collected leading to the conclusion "that improved guidance services and employment selection techniques were needed to establish a more stable labor force and to aid business recovery" (Borow, 1964, p. 53). In addition, the institute used the growing technology in aptitude tests and related their results to other personal characteristics of the people it studied. The institute also perfected the basic paradigm at the heart of vocational guidance practice. (See Chapter 5 for further discussion of this issue.)

In 1933, the National Occupational Conference was established as a clearinghouse of information in the field of vocational guidance. It evaluated programs, disseminated information about those programs, and provided informed advocacy for the further development of the field. Ultimately, the Occupational Information and Guidance Service was established in 1938 to carry on many of the same services as the National Occupational Conference, including the sponsorship of national conferences to recommend policies on vocational guidance and vocational education. (The latter was succeeded in 1953 by the Guidance and Pupil Personnel Section of the U.S. Office of Education.)

Another major policy decision of the New Deal culminated in 1933 with the passage of the Wagner-Peyser Act, which created the United State Employment Service. The activities of this service contributed significantly to the development and refinement of instruments useful in counseling services, including the development of the General Aptitude Test Battery, one of the first factorially designed instruments of multiple aptitudes. The service also developed prototypical programs of "counseling, placement services, job analysis and worker analysis research. [Its activity in] occupational information counseling and publishing . . . is one of the largest and most developed to be found anywhere" (Borow, 1964, p. 54). The work of this organization was supplemented by the formation of the Occupational Outlook Service in the Bureau of Labor Statistics. The objective of the two agencies was to analyze occupational trends and opportunities, and they have published the *Occupational Outlook Handbook* over the years.

When the United States entered World War II, the need for selecting, classifying, training, and evaluating millions of men and women into hundreds of military occupational specialties called for the application of the most highly developed psychological technology available. Many psychologists who had gravitated toward the rapidly expanding synthesis of differential psychology, psychometrics, and vocational psychology came together to implement national policy in various areas of federal service. Their success contributed to a growing acceptance of the practice of vocational psychology.

The end of the war saw the public attempting to meet the problems of returning veterans. In 1944 Congress enacted Public Law 346, which extended education and training benefits, including counseling services, to all World War II veterans (Gazda, Childers, & Brooks, 1987). In this same year, the army separation-classification and counseling program was established. This program supplemented those that were operated by the VA and the employment service and

> made up the largest active network of vocational guidance and counseling in history. Vocational guidance became a potent force in the nation's economic strategy. A growing pool of trained counselors, sounder testing and counseling methods, growing interagency cooperation and improved occupational information tools, such as the Dictionary of Occupational Titles and cross-classifications of civilian and military occupations, aided immeasurably in the task of retraining and placing millions of returned veterans in employment [Borow, 1964, p. 58].

In the 1950s the country began turning its attention to the remarkable economic and military recovery of the Soviet Union. The launching of a Soviet space satellite created doubt about the readiness of the United States to deal with the scientific, educational, and diplomatic implications of that achievement. Accordingly, Congress passed the National Defense Education Act in 1958. One of its purposes was to identify talented students through assessment and to encourage them to enter higher education, particularly in the physical sciences. The legislation had a profound effect on counseling and guidance service, since it provided funds for the training of secondary school counselors to improve their quality and number (Gazda et al., 1987). Borow (1964) estimates that during the first five years of operation under this act (1958–1963), 14,000 people received education and training in counseling. The implications were staggering not only for secondary school counseling but also for counseling psychology and counselor education, because much of the training was in university departments populated by those professionals. Not only did the program strengthen the field, it also strengthened the departments and paved the way for the development of counseling psychology programs in the '70s and '80s. In 1964 elements of the National Defense Education Act enhanced guidance and counseling in elementary schools and postsecondary (nonbaccalaureate) education. Also in 1964 the Educational opportunity Act established the Job Corps, Vista, and Head Start programs and had a further effect on the development and expansion of guidance (Gazda et al., 1987). Head Start was added to the Manpower Development and Training Act, which had been established two years earlier to provide funds for "expanded institutional and on-the-job vocational training for the unemployed and underemployed, and providing also for a broad program of research in the field of manpower" (Borow, 1964, p. 62). Even though Head Start was a program for young children, it was conceived as a developmental activity with ultimate implications for work and productivity and hence deemed an appropriate supplement to the Manpower Development and Training Act.

Other legislation in the past two decades has served to expand the national policies for the development of counseling and guidance. The Elementary and Secondary Education Act of 1965 designated funds for guidance and counseling, and amendments to it in 1974 "legislated career education and initiated the Office of Career Education in the U. S. Office of Education" (Gazda et al., 1987). Additional amendments to the law in the late 1970s provided support for vocational guidance and funds to assess the status of guidance and counseling.

Although no national legislation has ever been passed that specifically mentions counseling psychology, the clear public policies in support of vocational psychology, counseling and guidance, and vocational education have had a cumulative effect on the evolution of a mandate for counseling psychology.

Legislation Affecting Rehabilitation

The Vocational Rehabilitation Act of 1918 established the Rehabilitation Division for Disabled Soldiers. The Smith-Sears Act of 1918 and the Smith-Fess Act in 1920 both added to the public policy mandate for vocational rehabilitation. The Rehabilitation division was administered by the newly established Veterans Bureau, which was the predecessor of the Veterans Administration. Ultimately, a board to supervise civilian rehabilitation was established.

In 1943 the Barden-LaFollette Act expanded the program of civilian rehabilitation. This law was an extension of the earlier Vocational Rehabilitation Act, which specifically included

> any services necessary to render a disabled individual fit to engage in a remunerative occupation. [It also] specifically authorized services that had previously been administratively prohibited, including, for clients in financial

need, such services as physical restoration, prosthetics, transportation, maintenance and such materials while in training as occupational licenses, tools and equipment. Medical examinations and vocational aptitude analyses would be provided without the evidence of financial need [Jaques & Kauppi, 1983, p. 226].

Also in 1943, the Disabled Veterans Rehabilitation Act provided rehabilitation, education, and training for those with a service-connected disability. Counseling and guidance services were specifically included in this act, leading ultimately to the expansion of services in vocational rehabilitation and education as well as increased services in VA hospitals. As we have pointed out, both these programs had a direct effect on the evolution of counseling psychology.

The passage of Public Law 565 in 1954 had a profound effect on the field of rehabilitation, with a particular impact on rehabilitation counseling. Under the research and demonstration program of what was then called the Office of Vocational Rehabilitation, programs of research and training were begun. The purpose was to increase the number of trained professionals in the field and the standards of training. Many counseling psychologists became involved in educating rehabilitation counselors. The Office of Vocational Rehabilitation was ultimately given independent status in the Department of Health, Education, and Welfare under the title of the Vocational Rehabilitation Administration. It is now known as the Rehabilitation Services Administration. "From its beginning in 1954, with Public Law 565, federal support for education and training in rehabilitation counseling grew. At its peak, nearly 100 university programs offered graduate degrees" (Jaques & Kauppi, 1983, p. 234).

The Education for All Handicapped Children Act, passed in 1976, "introduced the concept of special education in the 'least restrictive environment' and 'mainstreaming' became the order of the day" (Gazda et al., 1987, p. 11). Although this act has had its primary influence on school psychologists, it has had some modest effect on school counselors as well and, ultimately, on counseling psychologists as the principles are applied in postsecondary education.

Legislation Affecting Mental Health

Legislation dealing with mental health has had more significance for clinical psychology, social work, and psychiatry than for counseling psychology per se. As counseling psychologists have broadened their focus to deal with problems of general development, family problems, and life adjustment, however, they have become increasingly concerned with mental-health issues. In 1946, the national Mental Health Act was passed. The establishment of the National Institute of Mental Health was a direct outcome of this legislation. Research and training in clinical and counseling psychology and other professional groups has been supported by NIMH (Gazda et al., 1987).

In 1955 the National Mental Health Study Act created the Commission on Mental Illness, whose suggestions led to the passage of the Community Mental Health Centers Act of 1963. Legislation was developed to establish multidisciplinary teams of practitioners in the community. The extension of these principles was reinforced by legislation in 1970 and by an amendment in 1975 that provided additional mental-health services such as follow-up care, transitional living arrangements, treatment of children and adolescents, and programs in alcohol and drug abuse. Finally, the Mental Health System Act of 1980 (still in limbo because of funding issues) further extended services for children, youth, minority populations, the elderly, and the chronically mentally ill (Gazda et al., 1987).

The increased awareness of drug abuse has led to recent federal and state legislation expanding the area of practice and concern for counseling psychologists. Porter, Curran, and Arif (1986) summarize the efforts that have been made to provide central registration for drug and alcohol dependence. This makes it easier for agencies to exchange information and assess the scope of the problems treated. The increased awareness of the effect of drug and alcohol abuse has also led to a call for expanded treatment for relatives and offspring of drug and alcohol abusers. As McCabe (1977) notes, the laws in this area are changing with respect to the rights of relatives of drug and alcohol abusers. He observes that "there will undoubtedly be a greater and greater need for opening the gates of treatment to children" (p. 12). This will be a major area of involvement for counseling psychologists over the next decade.

Legislation Affecting Minority Groups

As a result of public policy mandates and the stance of an increasing number of professional organizations, including the American Psychological Association, it is clear that the United States is committed to developing positive programs to address the needs of minority groups. These populations had been excluded from access to training and education for some professions and occupations because of racial and ethnic discrimination. The passage of several federal and state antidiscrimination laws, human rights acts, and fair employment practice legislation culminated in 1964 with the passage of the Civil Rights Act. This law guaranteed that equal employment opportunities would be extended to all workers and, by extension, implied affirmative-action programs at work and in schools. The past 25 years have seen an increase in effort in this area. In addition, concern for equal opportunity for women has emerged. Success in these endeavors has been modest, however. Counseling psychology has been more successful than some professions in attracting women to its ranks and having them move into leadership positions. Yet it has been less successful with regard to racial and ethnic minorities.

Public Policy Mandates for the Future

John F. Jennings (1982), in assessing probable federal actions in the immediate future, makes the obvious point that the government's response will be related to the general economic trends in society. He stresses the need for all the constituents involved in the process of making public policy to exercise their political power:

> The federal disposition is not preordained. The activism of individuals and of their organizations will largely determine those results. In the days ahead

counseling must make the best possible case that its services make a difference, and that in these times of fiscal austerity a cutback in support for counseling will mean a real loss to individuals. If that can be made, and if the profession assumes an activist role, then support will follow [p. 129].

Credentialing and Licensure of Counseling Psychologists

The profession of counseling psychology itself may act to guarantee levels of competence by specifying the nature of formal training in a particular area. It may go further in establishing a process of accrediting programs to ensure that the standards are being met.

Credentialing refers to the authority to use the title of a particular profession and/or authority to engage in the practice of that profession (Herr & Pinson, 1982). It is generally a certificate attesting to a particular competence or sector of practice. Credentialing may be done by the profession itself or through public assessment.

One form of credentialing, *certification*, is normally conferred by state agencies or voluntary associations on counselors who are not required to have a Ph.D. Certification may also be granted by state governments as part of the public education law or by voluntary professional associations who verify the competence of a practitioner by assessing credentials or by examination. School psychologists are certified by the various states, reflecting a social mandate of sorts. Counseling psychologists are not affected by certification practices except when they seek to work in settings such as public schools that require certificates.

The fully trained counseling psychologist is most likely to be interested in *licensure* and *registry*. Licensure is normally established by state legislation that delegates to licensing boards the authority to establish the regulations and examine and assess the candidates. Licensed psychologists are authorized to represent themselves to the public as independent practitioners and are eligible to receive payments from organized mental-health plans such as those run by insurance companies—so-called "third-party" payments.

Registry, another approach to credentialing, has generally been used by national professional organizations as an inventory of those practitioners who by training and experience are qualified to offer the services overseen by that organization. A national registry provides the credentials of professional psychologists to institutions, government agencies, and others who want to employ them.

The National Register of Health Service Providers has been in existence since 1975. Its function is to provide interested parties such as consumers and health-service organizations with a register of psychologists who meet its criteria (Schmidt & Meara, 1984, p. 63). Current criteria for registration include licensure by a state board in psychology, an appropriate doctoral degree, and two years of supervised experience in an appropriate setting.

The APA in 1947 established a process of awarding diplomas that attested to special competence. The American Board of Professional Psychology issues these diplomas on the basis of depth of training, experience, and competence as it is measured by examinations in counseling, clinical, school, and industrial and organizational psychology (Schmidt & Meara, 1984).

Credentialing: Whom Does It Serve?

Ivey (1982) believes that the goals of the profession should be consistent with public policy and that credentialing should reflect the confluence of interest. The major objective of credentialing should be to safeguard public welfare. As Ivey notes, "the prime responsibility of the government and the profession is to represent and protect the public, the people whom both serve" (1982, p. 132). This position is based on the assumption that if some effort is not made to assess the services delivered by those who are credentialed, the only effect of credentialing is to protect the members of the profession and restrict access to professional status. To this end, Ivey suggests an extended credentialing process that would include human-service agencies and professionals that are now excluded from third-party payments. He recommends that such accreditation be tied to demonstrated competence in service delivery. He is suggesting a much broader base to credentialing than most counseling psychologists are probably ready for.

Counseling Psychology and Credentialing

Counseling psychologists are not particularly sanguine about their own licensure status. It has not been long since it was necessary for the Division of Counseling Psychology of the APA to point out the diversity among counseling psychologists. They are trained in many different areas in the universities, including departments of psychology and schools of education. Division 17 maintained that state examining boards in psychology that denied licensure or certification to counseling psychologists because of the source of their training might be denying the right of these psychologists to practice their profession. The issue is the quality and accreditation of the program, not its location (American Psychological Association, 1975).

   The issue is still a relevant one. A survey of Division 17 members and their colleagues revealed close to 200 who had sought licensure unsuccessfully. Reviewing those already licensed and assuming graduates of all kinds have sought licensure in equal proportions, "it seems likely that most difficulties would be experienced by graduates of counseling and guidance departments with Ed.D. degrees" (Apanaitis, Ference, & Sturgis, 1980, p. 19).

   In this transition period in which affiliation is divided between the fields of counseling and psychology (see Chapter 1), these issues will continue to exist. While a relatively clear social mandate exists for psychology as a profession, there is a much more ambiguous status for counseling per se. It is clear that counseling psychology programs are moving with increasing intensity toward seeking accreditation by the APA and toward a closer identification with psychology. Fretz and Mills (1980) take a rather strong position endorsing this movement:

We think it is time for counseling psychology to identify clearly with psychology rather than with counseling. To do so runs the risks . . . of cutting us off from some of our history and our allegiance with the counseling and guidance professions. However, if we are going to have any impact as a viable professional specialty, we are going to have to concentrate our efforts, and psychology seems most appropriate for such concentration [p. 16].

The real issue underlying this dilemma is the perceived need for a social mandate. Psychology as a profession seems closer to having such a mandate than does the more ambiguous and diversified field of counseling and guidance. Moving in this direction may have "unintended consequences," as pointed out by Danish (1980): "The uniqueness and strength of our training programs may be diluted, our potential to deliver new developmental-preventive services will diminish if not disappear entirely, and the consumers of our services will receive more expensive services which actually may be more harmful than helpful" (p. 37).

There is no easy solution to this problem. Certainly closer identification with psychology will make it less likely that counseling psychologists will advocate the broader social policy suggested by Ivey. They will also be less likely to make common cause with colleagues in counseling and guidance programs who remain outside the APA fold. It certainly creates a dilemma for those who split their loyalties between subdoctoral training programs in rehabilitation counseling and school counseling and the more standard program of the doctoral-level counseling psychologists. If the gap increases, what will become of the subdoctoral counseling programs? Whatever happened to subdoctoral affiliation with the APA as a possibility?

The trend is clear. To obtain an unmixed social mandate, counseling psychologists will move inevitably toward identification with psychology. But as they gain stature, they may lose counseling psychology.

Summary

The social problems of providing counseling services have existed for most of this century, and the efforts of the profession at competent and effective delivery of services have not seemed to improve significantly over the last half-century. We examined the issue of the origins of public policy and suggested a model by which perceived social needs might get translated into applied social policy. This model included the interaction among professionals, public interest groups, and political agents to evolve objectives in the area of social need. In examining the origins of public policy we considered the diverse social and political forces that lead to eventual political compromises that constitute social policy. These forces included professional organizations, consumer groups, clients, public and private agencies, and political parties and their agents. Those social mandates that do exist for counseling psychology have emerged as the cumulative and sometimes random interaction among developments in counseling and guidance, including vocational psychology, rehabilitation psychology, developments in mental health, and certain social and political events.

We traced the legislative effects of developments in each of these fields and considered the likely direction of such efforts in the future. We also examined the credentialing of counseling psychologists as an additional source of a social mandate for professional activity in this field. We noted the positive changes that have been brought about already by broadening the target populations, specifying practice and increasing resources for mental-health activities. We also suggested that the future will increase the eligibility for service under the terms of this legislation and will likely lead to expanded professional practice, including an increased demand for counseling psychologists. The credentialing dilemma is involved with the continuing issue of our status as a specialty of psychology and carries with it some potential danger of losing our identity.

References

American Psychological Association, Division of Counseling Psychology. (1975). Licensing and Certification of Psychologists: A Position Statement by the Division of Counseling Psychology of the American Psychological Association. *The Counseling Psychologist, 5*(3), 135.

Apanaitis, B. E., Ference, C. M., & Sturgis, D. K. (1980). Licensure Status of Division 17 Members. *The Counseling Psychologist, 9*(1), 18–19.

Borow, H. (1964). Milestones: A Chronology of Notable Events in the History of Vocational Guidance. In H. Borow (Ed.), *Man in a World at Work*. Boston: Houghton Mifflin.

Danish, S. J. (1980). Considering Professional Licensing From a Social and Historical Context. *The Counseling Psychologist, 9*(1), 35–38.

Fretz, B. R., & Mills, D. H. (1980). Professional Certification in Counseling Psychology. *The Counseling Psychologist, 9*(1), 2–17.

Gazda, G. M., Childers, W. C., & Brooks, D. K. (1987). *Foundations of Counseling and Human Services*. New York: McGraw-Hill.

Herr, E. L. (1982). The Effects of Counseling and Guidance—Three Domains. In E. L. Herr & N. M. Pinson (Eds.), *Foundations for Policy in Guidance and Counseling*. Washington, D.C.: American Personnel and Guidance Association.

Herr, E. L., & Pinson, N. M. (1982). Foundations for Policy in Guidance and Counseling: An Introduction. In E. L. Herr & N. M. Pinson (Eds.), *Foundations for Policy in Guidance and Counseling*. Washington, D.C.: American Personnel and Guidance Association.

Ivey, A. E. (1982). Credentialism: Protection for the Public or for the Profession? In E. L. Herr & N. M. Pinson (Eds.), *Foundations for Policy in Guidance and Counseling*. Washington, D.C.: American Personnel and Guidance Association.

Jaques, M. E., & Kauppi, D. R. (1983). Vocational Rehabilitation and Its Relationship to Vocational Psychology. In W. B. Walsh & S. H. Osipow (Eds.), *Handbook of Vocational Psychology* (Vol.2). Hillsdale, NJ: Erlbaum.

Jennings, John F. (1982). A Federal Perspective on Guidance and Counseling. In E. L. Herr & N. M. Pinson (Eds.), *Foundations for Policy in Guidance and Counseling*. Washington, D.C.: American Personnel and Guidance Association.

Levine, M., & Levine, A. (1970). *A Social History of Helping Services*. New York: Appleton-Century-Crofts.

McCabe, J. (1977, Fall). Children in Need: Current Issues in Treatment. *Alcohol Health and Research World*, pp. 2–12.

Perry, L. (1982). Special Populations: The Demands of Diversity. In E. L. Herr & N. M.

Pinson (Eds.), *Foundations for Policy in Guidance and Counseling.* Washington, D.C.: American Personnel and Guidance Association.

Pinson, N. M. (1982). The Ingredients of Policy: Traditions Power, Expediency, Morality. In E. L. Herr & N. M. Pinson (Eds.), *Foundations for Policy in Guidance and Counseling.* Washington, D.C.: American Personnel and Guidance Association.

Porter, L., Curran, W. J., & Arif, A. (1986). Comparative Review of Reporting and Registration Legislation for Treatment of Drug and Alcohol Dependent Persons. *International Journal of Law and Psychiatry,* 8, 217–227.

Schmidt, L. D., & Meara, N. M. (1984). Ethical, Professional and Legal Issues in Counseling Psychology. In S. D. Brown and R. W. Lent (Eds.), *Handbook of Counseling Psychology.* New York: Wiley.

Szasz, T. (1961). The Myth of Mental Illness. *American Psychologist,* 15, 113–118.

Whiteley, J. M. (1984). A Historical Perspective on the Development of Counseling Psychology as a Profession. In S. D. Brown & R. W. Lent (Eds.), *Handbook of Counseling Psychology.* New York: Wiley.

3

Critical Theories of Counseling

If mental healers were to be summoned to the patient's bedside in the order of their appearance in history, the magician or medicine man would be the first one to answer the call. He would be followed by the philosopher-priest of various religious denominations, who would, in turn, yield his place to the scientifically oriented psychotherapist. There would be a world of difference between their underlying philosophies and the way they minister to their patients' needs [Ehrenwald, 1976, p. 6].

The underlying philosophies and values to which we adhere color our beliefs and actions. Indeed, as Naroll (1983) writes, "the human situation may perhaps best be understood in terms of cosmology. If there is a meaning to human history, it may well be found there" (p. 24). Furthermore, he implies that the understanding of every moral order should probably begin with an examination of the underlying cosmology that informs it. This is certainly true of the scientific moral order of which psychology is a part. However, it is far beyond the scope of this discussion to reach into the complexities of cosmology as a means of clarifying the critical issues and theories facing counseling psychology.

It is not beyond the scope of this presentation, however, to consider a very special subset of the cosmic situation—namely, conflicts over values in psychology. Values certainly account for decisions to act in society. The mandates and goals of society are clearly dictated by the prevailing set of core values that inform the most powerful sectors of society. As Naroll observes,

The ideals of medieval Europe were far different from the ideals of modern European humanism. On the one hand, medieval Europe in its churches believed that the present happiness of mankind was a thing of little consequence; what really mattered was the eternal life of the soul in the hereafter. On the other hand, medieval Europe in its castles and manorial halls believed in the glories of warfare above all other things. Peace was but a time to prepare for war. Modern humanistic Europe looks to an ideal future and seeks to attain it through rational progress [1983, p. 43].

Societies organized around such fundamental differences in philosophical assumptions and values will probably behave quite differently, at least in terms of their stated objectives and in their rationale for action. Professional subsets within society are nothing more than microcosmic settings for the acting out of value conflicts in the larger society. Our values and beliefs will influence the manner in which we deal with all social problems, organize social networks to respond to needs, allocate social resources to solve problems, and evolve social rationales to explain and justify the actions.

The illustration with which we opened this discussion is a particular case in point. History reflects sequential responses to calls for help in the solution of "mental-health" issues down through the ages. The appearance, in order, of the magician, medicine man, philosopher-priest, and, ultimately, the scientifically oriented psychotherapist is a march through the history of philosophy and values in the treatment of mental disorders. Indeed, the manifestation of the particular disorder may be relatively constant from age to age. The difference is in the way society is organized to respond to the issue.

Frank notes that there is an anthropological and historical constant to this organization and that every society has organized to solve these problems down through the ages. The names of the actors have changed from epoch to epoch, and the action is altered according to the prevailing belief system in place at the time (Frank, 1973).

The Two Cultures of Psychology

Psychology continues to deal with value conflicts within its ranks. Kimble notes that "psychology has an identity problem. After more than a century of official existence, it still lacks a coherent set of values, there is little harmony among groups of us who practice very different professions, and there is even debate over the definition of our subject matter" (Kimble, 1984, p. 833).

There are those that argue that even though psychology has been independent from philosophy for almost 100 years, the separation was premature and that we are very much in need of the skills and techniques of the philosophers to resolve some of our epistemological dilemmas. The most cogent exponent of this position states, "for some years I have argued that psychology has been misconceived, whether as a science or as any kind of coherent discipline devoted to the empirical study of human beings. That psychology *can* be an integral discipline is the 19th-century myth that motivated its baptism as an independent science—a myth which can be shown to be exactly that, both by *a priori* and by empiricohistorical considerations" (Koch, 1981, p. 268).

Koch's indictment is powerful and pessimistic with respect to the basic viability of psychology as an independent area of study and practice. Others are more optimistic about the possibility of a resolution of these issues. Kimble points out that "psychology's splintered condition results in part from the existence of sharply polarized opinion about the epistemological underpinnings of psychology" (Kimble, 1981, p. 833). Koch believes that the polarization simply cannot be resolved. Others are much more optimistic and believe that resolution is possible (Staats, 1981). Royce points out that by applying philosophical principles and methodology to the "conceptually pluralistic" discipline of psychology, it is possible to organize, describe, classify and identify the "epistemic and theoretic framework" of psychology (Royce, 1982). Royce makes the point that "the major consequence of the psychologist's lack of sophistication in philosophy is that foundational issues continue to plague us" (Royce, 1982, p. 264). However, he is essentially optimistic about the possibility of bringing order to what he describes as the "multimethodological, multivariate, multiepistemic, multiworld, and multidisciplinary" science of psychology (Royce, 1982, p. 259).

It is possible to simplify the issues somewhat by examining, as Kimble does, the "two cultures" of psychology (Kimble, 1984). Obviously, by reducing Royce's complexities to a bipolar presentation we are not suggesting an either/or scenario. Rather, the adaptation of Kimble's classification system provides us with a means to describe the extremes of the epistemic differential. Table 1-1 presents a summary of the bipolar nature of the differences.

Incidentally, we agree with Kimble's observation that "nature appears to abhor dichotomies with as much passion as she detests a vacuum. In the case of psychology's two cultures, there is in fact a sense in which they do not exist" (Kimble, 1984, p. 838). As a matter of fact, in collecting data about these bipolar issues Kimble reports that these data were continuous (Kimble, 1984). However, he also notes that socialization into camps, organizations, and other manifestations of institutionalized bias is obvious, and "the biases that made the organization attractive in the first place are nurtured and strengthened. In short, the dual processes of selection and emphasis, rather than a preestablished epistomological typology, are the bases for psychology's two cultures" (p. 838). As a matter of fact, in collecting data about these bipolar issues Kimble reports that these data were continuous (Kimble, 1984). "The dual processes of selection and emphasis, rather than a preestablished epistomological typology, are the bases for psychology's two cultures" (p. 838).

In short, it appears that members of the psychological enterprise have anchored their beliefs somewhere near the extremes of the continuum. There is a sense of opposition and antagonism vis-à-vis values. Arguments in organizations from political perspectives tend to polarize positions even further. Struggles for control over direction of professional organizations may be colored by a process that seems to impel protagonists toward the most extreme manifestations of their position. Hence major points of disagreement become translated into significant splits over fundamental issues. For example, the issues at the source of our most important values (scientific vs. human), the source of basic knowledge (objectivism vs. intuitionism), and the generality of laws (nomothetic vs. idiographic) appear regularly to power disagreements in organizational and academic enclaves (Kimble, 1984).

In a study dealing with the difference in values between a group of behavioral scientists (those associated with the behavior modification movement) and a group of nonbehavioral scientists, Krasner and Houts (1984) confirmed many of the observations made above. They concluded that "psychology as a science is not value free" and "that different groups of scientists within a discipline have very different basic assumptions about their common discipline" (pp. 847–848). As one might expect, due to the prevailing stereotype, the be-

TABLE 1.1 Scales and Subscales of the Epistemic Differential*

Scale	Related opposing ideas
1. Most important values: scientific vs. human	Increasing knowledge vs. improving human condition; methodological strength vs. relevance; obligation to apply vs. no such obligation
2. Degree of lawfulness of behavior; determinism vs. indeterminism	Lawful vs. not lawful; understanding vs. incomprehensible; predictable vs. unpredictable; controllable vs. uncontrollable
3. Source of basic knowledge; objectivism vs. intuitionism	Sense data vs. empathy; observation vs. self-report; operational definition vs. linguistic analysis; investigation vs. common sense
4. Methodological strategy: data vs. theory	Investigation vs. interpretation; induction vs. deduction; evidence vs. argument
5. Setting for discovery; laboratory vs. field	Experimentation vs. survey/case study; manipulation vs. naturalistic observation; hypothesis testing vs. correlation; control vs. ecological validity
6. Temporal aspects of lawfulness; historical vs. ahistorical	Developmental vs. descriptive approach; longitudinal vs. cross-sectional study
7. Position on nature/nurture issue; heredity	Physiology vs. situation; biological vs. social science
8. Generality of laws; nomothetic vs. idiographic	Species general vs. species specific; "standard man" vs. individual's uniqueness; universalism vs. contextualism
9. Concreteness of concepts; hypothetical constructs vs. intervening variables	Biological reality vs. conception
10. Level of analysis: elementism vs. holism	Molecular vs. molar; part vs. whole
11. Factor leading to action: cognition vs. affect	Reason vs. emotion; thinking vs. motivation; intellect vs. impulse; rational vs. irrational
12. Conception of organisms; reactivity vs. creativity	Automaticity vs. voluntary control; associationism vs. constructivism

*Table reproduced with the permission of the author.

havioral group endorsed "factual, quantitative, empirical, and objectivist approaches to the study of human behavior. In contrast, the comparison group was characterized by a more humanistic and subjectivist approach to psychology" (p. 847). That finding is not surprising in view of the ubiquitous operation of the old trait and factor notion that "birds of a feather flock together." The finding reflects a common sense variant of the socialization of values phenomenon that we referred to earlier. More important than this finding was the observation that psychologists holding these "polarized views may separate what they believe about their discipline from beliefs about the nature of the world in general" (p. 848). If the latter is true, there is probably room in the future for Royce's optimistic view regarding the possibility of the resolution of value differences. For the present, however, we think it is safe to proceed under the assumption that generally held values and beliefs infuse and inform the theories and practices of present-day psychology.

The Science of Behavior and the Image of Humankind

Isodor Chein (1972) suggests that psychologists must choose between two images of humanity. The first image portrays human beings as active, responsible agents. These agents are motivated (Homo volens) and knowledgeable (Homo sapiens). Such human beings not only respond to things that happen to them but also act in ways that increase the likelihood that some things will happen and decrease the likelihood that other events will occur. This is a being

> who tries to generate circumstances that are compatible with the execution of his intentions, a being who may try to inject harmony where he finds disharmony or who may sometimes seek to generate disharmony, a being who seeks to shape his environment rather than passively permit himself to be shaped by the latter, a being, in short, who insists on injecting himself into the causal process of the world around him [Chein, 1972, p. 6].

The competing view that Chein proposes is of the human being as impotent reactor. In this concept, people are merely responsive to the forces that impinge upon them, both external and internal. These responses are conceived of as an automatic consequence of the interaction of body and environment. In contrast to the image described above, such people play no role in determining the outcome of the interplay between their body and the environment. Instead, human beings are portrayed as robots, "a complicatedly constructed and programmed robot perhaps, but a robot nevertheless" (Homo mechanicus) [p. 6].

Others have considered the competing nature of human beings in similar fashion. Hitt (1969) presents a list of the consequences of these same two contrasting views of human beings:

1. "Man can be described meaningfully in terms of his behavior; or man can be described meaningfully in terms of his consciousness.
2. Man is predictable; or man is unpredictable.
3. Man is an information transmitter; or man is an information generator.
4. Man lives in an objective world; or man lives in a subjective world.
5. Man is a natural being; or man is an irrational being.
6. One man is like other men; or each man is unique.
7. Man can be described meaningfully in absolute terms; or man can be described meaningfully in relative terms.
8. Human characteristics can be investigated independently of one another; or man must be studied as a whole.
9. Man is a reality; or man is a potentiality.
10. Man is knowable in scientific terms; man is more than we can ever know about him" (p. 652).

The specific models presented by Hitt inform perception, research, and intervention. One can define behaviorism, humanism, and other contrasting views of psychology by model building, using these basic views. For example, the prevailing model underlying behaviorist assumptions would focus on descriptions of behavior, predictability of behavior, inferences from information transmitted, objectivity, rationality, and so on. Many of these models have been criticized as simplistic or as forcing the observer to think in an either/or way. Actually, it is possible to describe models that deal with the nature of human beings in dynamic, rather than bipolar, terms. For example, in a dialectic view of human beings, individuals interact in a variety of ways to inner drives, external demands, physical conditions, and adventitious events in an unpredictable way. What is predictable is that interaction precipitates a pattern of action, reaction, and the reestablishment of stability at a new plateau. This interactive dialectic may lead individuals to evolve in ways that transcend the possibilities of many of the bipolar models. Other attempts at broadening that bipolar view include the ideas of Allport.

Allport (1962) presents a three-pronged approach to this debate. His first approach sees the human "as a reactive being." Allport describes this model as a positivistic view "that man is in some aspect of his being, a simple respondent to simple pressures" (1962, p. 375). He includes materialistic, positivistic, and behavioristic approaches under this rubric.

In his second descriptive model "man is seen as a reactive being in depth" (p. 373). The psychoanalytic defense mechanisms help to define the added dimension of depth. There is strong emphasis on the person's past history in the search for causation and maturation. This emphasis leads to the postulation of a repository of memories, that is, the unconscious, a mechanism that banishes memories from awareness and also brings the information back into consciousness. This doctrine of recall and recovery is central to depth psychology. In this model Allport includes psychoanalysis, depth psychology, and a wide variety of other psychodynamic approaches.

The third model presented by Allport differs quite markedly from the other two. In fact, as we have indicated, there is a close affinity between the construct of the "reactive being" and the "reactive being in depth." The basic assumption of the ways of humankind are quite similar. The separation occurs over the issue of depth, not over the basic philosophical tenets. However, in the third model there are drastic departures in belief. "Man is seen as a being-in-the-process of becoming" (p. 373). Allport sees this model as contributing to a "shattering transformation" and as throwing basic assumptions open to questions. All fundamental beliefs are attacked.

In rather dramatic fashion, Allport declares that modern humanity no longer remains within the confines "of Victorian decorum, theological certainties, or the Pax Brittanica. . . . The comfortable stabilities of culture, caste, the gold standard, and military supremacy are no longer ours. Nor are the comfortable stabilities of traditional psychology adequate" (p. 377).

His view of the person in the process of becoming reflects completely different underpinnings. In the first place, this view falls more clearly in Chein's image of the motivational and knowledgeable person. It emphasizes elements in Hitt's descriptive categories, such as humans' concern with consciousness, their unpredictable nature, their subjective world, their irrationality, and their holism and potentiality. For example, Allport argues that this worldview makes it possible for people to maintain both "a tentativeness of outlook" and the ability and freedom to make strong commitments. "We can be at one and the some time half-sure and whole-hearted" (p. 377). Included in this third model are such views and approaches as self theory, existential psychology, and holistic approaches to human behavior.

The Issue of Determinism and Freedom

One of the fundamental issues underlying these varying views and images of humankind is that of freedom versus determinism. It appears that every generation of psychologists confronts this issue, finds it difficult to resolve, and subsequently backs away from it. But it simply will not leave. This issue is implied in the difference between Chein's images of humankind and is certainly at the bottom of the differences between Allport's reactive being and his being in the process of becoming.

For theorists with a clear notion of where they stand, there is generally a satisfactory resolution of the issue. Radical behaviorists have no problem accepting the determinist position. Self theorists are equally comfortable with the argument for full freedom. Indeed, as Immergluck says, a large number of psychologists, probably the majority, are comfortable with the determinist model. After all, scientific method (as traditionally defined) has produced much solid knowledge and has classified a good deal about the courses of behavior. Immergluck (1964) maintains, however, that even those who profess to be comfortable with the determinist model still struggle with "the nagging conviction that man must somehow be personally free" (p. 270).

Gelso (1970) reflects this persistent paradox by suggesting that "strict determinism and free will are both valid and necessary assumptions" (p. 275). He justifies this assertion by contending that freedom and determinism exist along "different dimensions of human experience," and consequently the sources of information for each are different. He postulates "an objective scientific outer dimension" and "a subjective ascientific inner dimension." On the outer dimension freedom is an illusion, and on the inner dimension freedom is both necessary and possible.

Immergluck (1964) describes this effort to reconcile the two positions as an attempt to bridge the gap between two divergent views in modern psychology; "both are somehow right within their own limited frameworks in that they really complement one another in jointly reflecting the total realities of psychological life" (p. 271).

Immergluck rejects this notion as having serious flaws, particularly since he concludes that the experience of inner freedom is essentially a distortion of reality, an illusion. However, he is human enough to understand that although "the free-will character of our action is an illusion . . . it may well turn out to be a necessary illusion'' (p. 279). His conclusion is based on the belief that perhaps determinism does make too harsh an assault on human dignity and that to maintain their dignity, people must accept illusion, at least until scientific knowledge leads us to an altered view of human nature.

Perhaps there is another option in this continuing controversy between freedom and determinism. Phillips and Torbet (1968) suggest that we may need to define freedom in more specific terms before drawing conclusions about the issue. They examine freedom as indeterminacy and conclude that it would lead to a concept of unsystematic behavior and consequently to people who were not responsible. They examine the notion of freedom as ignorance and maintain that ultimately, when we know the facts, we shall have to reject this notion of freedom. Finally, they offer an analysis of freedom as control by goals. ''According to this image, a person is free when his actions are related to his goals by reasons'' (Phillips & Torbet, 1968, p. 370). They suggest, however, that the goals themselves may be determined. Finally they conclude that ''freedom as ignorance is an illusion; freedom as indeterminacy is sheer nonsense; . . . The kind of freedom that is most important . . . is control by goals: that person is freest who has the most information about his problem and the best ability to relate that information to his goals'' (p. 371).

We are certainly unable to offer a resolution of this issue, which has been perplexing psychology for as long as the discipline has existed. Certainly Phillips and Torbet's conception of freedom as controlled by goals places the concept within an essentially deterministic framework. It provides a concept that makes it possible to conceive of a limited amount of conscious control even within a largely deterministic framework. It is a step beyond the concept of a ''necessary illusion,'' and it does contribute to the maintenance of human dignity.

Value Orientations

The adoption of a particular theoretical orientation by psychological practitioners is in many ways as much an ethical decision as it is a rational selection among academic options. As Peterson (1976) notes, ''to take refuge in a claim of being scientific and thus unbiased is to deceive one's self, and to avoid the issue by claiming neutrality is to take a position of naive realism'' (p. 2)

Every decision, every act, every intervention that the counselor selects is filled with personal and moral decision making. Ultimately all counselors have to choose for themselves a position of morality to which they are committed. This morality stems from their values and beliefs. Every aspect of their professional behavior is value laden. The very act of assuming a professional role and offering their services implies that they value *what they are doing*. Their specific choices among therapeutic options emanate from their belief and value systems. London (1964) writes that

> many psychotherapists are poignantly unaware of this. Students of mental health find that it is difficult even to define such terms as ''health,'' ''illness,'' and ''normality'' without some reference to morals; and worse still, they cannot discuss the proper treatment of what they have defined without recognizing and involving their own moral commitments [p. 5].

This lack of awareness is particularly distressing in view of the fact that consistent reports of research over the years tend to confirm that the various psychotherapeutic approaches apparently produce the same level of outcome irrespective of theoretical orientation (Fiedler, 1950; Masling & Cohen, 1987). In addition, most psychotherapists seem to generate support for their own theoretical orientation in reporting success (Masling & Cohen, 1987). This tendency is described by Masling and Cohen as evidence of "therapists' belief in their own theories" that "serves as a self fulfilling prophecy, both to produce change in clients and to confirm the theory" (1987, p. 65). The point seems to be that counselors and therapists do make moral judgments and commitments without subjecting them to empirical testing. Frequently, it is the belief system of the therapists that determines the nature of intervention, rather than experimental evidence.

There is a good deal of convincing evidence that improvement in counseling and therapy is related to a convergence of values between counselors and clients (Rosenthal, 1955). This startling observation certainly reinforces the notion of the therapist or counselor as a member of a new secular priesthood. The point is that counseling is not neutral in terms of morals and values. The counselor's personal value system contributes to his or her functioning as a moral agent. Although the issue of conscious interjection of values by the counselor may be arguable, the process of subtle reinforcement may be inadvertent or deliberate. The conscious or unconscious nodding of the head, the barely perceptible forward lean of the body, the audible "uh-huh" may all serve to shape the client's response and reflect his/her values. However, such reinforcement appears to be present to a very significant degree in every counselor-client interaction. There are many apocryphal tales about why Freud moved from facing his patients to a position out of their view. We have no special insight into which of these tales is most accurate. Today, however, analysts sit behind the client to try to reduce the latter's ability to deduce their reactions and judgments. The practice is followed in order to mask the therapist's value system as much as possible for as long as possible. Perhaps this is as close to neutrality with respect to conveying values as counselors can come.

We know that the opposite extreme—namely, self-disclosure—is a very potent therapeutic force. It must be used in a controlled and deliberate fashion to maximize its effectiveness and to prevent it from becoming a liability rather than a therapeutic asset (Halpern, 1977).

It would appear that, like it or not, counselors intervene in the moral positions of their clients. Lowe's notion of the therapist as secular priest is not inconceivable considering the similarity between the two historical roles in society. Lowe (1976) identifies the therapist as

> mediating between man and society, conveying meaning of that social world whose confrontation is so bewildering to modern man. To the therapist belong the keys of a new kingdom, whose gates are opened not by faith in the supernatural, but by faith in science as interpreter of social reality [p. 16].

Critical Philosophical Value Systems

There are various approaches to classifying counseling theories within a framework of philosophical value systems. Although several have merit and are certainly adequate to the task at hand, we will concentrate on the system put forth by C. Marshall Lowe (1959, 1976), with references to some of the conceptions of James R. Barclay (1971). Lowe identifies four major streams of value orientation that compete for the counselor's attention: naturalism, culturalism, humanism, and theism.

Naturalism. For Lowe, "a naturalistic world view assumes that scientific laws can account for all phenomena . . . (and thus) limits psychology to the study of behavior" (1959, pp. 687–688). This view leads to the behaviorist approach to psychology, and Lowe identifies B. F. Skinner as the foremost proponent of this approach to human behavior. Naturalism, or rationalism, implies that logic is the basic source of truth and that knowledge in this framework is public and verifiable. Knowledge can be verified through the scientific method, and logical positivism is the primary scientific method to be employed. Barclay (1971), by extending the notions of naturalism and rationalism to an environmentalist approach to counseling and psychotherapy, includes the psychoanalysts (Freud and his disciples), the neo-psychoanalytic group (Horney and Sullivan), as well as behaviorists from a variety of orientations. For example, the experimental behaviorists such as Skinner, the behavior learning therapists (Eysenck and Wolpe) and the behavioral engineering group (Krumboltz and Bandura) are also included under this rubric (Barclay, 1971). Indeed, by extending the notion of naturalism to rational and environmental approaches, Barclay also includes experimentalists such as Williamson and Robinson.

Obviously, there are wide differences among these approaches to counseling and psychotherapy, but they are essentially congruent with respect to their theoretical underpinnings.

Culturalism. In the culturalist approach, those who contemplate issues of value in the realm of counseling and psychotherapy are concerned with the social needs of human beings and their manifestations. The focus here is on the social nature of the individual and the manifestation of problems arising from social needs rather than from physical needs. Lowe notes that "culturalism makes loyalty to the culture from which man is derived the supreme value" (1959, p. 689).

In this frame of reference issues are almost always rooted in social and interpersonal experiences. There is a strong commitment to social change as well as to personal adjustment. Indeed, in more radical manifestations of culturalism, the assumptions of adjustment with emphasis on adaptability to social conditions may be rejected in favor of a more socially activist position. From this perspective the basic source of the problem is the existing social situation, and the therapeutic imperative to a great extent is devoted to changing those social conditions.

From more traditional culturalist viewpoints, people's difficulties can be viewed as part of a complex of interactions among social conditions and interpersonal relations. Lowe notes that "we see this emphasis in such social psychoanalysts as Adler, Sullivan and Horney who see the cause of neurosis as isolation from other people and who see the cure in being led back to other people" (1959, p. 689).

The source of knowledge for the culturalists is usually public. The validation of that knowledge is usually empirical and results from a search for consensus. Culturalism is not as closely reliant on the scientific process as is naturalism, in that some elements of personal experience are accepted as valid sources of data. It is an approach that attempts to bridge the gap between scientific logic and empirical consensus. Social science is built on these premises.

Humanism.   Humanists view the human being as the major source of knowledge and values. Humanist values are based on the inherent dignity and worth of the person. As Lowe notes, ''the first humanistic value is that man is a rational being. If man is valued as a creature who above all is good, then the rationality which sets him apart from the animal is her crowning glory'' (1976, p. 99).

The second humanist value stems from commitment to the actualization potential of human beings. ''Humanists continue to emphasize individual initiative and to believe in progress and in man's ability to perfect his world'' (Lowe, 1976, p. 100). The ultimate manifestation of these two humanist values is the belief that people can control their own destiny through rationality and the exercise of will. Indeed, people are conceived of as having an internal drive to actively pursue positive growth. In some views of the humanist philosophy the drive takes on an imperative of its own. Among humanist psychologists, the equating of activism with mental health is the same whether the object of therapy be termed ''self-actualization,'' as by Goldstein, or ''emergent value-attitudes'' or the ''growth potential,'' as by Rogers.

Self-fulfillment, insight, and subjective evaluation processes are characteristic of the humanist approaches to counseling and psychotherapy (Barclay, 1971). Carl Rogers represents one of the major approaches to a counseling theory derived from humanism. Some of the work of Erich Fromm was also influenced by this philosophy. In addition, both religious and nonreligious existential views are reflective of humanist philosophies. As Barclay notes, ''existentialism is a philosophy that focuses on experience and experiencing'' (1971, p. 329). It also focuses on the nature of existence and the issues of being and attempts to bridge the gap between subject and object. Existential philosophy translated into a psychology attempts to understand human beings in their own world, their experience in this world, and their confrontation of problems.

The source of truth and knowledge in this perspective is more private than public. There is a basic faith in the capacity of human beings to direct themselves, free of restraints and external guidance. Religion and religious beliefs are possible but not necessary when humans are self-directing. The emphasis is on idiosyncratic experiencing of religion. Although reason is respected, there is also room to accept action based on intuition and feeling. Therefore a romantic and spiritual view of the world is compatible with this viewpoint.

Theism.   For theists, the problems that people face have their solution in religious faith. Despair, loss, meaninglessness, and interpersonal strife all have solutions within the context of religious beliefs. The supernatural and the spiritual transcend everyday concerns.

Obviously, knowledge and truth, in this frame of reference, are quite private. Light and truth are derived from religious faith and frequently emanate from supernatural sources. Although reason is certainly useful and acceptable, it is ultimately secondary to faith and intuition as a source of energy for action.

In the contemporary social context, issues of values and morals seem to pervade many of the problems of everyday living. In the contemporary professional situation for psychologists, the same situation prevails. Indeed, as we have already noted, while clients and counselors rarely deal with problems that are presented in clearly moral terms or as problems involving value resolution, much of what is presented and dealt with in counseling and psychotherapy involves both morals and values. Lowe believes that "therapy can be regarded as a process in which the client searches for significant values while the therapist responds either actively or passively by providing moral direction" (1976, p. 273). We are inclined to agree with this view. For this reason, counselors' knowledge of their own values and the values and moral options open to their clients is critical to the process of therapy.

Peterson (1976) offers the following "vital considerations" for counselors:

1. Counselors should as far as possible attempt to understand the society of which they are a part and especially the value conflicts stemming from it.
2. The quest for identity is in reality a search for meaning and significance; counselors should be mindful that it is a value-laden quest.
3. Counselors cannot avoid influencing their clients and must be aware of and concerned about the direction of their influence.
4. Counselors must make their values explicit to themselves and, when appropriate, to their clients (pp. 230–236).

Implications for Human Development

The philosophical value systems we have just examined have implications for human development. Although a complete explication of the issues of human development is beyond the scope of this presentation, it may be useful to examine some basic principles that inform counseling theory in the three orientations that are central to our presentation—namely, the psychodynamic, behavioral, and humanist perspectives.

Psychodynamic Views. The essence of the psychoanalytic perspective is that human beings are complicated and are impelled to action and growth by drives and passions as well as by external demands. The basic Freudian model portrays human beings propelled more by pleasure than by reason (Langer, 1969). Human development in this framework proceeds through a series of predictable stages that are biologically determined and psychologically modified by experience. They are the same for all human beings.

The structure of the mind is universal and consists of the id, which is the source of energy and instincts, the superego, which introjects social norms and restrictions, and the ego, which mediates between the two. In a classical modification of Freudian theory, C. G. Jung postulated an "impersonal" psychic system that existed in all people as "the collective unconscious" (Langer, 1969). Freud, of course, believed in the existence of the individual unconscious, a repository of information, memory, and motivational vectors beyond the conscious awareness of the person.

Modern psychodynamic thinkers have modified some of these beliefs in recent years. The ego psychologists ascribe much more importance and independence to the ego itself. They assume that the ego is capable of action independent of the id and superego and that it has an organizing directive and integrating function much broader than that conceived by Freud (Ford & Urban, 1963).

Psychologists such as Loevinger and Erikson have extended the developmental stages that were originally proposed by Freud to be more consistent with modern notions of ego psychology and more consistent with cultural awareness (Langer, 1969). These views are consistent with Allport's (1962) notions of a "reactive being in depth."

Behavioral Approaches. At the core of the behavioral model of human development is the belief that humans grow to be what they become by virtue of responding to forces that impinge on them from their environment. This view is consistent with Allport's notion of a reactive being.

Langer (1969) refers to this model as the mechanical mirror. Human beings reflect, behaviorally, that which stimulates them. The behavior is triggered by an external stimulus (agent), and the response is virtually automatic. Behavior in later life is the cumulative, quantitative, continuous aggregation of reactive behavior.

Modifications are certainly possible within this system. Psychologists such as Bandura and Vygotsky have postulated a process of mediation that changes the purely reactive responsiveness by incorporating a role for cognition. But it remained for Piaget and Werner to evolve a view of behavioral consciousness that truly transcends the simple reactive notions of earlier behavioral models. From their perspective development is a self-evolving psychological process that far exceeds the single stimulus/response association of traditional behaviorism. Vygotsky, Luria, Bandura, and others stand somewhere between the Skinnerian notion of a "mechanical mirror" and the more dynamic Piaget/Werner viewpoint (Langer, 1969).

The behavioral conception of learning is based on a perception of human beings as active agents and on a view of development as a self-constructive process. The human being is essentially self-generating, powered by genetic forces through a series of predictable evolutionary stages of mental and physical development (Langer, 1969). There is a heavy emphasis on cognition, perception, judgment, and operational activity.

Humanistic Viewpoints. The humanist perspective on development places a much stronger emphasis on human goals and perspectives. Charlotte Buhler is one thinker in this field who has raised the question of human volition and the impact of that motivation on behavior (Buhler & Musserick, 1968). This approach is less concerned with the biological basis of behavior and more with the impact of human motives and drives implementing human potentialities at all ages.

Humanism ascribes psychological motivations to development at each stage of life from early infancy onward. Buhler speculates that differences in behavior in infants, such as relative passivity versus relative activity, are not merely biological but reflect a volitional element at whatever level of symbolic behavior is possible at each age. She postulates that goal-setting behaviors may be infused in very young children. This system proposes a model in which children, rather than reacting to external stimulation, create the kind of environment they wish to have by engaging in behaviors that they select. Buhler incorporates the notion of mastery of the environment as part of this process and proposes that at all stages of development individuals are engaged in an interactive process with the forces around them.

These three varying views of human development have obvious implications for the critical theories of counseling, which follow in the next section.

Critical Counseling Theories

Approaches to counseling and psychotherapy have proliferated ad infinitum over the past half century. As Moursand (1985) notes, "In 1920 there was one psychotherapeutic approach; in 1930 there were, perhaps, half a dozen, all but one of only minor influence. Then explosion— . . . therapies piled upon therapies. Parloff reported more than 130 systems in 1976 and the number has continued to grow" (p. 5).

The purpose of our presentation is to provide a set of beginning guidelines to enable the psychological consumer to distinguish among these various systems. More than that, our goal is to suggest an approach that may enable us to identify the commonalities among the critical systems that clamor for our attention. Are there general theoretical assumptions that blend varying views of counseling and psychotherapy? Are there similar perceptions of the nature of human beings that will enable us to set up classification systems that identify theories with consistent baselines?

There have been a number of systematic attempts to bind viewpoints together in this fashion based on underlying assumptions and principles of practice. For example, Moursand reports a classification system of psychotherapy based on behavioral and verbal premises. Under the behavioral classification she lists such approaches as operant and classical behaviorism, conditioning, behavior modification, systematic desensitization, and cognitive behavioral methods. Under verbal approaches, she includes such theoretical orientations as rational-emotive therapy, psychodynamic therapies, humanistic approaches, client-centered therapy, and the like. This classification approach is very reminiscent of the system proposed by London (1964), which divided counseling and psychotherapy into insight and action orientations.

Barclay (1971) also offers a bipolar classification system, focusing on the distinction between an environmentalist approach (psychoanalysis, behavior learning therapy, experimental behaviorism, neo-psychoanalytic therapy) and a humanist approach (self theories and existential therapies). He recognizes that bipolar classification systems of this sort may be too simplistic for the complicated task of classifying approaches to counseling and psychotherapy. He presents evidence that it is probably necessary to analyze each theorist with respect to a variety of theoretical variables such as conscious processes, unconscious processes, self-concept, social determinants, emotion, learning, influence of the past, and biological determinants.

Our purpose in this presentation is to relate basic mainline theories to the fundamental philosophical belief systems of the main protagonists of the field. We recognize that variations and imitations exist within the three mainstream critical approaches to the theory. However, the fundamental assumptives remain reasonably constant.

The three mainstream approaches that we consider are the behavioral, the psychodynamic, and the humanist. Theories that share the same philosophical underpinnings tend to view the nature of humankind in a similar fashion. Their approaches to human development are also roughly congruent, although it is true that their techniques may differ. Techniques appear to be less significant than the fundamental applications of particular techniques. The latter can only be understood in terms of the assumptions and goals of the system, which, in turn, involves comprehending the action of practitioners within a system.

Our approach to understanding critical theories of counseling is based on the belief that counseling and psychotherapy represent the crystallization of belief systems rather than a technology. Even in the behavioral approaches, where the technical crafting of programs for change is critical, the techniques are much more clearly understood and delivered in the context of the beliefs and philosophy of the system.

Earlier in this chapter, we presented a variety of views of the nature of humankind. We shall use the Allportian system as a framework for our presentation of the critical theories of counseling.

Behaviorism: Modifying the Reactive Being

Most forms of behavior therapy adopt Allport's view of humans as reactive beings. The man who most clearly personifies this belief system is Burrhus Frederic Skinner, whose theories have informed the approach to therapy that has been labeled radical behaviorism.

Skinner's Radical View.   Skinner is not only a radical behaviorist but also a radical determinist: "Skinner does not look within the human psyche for any of the causes of behavior, and he denies the necessity of postulating states of mind and internal motives for exploration purposes" (Nye, 1981, p. 49). As indicated earlier in our presentation, this viewpoint derives its philosophical assumptions from essentially naturalistic and rationalistic roots. Its view of human development is presented in the framework of a responding organism that is acted on and shaped by the environment. Skinner and the radical behaviorists would view the process of human development as consistent with Langer's (1969) concept of the mechanical mirror. According to Nye, "Skinner says that mentalistic concepts only confuse and mislead, drawing attention away from real causes such as punishment. . . . In Skinner's view, there is also no place in scientific psychology for an assumption that human behavior is governed by 'individual choice' as that phrase is commonly used" (1981, p. 51).

Treatment in this system involves identifying the goals of the therapeutic situation, developing an understanding of the manner in which the original or undesirable behavior was shaped and maintained, and intervening in the process by using the same principles to alter behavior. Skinner's contention is that all behavior is learned, including behavior identified as mentally ill, neurotic, destructive, and so on. He has suggested "that the explanation for neurotic, psychotic, and other problem behaviors often may be found in environmental factors such as unique histories of reinforcement, conditions of extreme deprivation or satiation, intense aversive control, and harsh punishment" (Nye, 1981, p. 93).

Skinner suggests that the focus for changing these behaviors should be on the observable behaviors and conditions themselves. The development of the process for redirecting behavior involves an analysis of the existing contingencies of reinforcement in the person's life and the subsequent design of effective shaping techniques, new conditions of reinforcement, and environmental control to produce the desired result. Skinner believes that changes in behavior will lead to changes in feeling, not the reverse. According to his view, "the problem is the behavior and not the person" (Nye, 1981, p. 94).

Other Applications of Learning Theory to Counseling. Other important practitioners have applied learning or behavioral approaches to counseling and psychotherapy. These include Albert Bandura, Joseph Wolpe, Leonard P. Ullman, Leonard Krasner, John Krumboltz, and Carl Thoresen. They adhere to the fundamental principles of learning theory and the assumptions outlined above. But each has offered significant modifications to both Skinner's assumptions and his techniques.

Bandura, for example, recognizes that the selection of goals involves value choices and that even so-called objective behavior modifiers may run the risk of having their values intrude on the goal-selection process (Huber & Millman, 1972, p. 327). Bandura has applied a more subtle application of morality to the process of behavior modification than has Skinner and has focused on social initiation. Wolpe has developed his approach to behavior modification and theory from a classical conditioning viewpoint. He evolved a process of systematic desensitization based on relaxation (Huber & Millman, 1972).

Ullman and Kramer have done an excellent job of synthesizing the process and the issues in behavior modification. Krumboltz and Thoresen have evolved an approach to the application of behavior-modification techniques that is in the mainstream of verbal approaches to counseling while remaining clearly in the behavioral camp (Huber & Millman, 1972).

Psychodynamic Approaches:
Understanding the Reactive Being in Depth

The major proponent of the psychodynamic approach was Sigmund Freud. Freud and most of his disciples share with the behaviorists a deterministic view of the world. Whereas the behaviorists view human beings as passive, reactive, and essentially neutral, the psychodynamic position pays much more attention to what is going on inside the person. Psychodynamics, particularly as espoused by Freud, focuses on feelings and passions and identifies the essentially conflicted nature of human beings.

In his adherence to a deterministic viewpoint, Freud believed that all behavior was caused and could be accounted for, although the clear relationship between the causes of behavior and their consequences was regularly masked. According to Nye,

> If humans remain a mystery it is because of inadequacies in uncovering the driving forces within them and the experiences that have influenced their behavior. Nevertheless, these forces and influences do exist and they do determine the person's functioning. It is the role of psychoanalysis to uncover the mystery by seeking the sources of thoughts, feelings, and actions in hidden drives and conflicts [1981, p. 3].

Freud postulated a developmental process that was predictable and ubiquitous. He posited the psychological nature of development and formulated a set of constructs to account for the social manifestations of neurosis. Among his more controversial ideas were the theory of infantile sexuality and the Oedipal conflict. He proposed that pleasurable sensations were related to the normal psychological development of the child and that affect and meaning became fused during this process. The Oedipus complex resulted from a rivalry between a male child and his father because of the increasingly erotic nature of his love for his mother. Both these hypothetical constructs led to great controversy in mid-Victorian Vienna.

Freud also postulated a topography of the mind that rested on his notion of the unconscious. The unconscious was the repository of all aspects of our behavior of which we are unaware. As we have said, he also proposed the existence of an id, the site of basic drives, including the sexual and the aggressive; a superego, which introjected social constraints and constrictions; and an ego, which mediated between the two.

Freud's system of treatment was predicated on helping his patients gain access to the unconscious through the mechanism of free association and thereby uncover the connections and motives that were heretofore masked. This uncovering of the connections between early events and later behavior and the insight that results from it would lead to changes in behavior, in the Freudian view. The analyst works with transference, the client's unrealistic perception of the therapist as having the characteristics of significant figures in the patient's past, and with resistance, the mechanism by which patients avoid facing the truth about themselves. Interpretation of behavior is critical to this approach.

Modern psychodynamic approaches to therapy in depth may have modified Freud's premises to some extent. However, the basic structure remains relatively intact. There were early splits with colleagues and disciples such as Jung and Alfred Adler. Adler split with Freud by emphasizing the influence of social forces in causing behavioral problems rather than the unconscious of the individual. He came to believe that forces external to the individual played a major part in shaping behavior. Adler also ascribed a great deal of motivation to the individual's striving for superiority over external and internal forces. Freud ultimately dismissed his work as counterproductive to the psychoanalytic movement.

Jung evolved a metaphysical system that depended on constructs such as archetypes and developed a symbolism that Freud saw as unacceptable (Brown, 1964). His conception of the structure of the mind was much more complex than Freud's. He saw Freud's elements as merely the tip of the iceberg,

> a relatively insignificant fraction of the total mass of unconscious material. . . . That which lies below the personal unconscious is known as the collective or social unconscious, since it contains the collective beliefs and myths of the race to which the individual belongs. The deepest levels of the collective unconscious are the universal unconscious common to all humanity and even, it would appear, to man's primate and animal ancestry [Brown, 1964, p. 45].

Freud split with Jung and with other early associates who developed views of the application of the psychoanalytic process at variance with his own ideas. The British psychoanalyst Melanie Klein accepted orthodox Freudian theory but expanded it to include a more detailed study of the very early years of life. She believed that the first two years were particularly important (Brown, 1964).

Freud's daughter, Anna Freud, may also be viewed as a significant post-Freudian; she, too, accepted the basic orthodoxy of psychodynamics "while attaching more significance to the ego and its defenses than was formerly the case" (Brown, 1964, p. 37). Like Klein she focused her attention on the treatment of very young children. Both Klein and Anna Freud extended orthodox analytic theory to the treatment of very young children, 2 years of age in the case of Klein and about 3 in the case of Anna Freud.

Other post-Freudians included Karen Horney and Erich Fromm. Both practiced psychoanalysis in Berlin before the onset of Nazism. Horney ultimately moved to the United States, where she concentrated on the contribution of social factors to neurosis. Fromm, somewhat more politically radical than Horney, was concerned with the essential relationship between the individual and society, the nature of authoritarianism, and the emphasis on a social etiology of development rather than a biological one. Fromm has been adopted by the humanists, the existentialists, and even the Marxists as one of their own. This is undoubtedly due to his concern with what he labeled the "existential dichotomy" of living and his observation that there is a significant relationship between "cultural attainment" and neurosis (Brown, 1964, p. 155).

Another post-Freudian is the American psychologist Harry Stack Sullivan. Like Horney and Fromm, Sullivan differed from Freud in particular areas, but his position remained within the general purview of psychoanalytic theory. Sullivan, too, was influenced by social psychology and believed that personality was shaped by personal relationships. In Sullivan's view "we do not merely have experiences, we are our experiences'' (Brown, 1964, p. 166). Indeed, Sullivan believed that as we pursue satisfactions in meeting our basic physical needs and as we seek security in the cultural context of our existence, we form those aspects of personality that motivate our interpersonal behavior. Like Horney and Fromm, he was less concerned with the inevitability of particular biological influences on personality development and more concerned with the social manifestations of the interactions among people in the search for satisfaction and security.

The neo-Freudians, essentially ego psychologists, were influenced by Freud and the post-Freudians. Among the most significant of this group is Erik Erikson, who trained with Freud in Vienna, worked with Anna Freud and ultimately came to the United States. According to Nye (1981), Erikson emphasized the social influence impinging on the various developmental stages. He also added to Freud's developmental constructs by describing the three stages that covered young adulthood, the middle years of adulthood, and old age. Erikson is one of the first of the psychoanalytically influenced writers to propose a developmental system that spans the person's entire life and entertains the real possibility that development continues throughout a person's life. He labeled his developmental conception ''epigenetic.'' Erikson was also an ego psychologist, and he believed that the ego ''has the potential to deal creatively with life experiences and to produce such positive outcomes as competency, a sense of purpose, the ability to love and wisdom in old age'' (Nye, 1981, p. 42).

The manifestations of the influences of Sigmund Freud are found in the current practice of a wide variety of practitioners who consider themselves psychodynamically oriented. They believe in many of Freud's basic premises about the unconscious and the mechanisms of defense. They are essentially biologically oriented with respect to human development. They accept the Freudian wisdom about the role of insight in therapy and utilize variants of his analysis of transference and resistance in treatment.

However, they are much more attuned to social influences on behavior. They are aware of the relationship between culture and neurosis. In addition, they have more confidence in the ability of the ego to deal with circumstantial problems and to advance individual development without the need for the complete uncovering demanded by orthodox Freudians. Psychodynamic counseling and psychotherapy are optimistic, present- and future-oriented, competency-based, and generally committed to shorter periods of treatment than their parent, psychoanalysis.

Humanism: People in the Process of Becoming

Humanist counselors and psychotherapists are deeply committed to the idea of possibility. They perceive themselves as the ''third force'' in American psychology, after behaviorism and psychoanalysis. As we have said, humanism is based on a conception of human nature that is positive, with people having the capacity to make free choices with respect to their goals. There is a strong belief in the Maslovian notion of a natural tendency in people toward actualization. According to the humanist perspective the inherent drive toward actualization is impaired by people's social experiences and by the conditions placed on them by the society in which they live. The goal of treatment is to create conditions that remove the impediments to growth and freedom. This essentially optimistic view of the world promotes the idea that helping people overcome the blocks to growth that have accompanied their development will free them to make positive choices for growth. Moreover, it will put them in touch with their essential compassion, will lead them to a nonjudgmental acceptance of others, and will leave them comfortable with the tentative state of the world.

Rogers's Approach. The foremost proponent of this viewpoint was Carl Ransom Rogers, who, along with Freud and Skinner, was one of the most influential figures in psychology during the past half century. Rogers, an American midwesterner, was engaged in the practice of counseling and psychotherapy from the late 1920s until his death in 1987. He began publishing in the early 1930s and continued adding to his psychological social commentary for more than 50 years. A consistent theme running throughout his observations was essentially congruent with a humanist phenomenological perspective. Rogers stated his essential beliefs about the human condition in a retrospective written a few years before his death: "The individual has within himself vast resources for self understanding, for altering his self concept, his attitudes, and his self directed behavior—and . . . these resources can be tapped only if a definable climate of facilitative psychological attitudes can be provided" (1980, p. 49).

Rogers worked clinically for more than 20 years before he finally decided to advance a theory of therapy and personality (Rogers, 1959). However, he had already created a sensation among counselors and therapists with his publication of a series of observations on "the necessary and sufficient conditions of therapeutic personality change" (Rogers, 1959). These conditions were essentially designed to provide clients with the optimal environment in which to grow. Rogers believed that if clients enter counseling in a state of incongruence* and make contact with a counselor, the process will commence. Counselors need to be reasonably congruent and to have the capacity to communicate empathetically with clients. Moreover, they must have unconditional regard for clients as people. If those facilitative conditions are met the clients will probably feel increasingly free to express their feelings, accurately symbolize and visualize their experience, and reorganize their self concept. In the absence of conditions of worth,† the locus of evaluations will become internal, and clients will evolve the capacity to take responsibility for their actions and life in general (Rogers, 1959). That seminal approach led to a considerable amount of research in this system (actually, the self-therapists have generated more empirical research evaluating their system than the other critical approaches to counseling have; research in this area goes back to 1949). Rogers asserted that "there is a body

---

*Rogers used the term *congruence* to describe the relationship between perceived needs and their satisfaction. If there was a close relationship between that perception and the individual's actual experience, relative congruence eisted. Converesely, if an individual experienced a major discrepancy between perception and experience, he/she might be described as being in a state of *incongruence.*
†By *conditions of worth,* Rogers meant that in many interpersonal situations an individual received love, acceptance, or positive regard only if he/she conformed to certain expectations. The "condition" for receiving the approval was conforming to the expectations of the other. Conditions of worth are in effect a *quid pro quo.*

of steadily mounting research evidence which by and large supports the view that when these facilitative conditions are present, changes in personality and behavior do indeed occur" (1980, p. 117). He ascribed much of the nurturant quality of his therapeutic approach to the facilitative condition of empathy. While emphasizing the importance of the other factors, he maintained that the empathic process was the one indispensable ingredient in the evolution of the self. He noted, in reference to the therapeutic process in a person-centered approach, that "the individual in this nurturing climate is free to choose any direction, but actually selects positive and constructive ways. The actualizing tendency is operative in the human being" (1980, p. 134).

Rogers' best-known contributions to psychology are the development and refinement of client-centered therapy. However, he extended his worldview to include encounter groups, family relationships, and general human relationships (Nye, 1981). The original therapeutic approach

> was called nondirective. Later it became widely known as client-centered [and most recently] Rogers and his colleagues, since the middle 1970's, have used the name person-centered. The point of the name change is to reflect more strongly that the person, in his or her full complexity, is at the center of focus. Also, Rogers and his colleagues want to emphasize that their assumptions are meant to apply broadly to almost all aspects of human behavior and are not limited to therapeutic settings [Nye, 1981, p. 14].

Existential Approaches.   The humanist viewpoint is also reflected in the therapeutic views of existentialist writers, most notably Rollo May. Existential thinking is similar to Rogers's notions, in that it is a protest directed against traditional philosophy on the one hand and toward traditional psychology on the other. Many existentialists have claimed that Rogers is a part of their camp, but he did not readily associate himself with any particular school.

In any event, the existentialists have been concerned with such person-oriented issues as the nature of existence, the limitations of reason and rationality, anxiety, freedom, and life-and-death issues. In May's terms, the goal of existential therapy is "the achieving of a sense of being . . . a relation to one's self and one's own identity, which is a prerequisite for the working through of specific problems" (Huber & Millman, 1972, p. 238).

Existentialists in general, and May in particular, are concerned with issues of humanity. They accept the philosophical view that human beings have the capacity and power to influence their own destiny.

The relationship between therapist and client involves two real people, and the interaction between the intrapsychic processes of client and therapist is the focus of the therapy. In fact, there is a great deal of concordance between this approach and that of person-centered systems in which both counselor and client are seen as people in the process of becoming. Since the therapeutic situation is real rather than contrived, both therapist and client are affected in real and significant ways. In effect, the real "care" of the relationship is reflected in the true inclusion of each other in a significant existential encounter. The existential viewpoint shares humanist values and beliefs with Rogers's person-centered therapy.

Summary

Our primary thesis is that an analysis of theories of counseling and psychotherapy must take place in the framework of the underlying philosophy, values, and beliefs of the protagonists of those theories. We have noted that there are more than 130 separate theories of counseling and psychotherapy. Most can be classified within the framework of the three viewpoints we view as the critical theories—namely, the behaviorist, psychodynamic, and humanist models—although some approaches may be hybrids of two critical theories.

We have presented the fundamental beliefs underlying these three critical streams of ideas. We have indicated that the behaviorists function in the mainstream of naturalist thought. They are scientifically oriented and believe wholly in the biological nature of human beings. Behaviorists are committed to an empirical model of the verification of ideas and view human beings as essentially reactive to their genetic heritage and to the environment.

The psychodynamic point of view shares many of the scientific beliefs of the behaviorist but focuses on the inner domain of the individual and presents a conception of human motivation based on the unique conception of the unconscious. Psychodynamicists also believe in the limited freedom of humankind.

In contrast, the humanist view, the final set of critical theories considered, presented a set of conceptions based on the belief in the freedom of the individual to control his/her life experiences and in a system of personality and motivation based on personal control and volition.

Finally, it is our contention that all theories of counseling and psychotherapy derive from one of these critical streams of thought.

References

Allport, G. (1962). Psychological Models for Guidance. *Harvard Educational Review, 32*(4), 373–382.

Barclay, J. R. (1971). *Foundations of Counseling Strategies.* New York: Wiley.

Brown, J. A. C. (1964). *Freud and Post-Freudians.* Middlesex, England: Penguin.

Buhler, C., & Musserick, F. (Eds.). (1968). *The Course of Human Life: A Study of Goals in the Humanistic Perspective.* New York: Springer.

Chein, I. (1972). *The Science of Behavior and the Image of Man.* New York: Basic Books.

Ehrenwald, J. (1976). *The History of Psychotherapy.* New York: Aronson.

Fielder, F. E. (1950). A Comparison of Therapeutic Relationships in Psychoanalytic, Non-Directive, and Adlerian Therapy. *Journal of Consulting Psychology, 15,* 32–38.

Ford, D. H., & Urban, H. B. (1963). *Systems of Psychotherapy.* New York: Wiley.

Frank, (1973) Gelso, C. (1970). Two Different Worlds: A Paradox in Counseling and Psychotherapy. *Journal of Counseling Psychology, 17*(3), 271–278.

Gelso, C. (1970). Two Different Worlds: A Paradox in Counseling and Psychotherapy. *Journal of Counseling Psychology, 17*(3), 271–278.

Halpern, T. (1977). Degree of Client Disclosure as a Function of Past Disclosure, Counselor Disclosure, and Counselor Facilitativeness. *Journal of Counseling Psychology, 24,* 41–47.

Hitt, William D. (1969). Two Models of Man. *American Psychologist, 24,* 651–658.

Huber, J. T., & Millman, H. J. (Eds.) (1972). *Goals and Behavior in Psychotherapy and Counseling.* Columbus, OH: Merrill.

Immergluck, L. (1964). Determinism-Freedom in Contemporary Psychology: An Ancient Problem Revisited. *American Psychologist, 19*(4), 270–281.

Kimble, G. A. (1984). Psychology's Two Cultures. *American Psychologist, 39*(8), 833–839.

Koch, S. (1981). The Nature and Limits of Psychological Knowledge. *American Psychologist,* 1981, *36*(3), 257–269.

Krasner, L., & Houts, A. C. (1984). A Study of the "Value" System of Behavioral Scientists. *American Psychologist, 39*(8), 840–850.

Langer, J. (1969). *Theories of Development,* New York: Holt, Rinehart & Winston.

London, P. C. (1964). *The Modes and Models of Psychotherapy.* New York: Holt, Rinehart & Winston.

Lowe, C. M. (1959). Value Orientations: An Ethical Dilemma. *American Psychologist, 14,* 687–693.

Lowe, C. M. (1976). *Value Orientations in Counseling and Psychotherapy* (2nd ed.). Cranston, RI: Carroll Press.

Mahrer, A. R., & Pearsons, L. (Eds.). (1973). *Creative Developments in Psychotherapy* (Vol. 1). New York: Aronson.

Masling, J., & Cohen, I. (1987). Psychotherapy, Clinical Evidence and the Self-Fulfilling Prophecy. *Psychoanalytic Psychology, 4*(1), 65–79.

Moursand, J. (1985). *The Process of Counseling and Therapy.* Englewood Cliffs, J: Prentice-Hall.

Naroll, R. (1983). *The Moral Order.* Beverly Hills, CA: Sage.

Nye, R. D. (1981). *Three Psychologies: Perspectives from Freud, Skinner, and Rogers.* (2nd ed.). Pacific Grove, CA: Brooks/Cole.

Peterson, J. A. (1976). *Counseling and Values.* Cranston, RI: Carroll Press.

Phillips, J., & Torbet, D. (1968). Determinism, Freedom and Counseling Psychology. *Journal of Counseling Psychology, 15*(4), 368–371.

Rogers, C. R. (1959). A Theory of Therapy, Personality, and Interpersonal Relationships. In S. Koch (Ed.). *Psychology: A Study of Science.* New York: McGraw-Hill.

Rogers, C. R. (1980). *A Way of Being.* Boston: Houghton Mifflin.

Rosenthal, D. (1955). Changes in Some Moral Values Following Psychotherapy. *Journal of Counseling Psychology, 19,* 431–436.

Rosenthal, D., & Frank, L. D. (1956). Psychotherapy and the Placebo Affect. *Psychological Bulletin, 53,* 294–302.

Royce, J. (1982). Philosophic Issues, Division 24, and the Future. *American Psychologist, 37*(3), 358–266.

Staats, (1981) Wachtel, P. L. (1977). *Psychoanalysis and Behavior Therapy: Toward an Integration.* New York: Basic Books.

Warner, D. E. (1956). Carl Rogers and the Nature of Man. *Journal of Counseling Psychology, 3*(2) 89–92.

Individual Counseling
and Therapy

Novice counselors are generally encouraged to adopt one of the major theoretical positions we outlined in Chapter 3 and apply that approach to all the clients' problems they encounter. However, a single way of understanding human behavior and the use of techniques from that approach do not adequately meet everyone's psychological problems. After gaining some experience, most counselors encounter the perplexing problem of sorting out which therapeutic concepts and techniques to use with their clients. Theory is, in fact, integral with practice. The major theories in the field of counseling psychology were put forth by individual theorists and evolved from their own practices. These theorists continually revised their theories on the basis of experience and new findings. What today is called a major theoretical approach to counseling was once an individual's approach to working with his or her clients.

The field of psychotherapy has gone through periods in which a specific theoretical approach gained popularity and the numbers of practitioners aligning themselves with that position increased. Although several major theoretical positions are popular today, there are larger numbers of therapists identifying with some form of eclecticism (Howard, Nance, & Myers, 1986; Norcross & Prothaska, 1983; D. Smith, 1982). Smith defines eclecticism as a comprehensive theory based on a "unified and well-organized body of knowledge and strategies" (1982, p. 802). Brammer (1986) points out that *eclecticism* was once a "closet" word. At times the word has suggested laziness on the part of counselors who applied methods from different theoretical approaches without making a serious study of the assumptions behind those methods or without trying to find consistent theoretical elements.

Some believe that counselors should develop their own position. Counselors usually do this by modifying a major position rather than by integrating several different theories into their own eclecticism. Brammer (1986) indicates that these individual integrations are "not giant conceptual leaps; yet they [are] bold departures from a home base in behavioral, client-centered, or analytic position" (p. 444). Robinson (1950) wrote that eclectic counselors examined a variety of theories, and took from them the valid ideas and molded them into a consistent approach. This procedure is very different either from simply using ideas from many positions without attempting to integrate them of from rejecting theory as having no place in counseling. It is thus the task of truly eclectic counselors to choose techniques that they believe will work with a particular client with a particular problem. Actually, few counselors use a pure theoretical approach; most develop their own eclectic position.

It is not our purpose in this chapter to propose an organizing framework for a new, systematic eclectic position. Instead, we present the major dimensions in the counseling process that are significant in most approaches. We focus on the therapeutic processes and the relationship between counselor and client. The chapter begins with a description of the therapeutic relationship, followed by an examination of the therapeutic skills involved in establishing and maintaining the counseling relationship. Finally, we discuss the social dimensions that influence the therapeutic relationship.

The Therapeutic Relationship

Most theoreticians and practicing therapists believe that the counseling relationship is important to the outcome of all counseling efforts, because it provides the atmosphere in which the counselor uses specific strategies and techniques to help the client change.

Components of the Counseling Relationship

In examining the components of the counseling relationship, Gelso and Carter (1985) acknowledge Greenson's (1967) division of the analytic relationship into the *working alliance,* the *transference relationship,* and the *real relationship.* Gelso and Carter extend Greenson's conception by proposing that "all therapeutic relationships consist of three components, although the salience and importance of each part during counseling or therapy will vary according to the theoretical perspective of the therapist and the particulars of the given theory" (p. 161). In recent years, the concept of the working alliance has been extended beyond its psychoanalytic origins and is considered as important in short-term counseling as in long-term therapy.

The Working Alliance.   The counseling relationship is a working alliance developed to help clients move toward an agreed-on goal. Clients are able to try new behaviors through an internalization of this therapeutic relationship. The internalization is made possible when they feel accepted as a person and the counselor is helping them resolve the problem. Feeling accepted despite inappropriate behaviors is a corrective emotional experience for clients, and it helps increase their self-esteem and encourages them to work toward improvement. They may only identify with the counselor's attitudes at first; however, they eventually internalize that they are accepted and can really change, and they personalize the new attitudes and behaviors.

The Transference Relationship.   Gelso and Carter (1985) suggest that a transference relationship occurs with all types of counseling, regardless of the length of treatment. They describe transference as the repetition in therapy of past conflicts with other significant individuals, in which feelings, behaviors, and attitudes from those earlier relationships are reproduced. Transference involves a misperception or misinterpretation of the counselor by the client, whether it be positive or negative. Whereas transference refers to a client's response to a counselor, countertransference refers to the counselor's inaccurate emotional response to the client. Transference and countertransference are known as the "unreal relationship" within the total counseling relationship.

The Real Relationship.   Gelso and Carter also emphasize that a real relationship exists in all theoretical approaches. The counselor's understanding of the client's behaviors is realistic, and the counselor has genuine feelings and behaviors that are congruent with those feelings. The real relationship increases and deepens as client and counselor come to know each other as individuals and not just as the roles they play in counseling.

The interrelationship of the working alliance, the transference relationship, and the real relationship varies between each client and counselor. The working alliance is an essential component in the counseling relationship, as is the working agreement outlining tasks and behaviors. Both client and counselor bring to their new relationship certain emotional expectations that are placed on each other, and new transference feelings are stimulated as the two begin their relationship. As the two people come to know each other more personally, there will be less transference, and the strength of the real relationship will increase.

Parts of the Working Alliance

Horwitz (1974), Bordin (1979), and Gelso and Carter (1985) emphasize the importance of the working alliance. The goal of helping clients is dependent on two major factors, one in the clients and the other in the process that permits the alliance to develop. It is important that clients have a basic level of skill in establishing interpersonal relationships and that they expect counseling to be helpful and the counselor to be a helpful person.

Bordin (1983) attributes the impetus for change to the strength of the working alliance between the client and counselor and to the tasks that are incorporated in that alliance. The working alliance involves a collaboration for change, and Bordin identifies three aspects of the alliance. First, there must be mutual understanding about the goals of the counseling process. Second, there must be a clear description of the tasks of both the client and the counselor. And third, a bond between the client and the counselor is necessary to sustain the experience.

Mutual Goals.   The counselor and client must have a general agreement about the goals they hope to reach. The working alliance is strengthened when their goals are clear and mutual. These goals should include the thoughts, feelings, and actions that they believe will contribute to change.

Tasks.   Likewise, mutual understanding of the tasks of each person will improve the working alliance. The counselor's tasks are generally based on his or her theoretical orientation and personal style. It is important that clients understand their assigned tasks and how those relate to the desired goals. Since their performance of the tasks will be determined by how well the tasks fit their abilities, it is important that the counselor be sensitive to their skills in doing those tasks.

Bonds.   The bond in the alliance is made up of the feelings of liking, caring, and trusting that the counselor and client share. Different goals and tasks will determine how much liking, caring, and trusting need to exist to sustain the collaboration. Usually, the amount of time people spend together influences the quality of the bond. For example, short-term vocational counseling is less likely to develop the same bonds that a longer, more personal counseling relationship does.

The Process of Internalization

The general model of the working alliance suggests that when clients are positively disposed to counseling with a good counselor and receive sufficient gratification of their needs early in the process, the desired internalization of the alliance takes place. Numerous changes associated with the development of a favorable therapeutic relationship result from this internalization. Internalization is a process in which the representation of the counselor and the gratifying relationship between the client and the counselor become assimilated into the client's inner world. This dynamic is similar to an ordinary developmental process in which children begin to make their first internal judgments about their worth (their essential ''goodness'' or ''badness'') and about the dependability and trustworthiness of their caretakers.

Horwitz (1974) proposes four factors as subprocesses that contribute to internalization: corrective emotional experience, increased self-esteem, a transference improvement, and identification with the counselor. The subprocesses of internalization contribute to the growth of the therapeutic alliance and, in return, tend to be enhanced by the growing quality of the relationship. Part of the mutual understanding involves the counselor's accepting the client as a person while trying to help him or her behave more appropriately.

Corrective Emotional Experience.   A counselor's commitment to clients and their ability to perceive this commitment enhances their self-esteem (see below) and can also modify their special problem behavior. Clients experience the alliance as a corrective emotional experience because the counselor responds differently to certain aspects of their behavior than they had expected. For example, if there is no retaliation after their inappropriate behavior, the relationship grows, they develop trust in the counselor's intentions, and they are encouraged to hope that the relationship will be better than previous experiences. As the counseling relationship improves, clients feel safe enough to reveal more of themselves, and they internalize enough learning from the counselor to try new behaviors. When other significant individuals responded with criticism or acceptance, clients' internalization of those feelings resulted in lower self-esteem. Those experiences also contributed to the clients' inability to accept themselves. As clients gradually learn that those expectations are inappropriate, they can modify the misperceptions, reduce defensiveness, and have more positive expectations of the counseling relationship.

Increased Self-Esteem. When clients feel accepted despite inappropriate thoughts or behavior, they will have heightened self-esteem. The counselor's ability to accept the inappropriateness of clients' behavior also reduces the pressure on them to defend themselves and provides an opportunity for them to internalize the counselor's attitudes.

Transference Gains. Another aspect of an internalized relationship involves clients' efforts to please the counselor by trying more adaptive behavior. Although these changes in behavior may be temporary when they are not based on a sufficiently strong and positive internalization, when clients have a positive reaction to the counselor and attempt new behaviors to please the counselor, they can receive enough internal and external reinforcement to stabilize this behavior. For example, an improvement that occurred through transference during counseling can persist and become part of their behavior pattern.

Identification. Clients' identification with the counselor's attitudes is both the cause and the product of the internalization process. Clients may begin by identifying with some of the attitudes and feelings that the counselor had demonstrated toward them. Through this process they assimilate some of the essential ingredients of the counselor's attitudes into feelings about themselves. The process of identification is a basic part of normal development, and in the counseling relationship it represents an acquisition in an area where normal development has failed.

Clients' identification with specific attitudes of the counselor is a by-product of internalization. The counselor does not impose values on clients, but exemplifies attitudes and behaviors consistent with their goals for themselves. Identification is a process of becoming like an external model and thereby involves a modification of the self-representation.

Conclusion

Bordin (1983) writes that the building of a strong working alliance is a major feature in therapeutic change. He believes that the amount of change is based on both the construction and the maintenance of strong alliances.

The problems that stimulate people to seek counseling often include thoughts, feelings, or behaviors that are self-defeating. As the counseling process taps into such self-defeating behaviors, interferences in the working alliance that parallel self-defeat in other experiences are likely to occur. As these situations are resolved, clients can perceive a new way of thinking, feeling, and acting, and in many cases they can generalize these changes beyond the working alliance to other parts of their life. It is important to recognize that the working alliance goes beyond the rapport that is needed in early treatment and includes development throughout the counseling process.

The concept of a working alliance grew from psychoanalytic theory; however, it has been extended and appears to have broad acceptance within the counseling field. Gelso and Carter (1985) present several propositions concerning the working alliance and review some research that supports their positions:

1. It is important that a working alliance be established as early as possible to stimulate successful counseling. This appears to be important regardless of the length of counseling. The authors conclude that the working alliance is important early in short-term counseling and develops more slowly as the counseling relationship is continued.

2. The strength of the alliance varies according to the clients' problems and the type of counseling approach. A behavioral approach to counseling, for example, might place somewhat less emphasis on the alliance than would a psychodynamic approach. Whether the client was presenting an educational or vocational problem or a personality reconstruction issue would also affect the type of alliance.

3. There is a need for early bonding between the participants. However, it is important that they have an agreement about the goals for counseling and the tasks that each person will perform.

4. The strength of the working alliance is apt to ebb and flow during the counseling relationship.

Skills Used in the Therapeutic Relationship

Although the working alliance is the foundation, there are numerous dimensions in the counseling process. Counselors communicate their thoughts, feelings, and behaviors through their skills, which are often described as the methods, or techniques, needed in counseling. The skills are the skeleton of the interpersonal interaction that helps clients explore themselves and their situations, make decisions, and take action.

Facilitative Conditions

Since Rogers's (1957) assessment of the necessary and sufficient conditions for therapeutic personality change, the counselor attitudes and behaviors of positive regard for and empathic understanding of the client and counselor congruence have been believed important in the counseling relationship. In Rogers's view, clients change only in a relationship in which the two persons are in psychological contact; that is, both the client and counselor are truly aware of the presence of the other. Although counselors' acceptance of these facilitative conditions has varied over the years, they are still considered helpful in developing the therapeutic relationship.

The first facilitative condition is the counselor's warm, positive, accepting attitude toward the client. Through the early part of the relationship, counselors try to communicate that they like the client as a person and care about him or her in a nonpossessive way. This condition of positive regard means that counselors respect the client as an individual.

Rogers originally hypothesized that the relationship would be effective to the degree that this positive regard was unconditional. Counselors were not to accept certain feelings and disapprove of others. They were to provide unconditional acceptance to the degree that it was nonjudgmental. There were no conditions attached to their respect of the client. When clients feel this kind of acceptance, they do not have to conceal certain parts of themselves or behave in certain ways to gain the counselor's attention or acceptance. When researchers investigated the facilitative conditions, the aspect of unconditionality was soon deleted from the research, because it was not found to be statistically significant to counseling outcomes. Unconditionality is generally not included in the facilitative conditions. Even so, the degree to which clients experience restricted acceptance by the counselor will restrict the freedom they feel to explore their life situation and inner self. Therefore, the more the counselor can communicate an unconditional positive regard, the more the counseling relationship will be improved.

The counselor's empathic understanding of the client's views and feelings has to be accurately communicated. The counselor becomes aware of the client's private feelings and meanings as if they were his or her own, without losing the "as if" quality. It is important that the counselor not only sense these internal meanings of the client but also successfully communicate this understanding. This condition has received a vast amount of research attention over the years and is probably the most important of the facilitative conditions.

Rogers also asserted that counselors must be congruent. What they communicate verbally and nonverbally needs to be consistent with their internal feelings. The client's perception of their ability to be genuine in behavior, feelings, and attitudes is the only way to guarantee reality in the relationship.

To the core conditions of empathy, positive regard, and congruence, Carkhuff (1969) added concreteness, immediacy, and confrontation. Concreteness is sometimes described as the specificity of expression. It involves focusing not only on the feelings and experiences the client is expressing but also on the immediate interaction between the client and counselor. Being concrete contributes to the relationship by requiring complete, comprehensive, and relevant material about the client's problems. It also contributes to selecting a definite action to help the client resolve problems. Concreteness is important in the early stages of the relationship, when the counselor is helping the client focus on specific aspects of the problem, and then again in the later phases, when the counselor is helping the client focus on specific courses of action.

The condition of immediacy involves the counselor asking "What are clients trying to tell me that they can't tell me directly?" The counselor's immediate behavior, then, reflects directly to clients the message he or she thinks they are trying to communicate.

The addition of confrontation to the facilitative conditions brings more assertiveness to the counselor's role. Confrontation involves the counselor's communicating his or her observation and evaluation of clients' behavior by focusing on the discrepancies between their real self and their ideal self, between their insight and their behavior, and between their self-perceptions and the perceptions of others. Effective confrontation helps clients make a change. It is more likely when the relationship contains higher degrees of empathy and positive regard. As a result, clients engage in deeper self-exploration and move toward a better understanding and, eventually, more appropriate behavior. (The use of confrontation as a therapeutic skill will be addressed in detail later in this section.)

Evaluation.   In the 1960s and early 1970s there was considerable research into the facilitative conditions. Nearly all of the reported studies indicated that higher levels of the conditions were related to a variety of positive outcomes. Truax and Mitchell (1971), in a review of research conducted up to 1970, concluded that there was clear evidence that counselors who were accurately empathic, warm, and genuine provided the necessary and sufficient conditions for effective counseling regardless of the kind of problem or theory of counseling. They concluded that clients who received lower levels of facilitative conditions not only tended to fail to improve but even became worse. However, Parloff, Waskow, and Wolfe (1978) contended that some of the research included in the Truax and Mitchell review had been seriously questioned and that the earlier assessment had not given sufficient weight to obvious inconsistencies among the reports. They went on to challenge the idea that empathy, warmth, and genuineness were prerequisites for change. They maintained that these conditions should not be dismissed but should be considered as among a number of important factors. In a 1977 review, Mitchell, Bozwarth, and Krauft concluded that there had been conflicting evidence regarding a direct relationship between facilitative conditions and outcome. Although a number of studies suggest that one or more of the conditions are related to positive outcomes, other studies report little or no evidence of such a relationship: "The recent evidence, although equivocal, does seem to suggest that empathy, warmth, and genuineness are related in some way to client change, but that their potency and generalizability are not as great as once thought" (Mitchell et al., 1977, p. 181).

From their review of the counseling relationship, Gelso and Carter (1985) assert that "the conditions originally specified by Rogers are neither necessary nor sufficient, although it seems clear that such conditions are facilitative." They acknowledge that there is a modest relationship between the level of facilitative conditions and clients' behaviors and outcomes in counseling. Also, there is support for the finding that under certain circumstances lower levels of facilitative conditions may contribute negatively to client behavior.

It is apparent that the facilitative conditions of empathic understanding, respect for the client, and honest communications are important characteristics in establishing a counseling relationship. However, numerous other dimensions involving interpersonal skills are necessary for an effective relationship. The manner in which the counselor behaves in the relationship and uses various dimensions of interaction is related to this effectiveness.

Ambiguity

Ambiguity refers to the amount of structure the counselor provides in the therapeutic relationship. It is assumed that clients react to a stimulus situation in a way that communicates their needs. If the counselor provides a structure and asks questions in the interview, clients respond only in the areas established by the counselor. When the counselor presents a more vague stimulus situation, clients' responses are more likely to involve the unique aspects of their life history. A more ambiguous counseling situation leads clients to express emotional and motivational material that is usually repressed, thus allowing the counselor a deeper understanding of their behavior. Bordin (1968) identified three areas in which the counselor communicates the degree of ambiguity: "(a) The topic he considers appropriate for the client to discuss; (b) the closeness and other characteristics of the relationship expected; and (c) the counselor's values in terms of goals he sets up toward which he and the client should work as well as his values in general" (p. 150). The degree of ambiguity when the counselor opens the interview with "What would you like to talk about today?" is very different from that when the interview starts with "How are things going on your job?" If the counselor provides the topic for the interview, he or she structures the degree of ambiguity. When the counselor permits any topic to be discussed, the greater degree of ambiguity allows clients to project the area of their interest. The selection of topic is often related to whether the counselor establishes the goal or works with the client's values.

The counselor's decision to heighten the ambiguity in the relationship should be based on the needs of the individual client. Ambiguity produces anxiety, and while anxiety is an important aspect of effective therapy, there is an optimal level of anxiety that each person can use. If anxiety exceeds this point, clients may be so overwhelmed that they will use their energy for self-protection rather than therapeutic progress. Clients with schizoid tendencies need less ambiguity, because they are working to maintain contact with reality and actually benefit from a more structured situation. The counselor does not need to introduce a high degree of anxiety in an interview with a relatively well-adjusted person who is seeking consultation for a decision-making process.

It is also important that the counselor recognize his or her tolerance level for ambiguity. A counselor who becomes more anxious when control of the interview is maintained by the client is more likely to try to maintain control. Counselors' difficulties with ambiguity are evidenced by an avoidance of self-disclosure to the client or by an expression of uncertainty and concern about making a wrong move. The counselor's self-awareness and awareness of the client's present level of stress will be important in providing the most appropriate level of ambiguity.

Self-Disclosure

It is desirable for the client to reveal personal information, because such disclosure has been positively related to personal adjustment and successful counseling. In addition, the level of counselor disclosure is important, because self-disclosure occurs in a reciprocal fashion (Jourard, 1964). In dyadic relationship there is a high correlation between self-disclosure to a person and the amount of disclosure received from the person. Several studies reported evidence of the efficacy of reciprocal self-disclosure between the counselor and client (DeForest & Stone, 1980; Gary & Hammond, 1970; Graff, 1970; Worthy, 1969). They found a linear relation from low to medium and medium to high with counselor/client disclosures.

Although the literature strongly supports the value of counselors' self-disclosure, there is some evidence that it can be detrimental. It may cause negative reactions by the client and lead to feelings that the counselor is guilty of improper conduct by not remaining in a professional role. The self-disclosing counselor may violate the client's role expectations, and the client may view the counselor as less relaxed, strong, stable, or sensitive (Dies, 1973; Weigel, Dinges, Dyer, & Straumfjord, 1972).

Jourard (1971) suggests that the relationship between self-disclosure and mental health is nonlinear, indicating that there is an optimum level of disclosure and that when the counselor goes beyond that it may be destructive to the interpersonal relationship. We conclude that too little counselor self-disclosure may fail to produce client disclosures and that too much may decrease the time available to the client or cause the client to have concern about the counselor.

In recent years attention has been directed toward a more specific investigation of *self-involving statements.* Whereas self-disclosing statements refer to past history or personal experiences, self-involving statements are present expressions of the counselor's feelings about or reactions to the client's statements or behaviors (Danish, D'Augelli, & Hauer, 1980). McCarthy and Betz (1978) and McCarthy (1982) report that self-involving counselors were perceived more favorably by their clients than self-disclosing counselors in terms of expertness, social attractiveness, and trustworthiness. Self-involving counselor responses elicit client responses that tend to focus on greater exploration in the present, whereas self-disclosing responses are more likely to elicit responses focusing on the counselor that do not help the client concentrate on the present. It appears that self-involving disclosures keep the focus on the client and that self-disclosing statements may provide a conversational shift to the counselor. Reynolds and Fischer (1983) confirm these findings. McCarthy (1982) reports such results across all possible counselor/client gender pairings. We can conclude that it is more effective for the counselor to use self-involving statements than self-disclosing statements in keeping the client focused on self-exploration and understanding.

Transference

We have identified transference as an important aspect of the therapeutic relationship. Psychodynamic counselors may be more interested in analyzing transference as a way of understanding other client relationships. At the other end of the continuum, behaviorally oriented counselors are more apt to regard the therapeutic relationship as a vehicle for effecting behavior change or cognitive change and are not concerned with the transference phenomenon.

In psychoanalysis, the client lies on a couch, not seeing the therapist, and in this unstructured situation he or she is able to project onto the analyst earlier struggles with significant others. The process of transference allows the client to relive developmental periods in which basic patterns were established and also to modify these patterns through the new emotional experience with the analyst. The resolution of earlier conflicted relationships with parental figures is important in the personality reorganization. The insights that are achieved in therapy are then worked through by the client in relationships outside therapy.

Counseling psychologists, even those with a psychodynamic orientation, do not use a strictly psychoanalytic approach to therapy and therefore would not work through transference in the same way. Even though the counselor and client face each other in a relationship to resolve whatever the client's problem may be, some transference feelings may exist. Even Rogers (1951) acknowledged that transference occurred in client-centered relationships; however, he contended that this did not mean the transfer of infantile attitudes into the present relationship. Brammer and Shostrom (1982) describe transference as a type of projection of the client's past or present unresolved and unrecognized attitudes toward authority figures and love objects. In other words, clients respond to the counselor similarly to the ways in which they respond to other significant individuals. In this transference process clients build certain expectations of the counselor's role. The intensity of the transference depends on the type of client, the setting, the length of counseling, the extent of emotional involvement, the counselor's personality, and the counselor's techniques. The counselor does not depend on transference for effective counseling but needs to be aware that transference is present in varying degrees.

Cerney (1985) writes that transference occurs on an unconscious level and also that not all reactions or feelings toward the counselor can be labeled transference. Many behaviors are responses to reality, and counselors must be cautious in their interpretations. As an example, when a client expresses displeasure about the counselor's being late for an appointment, it may not be transference but an appropriate response to the reality of the counselor's behavior. A counselor is not really a blank screen. Through his or her personality and theoretical approach to counseling, the counselor creates an image that affects the intensity of the transference.

Gelso and Carter (1985) note that even though the client may have some conscious awareness of the feelings and perceptions that are being transferred to the counselor, the client's misperception is not conscious. They also suggest that clients have predispositions to certain distortions about other people and that certain aspects of the counselor may stimulate in clients those perceptions to which they are predisposed.

Mendelsohn (1981) describes an active approach to the exploration of transference and countertransference. The approach encompasses two techniques: active attention and focusing. Active attention is defined as the use of a mental set in which material is continuously sorted and categorized by the counselor. Focusing is a technical modification suggested for short-term therapy. It also emphasizes an active stance, in which the counselor focuses on one or two major conflicts to work on in the counseling process. The counselor is more active in directing the client toward material that highlights these chosen conflict areas. This process is different from the standard analytic technique of allowing the treatment session to evolve out of the transference; therefore, focusing is an active pursuit of selected material within counseling.

A more nurturant technique for working with transference is accepting clients' feelings and attitudes, thus allowing them to experience the projected feelings in the interview. The counselor may reflect clients' feelings but will seldom directly interpret the transference feeling (Brammer & Shostrom, 1982).

Countertransference

Countertransference is the counselor's emotional reactions toward and projections onto the client. The anxiety patterns in countertransference can be divided into three classifications: unresolved personal problems, situational pressures, and the client's communication of feelings to the counselor by empathic means. Both transference and countertransference typically refer to the interplay of irrational forces occurring when the client and counselor become intimately involved in the relationship. These phenomena operate as modes of illogic and a denial of reality (Kwawer, 1980).

Peabody and Gelso (1982) discuss a subtle but important change in the attitude toward countertransference over the years. Earlier definitions focused on the counselor's manifest behavior, whereas a more current definition stresses the counselor's internal reactions, feelings, and attitudes. Peabody and Gelso's study indicated that the counselor's empathic ability was positively related to reports of openness to countertransference feelings. They suggest that there is a limit to how often countertransference can be expressed without spilling over into behavior. It is important for the counselor to be aware of countertransference feelings but not necessarily to always express them. Cerney (1985) also writes about countertransference involving the feelings of empathy that develop in the counselor. When counselors become aware of growing feelings of irritation or annoyance, they might consider whether the client is communicating, even at a nonverbal level, in an attempt to get others to feel as the client feels—annoyed and irritated. If counselors can set aside their own feelings and just experience the client's feelings, the process is more similar to empathy, allowing them to sense the underlying feelings of the client.

Acting out is a description that is usually applied to a client's behavior; however, Watkins (1983) suggests that counselors may also act out. Although the term *acting out* lacks a clear definition, it does involve people acting or behaving as a result of conflicts in feelings. Watkins describes five counselor acting-out behaviors: attentional failures, empathic failures, aggressiveness, sexual and seductive behaviors, and logistical failures. Attentional failures involve the counselor's "tuning out" temporarily and missing the client's communication. Empathic failures involve a misuse of empathic responses, such as indiscriminate or uncritical use of empathy that is not helpful in the therapeutic relationship. Aggressive behaviors such as verbalizing anger or sarcasm or teasing the client are more blatant examples of acting out. Inappropriate touching or sexual innuendos are categorized as sexual or seductive acting out. Being late, missing appointments, and premature termination of a session or the counseling relationship constitute logistical failures. Any of these acting-out behaviors can be defined as countertransference and are appropriate topics for supervision.

Developing an effective counseling relationship involves becoming aware of and resolving countertransference feelings. The traditional approach to dealing with countertransference is through supervisory assistance, which focuses on locating the source of the feelings and attempting to resolve them. The counselor may also be referred to another professional to resolve problem situations. The use of audio and videotape recordings has become a major source of developing awareness of one's behaviors and feelings in the counseling relationship. A more recent approach is dealing with countertransference issues by discussing them with the client. We suggest that the counselor discuss this approach in supervision before bringing countertransference issues into the counseling relationship.

Resistance

Resistance is the client's tendency to defensively oppose the purposes of counseling. The counselor's skill must overcome this resistance by building and maintaining an effective relationship. One view of resistance describes it as coming from within the client. As clients approach a topic that causes anxiety, they will defend themselves by avoiding the topic or possibly the whole counseling situation. Another view of resistance suggests that it is caused by an external threat such as the counselor's behavior. Resistance will occur when the counselor's attempts to influence the client are perceived as manipulative or aggressive. Ruppel and Kaul (1982) report that counselors who were perceived as illegitimate in role, behavior, or attempts to influence elicited more resistance than counselors who were perceived as legitimate.

Resistance generally exists to some degree in all counseling relationships. The resistant client does not cognitively express doubts, fears, and other concerns. Resistance varies from outright rejection of counseling to subtle forms of inattention, and the client generally does not recognize it. It is an ambivalent attitude toward counseling, in that the client wants help yet resists it.

Lerner and Lerner (1983) describe a concept of resistance based on family-systems theory that they believe is relevant to individual therapy. In a family-systems perspective, one person's resistance serves as a positive and adaptive function within the context of the person's family. Often one family member attempts to protect others by not changing his or her own behavior, because the person unconsciously associates change with being disloyal to the family system. In individual counseling that person's resistance could be involved with the rest of the family system. When the counselor becomes aware of resistance in the counseling relationship, the client may be at the center of a tug of war, feeling a need to be loyal to the family and remain the same and also a need to work toward a change with the counselor. If the counselor can understand the client's predicament and view the resistance more positively, this understanding and positive behavior may help reduce the resistance impasse.

Working with resistance in the interview is one of the most taxing situations confronting counselors. It is important that they become aware of any external causes that may be contributing to the client's resistance, including the influence of their own behavior. Since resistance is a normal part of the struggle of change, they need to be aware of the client's feelings but not respond to them. They focus only on accepting and understanding the client. Should the level of resistance increase or become prolonged, they may need to become more active in reducing the client's resistance. They can move the discussion to a more intellectual level to reduce the tension and provide some support as well as clarification. Sometimes a temporary diversion can reduce the intensity of the client's feelings. If the client appears to be aware of the resistance and if a good relationship exists, counselors may offer an explanation of what they think the client is doing. Such an interpretation may help the client achieve at least an intellectual understanding of it. Empathic expression of the feelings of resistance may be helpful before even a slight interpretation.

Confrontation

The term *confrontation* all too often conjures up a hostile act. In counseling, however, confrontation challenges clients to examine, modify, and control aspects of their behavior. It helps them understand what they are doing and what the consequences may be and encourages them to assume responsibility for the change. A good confrontation promotes clients' self-examination. If a counselor fails to confront when it is needed, this failure allows clients to continue their self-deceptive behaviors. A good confrontation does not pit the counselor against the client but promotes the client's self-confrontation (Tamminen & Smaby, 1981).

Leaman (1978) identifies three purposes for confrontation. First, it helps clients recognize manipulations and ineffective communication patterns. Clients may be unaware that these patterns are an integral part of their defense mechanisms and are frustrating their fulfillment. Another purpose is to assist clients in evaluating the consequences of such maladaptive behaviors, because they may not recognize the cause/effect relationship between their patterns and the responses of other people. A third purpose is to help clients "own" their feelings and take responsibility for their actions.

Berenson (1968) described the five types of confrontation as experiential, didactic, strength, weakness, and encouragement to action. Experiential confrontation involves the counselor's response to any discrepancy between what clients say about themselves and how the counselor experiences them. A didactic confrontation is the counselor's offer of correct information when clients lack such information—for example, regarding education, vocational, or social areas. When clients talk about not being able to do anything, a counselor may confront them by stressing the strengths they have to act and move toward their goals. A confrontation of client weakness is used very seldom. It may be used when clients are unrealistic in their self-appraisal and the counselor points out some characteristics that are interfering with their success. Encouragement involves the counselor's pressing the client to act in some constructive manner.

Leaman (1978) asserts that confrontation and interpretation are closely related techniques, because both are direct statements to the client that define specific behavior patterns. A major difference involves the source of meaning. Interpretation involves assigning a meaning to a behavior from the counselor's theoretical framework, whereas confrontation allows the client to assign a meaning to this behavior. Therefore, a confrontation allows greater flexibility for the client than does an interpretation.

Egan (1976) emphasizes that the manner of the counselor's confrontation is as important as the type of confrontation and offers some guidelines on how confronting should be done. It is important that confrontation be offered in a spirit of empathy. The confrontation should be offered tentatively, particularly in the early stages of counseling. A tentative observation gives clients an opportunity to hear and examine a different perspective without having it thrust on them. A caring confrontation presupposes the development of a working alliance, and it is another way for counselors to communicate that they care enough to help.

Communication Techniques

The counseling relationship with all its social variables and relationship techniques involves verbal and nonverbal communication. The skills of counseling entail both receiving information from clients and communicating to them. Clients present their current state of behavior, organize difficulties, and begin to state more clearly what has been confusing. Clarity of language is an objective way of helping identify problem areas, interpret facts and feelings about themselves and their situation, and gain a better perspective on which decisions to make.

Degree of Leading. A specific skill in communication is the degree of leading used by the counselor in stimulating clients' exploration of their problems and development of insight. Some early research in communication indicated that counselors' verbal techniques tended to fall into definite categories (Robinson, 1950). Awareness of the different degrees of leading lets counselors enlarge their repertoire of techniques. The categories of verbal responses can be labeled and placed on a continuum. Responses with the least degree of leading include silence, acceptance, restatement, clarification, and summary clarification. The first three of these involve communicating understanding, acceptance of what the clients are saying, and encouragement for them to continue. Counselors do not communicate about themselves but give attention to the client. Even when they clarify the client's rambling comments, they are only making a more precise statement about the situation. The focus is still on the client, and they have not communicated anything about themselves. Assuming the clarification is accurate, this is an example of empathic communication.

A greater degree of leading involves giving a general lead. When counselors would like more information about a topic, they can respond by saying "Can you tell me a little more about that?", which leads the client into further description of the topic. This is not a very strong lead, but it does encourage the client to tell more about the previous statement.

Much stronger leading techniques are tentative analysis, interpretation, and urging. Counselors go beyond communicating that they understand the client and introduce some new ideas. They may tentatively encourage the client to look at the problem or a new solution in a different way, still leaving the client free to accept, modify, or reject this communication. When they offer an interpretation, they are making an inference from what the client has said. Although an interpretation may speed up insight, it should be given at a time when the client is ready to see the relationship between what he or she has said and the insight the counselor is presenting. If the client is not ready or the interpretation is too great a lead, it may lead to the client's resisting what the counselor has said. Urging the client to reveal something or make a certain decision may not be helpful. Clearly, the verbal methods of tentative analysis, interpretation, and urging involve the counselor much more in the process than milder techniques. It is possible to see how these verbal skills are involved in aspects of transference, countertransference, resistance, and confrontation.

Methods such as depth interpretation, rejection, assurance, and introducing an unrelated aspect of the subject have the greatest degree of leading, and they may be detrimental in the counseling relationship. A depth interpretation is made from the counselor's theory of personality dynamics and, therefore, may lead far beyond clients' present thinking. Even when the counselor feels that client attitudes or decisions may be wrong, rejection of their view would only hurt them or increase resistance. More effective communication would involve bringing them to a self-realization with more gradual degrees of leading. It is interesting reassurance may also feel like rejection to clients, because they feel that the counselor is belittling their problems. When counselors say "I'm sure everything will work out OK," they are also conveying a rejection of the topic that the client has been discussing. This clearly communicates that they are not interested in understanding what the client is talking about or feeling.

Types of Response.   Other systems have been developed to categorize counselors' responses. Hill (1978) developed such a categorization by incorporating parts of existing systems. Hill's system contains 14 types of responses: minimal encouragement, approval/reassurance, information, direct guidance, closed question, open question, restatement, reflection, nonverbal referent, interpretation, confrontation, self-disclosure, silence, and "other." This system is not based on a degree of leading, but it does define a large range of counselor responses that may be helpful in researching counselor/client communication.

Elliott (1979) conducted a content analysis of the literature on how clients and helpers perceive particular helper behavior. He reported the most typical: advice was perceived as guiding the client; acknowledgment—for example, "uh-huh"—as reassuring the client; reflection, as communicating understanding of the client's statement; interpretation, as explaining clients to themselves; questions, as gathering information; and self-disclosures, as helpers using themselves to help the client.

Elliott, Barker, Caskey, and Pistrang (1982) used an analog sample and a counseling sample to study the helpfulness of counselor responses. Clients rated interpretations as the most helpful type of counselor response, with trained raters ranking advice and interpretation as the most helpful responses.

Several other studies focused on counselor interpretation. Strong, Wambach, Lopez, & Cooper (1979) reported that students perceived interpretations as conditional and evaluative. However, the research did indicate that interpretation motivated change by making the problem behavior more serious, more relevant, and more threatening to the client's self-esteem. The researchers suggest that when clients see problems as caused by a factor they can directly affect, such as lack of effort, they are able to exert themselves to correct the situation. However, an interpretation that identifies causes of a problem that they cannot do anything about, such as past events, does not provide them with tools they can use to change. The type of interpretation has differing effects on their motivation to change.

Although counselors using different theories may offer different opinions and descriptions of interpretation, it is counseling skill that is generally thought to be essential in the counseling relationship, not one's theoretical approach. Claiborn's (1982) review of the literature indicates that interpretations are equally effective across theoretical approaches, suggesting that no theoretical framework has been superior to any other in promoting the therapeutic process. Claiborn suggests that providing clients with a different meaningful perspective on their situation is more helpful than not doing so. In this light, interpretation is described as providing clients with a viewpoint that is discrepant with their own, with the intent to induce them to adopt a new perspective.

Claiborn, Ward, and Strong (1981) examined the extent to which the counselor's interpretation of the problem differed from the client's belief and how much that difference affected the client. They found that interpretations that were congruent with or only slightly different from the client's produced somewhat more change than interpretations that were highly discrepant. Clients who received more congruent interpretations expected to change more and tended to show greater change and greater satisfaction than those who received more discrepant interpretations. A further important finding in this study was that even though congruent interpretations were viewed more positively, they still tended to arouse resistance to the client. The resistance appeared to reflect an awareness of the counselor's discrepant opinion and intent to influence rather than a rejection of the counselor's interpretation.

Nonverbal Communication. Nonverbal behaviors emphasize or accent the verbal message; such behaviors may amplify part of the message, explain a silence, add new information, or distort the verbal message. Several studies have reported on the importance of nonverbal clues. In a review of the literature regarding nonverbal involvement in social behavior, Edinger and Patterson (1983) suggest that nonverbal behaviors play an important role in changing attitudes and opinions. Gesturing, paralinguistic expressiveness, and looking at the client were generally found to increase the effectiveness of an attempt to persuade. Also, nonverbal reinforcements such as increased eye contact, smiling, and a positive head nod were effective in improving learning, test performance, and applicant performance on employee interviews. Edinger and Patterson concluded that gaze and facial expression were the most prominent nonverbal behaviors contributing to social control.

In a study of verbal interventions and nonverbal behavior, Claiborn (1979) reported that clients perceived the counselor's use of responsive nonverbal behaviors such as more vocal variation, facial expressions, eye contact, and gestures as more expert, attractive, and trustworthy than the use of comparatively unresponsive nonverbal behavior. Roll, Crowley, and Rappl (1985) found that clients perceived no significant differences in effectiveness, attractiveness, trustworthiness, and helpfulness between counselors who used a high frequency of nonverbal communication and those who used a moderate frequency.

Lee and Hallberg (1982) report that nonverbal communication had no impact in an evaluation of counselor effectiveness. The counselors' frequency of nonverbal behaviors as well as their decoding and encoding skills did not determine the effectiveness of the counseling session. However, counselors' verbal and nonverbal congruence was positively related to their effectiveness. This finding indicates that nonverbal communication should be examined not in isolation but with verbal communication, because the two seem to work together. The two methods of communication may be congruent, or nonverbal communications may deny or distort part of what is being verbally communicated. Tyson and Wall (1983), using an analog study, reported that nonverbal behavior seemed to increase the impact of congruent verbal communication. When there was an incongruence between the verbal and nonverbal method, however, the communication was altered in the direction of the nonverbal cue. Nonverbal behaviors appeared to make the verbal message believable or unbelievable.

Social Factors Influencing the Therapeutic Relationship

Several social factors affect the counseling relationship. In recent years considerable attention has been given to such variables as perceived competence, power, expertness, intimacy, attractiveness, and trustworthiness. Social factors, as perceived by a client, appear to have an impact on the early stages of the counseling relationship and on the effectiveness of counseling. There seems to be a relationship between counselor skills and client perceptions of these social factors. When clients rate their counselors higher on the social factors, the counselors are also rated as more successful.

Dixon and Glover (1984) report that counseling research has shown that counselors' influence over a client is affected by the client's perception of their expertness, attractiveness, and trustworthiness. Also, their influence is enhanced and they are more able to influence client change when they are perceived to be high in these social variables.

Expertness

Evidence suggests that clients' respect for the counselor increases proportionately with their perception of the counselor's expertise (Goldstein, 1980). Egan

(1985) uses the term *competence* to describe clients' belief that the counselor has the necessary information and ability to be helpful. Their perceptions of the counselor's competence or expertness increase their confidence in the counselor and help them accept and work with the counselor.

Egan (1985) lists three variables relating to clients' perception of a counselor's competence: reputation, role, and behavior. The counselor's *reputation* is established by other people stating that he or she is competent. Such communication comes from friends, colleagues, and former clients. When seeking a counselor, people may be referred by another professional or seek the advice of their friends. Although a reputation communicated in this manner may not always be a reliable indicator of a counselor's actual expertise, when a very positive referral is made, the client enters the relationship with an expectation of successful treatment. First indications of a counselor's *role* are communicated through his or her introduction, dress, demeanor, office, and diplomas. The counselor's personal demeanor in responding to clients will have an impact on their perceptions of his or her expertise. Clients also will notice office decor, including diplomas and certificates, which are interpreted as a statement of expertise. Although a counselor's reputation and role are influential, it is really the *interaction* with clients that has the strongest impact on their perception of competence. Effective counselors demonstrate their skills and professional knowledge by providing help to their clients. It is also through the behavior of the counselor that clients develop a sense of trust. As Egan (1985) notes, "Trust in a helper can evaporate quickly if little or nothing is accomplished" (p. 139).

Schmidt and Strong (1970) report college students' descriptions of expert and inexpert helpers. Expert counselors appear confident and seem interested and relaxed. They align themselves with the client by shaking hands and greeting him or her by name. They talk on the client's level and do not behave arrogantly. They can assume a comfortable, attentive position to focus attention on the client and can listen carefully. Their voice, facial expression, and gestures convey confidence and a clear focus on the client's problem. Their questions are to the point and thought provoking, and they follow a logical progression to the root of the problem, followed by some recommendations and possible solutions. Less expert counselors are more tense and uneasy, appearing to be afraid of the client. They may present a more formal bearing that appears cold, strict, and dominating. They are described as slouching in the chair and as acting too casual and relaxed, with a voice that is without inflection, giving an appearance of lack of interest and boredom. Their questions may be vague and appear trivial or irrelevant, seeming to have no common connection or aim. They are slower in getting the point across and are more confusing in their discussion of the client's problem. Therefore, the client feels that he or she is not getting anywhere.

Trustworthiness

Trustworthiness is another characteristic that increases the effectiveness of the counseling relationship. Rotter (1971) defined trustworthiness as the expectancy of one person that the word, promise, or written statement of another person can be relied on. The client's respect for the counselor and involvement in the counseling process will be greater when the counselor is perceived as highly trustworthy.

Trustworthiness, like expertness, may come as part of the counselor's reputation. For a meaningful counseling relationship to occur, however, the counselor must continuously behave in a credible manner. Egan (1985), Johnson (1981), and Strong (1968) have suggested counselor behaviors that communicate trustworthiness. It is important that the counselor provide accurate and reliable information. If clients detect errors, they may doubt other aspects of the counseling relationship. It is important to be dependable, because dependability builds trust. Dependable behaviors such as being on time, returning phone calls promptly, and living up to all the provisions of the client/counselor agreement will increase the feeling that the client can depend on the counselor. Maintaining the confidentiality of the client's communication is probably the most important aspect of trustworthiness. Learning that a counselor shared information without permission will quickly destroy the client's trust. Other counselor behaviors that enhance credibility involve being dynamic and active in the relationship, rather than passive and lethargic. Clients assume that frequent and dynamic responses indicate a sincere involvement by the counselor. Egan (1985) suggests that any evidence of ulterior motives such as voyeurism, selfishness, or superficial curiosity will certainly erode trust. Therefore, it is important that counselors communicate sincerity in their behavior in order to be trusted by clients.

Clients will be more cooperative when they trust the counselor. They will also learn to trust themselves and to communicate more openly and fully what they are thinking and feeling. This learning will help them understand themselves and the situations in which they live. By trusting the counselor, clients will also trust the solutions that they and the counselor establish for them to work through.

Interpersonal Attractiveness

Social-influence theory suggests that when clients perceive the counselor as attractive, the therapeutic relationship will be strengthened, and they will like and cooperate more with the counselor. Strong (1968) described interpersonal attractiveness as clients' perceived similarity to, compatibility with, and liking of the counselor. Interpersonal attractiveness involves more than physical characteristics and general appearance of the counselor. Although these variables may have some impact on clients' perceptions, the role, reputation, and behavior of the counselor are important variables. A behavior such as appropriate self-disclosure may help clients see the counselor as being compatible with them. The counselor's disclosure of similar attitudes and opinions about a situation may increase his or her perceived attractiveness to clients.

Structuring the interview is another way to enhance interpersonal attractiveness. Goldstein (1980) describes trait structuring and role structuring in interviewing situations. Trait structuring involves a third person describing to the client particular traits or characteristics about the counselor before the initial interview. This type of structuring will give the client an idea of the new person's qualifications and set the stage for an initial interaction. Although counselors will not be able to do this in their own interview, they can help the counseling process when they make referrals to other professionals. The counselor can use role structuring by clarifying what clients can realistically expect to occur in their interviews. When clients understand what their role and the counselor's role will be and what will transpire during the relationship, they will feel less apprehensive and develop realistic expectations for what will occur. This behavior will also be related to trustworthiness and a perception of competence.

Gender Roles

After years of research into sex bias in counseling, there is a tremendous diversity of findings and interpretations. Reviews of the literature have reached different conclusions even when the same research was considered (Lichtenberg & Heck, 1983). M. Smith (1980) writes that despite a prevailing attitude that gender biases are widespread in therapy, a meta-analysis of the research literature suggested an absence of such biases against women in counseling psychotherapy. Hare-Mustin (1983) maintains that problems specific to women, such as marital and family relationships, reproduction, surgical and sexual abuse, depression, and eating disorders, are still widely neglected in the development of counseling theory and practice despite the fact that women use mental-health services more than men. She also notes that research in this area has been inconclusive, with analog studies indicating no pattern of bias or stereotyping, whereas naturalistic data suggest that women are seen more often and given more potent medications than are men (Brodsky & Hare-Mustin, 1980).

Kaplan (1983) argues that traditional standards for diagnosis in psychology have the effect of overemphasizing women's pathology. She asserts that it is clearly a bias to diagnose women who have been socialized to be more dependent and more emotionally expressive than men as having personality disorders. With regard to sex bias in the diagnosis of mental-health problems, Wakefield (1987) notes that "women's biology and socialization are in many ways different than men's, and a diagnostic criterion that ignores these differences could end up unjustifiably classifying many more women than men as disordered" (p. 465). Baruch, Biener, and Barnett (1987) observe that research on stress in the workplace has been conceptualized in almost exclusively male terms, with the result that the interventions typically recommended may be inappropriate for women. For a number of years there has been a movement to develop mental-health practices that incorporate feminist principles. In some areas of the United States, formal and informal lists of feminist therapists are available.

In addition to problems of bias in the areas of counseling theory and diagnostic criteria, there has been considerable interest in the question of how gender differences influence the counseling process. Buczek (1981) found that male counselors asked female clients more questions related to their family relationships than they did male clients. She suggests that male counselors expected that family issues would be more important in the treatment of women than in the treatment of men, even when the presenting problems were virtually identical. Jones and Zoppel (1982) found that male and female counselors often perceived the same behaviors in female clients yet described the clients differently. Male therapists tended to be more negative in their descriptions of female clients.

The problem of sex bias in counseling, however, is further complicated by the biases that clients bring to the counseling situation. Feldstein (1982) found that male counselors were consistently rated higher than female counselors in terms of expertness, trustworthiness, and attractiveness by both male and female clients. Kunin and Rodin (1982) found, in an analog study, that clients rated male counselors significantly higher in intelligence than female counselors. In addition, they found some evidence that clients engaged in self-disclosure more frequently with male than with female counselors, even when the counselor variables of expertness and attractiveness were controlled for.

As we noted earlier, it is difficult to draw any firm conclusions from the large, varied, and frequently contradictory research literature. It seems likely that counseling theory and practice are not immune to cultural attitudes and beliefs that are biased against women. Counselors need to be sensitive to gender and sex-role issues and to be better informed about the psychology of women and the role of social and environmental factors in women's problems. Parloff, Waskow, & Wolfe (1978) note that it may well be the attitudes and values of the counselor that are important in successful, unbiased treatment, rather than the gender of the counselor or client.

With increasing interest in the problems of bias against women in counseling, there has also been some exploration of the special issues and needs of male clients. It has been recognized that the demands and constrictions of the masculine role may lead to psychological dysfunction. Much less attention, however, has been given to such issues. An idea that has received increasing attention lately is psychological androgyny, which refers to a union of the instrumental/masculine and expressive/feminine personality styles. Cook (1987) has suggested that androgyny can be viewed as an ideal state of psychological development, in that androgynous people are capable of achieving an identity that is unbound by sex-role stereotypes. Androgyny has been posited both as an indicator of the "health" of the client's personality and as a predictor of the potential effectiveness of the counselor. Further research, however, is needed to support such assertions.

Cross-Cultural Counseling

Concern for racial and cultural differences has become increasingly apparent in the professional literature. One's culture consists of all that one has learned to do, believe, value, and enjoy. It involves the ideals, beliefs, skills, tools, customs, and institutions into which one is born. Most, if not all, current theories of counseling have developed from a Western European, postindustrial knowledge base. Many of the philosophical assumptions inherent in modern culture contribute to difficulties in counseling individuals from other cultures.

Derald Sue (1981) points out that counselors, as a result of their education and training, often inherit the "racial and cultural bias of their forebears" (p. 5). He notes that the standard tests of intelligence and other personality factors are based on white, middle-class norms and that there has been a consistent equation of cultural, ethnic, or racial differences with deficiency or pathology. He warns counselors that, without a conscious awareness and appreciation of cultural differences, they can become unwitting enforcers of political and social inequities.

Traditional counseling approaches emphasize self-disclosure, insight into personal dynamics, and increased verbal, emotional, and behavioral expression. These goals, however, are not always consistent with the value systems of other cultures. In fact, some cultures emphasize behaviors that are in virtual opposition to those of traditional counseling approaches. It is also important to recognize that different cultures have different conceptions of mental health, emotional disturbance, and the process of adjustment.

For Asian Americans, especially those of Chinese or Japanese ancestry, obedience, conformity, and loyalty to the family are extremely important. Admitting emotional difficulty is likely to be avoided, as a way of protecting family honor. In addition, the restraint or repression of strong feelings is valued and is thus viewed as normal rather than pathological (Sue, 1981). It may be more acceptable for Asian Americans to express physical symptoms than emotional ones. Asian-American clients may also be experiencing serious identity confusion as they attempt to find an individual solution to the problem of acculturation. Each Asian American has to confront difficult decisions about how to incorporate modern values of freedom and individualism into the conservative values of the parent culture.

Elsie J. Smith (1981) has written that "the crises observed between blacks and whites . . . in the broad American society are reenacted daily in the counseling interview" (p. 141). Smith points out that black people place more emphasis on nonverbal behavior than do white people, and that black people of lower socioeconomic background have a different style of listening. Other differences must be taken into account by counselors if they are to provide appropriate and effective services to black people. One critical difference is that many black people see mental-health problems as being caused by a particular situation or the environment, rather than by intrapsychic conflicts or unresolved family problems. As a result, black people may often come into counseling seeking advice about a specific problem or assistance in dealing with a discriminatory institution. Counselors who are unaware of this and assume that intrapersonal conflicts are the "real" problem will not be able to provide appropriate services.

Hispanic culture is based on a common language and a shared history in the New World. Ruiz (1981) points out, however, that the Hispanic culture is far from being homogeneous and is, in fact, more accurately described as "an aggregate of distinct subcultures, each emanating from a different geographic area" (p. 187). Ruiz suggests that counselors must assess the extent to which a particular Hispanic client feels a part of his or her unique subculture and the larger Anglo culture. Dillard (1983) has noted some dimensions of the Hispanic/Anglo continuum that are especially relevant in working with Mexican-

American clients: the degree of fluency in both Spanish and English; the level of involvement in a large, extended family; the extent of personal commitment to a distinctly Mexican-American community; and the importance of traditional Roman Catholic religious beliefs.

There are, of course, several other cultural groups for which an understanding of their unique worldview and value system would be crucial in a counseling relationship. Native American, Vietnamese, Arabic, and numerous African tribal cultures are fully developed and distinctive systems that are quite different from a white, middle-class perspective. A thorough discussion of the complexity and diversity of all these cultures and the implications for counseling is beyond the scope of this book, so these examples are intended to be suggestive rather than definitive.

A serious pitfall for the counselor seeking cross-cultural competence is stereotyping. Lloyd (1987) suggests that the range of individual variation within any specific cultural group may be greater than the differences between cultural groups. He cautions counselors against insidiously accepting stereotypes in the hope of becoming culturally sensitive. Smith (1981) asserts that each client is like all people in some respects, like some other people in a few respects, and like no other person in many respects. Pedersen (1977, 1981) has developed a model for improving cross-cultural skills in counseling trainees. The model involves role playing and helps trainees increase their awareness of cultural variation through gaining specific knowledge about a given culture.

Sue and Zane (1987) note that even if counselors gain in sensitivity and knowledge about cultures other than their own, neither sensitivity nor knowledge leads directly to effective counseling. Cultural sensitivity and knowledge are thus necessary, but not sufficient, conditions for beneficial change. Sue and Zane stress credibility and giving. Counselors can use specific cultural knowledge to enhance their credibility with minority clients. Cultural knowledge is important so that the counselor's conceptualization of a problem, its solution, and the intermediate goals are congruent with the beliefs and values of the client. With the establishment of credibility, counselors must provide the culturally different client with some immediate benefit in the initial sessions. Sue and Zane suggest that letting clients know that they are not alone in having such problems, giving them reassurance, and instilling hope and faith are examples of such benefits.

Cross-cultural situations place additional demands on the practitioner if counseling is to be effective. Counselors must be aware of and positively value the cultural differences of clients and must also be aware of their own residual biases and prejudices. They must be sensitive to sociopolitical realities, especially as they negatively affect minority clients. The counselor must select treatment options that fit the culturally different client, rather than expect the client to adapt to a counseling process constructed on the basis of white, middle-class values.

Summary

Counseling is an interpersonal process between the counselor and the client. The process involves establishing a cooperative relationship and using the interaction to help clients explore themselves and their situations, gain a clearer understanding, and try appropriate behaviors. This process is used with a wide range of client concerns, from developmental decisions to personality changes.

The working alliance lets the client experience a corrective emotional experience, internalize the therapeutic relationship, and develop self-confidence. Numerous relationship skills are used in the process of building and maintaining the alliance. The degree of structure that counselors provide in their sessions and the amount of self-disclosure or self-involving material that they use have an impact on the working alliance. Counselors' thoughts and behaviors about transference and countertransference and their use of concreteness, immediacy, and confrontation also contribute to the counseling interaction. Most of the relationship skills are applicable in all theoretical approaches, and each skill involves counselor/client verbal and nonverbal communication. Social factors also influence this relationship. Counselors' impact on the client is increased when they behave in ways that the client perceives as more expert, interpersonally attractive, and trustworthy. Other social factors—that is, the culture and gender of the client or counselor—will influence the counseling process. Counselors must be aware of and positively value the individual difference of clients and modify their counseling process accordingly. A counseling relationship is not a standard recipe but an individually developed concoction mixed and measured by the two participants.

References

Baruch, G. K., Biener, L., & Barnett, R. C. (1987). Women and Gender in Research on Work and Family Stress. *American Psychologist, 42,* 130–136.

Berenson, B. (1968). Level of Therapist Functioning, Patient Depth of Self-Exploration, and Type of Confrontation. *Journal of Counseling Psychology, 15,* 317–321.

Bordin, E. (1968). *Psychological Counseling.* New York: Appleton-Century-Crofts.

Bordin, E. (1979). The Generalizability of the Psychoanalytic Concept of the Working Alliance. *Psychotherapy: Theory, Research and Practice, 16,* 252–260.

Bordin, E. (1983). A Working Alliance Based Model of Supervision. *The Counseling Psychologist, 11*(1), 35–42.

Brammer, L. (1986). A Paradigm Shift in Counseling Theory. *The Counseling Psychologist, 14,* 443–447.

Brammer, L., & Shostrom, E. (1982). *Therapeutic Psychology.* Englewood Cliffs, NJ: Prentice-Hall.

Brodsky, A., & Hare-Mustin, R. T. (Eds.). (1980). *Women and Psychotherapy: An Assessment of Research and Practice.* New York: Guilford Press.

Buczek, T. (1981). Sex Biases in Counseling: Counselor Retention of the Concerns of a Female and Male Client. *Journal of Counseling Psychology, 28,* 13–21.

Carkhuff, R. (1969). *Helping and Human Relations* (Vols. 1 & 2). New York: Holt, Rinehart & Winston.

Cerney, M. (1985). Countertransference Revisited. *Journal of Counseling and Development. 63,* 362–364.

Claiborn, C. (1979). Counselor Verbal Interaction, Non-Verbal Behavior, and Social Power. *Journal of Counseling Psychology, 26,* 378–383.

Claiborn, C. (1982). Interpretation and Change in Counseling. *Journal of Counseling Psychology, 29,* 439–453.

Claiborn, C., Ward, S. R., & Strong, S. R. (1981). Effects of Congruence Between Counselor Interpretations of Client Beliefs. *Journal of Counseling Psychology, 28*(2), 101–109.

Cook, E. P. (1987). Psychological Androgyny: A Review of the Research. *The Counseling Psychologist, 15,* 471–513.

Danish, S., D'Augelli, A., & Hauer, A. (1980). *Helping Skills: A Basic Training Program* (2nd ed.). New York: Human Sciences Press.

DeForest, D., & Stone, G. (1980). Effects of Sex and Intimacy Level on Self Disclosure. *Journal of Counseling Psychology, 27,* 93–96.

Dies, R. R. (1973). Group Therapist Self-Disclosure: An Evaluation by Clients. *Journal of Counseling Psychology, 20*(4), 344–348.

Dillard, J. M. (1983). *Multicultural Counseling: Toward Ethnic and Cultural Relevance in Human Encounters.* Chicago: Nelson Hall.

Dixon, D., & Glover, J. (1984). *Counseling: A Problem-Solving Approach.* New York: Wiley.

Edinger, J., & Patterson, M. (1983). Non-Verbal Involvement and Social Control. *Psychological Bulletin, 93,* 30–56.

Egan, G. (1976). Confrontation. *Group and Organizational Studies, 1,* 223–243.

Egan, G. (1985). *The Skilled Helper: Model, Skills and Methods for Effective Helping* (3rd ed.). Pacific Grove, CA: Brooks/Cole.

Elliott, R. (1979). How Clients Perceive Helper Behaviors. *Journal of Counseling Psychology. 26,* 285–294.

Elliott, R., Barker, C., Caskey, N., & Pistrang, N. (1982). Differential Helpfulness of Counselor Response Modes. *Journal of Counseling Psychology, 29,* 354–461.

Epstein, L., & Feiner, A. (Eds.). (1979). *Countertransference: Therapist Contributions to the Therapeutic Situation.* New York: Aronson.

Feldstein, J. C. (1982). Counselor and Client Sex Pairing: The Effects of Counseling Problem and Counselor Sex Role Orientation. *Journal of Counseling Psychology, 24,* 418–420.

Gary, A. L., & Hammond, R. (1970). Self-Disclosure of Alcoholics and Drug Addicts. *Psychotherapy: Theory, Research, and Practice, 4,* 142–146.

Gelso, C., & Carter, J. (1985). The Relationship in Counseling Psychotherapy: Components, Consequences, and Theoretical Antecedents. *The Counseling Psychologist, 13,* 155–243.

Goldstein, A. P. (1980). Relationship-Enhancement Methods. In K. F. Kanfer & A. P. Goldstein (Eds.), *Helping People Change* (2nd ed.). New York: Pergamon Press.

Goodman, M. (1981). Group Processes and Induced Countertransference. *Psychotherapy: Theory, Research and Practice, 18,* 478–486.

Graff, R. W. (1970). The Relationship of Counselor Self-Disclosure to Counselor Effectiveness. *Journal of Experimental Education, 38*(3), 19–22.

Greenson, R. (1967). *The Technique and Practice of Psychoanalysis* (Vol. 1). New York: International Universities Press.

Hare-Mustin, R. T. (1983). An Appraisal of the Relationship Between Women and Psychotherapy: 80 Years After the Case of Dora. *American Psychologist, 38,* 593–601.

Heilburn, A. (1982). Tolerance for Ambiguity in Female Clients: A Further Test of the Catharsis Model for Predicting Early Counseling Dropout. *Journal of Counseling Psychology, 29,* 567–571.

Hill, D. (1978). Development of a Counselor Verbal Response Category System. *Journal of Counseling Psychology, 25,* 461–468.

Holland, G. (1965). *Fundamentals of Psychotherapy.* New York; Holt, Rinehart & Winston.

Horwitz, L. (1974). *Clinical Prediction and Psychotherapy.* New York: Aronson.

Howard, G. F., Nance, D. W., & Myers, P. (1986). Adaptive Counseling and Therapy: An Integrated, Eclectic Model. *The Counseling Psychologist, 14,* 363–442.

Johnson, D. W. (1981). *Reaching Out: Interpersonal Effectiveness and Self-Actualization* (2nd ed.). Englewood Cliffs, NJ: Prentice-Hall.

Jones, E. J., & Zoppel, C. L. (1982). Impact of Client and Therapist Gender on Psychotherapy Process and Outcome. *Journal of Consulting and Clinical Psychology, 50,* 259–272.

Jourard, S. M. (1964). *The Transparent Self.* New York: Van Nostrand Reinhold.

Jourard, S. M. (1971). *Self-Disclosure: An Experimental Analysis of the Transparent Self.* New York: Wiley.

Kaplan, M. (1983). A Woman's View of DSM-III. *American Psychologist, 38,* 786–792.

Kunin, C. C., & Rodin, M. J. (1982). The Interactive Effects of Counselor Gender, Physical Attractiveness, and Status on Client Self-Disclosure. *Journal of Clinical Psychology, 38,* 84–90.

Kwawer, J. (1980). Transference and Countertransference in Homosexuality: Changing Psychoanalytic Views. *American Journal of Psychotherapy, 34,* 72–79.

Leaman, D. (1978). Confrontation in Counseling. *Personnel and Guidance Journal, 56,* 630–633.

Lee, D., & Hallberg, E. (1982). Non-Verbal Behaviors of a "Good" and "Poor" Counselor. *Journal of Counseling Psychology. 29,* 414–417.

Lerner, S., & Lerner, H. (1983). A Systematic Approach to Resistance: Theoretical and Technical Considerations. *American Journal of Psychotherapy, 37,* 387–399.

Lichtenberg, J., & Heck, E. (1983). Sex Bias in Counseling: A Reply and Critique. *Personnel and Guidance Journal, 61,* 102–104.

Lloyd, A. P. (1987). Multicultural Counseling: Does it Belong in a Counselor Education Program? *Counselor Education and Supervision, 26,* 164–167.

McCarthy, P. (1982). Differential Effects of Counselor Self-Referent Responses and Counselor Status. *Journal of Counseling Psychology, 29,* 125–131.

McCarthy, P., & Betz, N. (1978). Differential Effects of Self-Disclosing Versus Self-Involving Counselor Statements. *Journal of Counseling Psychology, 25,* 251–256.

Mendelsohn, R. (1981). Active Attention and Focusing on the Transference/Countertransference in the Psychotherapy of the Borderline Patient. *Psychotherapy: Theory, Research, and Practice, 18,* 386–393.

Mitchell, K., Bozwarth, J., & Krauft, C. (1977). A Reappraisal of the Therapeutic Effectiveness of Accurate Empathy, Non-Possessive Warmth, and Genuineness. In A. Gurman & A. Razin (Eds.), *Effective Psychotherapy: A Handbook of Research.* New York: Pergamon Press.

Norcross, J., & Prothaska, J. (1983). Psychotherapists in Independent Practice: Some Findings and Issues. *Professional Psychology: Research and Practice, 14,* 867–881.

Parloff, M., Waskow, I., & Wolfe, B. (1978). Research on Therapist Variables in Relation to Process and Outcome. In S. Garfield & A. Bergin (Eds.), *Handbook of Psychotherapy and Behavior Change: An Empirical Analysis.* New York: Wiley.

Peabody, S., & Gelso, C. (1982). Countertransference and Empathy: The Complex Relationship Between Two Divergent Concepts in Counseling. *Journal of Counseling Psychology, 29,* 240–245.

Pedersen, P. (1977). The Triad Model of Cross-Cultural Counselor Training. *Personnel and Guidance Journal, 56,* 94–100.

Pedersen, P. (1981). Triad Counseling. In R. Corsini (Ed.), *Innovative Psychotherapies* (pp. 840–855). New York: Wiley Interscience.

Reynolds, C., & Fischer, C. (1983). Personal Versus Professional Evaluations of Self-Disclosing and Self-Involving Counselors. *Journal of Counseling Psychology, 30,* 451–454.

Robinson, R. (1950). *Principles and Procedures in Student Counseling.* New York: Harper & Brothers.

Rogers, C. (1951). *Client-Centered Therapy.* Boston: Houghton Mifflin.

Rogers, C. (1957). The Necessary and Sufficient Conditions of Therapeutic Personality Change. *Journal of Counseling Psychology, 21,* 95–103.

Roll, S., Crowley, M., & Rappl, L. (1985). Client Perceptions of Counselors' Nonverbal Behavior: A Reevaluation. *Counselor Education and Supervision, 24,* 234–243.

Rotter, J. B. (1971). Generalized Expectancies for Interpersonal Trust. *American Psychologist, 26,* 443–452.

Ruiz, R. A. (1981). Cultural and Historical Perspectives in Counseling Hispanics. In D. W. Sue (Ed.), *Counseling the Culturally Different: Theory and Practice* (pp. 186–215). New York: Wiley Interscience.

Ruppel, G., & Kaul, T. (1982). Investigation of Social Influence Theory's Conception of Client Resistance. *Journal of Counseling Psychology, 29,* 232–239.

Schmidt, L. D., & Strong, S. R. (1970). Expert and Inexpert Counselors. *Journal of Counseling Psychology, 17,* 115–118.

Smith, D. (1982). Trends in Counseling and Psychotherapy. *American Psychologist, 37,* 802–809.

Smith, E. J. (1981). Cultural and Historical Perspectives in Counseling Blacks. In D. W. Sue (Ed.), *Counseling the Culturally Different: Theory and Practice* (pp. 141–186). New York: Wiley Interscience.

Smith, M. (1980). Sex Bias in Counseling and Psychotherapy. *Psychological Bulletin, 87,* 392–407.

Strong, S. (1968). Counseling: An Interpersonal Influence Process. *Journal of Counseling Psychology, 15,* 215–224.

Strong, S., Wambach, C., Lopez, F., & Cooper, R. (1979). Motivational and Equipping Functions of Interpretation in Counseling. *Journal of Counseling Psychology, 26,* 98–107.

Strupp, H. (1978). Psychotherapy, Research, and Practice: An Overview. In S. Garfield & A. Bergen (Eds.), *Handbook of Psychotherapy and Behavior Change: An Empirical Analysis.* New York: Wiley.

Sue, D. W. (1981). *Counseling the Culturally Different: Theory and Practice.* New York: Wiley Interscience.

Sue, S., & Zane, N. (1987). The Role of Culture and Cultural Techniques in Psychotherapy: A Critique and Reformulation. *American Psychologist, 42,* 37–45.

Tamminen, A., & Smaby, M. (1981). Helping Counselors Learn to Confront. *Personnel and Guidance Journal, 59,* 41–45.

Truax, C., & Mitchell, K. (1971). Research on Certain Therapist Interpersonal Skills in Relation to Process and Outcome. In S. Garfield & A. Bergin (Eds.), *Handbook of Psychotherapy and Behavior Change: An Empirical Analysis.* New York: Wiley.

Tyson, J., & Wall, S. (1983). Effect of Inconsistency Between Counselor Verbal and Nonverbal Behavior on Perceptions of Counselor Attributes. *Journal of Counseling Psychology, 30,* 433–437.

Wakefield, J. C. (1987). Sex Bias in the Diagnosis of Primary Orgasmic Dysfunction. *American Psychologist, 42,* 464–471.

Watkins, C. E. (1983). Counselor Acting Out in the Counseling Situation: An Exploratory Analysis. *Personnel and Guidance Journal,* 417–422.

Weigel, R. G., Dinges, N., Dyer, R., & Straumfjord, A. A. (1972). Perceived Self-Disclosure, Mental Health, and Who Is Liked in Group Treatment. *Journal of Counseling Psychology, 19*(1), 47–52.

Worthy, G. (1969). Self-Disclosure as an Exchange Process. *Journal of Personality and Social Psychology. 13,* 59–63.

Career-Development Strategies

A man's closest link to his society is his job or profession. Dislocation in that area means trouble for both the community and himself. The health of the individual in a society and the breadth of the society depend on how they are linked to each other [Levenstein, 1964, p. 20].

That cogent observation has provided material for research and intervention by sociologists, anthropologists, economists, medical personnel, industrial managers, labor experts, and, of course, psychologists. For example, the psychological adjustment and adaptability of the individual in society is obviusly closely linked to satisfaction on the job, the experience of competence and success in work accomplished, and quality of peer relationships in the workplace. Counseling psychology has played a substantial role in this complex process. As industrial society expanded, there were demands to understand this area of activity and to develop the technology and skill to mobilize the human resources to power the workplace. The need attracted scholars, dreamers, idealists, realists, and, most significantly of all, a group of "earthly" pragmatists (Super, 1983, p. 5). They were the products of an early American psychology, and they founded a branch of that discipline known as vocational psychology. As we have pointed out, it was one of the fundamental antecedents of counseling psychology. As Super observes,

> what mattered to the founders of vocational psychology was what people do, why they do it, how well they do it, and what satisfactions they get from doing it. In a work-oriented society dominated by the Protestant work ethic, work was man's, and woman's, most important activity on 5 or 6 days of the week. Hence the focus on work of many applied psychologists in the United States, some concerned with personnel selection, job satisfaction, and productivity, some with occupational choice, satisfaction, and success [1983, p. 6].

The Role of Work in Society

Walter Neff observes that "we know very little about the beginnings of work. The historians of the ancient world give us little information about how people worked or what they thought about the work they did" (1985, p. 19). While we may not know the particulars of work in times gone by, we are least aware of the prevailing work ethic of significant historical eras and how it influenced culture. Whether or not one shares Marx's enthusiasm for a completely economic interpretation of history, he was certainly correct to call attention to the role that human labor played in the organization of society. Social structures, including family and tribal associations, and, ultimately, national structures emerged from the conditions under which goods and services were produced.

Levenstein describes the moral growth of the world in terms of the way in which people worked and survived (Levenstein, 1964). He believes that the world has evolved through four stages. In the first stage, human beings moved around the earth as nomads. Social organization was primarily centered on the traveling tribe. The present, or "immediacy," was the temporal norm. As Levenstein notes, "a creature that cannot look across the distance of time is tied to the present and has no sense of consequences. His only instrument is violence—the blow struck to attain the immediate objective. His only ethic is the exercise of force" (1964, p. 253).

As people learned that their survival could be enhanced by growing things, they slowly evolved into the second stage of social development, namely "the economy of agriculture" (Levenstein, 1964, p. 253). People's perspective on time was considerably altered in the contemplation of the paradigm of planting, care, growth, and harvest. Nomadic existence was not feasible in an agricultural economy. Roots had to be put down, literally and figuratively. Social structures changed, in that society evolved from being organized primarily around the tribe to being organized around the family. The land assumed greater economic and personal value. Area was circumscribed by boundaries, and the concept of ownership emerged. The rudiments of trade and barter began to emerge. Levenstein argues that these changes led to a significant shift in moral and ethical outlook. The new view included respect for property and person and a shift toward a less violent outlook, at least with respect to the immediate world. It also led to an increasingly complex division of labor. In any event, people's "survival depended on [their] ability to grow food and maintain the expanding population—a goal that could not be attained without a new moral outlook" (1964, p. 254).

The third stage, dominated by commerce, emerged from the needs of expanding populations and the discovery of resources and goods for both survival and pleasure that extended horizons and desires. The social alterations that accompanied this shift included the emergence of larger social organizations, ultimately including the nation. Although there were negative effects of this wider competition for the control of goods and markets, including increasingly destructive wars, a higher-order morality also emerged. Commerce "required an affirmative trust, extended even to strangers, an assumption that each of the parties would keep his pledged word . . . [in short] . . . the ethic of fair exchange and mutual obligation" (Levenstein, 1964, p. 252).

Work in this context continued to become more complex. The solidification of class along occupational lines emerged. The price of commerce and the industrial revolution was, in part, the expanding alienation of many workers from their products and the need to identify more complex sources of work satisfaction than that intrinsic to the activity. The rewards included advances in the quality of life and the evolution of leisure.

Levenstein suggests that we are currently in transition to another era, an age of altruism and cooperation. This is the notion of work based on the motive to give "without any promise of return" (p. 255). How long the transition will take is not clear, and there is even concern that it may be an illusion. In any event, it appears that we are caught in the grip of a moral crisis. Each transition era must have produced its own sense of the loosening of the foundations.

Whatever the age, whatever the prevailing ethical or moral system, work has provided a baseline for social structures, rewards, and values. Perhaps Freud said it best when he observed that "laying stress upon the importance of work has a greater effect than any other technique of learning in the directions of binding the individual more closely to reality; in his work he is at least securely attached to a part of reality, the human community" (1955, p. 34).

Work, according to Freud, provides an opportunity to meet basic psychological needs and gain social satisfactions. Despite this very fundamental role in the well-being of people, Freud noted that

> As a path to happiness work is not valued very highly by men. They do not run after it as they do after other opportunities for gratification. The great majority work only when forced by necessity, and this natural aversion to work gives rise to the most difficult social problems [1955, p. 30].

It is clear that social organizations down through the ages have been interconnected with work. It is also clear that the process of socialization into work roles, the selection of careers, and the nature of job satisfaction are complex areas for study. Major social-reform and revolutionary movements have been organized around the implications of work. In all of these concerns, there is a role for the counseling psychologist as researcher, facilitator, resource, and, perhaps, even as moral advocate.

Vocational Development and Career Patterns

Work and Human Life Stages

Just as Freud was one of the first psychologists to recognize work as important to human adjustment and as a possible source of conflict, he was also one of the first to propose an orderly progression of human development based on the interactions between internal biological forces and the environmental forces of culture, the economy, and interpersonal relationships.

Many other psychologists have expanded upon his early observations and have proposed sequences of development through the life span with appropriate developmental tasks at each age. Two of the developmental theorists who recognized the importance of work were Charlotte Buhler and Erik Erikson. As a matter of fact, Donald E. Super, who has formulated a comprehensive theory of vocational development, was originally influenced by Buhler's thinking in this area. Her five major life stages—growth, exploration, establishment, maintenance, and decline—exerted a significant influence on his later conception of the sequence of vocational development. He credits her work, particularly her collection of biographical and case-history materials dealing with the lives of men and women in Austria, England, and the United States, as an early influence on his life-stage conception of career (Buhler & Masserick, 1968; Super, 1942).

Erikson proposed an eight-stage system that contains the dynamic potential for altering behavior throughout a person's life. His stages of development are presented as a series of psychosocial crises to be resolved in sequence, with the resolutions having an effect on subsequent developmental stages.

The crises at each age are defined in general terms, and specific intervention in an individual's life is based on the normal expectations of conflict resolution at that stage. Vocational development is a very special case of general human development. In this context it is a process rather than a series of events.

Super's Approach to Vocational Development

As we indicated earlier, Super was one of the earliest to recognize the complexity of vocational development. He noted that he was searching for more than a concept of adjustment:

> I wanted a dynamic theory, and the concept of adjustment implied a capacity for change in persons, or the jobs which they obtain, and in the occupations they pursue. The makings of a dynamic theory of how people choose, enter, and progress in their occupations were then largely lacking, but I drew on what I could find not only in differential psychology, but also in developmental psychology, in personality theory, in sociology, and in economics, that seemed to me to throw light on these processes [1969, p. 2].

According to Herr & Cramer (1984), Super's approach to vocational development is the one

> that has received the most continuous attention, stimulated the most research, influenced most pervasively the field of vocational psychology, and is the most comprehensive. . . . He has characterized the career development process as ongoing, continuous, and generally invisible; as a process of compromise and synthesis within which his primary construct—the development and implementation of the self concept—operates. The basic theme is that the individual chooses occupations that will allow him to function in a role consistent with his self concept and that the latter is a function of his developmental history [pp. 123–124].

Following the lead of Buhler, Super proposed a conception of life stages and developmental tasks as follows (see Herr & Cramer, 1984, p. 125):

1. The *growth* stage (from birth to age 14) includes the developmental tasks that relate to role identification, social participation, self-direction, early work habits and goal-directed behavior, and early experiences with competency. The substages of development during this period include fantasy (4 to 10 years of age), interest (11 to 12 years), and capacity (13 to 14). The primary task of this

period is developing a sense of reality in relation to the self-concept as well as an orientation to the world of work.

2. The *explorative* stage (from 14 to 24) includes many of those developmental experiences that incorporate the work-related activities pertaining to school, leisure, and part-time employment. The substages of this period include "tentative" (15 to 17), which encompasses the early identification of possible areas of education and work, "transition" (18 to 21), in which specification of choice in relation to reality emerges, and "trial with little commitment" (22 to 24), in which an educational and career choice has been made at a provisional level. The primary tasks of this period involve moving from generalized to specific choices and actively pursuing those choices.

3. The *establishment* stage (24 to 44) involves establishing and solidifying one's place in a chosen occupation. The first substage of this period is trial with commitment and stabilization (25 to 30). This substage generally involves a "settling down," or some shifing may occur if the intitial choice proves to be unsatisfactory. Advancement (31 to 44) is the second substage of this period. The general tasks of the establishment stage involve demonstrating competence, establishing a position for oneself, and identifying the route for advancement.

4. The *maintenance* stage (46 to 64) is concerned with the task of holding on to what has already been accomplished and functioning at an acceptable level of competence. It is essentially a preservative stage.

5. The stage of *decline* (64 years and beyond) is a time of mental and physical weakening. The vocational actor must step aside and give way to new leadership, assuming a more passive role. The substages in this period are *deceleration,* which includes a general diminution of the pace of work, even shortened hours, and *retirement,* when the main work is no longer performed and either leisure activities or avocational interests hold sway. The major task here is the management of loss of status and the acceptance of "disengagement."

Other Approaches to Career Development

Herr (1986) suggests several other classifications of career development, including "trait and factor; actuarial or matching; decision; situational or sociological; [and] psychological or personality" (p. 176).

Trait and Factor Approach. This trait and factor* approach to career development is probably the oldest in the field. It traces its origins back to Frank Parsons' original paradigm of analyzing the individual, assessing the occupation, and engaging in "true reasoning" to match the person with the job (Herr, 1986). As more sophisticated techniques for analysis emerged, the trait and factor approach was refined and made more sensitive. The system is based on the logic of differential psychology, which assumes that the characteristics of the individual can be measured through testing and that the unique profile of the individual can be described and ultimately matched with a description of rele-

---

* *Traits* refer to the relevant characteristics of the individual such as interests, skills, aptitudes, and the like. *Factors* refer to the requirements of specific occupations or jobs—that is, what is required to perform them successfully.

vant occupations. Early approaches to vocational guidance were essentially derivations of this approach.

This cross-sectional approach takes a "snapshot" of the individual and compares it with a picture of appropriate options. It examines these options through counseling approaches that are primarily, but by no means exclusively, cognitive. It focuses on the identification of a choice. This static approach generally does not take into account the forces that brought the individual to his or her present state, the person's potential for change in terms of traits or motivation, and the possibility of alterations in the job environment. Herr asserts that

> at its worst, a trait and factor approach can be merely deterministic unless the individual involved is an active participant in the choice process, helping to decide not only what is the best literal fit of individual characteristics and the requirements of different alternatives but rather how available choices occurred with the particular person's assessments of what such a fit should be, given one's values, personal preferences, and willingness to make commitments at a particular point in time [1986, p. 178].

The advantage of this approach is its reliance on the ever-increasing accuracy in portraying the characteristics of the individual and the options available. In addition, early applications of the model provided insight into the nature of decision making as well as into the nature of the counseling process.

Decision Approaches. Decision approaches are found in the model of utility theory, which is concerned with weighing as much information as possible so that the resulting decisions enhance the organism to the utmost. Applied to an individual's occupational choices, "the assumption in such a model is that one chooses an educational or occupational goal that will maximize one's gain and minimize one's chance of loss" (Herr, 1986, p. 178).

Obviously, many complexities must be taken into account. One's personal style, proclivity to risk taking, value system, and unique motivations all contribute to the ultimate decision. Decision approaches have also focused on the steps necessary to reach a decision, which include "defining the problems, generating alternatives, gathering information, processing information, making plans and relating goals, [and] implementing and evaluating plans" (Herr, 1986, p. 181).

Decision theory also involves a good deal of social learning. The process itself may alter the individual's goals, change the basic nature of the information itself, and affect the goals themselves. The process, in behavorial terms, includes "constantly encountering learning experiences, each of which is followed by rewards or punishments that in turn produce the uniqueness of each individual" (Isaacson, 1985, p. 72).

One of the strengths of this approach is that it encourages the career seeker to project into the future and imagine sequences of events. It also encourages the person to consider a variety of alternate scenarios and outcomes as a consequence of options taken at various junctures. The decision approach is thus much less mechanistic than the trait and factor approach and allows for some degree of informed speculation in the evaluation of options. The system also provides for the extensive exploration of personal value systems and includes the option of using so-called "soft" estimates of information about the potential payoffs of particular decisions. These soft estimates are not dependent on hard, precise data but allow for impressions and hunches as part of the process. The ultimate utility of the decision is thus affected by emotions and feelings as well as by purely cognitive processing of information.

Sociological Approaches.   "Situational or sociological approaches to career development accentuate the reality that one's environment both provides the kinds of choices from which any individual can choose and also shapes the likelihood that persons holding memberships in different groups are likely to make certain choices and not others" (Herr, 1986, p. 182.) From an informational and historical point of view, approaches in this realm are particularly sensitive to the influence of gender, social class, and race on career development. The fundamental question of whether people are free to choose in the area of career development or whether there are powerful sociological forces that propel them toward inevitable vocational objectives has long been of concern to professionals. The issues are, in fact, much broader than sociological. They include political, economic, and historical forces as well. Were they merely sociological, the counselor would be justified in providing reality information to clients and delegating the responsibility to them for incorporating and processing that information. The present realities dictate that the counselor must be aware of the implications of these sociological factors but also be able to point out their origins and their political, historical, and economic implications.

Not too many decades ago, counselors were advised to point out to members of minority groups the difficulty of attaining particular occupational objectives. The data were presented in actuarial terms, and clients were left to their own devices. A more modern and sophisticated use of such sociological data would be to use the data as a starting point for discussions with clients but to indicate the process of change underway, to aid the clients by becoming an advocate for such change. The counselor probably has a responsibility to make certain that the client is aware of the implications of his/her interests for the "realities" of gender, race, and social class issues in career development and the process of confronting these realities.

In short, counseling psychologists have a professional obligation to be informed of the various sociological and situational factors that have an impact on career development. They have a personal and moral obligation to be certain that they encourage behaviors and outcomes that are designed to alter these realities in directions consistent with the human aims of their parent professional organizations. Indeed, professional detachment in particular areas of practice may be inimical to moral and ethical practices.

Personality Approaches.   Approaches to career development that evolve from a consideration of the personality of the career seeker obviously narrow the focus of concern. Herr notes that if sociological and situational approaches are macroapproaches to career development, "personality approaches might be considered microapproaches, attempts to identify individual as opposed to group mechanisms that shape career behavior" (1986, p. 184).

These approaches focus on the "intrinsic motivation" of each individual in the area of career development and derive from a "need/drive" approach to explain particular behaviors (Herr, 1986). Theorists from a variety of psychodynamic approaches postulate conscious and unconscious motivation for career behaviors. Individuals are either attempting to meet their needs through work-related activities or to reduce particular drives, centered in the various aspects of their psyches, in their search for work satisfaction. Theorists such as Maslow and Roe attempted in a general way to indicate how it is possible for an individual to attend to personal goals through occupational resolution (Herr, 1986). Holland proposed "a hierarchy of preferred methods for dealing with social and environmental tasks. These preferences are reflected in one's modal personal orientation" (Herr, 1986, p. 185). Maslow (1954) points out in his general treatise on motivation and personality that in making decisions about life that include work decisions, people are driven by their basic needs. Roe (1956), in a more focused treatise, notes the relationship between early personal experiences, evolving personal characteristics, and choice of occupational endeavor.

All these approaches are based on the assumption that personality characteristics are a product of early experiences and that these characteristics are part of the idiosyncratic evolution of each individual. In addition, both Roe and Holland believe that the emerging personality is a product of the interaction between heredity and environment. Both believe that early influences produce shaping behaviors that mold the individual's personality. Holland, while less specific than Roe with respect to early influences, agrees that early life history and the values it introduces permanently influence human perceptions and self-concepts and lead to the evolution of his six basic occupational types (realistic, investigative, artistic, social, enterprising, and conventional) (Isaacson, 1985).

As indicated, Roe's and Holland's approaches both focus on the effect that personality and early behavior have on vocational choice. We have also examined the trait and factor, decision, and sociological theories. We began with a presentation of the developmental approach, which we believe is the most comprehensive of the models of career development and behavior. We believe that aspects of each model are significant for the counseling psychologist in working with clients in vocational and educational counseling. The developmental approach has the capacity for incorporating the best features of the others. In addition, it provides a framework for counseling in this area of activity that extends across the life span of the individual and focuses on behaviors that are relevant at the various life stages. It includes the prevocational stages as well as disengagement and incorporates leisure and avocational activities. Finally, its broad framework is able to incorporate the unique status of each individual as determined by gender, race, and social status.

Developmental Counseling:
A Framework for Counseling Psychologists

A commitment to a developmental framework is essential to our conception of counseling psychology. In examining the historical development of the field as well as in considering the critical theories that inform its practitioners, we have pointed out that development through the life span has a central role for the counseling psychologist. Whether counseling psychologists work in higher education, hospitals, mental-health agencies, or private practice, they have a direct or indirect influence on clients throughout the life span. A developmental framework is therefore a useful structure in assessing strategies for intervention.

Selman points out that "the basic assumption of this approach is that social reasoning develops through an invariant sequence of stages; each stage is qualitatively distinct from the previous stage" (1977, p. 33). His research focuses on examining the relationships among children's experience in the physical, cognitive, affective, and social domains. He concludes that development is not parallel in these domains, even in normal children. He maintains that it is possible to affect development in one domain by structural stimulation in another domain. As an example of this principle, Selman notes "that even when interpersonal reasoning is at age normative levels, interpersonal relating may still be immature. In fact, in its strictest interpretation, this model implies that by generally improving the structure of interpersonal behaviors one is likely to improve reasoning, rather than the reverse" (1977, p. 6).

Examples of interventions and their implications exist at all levels of development. Cooney (1977) provides evidence for guidance and counseling at the elementary school level. Collins (1977) suggests that programs designed to promote cognitive growth may benefit from the intervention evaluation models employed by counseling psychologists, particularly if these interventions engage or involve children in the process. Bernier and Rustad (1977) suggest that applying a cognitive-developmental model to the school curriculum promotes growth in adolescents. They characterize their approach as combining counseling and teaching skills in a normal developmental framework. Some writers observe that the success of these interventions is directly related to the extent of student involvement through active participation, "responsible role taking and active reflection" (Cognetta, 1977, p. 24). Applications of these concepts to late adolescents and young adults have been suggested by Widick (1977) and Stephenson and Hunt (1977). Finally, several authors have suggested applying the general cognitive-developmental schema to career planning and decision making (Touchton, Wertheimer, Cornfeld, & Harrison, 1977).

Perhaps there is no more significant sector within which to apply these interactive developmental concepts than career development and decision making. As Herr notes, "Vocational guidance has historically experienced some difficulty in articulating what its purposes are in an operational way" (Herr & Cramer, 1964, p. 561). Indeed, criticisms of the field have included the observations that descriptions of these services are "frequently simple inventories of what will be done—e.g., individual counseling and testing—rather than an explanation of why anything is to be done or the behavioral changes in students or clients which are expected as a function of [this] intervention" (p. 561). The developmental framework provides a reasonable rationale within which to address the relationship between the type of intervention, the expected outcomes of that intervention, and appropriate age-related behavioral objectives.

Specific Interventions in Career Development

As Isaacson notes,

> all persons who survive to adulthood are involved in the career develop-
> ment process, just as they are involved in physical growth, personality
> development, and the educational process. Similarly, the career develop-
> ment process continues through adulthood just as physical growth and
> change, personality development, and the learning processes also continue
> as lifelong aspects of the human condition [1985, p. 38]

The differences in application of the specific interventions are related to the
life stage of the individual, the setting in which that intervention takes place,
and the special circumstances of the client. Beyond these differences, a number
of comprehensive, universal objectives of career development have emerged
in the last half century. They are listed succinctly by Herr and Cramer (1984):

1. *The development of decision-making skills.* People need to acquire skill
in identifying, collecting, and evaluating the information necessary for making wise decisions. They must develop an understanding of the process of decision making.

2. *Evolution of a self-concept.* People need to develop the capacity to
integrate information about relevant elements in their environment and to comprehend the impact of these elements on their sense of self. They must learn
to understand how their personal characteristics interact with the external
world. They need to experience those interactions in terms of their needs and
conceptions of self.

3. *Assessment of values, lifestyles, and preferred activities.* The general
goals and satisfactions that define a person's choice of educational, occupational, and leisure activities are likely to be bound together by a unique complex of values and beliefs. People need to be helped to identify and understand
their motivating value systems.

4. *The nature of choice.* People should have the opportunity to examine
the process of choice and to contemplate the options available to them. Within
this context, they should develop the capacity to assess the costs and benefits
of particular choices.

5. *The explanation of individual differences.* People should have the opportunity to examine their unique characteristics and the ways in which they
differ from other people. An exploration of their interests and capacities is the
main objective of this activity.

6. *Responding to a changing world.* "Career guidance must help persons consider contingency planning, multiple routes to goals, flexibility in goals,
and other notions of tentativeness and methods of coping with rapid change
in social and occupational conditions" (Herr & Cramer, 1984, p. 10). In addition to these issues, preparation for catastrophic personal and social events needs
to be incorporated into the developmental experience of the individual.

The tasks outlined above are universally applicable in a developmental
context of counseling and career development. As we noted, the specific attainment of each of these goals depends on the stage of development and set-

ting in which they are applied. Applications of these objectives will vary by age and setting; for example, if one is considering a career-development program in an educational setting such as an elementary or secondary school it would involve a very different set of applications than would be involved in a Veterans Administration counseling center. In addition, the needs of special populations have to be taken into account. Orthopedically handicapped clients will, of necessity, need to pay choser attention to the physical requirements and the environmental circumstances of work than will others. The issues of self-concept, assessment, and decision making are obviously quite different for a person entering the exploration stage (14 to 24 years of age)—with its sense of future, expanding horizons, and opportunity—than it would for a person in his or her middle years (maintenance stage), faced with a catastrophic loss of job, who must deal with the identification of new occupational objectives. While the circumstances and impact of a variety of intervention strategies are quite different in the examples given, however, the intervention areas are the same. Irrespective of the particular problem in career development, the issues of assessment, self-exploration, and decision making through individual and group intervention cut across all ages and all sectors.

Assessment in Career Development

One of the major sources of information about the characteristics of the individual client is standardized tests. The refinement of assessment techniques and the increased sophistication of differential psychology give the counselor a highly developed technical source of descriptive information. Tests provide "more reliable and valid assessments of certain human characteristics than would usually be possible or feasible on the basis of subjective judgment" (Prediger, 1974, p. 329). Some tests provide data unavailable in any other form. Information obtained from tests can help clients explore themselves, compare themselves to others, examine preferences and interests, assess relative strengths and weaknesses, and open up new areas of interest. Prediger suggests that

> the role of tests in career-guidance is therefore threefold: first to stimulate, broaden, and provide focus to career exploration; second to stimulate exploration of self in relation to career; and third to provide "what if" information with respect to career choice options. This role can best be performed in the context of a developmental career program [1974, p. 338].

Some tests are designed to provide rather specific data about the relationship between a person's skills and the accomplishment of specific tasks. These are referred to as "narrowed" instruments. They "focus intensive assessment on a specific, limited area of concern with the objective being highly accurate measures of those personal characteristics most relevant to that concern" (Predinger, 1974, p. 340). Instruments in this category answer a client's very specific questions about a focused objective or area of competence. Just as frequently these narrowed measures are used by institutions to help them place an individual in a specific level of activity. Wide-based instruments, on the other hand, include measures of interests, abilities, values, preferences, and personality. These are the major tests used in career counseling. Their purposes are prediction, diagnosis, monitoring, and evaluation (Isaacson, 1985).

Predictive tests can provide partial insight into questions about the client's ability to succeed in an activity. We say "partial insight" because of the complexities involved in accurate prediction and the difficulty in controlling unmeasurable variables such as maturation, effort, the nature of the particular experience, and chance factors. Nevertheless, "The evidence suggests that in spite of the limitations, predictions based on actuarial data seem to be stronger and more reliable than those based on clinical judgment alone" (Isaacson, 1985, p. 151). The more diffuse the activity, the larger the number of variables, and the more complex the intangibles, the greater the difficulty in making accurate predictions. As Herr and Cramer note, "it is safe to say that aptitude tests predict school performance and success in training better than they do performance in an occupation" (1984, p. 471).

Although many criticisms have been offered of the use of tests, particularly in prediction, we agree with Herr and Cramer that tests used in combination and added to other data about the individual "hold enough predictive power to be of practical value in the selection of personnel and of some value in counseling, depending on how they are used" (1984, p. 472).

Aptitude and interest tests can yield information for diagnostic purposes. Such tests frequently provide answers to clients' questions about the likelihood of their succeeding in a particular career or the similarity between their interests or abilities and those of people working in various fields.

Monitoring tests are usually concerned with appraising a person's progress in a particular activity. As Isaacson notes, these tests generally focus on "developmental processes or on skill acquisition. Achievement tests are the most typical kinds of tests used for monitoring purposes" (1985, p. 52).

Finally, evaluative tests are usually employed after training or educational programs to determine whether clients have accomplished what they set out to do. They are utilized more as part of a total career-development program than for individual counseling activities.

Interest inventories, ability and aptitude tests, and personality, temperament, and value inventories are the specific tests used most often in career-development assessment. In addition, there are several instruments specifically designed to measure "career maturity." At advanced levels of development, job-satisfaction measures may be useful. The selection of the appropriate assessment devices is, of course, a function of the education of the counseling psychologist. Zytowski and Borgen assert that

> too often vocational psychologists have only one or two assessment instruments in their repertory and fit their conception of the client's needs to what these instruments yield. . . . clearly the decision to use a particular assessment and which one to select depends on an exact understanding of what information is needed and intimate knowledge of tests that might provide it [1983, p. 26].

Individual Intervention in Career Development

Most counselors practice from a broadly conceived approach based on an amalgam of their philosophical viewpoints, beliefs, values, perceptions of human nature, and conceptions of human development. Career development frequently requires some adjustment of this perspective. Such adjustments stem from the realization that career counseling requires broad strategies to meet varying client needs. Some clients need the opportunity to explore their sense of self. Others need information about themselves and the world of work. Still others may need to identify their status with respect to the accomplishment of particular vocational-developmental tasks and, consequently, may discover that they need some degree of remediation in this area. Others may need help in processing and integrating all the relevant data that they use in a rational decision-making process that leads to a decision appropriate for their developmental level. In any event, individual intervention in career counseling requires the counselor, of whatever persuasion, to focus on the needs of the client in the context of the developmental tasks of career counseling.

As we have said, whatever the approach, the counselor must ensure that the client understands the nature of career development as a continuous process through the life span. In addition, clients must be given the opportunity to explore their interests, values, aptitudes, and goals. They must understand the relationship between their cultural background, values, and occupational goals and aspirations. In addition, they need the opportunity to learn the sources of information about themselves and the process of evaluating this information in the context of their own needs and satisfactions. Career counseling has a very powerful educational role to play. There are specific sources of data, well-defined processes, and identifiable entrance requirements to educational and occupational objectives. The cognitive content of career development and counseling is perhaps more easily identified than in any other area of counseling psychology.

One approach to career counseling involves a process of sequential decision making (Gelatt, 1978). The decision-making model can be integrated quite easily with cognitive-behavioral approaches and neo-analytic (particularly ego-psychology) approaches. A more subtle adjustment may be required for some humanist approaches to counseling, but combined cognitive and humanist principles are possible.

Gelatt (1978) suggests that the system requires information, a predictive system that includes the opportunity to assess alternatives and the opportunity to simulate these decisions and test them out. One such approach involves a gaming strategy wherein the player is able to devise a strategy to reach specific goals. The individual's values interact with alternatives and outcomes, and each decision may be evaluated with respect to the desirability of the outcome. The individual has the opportunity to collect more data, adopt a new strategy, and reassess goals. As Gelatt notes "a decision can be final only in the sense that an immediate goal is reached. But the achievement of this goal may itself influence or modify other related choices. The counselor's role in this process is to assist the individual through the cycle (1978, p. 404–405).

Group Intervention in Career Development

Herr and Cramer (1984) suggest several ways in which groups can be used to foster career development. Among these approaches, they suggest using the group to disseminate information. It should be clear that this will not necessarily reduce the need for individual follow-up. People frequently need data that are applicable only to themselves. In addition, idiosyncratic responses to information may need to be dealt with on a one-to-one basis.

Groups provide an excellent setting for teaching about the process of career development. Rehearsal of actions and reality testing can be carried out through role playing. Career-development groups can explore and develop attitudes, visit job sites and career conferences, and provide a source of motivation (Herr & Cramer, 1984, p. 413–414).

Group approaches are an additional strategy to be employed in a total program of career development. While most frequently employed in schools, this approach is useful with clients of all ages and at all stages of career development. It is frequently the best approach to initiate the process of career development with adults in a crisis stage—for example, employees in a company that has just shut down, veterans in a hospital, or retirees who need to consider leisure activities. In short, the teaching, information-dissemination, and motivational functions of groups apply across the spectrum of career development. The psychodynamics of the group process can be helpful at many stages of development.

The Settings of Vocational and Educational Counseling

Counseling psychologists work in a variety of settings that feature career development as one of their services. In addition, through their research programs and teaching activities, they influence career-development programs in a number of sectors of society. In this section we examine several of these activities in the schools, in the community, and in industry.

Career Development in School

Career development is a major endeavor at the elementary, junior high school, and senior high school levels. In addition, of course, significant career decisions are made in higher education.

Most of the work of career development through secondary school is carried out by master's-level school counselors and career specialty counselors. The student of counseling psychology may fail to see the relevance of examining the practice of career development and guidance at these levels. There is an important connection, however. One of the anomalies of counseling psychology is that the influence of this field far exceeds the number of practitioners in it. The basic research that informs the field of career development has, for the most part, been carried out by counseling psychologists. The significant theories of career development have evolved from the work of the vocational psychologists, many of whom metamorphosed into counseling psychologists (see Chapter 1). The primary life-stage approach to career development outlined in this capter was evolved by Super, one of the leaders in the field of counseling psychology over the past half century.

In addition, a significant number of the subdoctoral counselors who are responsible for devising career-development programs in the schools have been educated by counseling psychologists. These "counselor educators" are counseling psychologists either by training or by subsequent identification. The irony is that counseling psychology, in its professional manifestation, has failed to address its responsibility for this endeavor. Indeed, there is a good deal of looking the other way on this issue.

Ideally, programs in career development should begin in the elementary school with a curricular focus on work values, attitudes toward work, and the development of preliminary understandings of the relationship between the child's world and the world of work. In a broadly developmental sense, these are the years when work habits become reinforced and when Erikson's stage of industry versus inferiority should be worked through to resolution. These are the years when the early applications of a sense of mastery of the environment and the developing sense of competence begin to emerge. Herr and Cramer observe that

> the first few years of life have been called, correctly, the "nursery of human nature." This is the period of life when a child's goals, achievement motivation, and perceptions of self as worthy or inferior begin to be formulated. The concepts children acquire during this life stage directly influence both school success, career identity, adult interests and general perspectives on life [1984, p. 217].

The career-related activities of the elementary school need to reflect this profound truth and include opportunities for appropriate experiences throughout grade school. Such activities include opportunities for self-exploration and self-assessment, identifying occupational and role models, and developing insight into the relationship between these aspects of life and one's own values and attitudes.

Naturally the career-related tasks become more specific in middle school, or junior high school. The focus in the relationship between broad occupational goals and spcific interests, values, abilities, and personal characteristics is appropriate at this level. In addition, examining educational options at the next level of accomplishment is appropriate here. The implications of selecting one curriculum over another helps students clarify their understanding of themselves as well as learn something about the process of decision making. Information about occupational groups and the educational requirements for different levels of access to those groups is appropriate.

Specification increases again in senior high school. Assessment of the vocational maturity of students is appropriate. Concrete explorations of work values and work aspirations are timely. Herr and Cramer note that in high school there may need to be three separate emphases, namely, "stimulating career development, providing treatment and aiding placement (the latter refers to student movement to the next educational level or to the immediate life of the worker)" (1984, p. 262).

There are choices here for the counselor, depending on the readiness of the client to proceed with the process. The first emphasis, "stimulating career development," refers to helping students integrate career information with personal characteristics and make the necessary decisions about educational and occupational planning. "Providing treatment" may be necessary for those with lagging vocational maturity who need to acquire knowledge, skill, and improved attitudes in this area because they have not worked through the appropriate vocational-development tasks. Finally, the counselor at this level will need to be concerned with specific planning for those going on to college or into specialty training as well as those entering the world of work. Frequently, the latter group is left on its own by counselors and the school system.

Counseling psychologists are most likely to be involved in career development in colleges or universities. The issues here may be similar to those faced by secondary school students. Students frequently need assistance in making decisions as well as in gaining access to employment. Some of the most interesting work in career development is with the group of college students classified as "undecided." Their ranks are swelled by those who enter college with specific goals in mind but discover that they were misplaced. These clients frequently present serious problems of disillusionment. The skills of the counseling psychologist are necessary to integrate a remediation strategy with an effective career-development experience.

Career Development in the Community

Many counseling psychologists work with veterans in either hospitals or in the community. Their task is complicated by the fact that these veterans are in various life stages, ranging from early adulthood to the last years of life. In addition, many have had their careers interrupted by serious illness or injury. Still others may be unable to work anymore. In these last cases, counselors help clients develop alternative activities that can offer some of the satisfaction formerly provided by work.

Counseling psychologists may be called on to deal with community members who have suffered disruptions in their occupational life. Plant closings, company reorganizations, and shifting economic patterns have caused major career interruptions for a significant number of people. In addition, counselors who work in the community may also see people who have completed a career in one sector, such as the military or the civil service, and are considering a new career.

Vocational Psychology in Industry

Historically, counseling psychologists have been employed by industry in personnel selection and, occasionally, in remedial or therapeutic capacities with workers suffering from adjustment problems. The role of counseling psychologists in this sector has overlapped with those of industrial psychologists and sociologists. Shullman and Carder (1983) suggest that an integration of activities of these professionals may be taking place and that the future may provide an increased role for vocational/counseling psychologists in industry.

Shullman and Carder assert that an increasing perception of the large organization as a "career system" may create this demand. (They describe a *career system* as a dynamic setting in which workers are continually learning and evolving, moving from job to job, climbing occupational ladders, and experiencing all the concerns, satisfactions, and disappointments in microcosm just as they exist in the broader occupational world.)

> An organization requires adequate financial, physical, informational, and human resources to operate and a certain mix and relationship among them to be effective. Thus, acquisition and management of human resources and the establishment of organizational career systems are not purely in response to any particularly altruistic, "nice-to-do" organizational motives but represent the efforts of organizations to meet survival needs. . . . It is becoming a matter of economic necessity for organizations to successfully address these issues in the 1980's [1983, p. 146].

They also propose that this career-systems approach suggests the emergence of a "tripartite model" focusing on an industry's organizational aspects, the individual dimension, and the interactional processes linking the two. They note that

> traditionally, research at the organizational level has come from industrial/organizational psychology and sociology, whereas vocational (and counseling) psychology has dealt with the individual. The use of a tripartite model highlights the research gap between the two areas, while also providing a conceptual framework to organize existing research [p. 147].

In this context, it becomes apparent that the concerns of the industrial organization may expand to include ways of maximizing its talent. This effort may include examining the processes that lead to increased job satisfaction, productive career shifts, and minimization of career plateauing.* There may very well be an expanding role in industry for counseling psychologists in which they move beyond a selection and remedial role and introduce the concept of adult career development.

Special Concerns in Career Development

Counseling psychologists should be aware of the changing status of significant segments of the population with respect to career development and counseling. As more and more women enter the work force in a wide variety of jobs, the impact on planning for women's careers has shifted, as has the structure of the work force. In addition, with increasing access by the disabled to education and occupations, their role has broadened as well. Finally, with rising political and economic sophistication, there have been significant shifts in social attitudes toward minority groups.

Career plateauing refers to the situation of individuals who have the potential to advance but have not progressed according to expectations.

Women and Career Development

While women are still concentrated in the lower paid, often dead-end occupations, they have been gaining greater representation in previously male-dominated occupaitons such as law, engineering, and medicine (Cramer, Keitel, & Rossberg, 1986). The old assumption that the primary role of women in society was that of housewife and mother has shifted dramatically. In addition, the assumption long existed that when women did work outside the home, they served men or replicated their domestic and child-care responsibilities. As Fitzgerald and Betz (1983) observe, "women's place is clearly no longer exclusively in the home. . . . Not only will most women work outside the home, but the majority of young women now prefer to combine marriage and career pursuits in their adult lives" (pp. 84–85).

Counseling psychologists not only need to be aware of these changes in serving female clients but also need to increase their research into the process of career counseling with women. For the first half century of the existence of vocational psychology, the special concerns of women did not enter into the research considerations of the field. More recently attention has been paid to these issues. We now have research into such issues as societal sex-role stereotypes, occupational sex stereotypes, family background, the influence of marriage and children, and the influence of role models. In addition, there has been an increasing concern with the special nature of career patterns of women as well as with the impact of career counseling on them. This recent increase in concern for women's career-development patterns has also reestablished interest in examining the differences in interests and abilities of men and women.

The increased presence of women in the work force has led to the consideration of other complex issues, including the emergence of women in competing roles with men, the appearance of women in top leadership positions, and the impact on interpersonal relationships in the workplace, including the demands for an increased number of competent women role models. Certainly sexual harassment as an area of increased awareness and consciousness is part of this issue.

Much of the foregoing discussion has concentrated on the external barriers to the evolution of women's roles in the work force, such as discriminating attitudes, ancient stereotypes, and sexual harassment. Fitzgerald and Betz note that it seems clear that internal factors also play a critical role in preventing women from fulfulling their career potential and achieving vocational satisfaction: "Two major types of internal barriers salient during the career adjustment stage are role conflict and overload and the management of dual career issues" (1983, p. 135). The demands on women trying to perform the roles of both worker and homemaker lead to the notion of overload (Cramer et al., 1986). In dual-career families, the effects on the marriage and the impact on work satisfaction for husband and wife need to be examined and resolved.

Career Development for the Disabled

In this section we address the career problems of clients who are in need of the special services offered under the rubric of rehabilitation. Such clients may experience social, physical, and psychological barriers to development, including career development. Jaques and Kauppi (1983) point out that the rehabilitation process involves addressing the attitudes of society toward the particular disability, assessing and mobilizing the assets of the client; fostering the process of helping the client cope with personal barriers to development; helping the client develop functional skills necessary for successful living in the world; and aiding the client to become a responsible decision maker in his or her own behalf.

The rehabilitation process is developmental and may be entered at any stage of a person's life. Some individuals deal with genetic and birth defects. Other defects are acquired at an early age or occur later in life as a result of an accident or illness.

Society has provided social mandates for services to the disabled for most of this century through legislation mandating aid for the industrially injured, the war injured, and the genetically disabled. Social legislation provides service to people with specific disabilities ranging from physical handicaps to emotional difficulties to mental retardation. Much of this legislation has included provisions for the vocational rehabilitation of these populations (see Chapter 2). Recent federal legislation has mandated improvements in physical access to public buildings and transportation. Such legislation has also mandated equal access to educational programs specifically designed to meet the needs of the disabled. Furthermore, federal law has mandated the education of subdoctoral rehabilitation counselors, trained to provide vocational rehabilitation and general counseling services to the handicapped.

Counseling psychologists have long been engaged in the education of rehabilitation counselors and in providing theoretical and research contexts for their work. In addition, in such settings as Veterans Administration hospitals, they have been given the responsibility of providing direct care to veterans in need of psychological rehabilitation, including vocational rehabilitation. They have been involved with the direct and indirect treatment of the disabled over a long period of time.

Counseling psychologists need to be particularly aware of the need for special applications of the concepts of career development to the disabled. Hershenson (1974) proposes a model that includes many of the traditional components of vocational development but suggests the incorporation of constructs that focus on "the individual's background (physical and psychosocial), his work personality (his constellation of psychological traits and attitudes which mediate adaptation to work), his work competence, his work choice, and his work adjustment" (p. 487).

Counseling psychologists should be aware of resources in the community that provide special services and support to the disabled. In addition, the issue of placement and follow-up in employment may need to be more carefully considered in the case of handicapped clients. Hershenson also notes that

> aside from the usual practices of locating jobs or job producing resources
> and convincing employers of the work potential of the clients, vocational
> guidance with the handicapped has promoted the development of several

original placement strategies. Among these are the techniques of job engineering or structuring jobs to the capacities of workers [1974, p. 493].

Career development and rehabilitation with disabled workers frequently involves expanding the traditional approaches with a creative dimension to resolve specific problems.

Career Development for Minority Clients

The political changes that have occurred since the end of World War II have made us acutely aware of the exclusion of particular populations from normal access to the American dream. Some of these changes in attitudes and understanding relate to changing structures in the world at large, particularly the breakup of 19th-century colonial empires and the evolution of freedom and nationalist movements around the world. Another part of this process was the evolution of these same demands for freedom within the United States. Homegrown colonialism and the exploitation of many ethnic and social minorities was finally recognized. Populations like blacks, Puerto Ricans, Cubans, Native Americans, Mexican Americans, and, to some extent, Asian Americans were explicitly and implicitly excluded from the normal processes of development, access, and freedom of choice within American society.

During the past three decades demands for improved civil rights, human rights, and equal access to educational and occupational opportunity have been incorporated into the law of the land. The school-integration program is a result of these changes. The establishment of human-rights commissions, fair-employment-practices commissions, affirmative-action programs and the like are part of this necessary political change.

In the past, career development for minority groups ranged from neglect to benign reinforcement of the status quo. Even the most positively inclined counselors were likely to discourage minority-group members with extraordinary vocational aspirations because of "existing reality." These behaviors have been significantly altered with changes in social attitudes and practices. Counseling psychologists have a professional and moral responsibility, as members of a profession that has made affirmative action one of its significant social objectives, to implement those goals by adopting an active stance in the counseling of members of minority groups. As Gordon (1974) asserts, what is required is a change in focus and method,

> a shift from diplomacy to advocacy. Our clients do not need to be apologized for and to have their troubles explained away, they need to be more actively involved in the decision-making processes that control their lives. Their rights need to be more appropriately defended, and opportunities for meaningful involvement need to be more vigorously advanced [p. 472].

Summary

Vocational and educational counseling is a sector of professional activity that counseling psychologists, as they emerged from the old vocational guidance movement and incorporated the findings and research from vocational psychology, identified as their own bailiwick. We examined the critical role of work in society and pointed out how activity in the vocational area is related to reality. In addition, we examined the relationship between vocational development, career patterns, and general life stages. Vocational development is best understood in the context of general human development, but it has its own unique characteristics. We noted the parallels between vocational life stages and human life stages.

Donald E. Super's seminal role in this area was considered particularly with respect to the stimulus he gave to research in the field and to his monumental efforts at synthesizing data from several fields of study. We looked at Super's approach to vocational development as well as other developmental approaches, trait and factor approaches, and decision-making theories. We considered the role of counseling psychologists in these activities with respect to intervention, treatment, and counseling strategies. In addition, we examined some of the settings in which couseling psychologists might function in the area of career development.

We conclude with a note that although vocational and educational counseling have traditionally been the domain of counseling psychologists, interest may be diminishing in this sector of activity. Watkins (1981) suggests that there may be fewer professionals providing service in vocational appraisal and counseling. He also expresses concern that the research base in this important area might diminish because of "stunted" activity (1981, p. 87). Not all psychologists agree with Watkins. Some even suggest that increased demands in such settings as industry may contribute to a new sprint of growth in the field (Shullman & Carder, 1983). In any event, developments in this area will be critical to the continued identification of counseling psychology as a subspecialty.

References

Bernier, J. E., & Rustad, K. (1977). Psychology of Counseling Curriculum: A Follow-Up Study. *The Counseling Psychologist, 6*(4), 18–21.

Buhler, C., & Masserick, F. (Eds.). (1968). *The Course of Human Life: A Study of Goals in the Humanistic Perspective.* New York: Springer.

Cognetta, P. (1977). Deliberate Psychological Education: A High School Cross-Age Teaching Model. *The Counseling Psychologist, 6*(4), 22–24.

Collins, W. A. (1977). Counseling Interventions and Developmental Psychology: Reactions to Programs for Social-Cognitive Growth. *The Counseling Psychologist, 6*(4), 15–17.

Cooney, E. W. (1977). Social-Cognitive Development: Applications to Intervention and Evolution in the Elementary Grades. *The Counseling Psychologist, 6*(4), 6–9.

Cramer, S. H., Keitel, M. A., & Rossberg, R. (1986). The Family and Employed Mothers. *International Journal of Family Psychiatry, 7*(1), 17–34.

Danish, S. J., D'Augelli, A. R., & Ginsberg, M. R. (1984). Life Development Interventions: Promotion of Mental Health Through the Development of Competence. In S. D. Brown & R. W. Lent (Eds.), *Handbook of Counseling Psychology* (pp. 520–544). New York: Wiley.

Fitzgerald, L., & Betz, N. E. (1983). Issues in the Vocational Psychology of Women. In W. B. Walsh & S. Osipow (Eds.), *Handbook of Vocational Psychology* (Vol. 1) (pp. 83–160). Hillsdale, NJ: Erlbaum.

Freud, S. (1955). *Civilization and Its Discontents.* London: Hogarth Press.

Gelatt, H. B. (1978). Decision-Making: A Conceptual Frame of Reference for Counseling. In J. C. Hansen (Ed.), *Counseling Process and Procedures* (pp. 402–408). New York: Macmillan.

Gordon, E. V. (1974). Vocational Guidance: Disadvantaged and Minority Populations. In E. L. Herr (Ed.), *Vocational Guidance and Human Development* (pp. 452–477). Boston: Houghton Mifflin.

Hayes, R. L. (1985). Human Growth and Development. In M. D. Lewis, R. L. Hayes, & J. A. Lewis (Eds.), *An Introduction to the Counseling Profession* (pp. 36–95). Itasca, IL: F. E. Peacock.

Herr, E. L. (1986). Life-Style and Career Development. In M. D. Lewis, R. L. Hayes, & J. A. Lewis (Eds.), *An Introduction to the Counseling Profession* (pp. 167–214). Itasca, IL: F. E. Peacock.

Herr, E. L., & Cramer, S. H. (1984). *Career Guidance and Counseling Through the Life Span.* Boston: Little, Brown.

Hershenson, D. B. (1974). Vocational Guidance and the Handicapped. In E. L. Herr (Ed.), *Vocational Guidance and Human Development* (pp. 478–501). Boston: Houghton Mifflin.

Isaacson, L. E. (1985). *Basics of Career Counseling.* Boston: Allyn & Bacon.

Jaques, M. E., & Kauppi, D. R. (1983). Vocational Rehabilitation and Its Relationship to Vocational Psychology. In W. B. Walsh & S. Osipow (Eds.), *Handbook of Vocational Psychology* (Vol. 2) (pp. 207–258). Hillsdale, NJ: Erlbaum.

Jordaan, J. P. (1974). Life Stages as Organizing Modes of Career Development. In E. L. Herr (Ed.), *Vocational Guidance and Human Development.* (pp. 263–295). Boston: Houghton Mifflin.

Levenstein, A. (1964). *Why People Work.* New York: Collier Books.

Maslow, A. H. (1954). *Motivation and Personality.* New York: Harper.

Miller, C. N. (1971). *Foundations of Guidance.* New York: Harper & Row.

Neff, W. S. (1985). *Work and Human Behavior* (3rd ed.). New York: Aldine.

Prediger, D. J. (1974). The Role of Assessment in Career Guidance. In E. L. Herr (Ed.), *Vocational Guidance and Human Development* (pp. 325–349). Boston: Houghton Mifflin.

Roe, A. (1956). *The Psychology of Occupations.* New York: Wiley.

Selman, R. L. (1977). A Structural-Developmental Model of Social Cognition: Implications for Intervention Research. *The Counseling Psychologist, 6*(4), 3–5.

Shullman, S. L., & Carder, C. E. (1983). Vocational Psychology in Industrial Settings. In W. B. Walsh & S. Osipow (Eds.), *Handbook of Vocational Psychology* (Vol. 2) (pp. 141–180). Hillsdale, NJ: Erlbaum.

Spokane, A. R., & Oliver, L. W. (1983). The Outcomes of Vocational Intervention. In W. B. Walsh & S. Osipow (Eds.), *Handbook of Vocational Psychology* (Vol. 2) (pp. 99–140). Hillsdale, NJ: Erlbaum.

Stephenson, B. W., & Hunt, C. (1977). Intellectual and Ethical Development: A Dualistic Curriculum Intervention for College Students. *The Counseling Psychologist, 6*(4), pp. 39–42.

Super, D. E. (1942). *The Dynamics of Vocational Adjustment.* New York: Harper & Row.

Super, D. E. (1969). Vocational Development Theory: Persons, Positions, and Processes. *The Counseling Psychologist, 1,* 2–9.

Super, D. E. (1983). The History and Development of Vocational Psychology. In W. B.

Walsh & S. Osipow (Eds.), *Handbook of Vocational Psychology* (Vol. 1) (pp. 5–38). Hillsdale, NJ: Erlbaum.

Touchton, J. G., Wertheimer, L. G., Cornfeld, J. L., & Harrison, K. H. (1977). Career Planning and Decision-Making: A Developmental Approach to the Classroom. *The Counseling Psychologist, 6*(4), 42–46.

Watkins, C. E., Jr. (1981). Counseling Psychology Versus Clinical Psychology: Further Explorations on a Theme. *The Counseling Psychologist, 11*(4), 76–92.

Widick, C. (1977). The Perry Scheme: A Foundation for Developmental Practice. *The Counseling Psychologist, 6*(4), 35–38.

Zytowski, D. G., & Borgen, F. N. (1983). Assessment. In W. B. Walsh & S. Osipow (Eds.), *Handbook of Vocational Psychology* (pp. 5–40). Hillsdale, NJ: Erlbaum.

Group Counseling
and Therapy

Over the last 25 years group counseling has become a preferred mode of treatment in resolving interpersonal difficulties. Group experience has also been used by people who are not experiencing specific problems to work on personal development. Group experiences have existed in various forms throughout history, but only recently have they been recognized as relevant and respected forms of counseling. Much of what people believe about themselves comes from feedback from interactions with others. However, everyday interactions do not allow people to check the reactions of others as they can in group counseling. By analyzing their behaviors in a group, people can see how they act in everyday life. The group is a microcosm of society, and the same characteristics displayed in the real world will emerge in the group.

In group counseling, the group is more than a collection of people. The members share some common attitudes and values, accept one another, and maintain an interaction. Cartwright and Zander (1968) defined the characteristics necessary to form a group. They wrote that a group was composed of people who engaged in frequent interactions, defined themselves as group members, were considered by others as belonging to the group, shared norms concerning common interests, participated in a system of interlocking roles, identified with one another, found the group rewarding, pursued interdependent goals, and had a collective perception of their unity. A synthesis of the definitions of groups could be: "an aggregate of people can be identified as a group when the group members see themselves and are seen by others as psychologically interdependent and interactive in the pursuit of a shared goal" (Dagley, Gazda, & Pistole, 1986).

Most groups start as just a collection of people because the members do not begin with the group characteristics. The more the characteristics of the group develop, the stronger the group will become. The group will pass through several stages of development in that process.

Types of Groups

Modern group work developed from diverse origins. J. A. Pratt used a class method for assisting tubercular patients in dealing with their common problem.

J. L. Moreno worked with children and adults in developing an active approach called psychodrama, which provided stimulation that is still continued today. Alfred Adler used group-guidance methods with families (G. Gazda, 1982). During the 1930s, Slavson in New York developed small, intensive, psychoanalytically oriented therapy groups. In the early 1940s Moreno founded the American Society of Group Psychotherapy and Psychodrama, and Slavson formed the American Group Psychotherapy Association. Following World War II social psychologists were actively involved in studying groups. Much of this research focused on effective functioning of democratic organizations. The collection of these research studies formed the basis of group dynamics and led to the interest in the human-relations movement of the 1960s. During this postwar period there was emphasis on teaching about groups by having individuals involved in the experience discuss what they were learning about themselves.

During the 1950s and 1960s there were two approaches to group experience. One approach involved T-groups, or sensitivity groups often conducted in laboratory training (see below). Another approach focused on the intellectual aspect of the individual and was represented by the psychoanalytic group (G. Gazda, 1982). The encounter-group movement was instrumental in merging the emotions and intellect into the full process of personal change. Today all of the types of experience are available. The groups differ in terms of goals, techniques, the role of the leader, and the membership involved in the group.

Encounter Groups

Encounter groups are person-growth groups offering an intense experience designed to help relatively healthy clients gain closer contact with themselves and others. The group activities are used to teach the members about growth and development as well as help them achieve these goals. Most people join the group intending to explore themselves and realize their full potentials. There is an emphasis on expressing their feelings, being spontaneous, and engaging in new behaviors as a part of the learning process. Numerous nonverbal techniques such as touching and sensory-awakening exercises are used in the process. Encounter groups are usually time-limited, and the members are encouraged to become increasingly aware of their feelings and to risk experimenting with behavior that might not feel appropriate to their roles. There are various types of encounter groups, but each has a focus on personal growth of the participants (Corey & Corey, 1987).

T-Groups

T-groups are laboratory training experiences that emphasize human-relations skills for successful functioning and organization. The emphasis is on learning by doing in an environment in which new behaviors are encouraged and analyzed and decisions can be made or problems resolved. These groups tend to be task oriented and to focus on specific organizational problems. T-groups emphasize group process more than personal growth, although members are taught to observe their own process and develop leadership (Corey & Corey, 1987).

Group Therapy

Therapists working with a small number of clients with a common problem assume a role similar to the one they play in individual therapy. They also find that the group offers support, caring, and consultation that are not available in individual therapy. In addition, within the group, members can practice new skills and apply their knowledge, so that more of the working-through process occurs in the group and not just on the outside. Group therapy is of a relatively long duration, aimed at correcting the specific emotional or behavioral disorders of the participants. The goals vary from solving relatively minor problems to reorganizing members' personality structures. As the group members work on specific symptoms and problems, some attention is focused on unconscious factors as well as their past behaviors.

Group Counseling

Group counseling differs from group therapy by dealing with more conscious problems that are not aimed at major personality reconstruction. It is aimed at resolution of specific short-term issues and frequently focuses on educational, vocational, social, or personal problems. Counselors establish a climate for group development and facilitate the members' interaction. They may use a variety of methods, both verbal and nonverbal, to assist the members in understanding themselves and the situations in which they live.

Group Dynamics

Cartwright and Zander (1968) defined group dynamics as a "field of inquiry dedicated to the advancing knowledge about the nature of groups, the laws of their development, and their interactions with other groups, and larger institutions" (p. 19). Considerable research has been conducted into the nature of group behavior. This information is used to prepare group leaders so they will understand what occurs during the life of the group. According to Knowles and Knowles (1959), the group "is always moving, doing something, changing, becoming, interacting, and reacting" (p. 12). Therefore, another definition of group dynamics is the interplay of internal and external forces affecting the group's behavior and movement. The group counselor needs to be aware of group dynamics to better understand the members' interaction in a specific group. Most books on group dynamics include materials on goals, structure, norms, cohesiveness, members' roles, and leadership.

Goals

Most counseling groups begin with an established goal focusing on some topic such as vocational, education, social, or personal issues. The group may deal with self-improvement, growth, improved communication, or a change in behavior. No matter what the goal, the group will become more effective in achieving it if subsidiary goals are established by consensus of the members. Although the group may begin with a general objective, the members usually evolve the meaningful goals for the group.

Goal setting evolves from the group's interaction and members' decisions about what they want to achieve. If a group has difficulty establishing clear goals, it will have more difficulty becoming a cohesive unit and will find the group experience less attractive, leading to a less effective interaction. Napier and Gershenfeld (1973) suggest that the goals reside "in the minds of individuals, as they think of themselves as a group or a unit" (p. 194).

Structure

A group's structure is seen in the patterns and interrelationships of its members (Luft, 1984). The group must establish a workable structure of interaction that will permit it to move toward its understood goals. An effective group structure changes through the life stages of the group because different interactions are necessary at the different stages.

At one time groups were described as structured or unstructured. That is not an accurate form of description, because all groups have structure. The intent was to indicate whether the counselor established a structure for the group or consciously refrained from doing so. Obviously if the leader does not establish something, the group will evolve its own interactional structure. Group leaders' participation in the structure can be seen in their definition of goals, their response to group expectations, and their defining of the basic rules and procedures for the group. Those actions will establish how the members interact, at least during the early stage of the group.

Research has indicated that structure is an important part of the group's early development. When counselors, in preparing members to start a group, clarify group goals, identify client behaviors, and explain the process, the members tend to focus on the group work more quickly (Bednar, Melnick, & Kaul, 1974). Pretraining for members in using positive and negative interpersonal feedback helps the group engage in higher levels of group process and reach higher levels of cohesiveness (Rose & Bednar, 1980). Structuring through topic training given at the group's developmental stage enhances both the process and outcome of group therapy (Kivlighan, McGovern, & Corazzini, 1984). By having clarity in the group goals and helping members establish a method of interaction in the early stages of counseling, the leader will push members to interact more appropriately and focus on moving toward their goal.

Norms

The rules for group behavior are described as its *norms.* Some of these rules are stated by the counselor: arrive on time, don't talk about group discussions outside, no hitting in the group. Other acceptable behaviors become established through spoken or less formal methods of communication. The counselor's stated ground rules serve as a preliminary basis for the group's normative system. But it is only when these rules become a part of the group members' internalized sense of operating procedures that they are truly the norms of behavior. After these norms have been established, there is usually group pressure on members to conform to them. Members are expected to behave in certain ways for the good of all in the group. Although the norms are important in the group's development and effectiveness, the counselor must be aware of pressures that could be detrimental to individuals or the full group.

Cohesiveness

Cohesiveness or a sense of bonding together into a unit is important to any group. The more a member is attracted to the group, the more he or she will actively participate in attaining the group's goals. There needs to be a strong sense of commonality in a group for the members to accomplish their tasks. A group's cohesiveness, or collective identity, is built on its acceptance of common goals and norms, so that members perceive it as important to belong to the group.

Group Membership

The effectiveness of the group is a function of the leader's ability, the quality of the relationships among the group members, and the interaction between the leader and the members. Membership roles and behaviors have been a major focus in the area of group dynamics.

The roles that individual members use in the group are not chosen randomly but are a product of four major influences: (1) the members' expectations of themselves and others, (2) personality factors, (3) the characteristics of the leader, and (4) the characteristics of the group. Aspects of these four areas produce the actual behavior of the individual group member. The members' expectations of themselves and others are influenced by past experiences and their role in society. Members entering a group usually attempt to behave in a fashion they feel appropriate to their social status. In other words, they try to fulfill their perceptions of their social role.

The member's underlying personality traits are another important factor in his or her interaction in the group. We would expect the dominant personality traits that an individual brings to the group to have both overt and covert impacts on other group members. It is that assumption that leads counselors to select members for groups. Those included in the group should have personal styles that interact beneficially for all members. It is important not to include a member who would be detrimental to group functioning because the reaction of others would also be detrimental to that individual.

The personality of counselors obviously affects the behaviors they will use in conducting groups. Their personal characteristics and style of leadership will also influence the roles that individual members adopt. One of the chief factors affecting the behavior of members is their concern with the internal and external prestige of the group. If they feel that they are valued members of the group they will participate and become more involved. Conversely, with greater external orientation, they are less interested in acceptance of other members.

There is also an issue of homogeneity or heterogeneity in the composition of the group. Should the group examine one problem or be composed of one gender or one age group; or should it have different types of people with different problems? Research has indicated that heterogeneous members encourage a wide range of group roles and that homogeneous groups may act to restrict the roles that are used. Homogeneous group members are more likely to use roles that are concerned with the social atmosphere of the group. If the members are to form a group with a therapeutic atmosphere, they need to establish norms for group behavior, which is more easily accomplished with a homogeneous membership.

Many writers in the field have developed lists of roles and group behaviors. Most of the lists have the same set of behaviors with different names to describe them. These lists stem from two early descriptions of membership roles. Benne and Sheats (1948) described three classifications: individual roles, group task roles, and group building and maintenance roles. A set of more specific roles was defined by Bales (1951), who classified roles into two areas: instrumental, or task, roles and social/emotional, or expressive, roles (Table 6-1).

Benne and Sheats' building and maintenance roles act to collect individuals into a group and then to maintain group cohesiveness. These roles include the facilitator or encourager, who encourages a feeling of friendship and security in the group; the gatekeeper or expeditor, who keeps the group operating within its norms; the goal setter, who pushes for a definition of the outcome; the harmonizer, who strives to mediate differences between group members; the promiser, who suggests alternatives; the group observer, who provides feedback to the group; and the follower, who swings with the group wherever it goes. These roles focus on the social/emotional atmosphere of the group and help develop a feeling of cohesiveness.

Once the social/emotional atmosphere of the group has been established, task roles become more important. The task may be specific, such as a plan of action for the group, or more subjective, such as personal tasks for each member in resolving his or her particular difficulty. Group task roles include the initiator/energizer, who prods for action from the group and confronts it for lack of action; the information or opinion seeker, who wants cognitive or affective information to be clarified; the information or opinion giver, who wants to provide his or her thoughts to others; the elaborator or coordinator, who tries to ensure that the ideas expressed are workable; the evaluator, who serves as a judge in terms of how close the group is to resolving the task and its level of quality in achieving the goals; and the procedural technician, who keeps the group operating on acceptable norms toward the achievement of its goals. The conduct of these roles often produces conflict in a group, but this conflict is necessary for the members' individual growth. If the group is not developing these roles, it will not progress beyond a stage of cohesion. Members will like one another, but they will not reach their individual or collective goals.

TABLE 6.1 Classification of Roles Within a Group

	Social/emotional roles	
Task roles	Positive	Negative
1. Provides orientation, information	7. Provides help, status	10. Shows passive resistance, disagrees
2. Gives opinions, evaluates and analyzes group data	8. Facilitates tension reduction	11. Creates tension, seeks help, withdraws
3. Directs and suggests	9. Shows understanding and compliance	12. Acts aggressive, antagonistic
4. Seeks information		
5. Seeks direction or action		
6. Encourages evaluation and analysis of group data and experiences		

Source: Based on Bales (1951).

Benne and Sheats defined some negative social/emotional roles as individual roles because they are counterproductive to the positive outcome of the group. These roles have been characterized as self-serving rather than group oriented. Individuals who act as blockers, recognition seekers, self-confessors, dominators, or monopolists do so in an attempt to fulfill individual needs. It is important that such individuals not be excluded from the group, because their personal needs are such that they may have difficulty in interpersonal relations. Their presence, however, will make a smooth operation of the group difficult.

Bales (1951) categorized membership roles as either task or social/emotional (see Table 6-1). Bales believed that a group moved in a cyclical motion between the task and social/emotional atmospheres. When the group works on a task, it creates at least some tension for the members, and when the tension mounts, it must be reduced. At that time roles come into play that act to reduce the tension and restore a more cohesive social balance within the group. Bales believed that a group must go through this cycle to be productive. If the group remains in a social/emotional atmosphere, it will not make progress toward the task. On the other hand, if it focuses only on the task, tension will be produced to such a degree that the group will disintegrate. A close examination of the Bales and Benne and Sheats classifications reveals that they are very compatible and are effective descriptions of member's role behaviors.

Leadership

The success of any group endeavor is highly dependent on the leadership. Although most counselors and writers agree with such a statement, leadership is one of the more complex concepts to understand or describe. Dagley, Gazda, and Pistole (1986) conclude that "leadership refers to the interactive influence of the leader's position, functions, traits, and style on group members, individually and collectively." Garetz and Fix (1972) suggest that counselors base their approach on four principles of leadership: (1) practically applying a solid theory of group dynamics, (2) encouraging maximum group self-direction, (3) showing high respect for the group members by being emotionally honest with them, and (4) serving as a behavioral model. What characteristics should counselors model?

Personal Characteristics.   Although many people believe that the personal characteristics of the leader are the most important determinants of group outcomes, it is difficult to achieve agreement on the list of traits of effective leadership, let alone on a particular personality type. Over the years numerous research studies have attempted to determine the personality traits of effective group leaders. However, Luft (1984) writes that "the search for special characteristics in the personality of the leader has failed to yield convincing results" (p. 118). Berger (1974) discusses the impact of the counselor's personality on the group and emphasizes the integrated use of the total person for constructive therapeutic purposes. The total person includes physical behaviors and sensations, emotional states, reactions to self and others, cognitive awareness, and all other thoughts or feelings, which are referred to as intuitive. The way counselors use their personality is a reflection of a whole life history as well as a professional technique. Their use of self involves what they do as well as who they are.

Leadership Functions.   Lieberman, Yalom, and Miles (1973) identify four leadership functions: emotional stimulation, caring, attribution of meaning, and executive duties. These dimensions were derived from their research on leadership in encounter groups; they suggest, however, that these dimensions are capable of discriminating among leaders from highly varied theoretical orientations to group counseling.

Emotional stimulation involves emphasizing that members should reveal their feelings, personal attitudes, and values; should participate frequently as members; and should draw attention to themselves. The leader emphasizes release of emotions by taking risks and expressing anger, warmth, and love. The leader stimulates the members and places a high value on personal confrontation as a primary condition to learning. Leaders who are high on stimulation are generally described as charismatic.

The function of caring involves protecting; offering friendship, love, or affection; inviting members to seek feedback; and providing support, praise, and encouragement. The leader expresses acceptance, genuineness, and concern for the group members.

The function of attributing meaning involves cognitive techniques. The leader gives the members concepts so they can understand what is happening as well as ideas for how to change. Leaders high on meaning attribution understand that how people are feeling is a major goal in their behavior change. Some leaders use interpretations that emphasize cognitive recognition of the group climate or ask the group to reflect on its behavior. Others direct attention to individual behavior and request similar information about interpersonal issues.

The executive function involves setting goals, suggesting rules or norms, setting limits, managing time, and otherwise interceding. Leaders invite, question, and suggest procedures for a person or the group. Counselors who are high on the executive function emphasize the expression of emotion through suggestion rather than demonstration. They function like movie directors, stopping the action and focusing on a particular behavior of an individual or the group. This behavior is intended to help members learn about particular cues, emotions, or personal behaviors. The executive behavior is directed toward directing the group as a social system achieving its goals.

Lieberman and his colleagues (1973) evaluated the four basic dimensions of behavior in relation to group outcome. They concluded that the most effective leadership styles were displayed by counselors who were moderate in the amount of stimulation, high in caring, and moderate in expression of executive functions and who utilized meaning attribution. Conversely, less effective leaders use either very high or very low stimulation, are low in caring, and provide little attribution of meaning.

Leadership at Various Stages. Dugo and Beck (1984) describe four leadership roles, which may be used by group members, not just the group counselor. They use the term *leader* for a person who has influence in determining the group's direction. The four major roles identified by Dugo and Beck are the task leader, the emotional leader, the scapegoat leader, and the defiant leader.

The task leader is the person from whom the group members seek help and direction. Early in the life of the group, the counselor generally fills this role. Later in the group process, however, members may assume task leadership. A member could be considered an emotional leader if he or she expresses concerns to other members or the counselor. These concerns usually focus on the emotional needs of that person but also serve to stimulate awareness of emotional needs in other members. A member assumes a scapegoat-leadership role by engaging in more self-disclosing behaviors than other members. Other members make that person the scapegoat by rejecting him or her or by pressuring the person to assume the role of deviant member. A member may assume a defiant-leadership role by resisting the help offered by the counselor or by more openly disagreeing with the counselor or other group members. These different leadership roles will be involved at different levels of development in the group's life stages.

Stages of a Group

Many social scientists have described the changes in the life of a group. The described stages vary according to the type of group being studied, the goal of the group, and the professional interest of the leader. Developmental stages have been identified in learning groups (Lacoursiere, 1974; Mills, 1964; Thelen & Dickerman, 1949); training groups (Dunphy, 1968; R. D. Mann, 1966, 1971; Miles, 1953); and counseling and therapy groups (Beck, 1981; Bonney, 1974; Brabender, 1985; L. M. Gazda, 1972; Heckel, Holmes, & Rosecrans, 1971;

MacKenzie & Livesley, 1986; Mahler, 1969; J. Mann, 1953; Martin & Hill, 1974; Shambaugh & Kanter, 1969; Whitaker & Lieberman, 1964).

Although the descriptions come from observation of a few groups and there are variations, certain basic patterns of development occur within most groups. Five stages are generally described: the initiation of the group, a conflict stage, the development of cohesiveness, productive behaviors, and termination. The organization of this section follows that structure, with an initial subsection on preparation for the group.

Preparing for the Group

Leaders' decisions before beginning a group are as important as their behaviors in the group. Decisions must be made regarding the size of the group, the process of selection, whether the group will be closed to new members, and the duration of the group.

Size.   Although not based on research, a consensus of scholars suggests that the ideal size for group counseling is seven to eight members, with a range of from five to ten. If the group is much smaller, it ceases to operate as a group, and individuals feel awkward at being involved in individual counseling within a group setting. Too many members would not provide adequate time for working through individual problems, and as the group size increases, it is more difficult for less active members to express their ideas. One or two individuals may drop out during the early stages of the group; therefore leaders often begin with a slightly larger group than is ideal.

Selection.   Careful selection of members will increase the chances of a successful group experience. The counselor should understand as much as possible about each member and, therefore, should review the history of the individual's family background, childhood, and adolescence and all aspects of his or her presenting problems. The intake meeting should also focus on the individual's stated goals so that both the counselor and the client are aware of some proposed personal changes. There is a great deal of anxiety in the early group meetings, and the relationship developed with the counselor will help members cope with this fear until they begin establishing relationships with other members.

Another questions for the counselor during the selection process is whether the group should be homogeneous or heterogeneous. That is, should it focus on one problem area and be made up of one sex, socioeconomic level, or age group? Or should there be varying elements within the group?

Homogeneous groups tend to become cohesive more quickly, offering more immediate support to members and providing more rapid symptomatic relief. However, homogeneous groups are more likely to remain at a superficial level and be less effective in changing the members' behavior. If the leader decides to select a heterogeneous group, clear understanding of the personality dynamics and behavior patterns of the individuals will be helpful in organizing the group.

Melnick and Woods (1976) suggest using compatibility rather than homogeneity. Compatibility would focus on personal attraction, cooperation, and productive interaction among the members. The authors suggest avoiding extreme heterogeneity to ensure a warm interaction while creating confrontations sufficient to provide alternative behavior modes.

Open versus Closed Groups. Before beginning the group the counselor must determine whether it will be an open or a closed group. A closed group will not add new members, and it may meet for a predetermined number of sessions or until the group decides to terminate. An open group replaces members as they leave the group, so that it continues to function without a predetermined conclusion. The advantage of a closed group includes the stable population and time limits; however, difficulties may occur as members decide to drop out or move. An advantage for the open group is that members have new individuals with whom to interact and from whom to receive feedback; however, the new members are not aware of the content that has been discussed or the functioning of the group.

Moreland (1985) notes that new members in an open group can isolate themselves by deciding to interact only with other new members, thus establishing themselves as an out-group within the group. He also reports that newcomers tend to begin with a pessimistic outlook, to interact with other new members primarily, and to perceive discrimination where there is none. However, these biases fade in time. He also acknowledges that some oldtimers in groups may act out biases to the behaviors of newcomers. The counselor's decision usually depends on the desire to have either changing group membership or a specific time limit.

Duration. One aspect of a group's duration involves the amount of time in each session. Usually some time is allotted for members to warm up to personal communication and then work through some of the major themes in the session before reaching closure. The folklore around conducting groups suggests that it is difficult to become personally involved and productive in less than 90 minutes to two hours. Therefore, most groups meet for about two hours. Even so, it is possible to have group counseling in one-hour sessions.

Another aspect of duration involves the number of times to meet each week. Most groups meet once a week, although some intensive groups meet two to five times. A final aspect of duration concerns how many times a closed group will meet. A cognitive, topic-oriented group may run 10 to 12 meetings, and some encounter, self-awareness groups are also short in duration. There is no set number of meetings, but it takes time for a group to move through the stages to become productive if the goals involve more personal insight and change.

Preparation Interview. Yalom (1975) suggests that the preparation interview be used to help clients recognize and work through misconceptions and unrealistic beliefs or expectations about group counseling. The counselor may help members participate more effectively by outlining a structure or some concepts about the group's behavior. The interview should focus on clarifying the client's role expectations, clarifying the counseling process, and providing video or audio models of desired client behaviors. Bednar and his associates (1974) recommended that a full explanation and description of the value of the expected behavior precede the vicarious learning situation. Cognitive learning should also precede such audio or video presentations.

Initiating the Group

During the first stage of the group, members get to know one another but reveal only their safer or more public information. They tend to describe previous experience that has been told before rather than personally relevant material. Members follow the usual social code of behavior with strangers, and from this socially appropriate behavior they begin to formulate an idea of the role each expects to play in the group. They often wonder if they will be liked and respected or rejected by the other group members, and they must deal with their social relationships in the group. They wonder what is expected, how much of themselves to reveal, and what type of commitment must be made to the other members.

People often behave almost entirely in terms of transference when they first meet new people. They project their unconscious fantasy objects onto one another and try to manipulate them accordingly. The members approach the situation by repeating old patterns of behaviors with new individuals, and this becomes the focus of future interactions.

The primary task in this first stage is to resolve the issue of engagement and detachment. The collection of people cannot emerge as a viable social system until they achieve this task. The realization that others have similar problems and experiences is the main mechanism for the development of engagement (MacKenzie & Livesley, 1984). The group needs to clearly identify the external boundaries between itself and the rest of the world. This stage establishes an identity of belonging to a separate group of people. The boundaries between individual members need to become blurred, so that members can stress their similarities. The demarcation of the external boundary combined with an experience of similarity indicates that they have become an established group and that the first task has been achieved.

The Undifferentiated Mass.   At first the group is an undifferentiated mass, and an individual member selects one or two others for attention. Since all members are having a similar experience, the group is rather tenuous. At first there is an opportunity for the members to play their favorite roles; however, more reality soon begins to intrude into their perceptions of one another. Since the leader is known to all members, they can have a shared fantasy about him or her, and it is through this process that a new reality is formed that permits the members to confront one another. The members try to keep the leader differentiated from the other members as a remedy for their confusion, wanting the leader to rescue them with enough direction to reduce their stress. A differentiated leader does not necessarily produce differentiations among the members. Groups often struggle with this process until there is a type of revolt against the leader that will bring out the differences in the members' attitudes toward the leader. However, the group cannot confront the leader as long as it perceives itself as a mass.

Watkins (1984) considers some of the unconscious aspects of communication. In particular, he describes transitional, derivative content, which is a communication among the group members that is symbolic of personal issues, disguised and indirect, and is used in a purposeful manner to test the group. For example, he describes an incident in the early stage of counseling in which a member discussed a woman in the neighborhood having been raped and other members became identified with this theme. This type of communication may be a disguised presentation of trust issues that the group members are feeling at this time. Although the example occurred in this first stage, the counselor should be alert for similar indirect presentation throughout the group process. Watkins discusses four interventions that counselors can use. They can remain quiet to permit the group to move at its own pace, but silence cannot be overused because of the danger of stagnation or superficiality. They can use reflective intervention to reflect a feeling related to a theme, but it should not exceed the group's level of awareness or readiness. If interpretation is used, it should be with extreme caution and with tentatively phrased statements so as not to create defensiveness in the members. Refocusing is an intervention that shifts the group's attention to another topic that involves a theme behind the transitional material. The purpose of this technique is to help the members refocus on their intended purpose at this time in the group. This intervention requires considerable inference, intuition, and appropriate timing.

Leadership Roles in the Initiation Stage. Dugo and Beck identify an emotional leader as important in the initial stage in providing expression to the members' concerns and questioning the task leader and the other members. The task leader is often the counselor during the initial stage, because the members have come to the group to get help from him or her. The task for this first stage involves the members' getting to know one another and their abilities to work in the group. The task leader (counselor) must help them begin the process of bonding with one another as well as with him or her. The other group members, including the emotional leader, help play a role in developing a feeling of closeness among the members.

The counselor's role during this initial stage is to reduce the threat to members and allow them further self-exploration. Counselors are encouraged to provide a relationship characterized by genuineness, positive regard for the members, and empathic understanding. The counselor will be instrumental in helping the members set goals, including process goals, general group goals, and individual goals. Process goals involve how the group will function, including the self-exploration and interpersonal interactions of the members. The more specific and operational the goals are, the more value they will have for the group. Effective development of the group requires that the members share an image of the group. Discussing their goals is one way for members to be involved in the process of achieving a common identity.

Engagement in the Process.   For the group to move forward and for members to achieve self-understanding and eventually change their behaviors, they must become involved in the process. The process involves the group in providing a facilitative relationship in which all members feel safe enough to explore themselves. The exploration and interpersonal feedback from other members will lead to a greater degree of self-understanding as well as a better understanding of the environment. The counselor encourages self-exploration as a major goal in the initial stage but keeps in mind the different levels of self-exploration of each member.

At this stage there is not much cohesion in the group. It is a group of individuals having little or no sense of shared identity. The members have their own private ideas and feel isolated from one another. The only justification for calling these people a group is that they meet regularly with a counselor, who is the primary person with whom they relate. Some members will try to establish a structure by assuming their own type of leadership. As members respond to their conceptions of the group, they will offend others, and it is not unusual that there is a "fight-or-flight" theme in the group. The fight mood involves aggressive attitudes, while flight is psychologically moving away from an unknown danger. At the conclusion of this stage the group members are generally disillusioned and confused. Their preconceived ideas have been inadequate, and they tend to withdraw from complex issues and suppress their personal feelings.

The Stage of Conflict and Confrontation

Conflict and confrontation occur because the members are dissatisfied with the operation of the group. After an initial acquaintance time, they are frustrated in their attempts to evolve new patterns of behavior and work toward group goals. The task of the group is to recognize that differences exist among the members. The recognition of differences generally leads to a challenge of previous functions, and confrontation and conflict develop (MacKenzie & Livesley, 1984).

The counselor is perceived as a frustrating figure, because he or she does not fit the stereotype and tell members what to do. Some members will try to force a leader to be more active, while others will respond with open hostility or silence. Considering the unrealistic attitudes that members often have toward their leader, their frustration and hostility are inevitable. Although the members' frustration is first directed at the leader, it soon extends to one another. Differences between the members' real selves and their stereotypical images in the group may lead to conflict. Members challenge one another's reactions and insist on their own rights. There is a time in the group when there may be some suspension of the usual social mores and appropriate social behavior. Responses may lead to hurt feelings if they are taken personally rather than as part of the process of moving through this stage. Seldom does the whole group attack the counselor. Generally, individuals and subgroups defend the counselor. Considerable counterdependency and independence arise from this stage.

Members' Leadership Roles.   During this stage a scapegoat leader may become prominent. This member may be more self-disclosing than others and thus model and mirror the conflict in relationship building. The other members may put negative pressure on this person and even convey rejection. During this stage the emotional leader is crucial in accepting and integrating the scapegoat leader into the group. The emotional leader does not attack others but is free to enter the dialogue in a focused and less negative way. These two leaders can be instrumental in forming a solution to the conflict and establishing a bond. The task leader is usually the counselor and the one who can intervene in the conflict. When the counselor is the task leader, his or her role is to identify the conflict and hostility, take the role of a referee identifying fair play, uncover stresses, and help members establish constructive interactions (Dugo & Beck, 1984).

A member may emerge as the defiant leader. When the counselor tries to help this person, he or she may ask for help but resist any therapeutic nurturance. This behavior may lead the counselor to feel either uncaring or impotent. If the counselor and group members are unable to resolve this dilemma, it will injure their chances of becoming effective. The best solution to this situation involves helping such defiant leaders become more specific about their needs and accepting them while they move toward greater clarity and willingness to modify the norms in an appropriate way (Dugo & Beck, 1984). Counselors also need to become more open about their limitations, serving as a model for all group members to explore their own weaknesses.

Resistance. Conflict and confrontation are demonstrations of the members' resistance to the topic, other members, or the leader. Misunderstanding of the goals and procedures or avoiding work in an effort to get more structure from the leader are other forms of resistance. Counseling groups that focus on self-disclosure, self-understanding, and behavior change are apt to face more resistance than those that are more cognitive or task-oriented.

In many groups this second stage may not emerge early or may be avoided completely unless group members have enough commitment to the group to risk a confrontation. The conflict frequently occurs in only one session, but some groups may continue with individuals in conflict for longer periods. Without working through this phase of group development to establish appropriate norms of behavior, groups can develop only a superficial level of cohesiveness. It is in the process of working through their differences of opinion that group members are able to accept one another as real persons rather than stereotyped images and to establish appropriate norms for behavior.

The Stage of Cohesiveness

Following a period of conflict, the group begins developing feelings of cohesiveness, with an increase of mutual trust and group morale. Cohesiveness refers to the level of "groupness," "we-ness," or solidarity. At times there may be a difference between an individual's level of cohesiveness and that of the total group.

During this stage the group will experience intimacy and explore its implications. This process can occur as members understand themselves and others in depth, since "intimacy" without mutual self-knowledge is only a facade (MacKenzie & Livesley, 1984). The members are in a here-and-now relationship with one another. The emotional leader can model the strain that group members feel between the wish for deeper bonds with others and the wish to deny this need. The emotional leader may seek acknowledgment of a special bond with the counselor. This allows the counselor to become involved in the group in a more human relationship, not only with the emotional leader but also with the entire group. The scapegoat leader's role at this time may be to openly acknowledge caring for the task leader.

Commitment to the Process.   In addition to complying with the norms established by the counselor and establishing their own norms at this stage, the members must be personally committed to the counseling process for any real behavior change to occur. Kelman (1963) wrote that the members' commitment to counseling took place through identification with the counselor and with the group. Successful individual changes depend largely on an association, however temporary, of those individuals involved in the group. Identification with one another leads to a commitment to work together.

Members come to accept the group and one another's idiosyncrasies, and they respond more readily to subtle cues. Rather than giving a flat acceptance or rejection, members indicate tentative agreement or disagreement. By virtue of the members' mutual acceptance, desire to maintain the group, and establishment of group norms, they become a unique social system with its own values and internal arrangements. Although cohesiveness is an important precondition for productive work in group counseling, it is not by itself a curative factor. Many counselors believe that when the group has reached this stage, they are successful, and they permit the group process to stagnate. Yalom (1975) suggests that only when all emotions can be expressed and worked through does the group become cohesive enough to be mature and productive.

The group may regress or enter a second stage of group conflict, which arouses hostilities that have not been completely resolved. Many of these conflicts center on dependency or counterdependency. Defiant leadership emerges in a member who is experiencing some fear, hostility, or ambivalence about participating in mutuality. Often, the person is defiant by presenting counterdependency behavior yet wants to maintain some dependency on the counselor. The defiant leader may well be mirroring the feelings of other group members. It is important for the counselor to accept the limits of the group's ability to change someone who is not ready. The counselor must accept the defiant leader's need to act independently without punishing him or her.

The real test for the group is its ability to move out of this stage and become an instrument of action directed toward individual goals. The members may find it difficult to move beyond this stage, in which they enjoy one another but do not really accomplish anything. Where the bonds are genuine and strong, a remarkable amount of cohesiveness develops, and group members give the mutual, evaluative support necessary for successful behavior change. As some members discover that other members are insightful and productive, they attempt to follow their lead.

The Stage of Productiveness

After the group achieves some stability in its patterns of behavior, a long working process begins. Because they are deeply committed to the group, members may reveal more of themselves and their problems in living. In fact, individual goals may be redefined at this point.

The transition to this phase is signaled by a shift from the excitement of interpersonal closeness to an awareness that such involvement, if it is continued, must be combined with a sense of interpersonal responsibility. The task of this stage is to develop such responsibility by conceptualizing an appreciation of the fundamental uniqueness of each member rather than increasing the sense of intimacy.

At this time the members function as a group. In the beginning the group was dependent on the leader, but now members have developed some effective leadership skills and a pattern of distributive leadership in which realistic individual roles are maintained. The roles of leadership are assumed by many members, and the counselor serves as only one source of leadership.

The group structure becomes functional, and the norms of behavior are useful rather than maintained simply for the sake of rules. The counselor and members remain aware of the structural patterns of behavior they have developed, and they give constant attention to the work process. The group directs itself to members as objects, since their subjective interpersonal relations have been established. Members view individual behaviors with greater objectivity and show greater ease in making decisions and more flexibility in controlling group processes. Despite this movement, groups frequently regress from constructive behavior and may revert to a lower level of functioning before they regenerate into a productive stage.

Corrective Emotional Experience. For lasting behavior changes to occur, the member must undergo what Kelman (1963) called "corrective emotional experiences." These experiences are based on the manifestations in the group of the members' distorted, self-defeating, and troubling attitudes that also occur in their real-life relationships. The corrective experience can occur when members experience feelings and attitudes in the group situation as intensely as they do under usual circumstances. The difference between the group setting and the life situations is that in the group the individual is simultaneously encouraged to examine the feelings as they are occurring. The counselor and other members help the individual see his or her attitudes in their true light, recognize that they are distorted and self-defeating, and gain some understanding into their origins. As the person experiences the feelings, it is more than an intellectual exercise. This type of experience can be the basis for new insight into the attitudes and behaviors that are used in interpersonal relationships and the result of those behaviors. The new insights should lead to more realistic attitudes and behaviors.

The group influences members to overcome resistances and allow themselves to experience some threatening feelings at the same time they are being felt. Davies and Kuypers (1985) report that during the productive stage members increase their feedback to one another and that feedback is mainly positive. It is the influence of the members that makes group counseling more effective than individual counseling for some people.

Insight is not sufficient. To be productive an individual must change behavior in daily life outside the group. Although new behaviors are tested within the group, the real payoff occurs from generalizing these behaviors to outside life.

Termination

Termination is an important part of the group process when members make a transition from the group to their daily lives and put their new learning into practice. This is easier when the counselor emphasizes the importance of taking action and making changes in attitudes and behaviors. The group members have given one another a good start and an incentive to continue the learning process after the group ends. During this stage the members may focus on ways of working through what they have learned when they no longer have the group situation for support.

The leader and members eventually deal with the ending of this temporary social system. During the termination stage the group must direct its attention to the external boundary of the group. Members frequently review the history of the group and recall critical incidents, and declare that the group has been a personally important and lasting experience. For many members termination is accompanied by a feeling of loss and separation, an analog of death (MacKenzie & Livesley, 1984).

The counselor must consider three forms of termination: that of the unsuccessful client, that of the successful client, and that of the entire group (Yalom, 1975). The unsuccessful member may leave early or remain in a closed group to the end without really making attitude or behavior changes. Very little is written about clients who continue through a closed group to termination and yet do not make changes. Most of the literature focuses on people who prematurely leave an open group. McGee, Schuman, and Racusen (1972) described three forms of premature termination. The first type involves the member's avoidance of dealing with the importance of the loss. The person may separate by denying or repressing and using a letter or phone call to the counselor. This type of separation usually occurs during the early stages of the group when there is an insufficient level of cohesiveness. A second type of termination is considered a "flight into health." The client has achieved some self-exploration and some understanding and has started experimental behavior changes. The person may feel no need to continue in the group. It is difficult to discourage an individual from termination; however, when the member has not successfully made the generalization to outside life, termination may be premature. A third level of termination occurs when a member has successfully developed insight and made some behavior changes and is now unwilling to proceed further. Such clients may feel that they will make future behavior changes on their own.

Terminating successful members from the group is an extended and comprehensive process. It involves their openly acknowledging what the group has meant and how they will function without it. The other group members should also acknowledge what the departing person has meant to them and how they will feel about functioning without him or her. The procedure may begin with the individual making some indication of an intent to leave the group. This is followed by a discussion of the client's plan and its implications for the individual and group members. The member attends his or her last meeting, and the aspect of finality forces the terminating member and the other group members to examine the concept of loss. The group members usually discuss the termination and its implications during the next few sessions.

In a closed group, the last meeting is fixed in advance. The members approach the last meetings by spending some effort generating new interpretations of problems, noting successful events, and examining the group's failures. It is common for clients to express their wish to have had a closer relationship with the counselor, and there is often pressure on the counselor to affirm the extraordinary quality of the group.

In their research into the developmental stages of a group, Davies and Kuypers (1985) reported a definite termination phase in which the members' behavior changes. There is an increase in the frequency of feedback at this point, with most of it being positive. In fact, their study reports that the amount of feedback tends to increase over the lifetime of the group and that the feedback tends to be more positive over time. However, frustration, insecurity, and anger sometimes emerge in the last sessions. Some of these feelings may have been unexpressed or dealt with through the group's sessions, but anxiety and hostility also serve as distancing devices for a separation. People frequently withdraw by first expressing their negative feelings and then their positive feelings. Although the group did not accomplish as much as the members had hoped, they generally express that knowing one another has been significant and confirm that their choice to be in the group was a good one.

Summary

Counseling provides many types of group experiences. Although counselors may conduct encounter groups or training groups, most will focus on group counseling and therapy. A thorough knowledge of group dynamics is imperative before starting to provide any of these services. Counselors need to understand the significance of group goals, structures, norms, and cohesiveness in the functioning of any group. In addition to knowledge and understanding, the counselor must have skills in helping the members establish goals, develop a structure and norms of behavior, and achieve the cohesiveness necessary for members to form an effective working environment to assist one another in achieving their goals.

The counselor is aware of the various membership roles that are necessary to help the group function appropriately and facilitate individual members in assuming new roles as well as those more natural for them. Likewise, counselors are aware of their own characteristics that they use in helping individual members as well as the whole group.

Groups go through a series of stages: initiating the process, experiencing conflict, becoming cohesive, focusing on productive behaviors, and terminating. Each stage finds both members and leaders performing leadership roles, including those of the task leader, the emotional leader, the scapegoat leader, and the defiant leader.

References

Bales, R. R. (1951). *Interaction Process Analysis.* Cambridge, MA: Addison-Westley.

Beck, A. (1981). The Study of Group Phase Development and Emergent Leadership. *Group, 5,* 48–54.

Bednar, R., Melnick, J., & Kaul, T. (1974). Responsibility and Structure: A Conceptual Framework for Initiating Group Counseling and Psychotherapy. *Journal of Counseling Psychology, 21,* 318–338.

Benne, K. C., & Sheats, P. (1948). Functional Roles of Group Members. *Journal of Social Issues, 4,* 2.

Berger, M. (1974). The Impact of the Therapist's Personality on Group Process. *American Journal of Psychoanalysis, 34,* 213–219.

Bonney, W. (1974). The Maturation of Groups. *Small Group Behavior, 5,* 445–461.

Brabender, V. (1985). Time-Limited Inpatient Group Therapy: A Developmental Model. *International Journal of Group Psychotherapy, 3,* 373–390.

Cartwright, D., & Zander, A. (1968). *Group Dynamics: Research and Theory* (3rd ed.). New York: Harper & Row.

Corey, G., & Corey, M. (1987). *Groups: Process and Practice* (3rd ed.). Pacific Grove, CA: Brooks/Cole.

Dagley, J., Gazda, L., & Pistole, M. (1986). Groups. In M. Lewis, R. Hayes, & J. Lewis (Eds.), *The Counseling Profession* (pp. 130–166). Itasca, Il: F. E. Peacock.

Davies, D., & Kuypers, B. (1985). Group Development and Interpersonal Feedback. *Group and Organizational Studies, 10,* 184–208.

Dugo, J., & Beck, A. (1984). A Therapist's Guide to Issues of Intimacy and Hostility Viewed as a Group-Level Phenomenon. *International Journal of Group Psychotherapy, 34,* 25–45.

Dunphy, D. (1968). Phases, Roles and Myths in Self-Analytic Groups. *Journal of Applied Behavioral Science, 4*(2), 195–225.

Garetz, C., & Fix, A. J. (1972). Difficult Problems in Therapy Group Leadership. *Hospital and Community Psychiatry, 23,* 248–250.

Gazda, G. (1982). Group Psychotherapy and Group Counseling: Definition and Heritage. In G. Gazda (Ed.), *Basic Approaches to Group Psychotherapy and Counseling* (3rd ed.) (pp. 5–36). Springfield, IL: Thomas.

Gazda, L. M. (1972). *Group Counseling: A Developmental Approach.* Boston: Allyn & Bacon.

Heckel, R. V., Holmes, G. R., & Rosecrans, C. J. (1971). A Factor Analytic Study of Process Variables in Group Therapy. *Journal of Clinical Psychology, 27*(1), 146–150.

Kauff, P. F. (1977). The Termination Process: Its Relationship to Separation-Individuation Phase of Development. *International Journal of Group Psychotherapy, 27,* 3–18.

Kelman, H. C. (1963). The Role of the Group in the Induction of Therapeutic Change. *International Journal of Group Psychotherapy, 13,* 399–432.

Kivlighan, D., McGovern, T., & Corazzini, J. (1984). Effects of Content and Timing of Structuring Interventions on Group Therapy Process and Outcome. *Journal of Counseling Psychology, 31,* 363–370.

Knowles, M., & Knowles, H. (1959). *Introduction to Group Dynamics.* New York: Association Press.

Lacoursiere, R. (1974). A Group Method to Facilitate Learning During the Stages of a Psychiatric Affiliation. *International Journal of Group Psychotherapy, 24,* 114–119.

Lieberman, M. A., Yalom, I. D., & Miles, M. D. (1973). *Encounter Groups: First Facts.* New York: Basic Books.

Luft, J. (1984). *Group Processes: An Introduction to Group Dynamics* (3rd ed.). Palo Alto, CA: Mayfield.

McGee, T., Schuman, B., & Racusen, F. (1972). Termination in group psychotherapy. *American Journal of Psychotherapy, 22,* 3–18.

MacKenzie, K., & Livesley, W. (1984). Developmental Stages: An Integrating Theory of Group Psychotherapy. *Canadian Journal of Psychiatry, 29,* 247–251.

Mahler, C. (1969). *Group Counseling in the Schools.* Boston: Houghton-Mifflin.

Mann, J. (1953). Group Therapy With Adults. *American Journal of Orthopsychiatry, 23,* 332–337.

Mann, R. D. (1966). The Development of the Member-Trainer Relationship in Self-Analytic Groups. *Human Relations, 19,* 85–116.

Mann, R. D. (1971). The Development of the Member-Trainer Relationship in Self-Analytic Groups. In C. L. Cooper & I. L. Mangham (Eds.), *T-groups: A Survey of Research.* London: Wiley Interscience.

Martin, E., & Hill, W. (1957). Toward a Theory of Group Development: Six Phases of Therapy Group Development. *International Journal of Group Psychotherapy, 7,* 20–30.

Melnick, J., & Woods, M. (1976). Analysis of Group Composition Research and Theory for Psychotherapeutic and Group-Oriented Groups. *Journal of Applied Behavioral Science, 12,* 493–512.

Miles, M. B. (1953). Human Relations Training: How a Group Grows. *Teachers College Record, 55,* 90–96.

Mills, T. (1964). *Group Transformation.* Englewood Cliffs, NJ: Prentice-Hall.

Moreland, R. (1985). Social Categorization and the Assimilation of the 'New' Group Members. *Journal of Personality and Social Psychology, 38,* 1173–1190.

Napier, R., & Gershenfeld, M. (1973). *Groups: Theory and Experience.* Boston: Houghton Mifflin.

Rose, G., & Bednar, R. (1980). Effects of Positive and Negative Self-Disclosure and Feedback on Early Group Development. *Journal of Counseling Psychology, 27,* 63–70.

Shambaugh, P., & Kanter, S. (1969). Spouses Under Stress: Group Meetings with Spouses of Patients on Hemodialysis. *American Journal of Psychiatry, 125,* 928–936.

Thelen, H., & Dickerman, W. (1949). Stereotypes and the Growth of Groups. *Education Leadership, 6,* 309–316.

Tuckman, B. W. (1965). Developmental Sequence in Small Groups. *Psychological Bulletin, 63,* 384–399.

Tuckman, B. W., & Jensen, M. A. (1977). Stages of Small Group Development Revisited. *Group and Organizational Studies, 2,* 419–427.

Watkins, C. E. (1984). Transitional Derivative Content: A Necessary and Facilitative Group Dynamic? *Journal of Specialists in Group Work,* 186–191.

Whitaker, D., & Lieberman, M. (1964). *Psychotherapy Through the Group Process.* New York: Atherton.

Yalom, I. (1975). *The Theory and Practice of Group Psychotherapy* (2nd. ed.) New York: Basic Books.

Family Therapy

The family counselor's theoretical conception is a guide to his or her methods. Theory does not reduce the intuitive, or artistic, component of a counselor's work, but a set of concepts functions as a map for the client's behavior and helps the counselor understand it. Theories of family therapy are considerably different from those used as the basis of individual and group counseling, and the names of the conceptual leaders are very different.

The Development of Family Therapy

The use of family therapy is relatively new. Before the 1950s there was no therapeutic approach that specifically involved work with families. During the 1940s and 1950s the psychodynamic orientation dominated mental-health practice. Psychoanalysts and psychiatrists refrained from having contact with the patient's family, because bringing family members into the therapy session would interfere with the patient's transference. Given this influence there is little wonder that the family field began by focusing on research about families with a schizophrenic member. This background also points out the role played by Nathan Ackerman (1958), a psychiatrist and psychoanalyst, in translating psychoanalytic thought into a family-oriented approach to therapy. He is generally considered the grandfather of family therapy.

Guerin (1976) describes the development of the family movement between 1950 and 1975. Due to its predominant theoretical orientation, family therapy was essentially underground between 1950 and 1954. Research was based on a view of the family as a unit with an emotionally disturbed individual. It was not reported at professional meetings or in the literature. During those years Gregory Bateson, an anthropologist, received a Rockefeller Foundation grant to study communication, and he is generally credited as one of the primary individuals in developing "systems" thinking about human behavior. Bateson hired Jay Haley and John Weakland to work on the communications research project. They were later joined by Don Jackson and Virginia Satir. This group contributed the notion of the double bind to the field of family communication. Their research also identified the concept of homeostasis, which implied that there was a relative consistency in the family's environment that maintained the continuous interplay of forces between the members. At the same time, in Topeka, Kansas, Murray Bowen was working on the concept of mother/child symbioses in schizophrenia. His research on distorted communication in families with a schizophrenic member resulted in a paper, "Toward a Theory of Schizophrenia," which was published in 1956. By the mid-1950s Bowen had moved to the National Institute of Mental Health in Washington, where he began working with whole families in a hospital.

In the mid-1950s the family movement became public. The first panel on family therapy to be presented at a national convention was organized in 1957 at the Orthopsychiatry Convention. A panel at the American Psychological Association's meeting later that year led to Jackson's book, *The Etiology of Schizophrenia,* which was published in 1960. At the same time Bowen (1960) published a paper describing a family concept of schizophrenia. By 1950 Ackerman had established the Family Institute in New York, and in 1962 he and Jackson produced the field's first journal, *Family Process.*

Numerous landmarks were established during the 1960s. The Hillcrest series of films was produced, in which Ackerman, Jackson, Bowen, and Carl Whitaker each interviewed the same family. A group of clinicians and researchers established the Philadelphia Family Institute in 1964. Nagy and Framo edited the book *Intensive Family Therapy,* which brought together much of the work done with schizophrenic families. In 1966 Bowen published "The Use of Family Theory in Clinical Practice," which is one of the first major theoretical papers on family systems. Satir (1967) wrote *Conjoint Family Therapy,* and Watzlawick, Beavin, and Jackson (1967) published *Pragmatics of Human Communication.*

Some of the early conceptualizations have been changed, and others have been retained. Most of the early leaders in the field of family therapy are still active. Bowen is at Georgetown University, continuing to offer training in family therapy. Whitaker has returned to Wisconsin after a period as interim director of the Philadelphia Child Guidance Clinic. Salvador Minuchin is living in New York City, continuing to speak, consult, and train. Satir resides in California and maintains an active schedule in speaking and training in family therapy. Watzlawick and Weakland are still involved with brief therapy at the Mental Research Institute, and Haley has developed the Washington Family Institute for Practice and Training.

The Family as a System

Not only are the names of the major theorists different, but the basic concept underlying family therapy is different from that of individual counseling. Family therapy is based on systems theory. Counselors oriented only to individual counseling focus on the individual as the site of the problem. They gather information primarily from one person or about that person or from that person's perception. This process is similar to using a magnifying glass: the details are clear but the field is small. Hoffman (1981) notes that family therapy is founded on different assumptions about human behavior and interaction. She identifies two emerging thoughts about the family as a system. The cybernetic model describes the family as a homeostatic system and stresses the idea that symptomatic behavior has the function of maintaining equilibrium. Another view, the evolutionary model, sees families as evolving, changing, and transforming systems. Hoffman describes circularity as the unifying notion of this new epistemology.

The systems theory is a break from the linear cause-and-effect concepts of medical or psychodynamic models of mental illness. Those models traditionally describe mental illness as having a cause based on an anomaly of either genetic, biochemical, or intrapsychic origin. Therefore, the identified client is the focus of the diagnosis and treatment. In contrast, the systems approach is circular. The behavior of the identified client affects and is affected by the other members of the system as a part of what Hoffman calls a "recursive dance."

General Systems Theory and Family Therapy

Systems theory has contributed the idea of understanding an individual in relation to his or her family and of understanding the family in relation to the larger community. French (1977) defines a system "as a structure composed of a set of elements and a set of rules that specify the relationship among the elements" (p. 20). In applying this theory to a family, the system can be interpreted as the family made up of a set of individuals whose behavior is governed by a set of rules. Most of the rules of interaction and behavior are unspoken and are only intuitive. Often family members cannot describe all the rules of interaction that have affected their behavior patterns.

Structural problem solving can be used on family problems because the family, like a formal organization, is characterized by (1) wholeness—the whole is greater than the sum of its parts; (2) transformation—it remains stable even though individuals within it are continually changing; and (3) self-regulation—it maintains order during the change.

From a family-systems perspective, pathology may be inside the individual, in his or her social context, or in the interaction between them. Clients are therefore counseled within their social system, the family, because their psychic life is not entirely an internal process. They are influenced by the social system of which they are a part, and changes in the family structure contribute to changes in each of the members. As the therapist works with the family, his or her behaviors become part of that system and can be influential in making changes.

Papp (1983) describes the key concepts of a systems approach as wholeness, organization, and patterning. The wholeness of the family system is considered greater than the sum of the family's parts, the members, and each individual is understood only in the context of the whole family. A change in one part or family member will affect every other member. The whole family regulates itself through a series of communication feedback loops whereby information goes back and forth between people in order to provide stability. The individuals are constantly changing in order to keep the family system balanced and consistent. It is this description of patterning and circular organization, rather than an individual, linear explanation, that has become the systems foundation for family therapy.

The systems theory states that no one person's behavior causes that of another but that behaviors are linked in a circular manner to many events and behaviors. Over time the events and behaviors become consistent, recurring patterns that balance the family system and allow it to evolve to another developmental stage. Individual members possess certain innate characteristics but manifest behaviors in relation to other family members' behaviors. Therapists do not look for the cause of an individual's behavior but attempt to understand the function of a behavior in the pattern from which it derives its meaning.

Change in the Family

Whether an individual's behavior is serving a homeostatic function and keeping the family pattern consistent or is serving an evolutionary function in encouraging the family to evolve to a different stage, some family members may find it inappropriate. At that point the behavior is described as a symptom and the person as an identified patient. When the symptom causes sufficient stress, the family may seek help. Increasingly, family therapy is being used as a preferred treatment, particulary when a child or adolescent is identified as the problem person.

The family usually wishes to see the problem behavior alleviated, but it does not want to change the family system. In other words, it wants to change the identified problem person, but the other members do not want to change. If one believes in systems theory, that is impossible. Change will have an impact on everyone, and the family and the therapist should consider the repercussions for the entire family. To ignore the impact on the entire family involves what Keeney (1983) terms "ecological ignorance." In recent years scientists in many fields have found that solving an immediate problem often creates another problem in the larger ecology. As Papp (1983) points out,

> The central therapeutic issue is not how to eliminate the symptom but what will happen if it is eliminated; the therapeutic argument is shifted from the problem, who has it, what caused it, and how to get rid of it, to how the family will function without it, what price will have to be paid for its removal, who will pay it, and whether it is worth it [p. 11].

A Variety of Approaches

Although all family therapy is conducted from a systems perspective, individual counselors base their practice on their own conceptualization of the problem and their own form of intervention. Minuchin looks at the family system as a hierarchical set of organizations, and he attempts to change the structure of the family. Haley describes the family system in terms of power and focuses his attention on changing the power structure. Bowen sees the family as a series of triangles and sees individuals according to their differentiation from the family system. Satir views family members as playing different roles and focuses attention on teaching them to communicate more appropriately for the common good as well as their individual benefit. An examination of the specific approaches of Minuchin, Bowen, and Satir will give you an idea of different family concepts and therapeutic interventions used in family therapy.

Minuchin's Structural Approach

Minuchin's structural conceptualization of family interaction developed while he was working with poor youths and families. Although he is trained as a psychiatrist and psychoanalyst, he broke away from that theoretical model and emphasized observable processes between the family members and subsystems. His approach to family therapy began with techniques in working with the families and then became more theoretical.

Family Concepts

Minuchin believes that the family is a system, with each member acting and reacting as a member of that system. He defines the family structure as an invisible set of functional demands that organizes the way in which the members interact. He believes that the only way to know a family structure is to see it in movement. Repeated transactions establish patterns of who will relate and how and when these patterns maintain the system. These transactional patterns regulate the members' behavior.

Minuchin's approach to therapy involves changing the family structure, because changing the transactions between individual members will change the structural positions of members. He writes that "a family is transformed over time, adapting and restructuring itself" (1974, p. 65). This transformation process occurs when the family reacts to inner stress, which comes from the developmental changes of individuals or subsystems in the family, or to outer pressure, which comes from the demands of other significant social structures.

Family Subsystems.   The family system carries out its functions through subsystems. An individual is a subsystem within the family, and subsystems can also be formed by generation, sex, or function. The three major subsystems of the family are the spouse subsystem, the parental subsystem, and the sibling subsystem. The spouse subsystem is created when two adults join to form a family. This subsystem is a refuge from the external stresses and is formed through a mutual accommodation to each other.

A parental subsystem is a new level that occurs when the first child is born. It is different from the spouse subsystem in that it needs to perform tasks of socializing the child. At times, children may cause confusion between the parents and set up different forms of subsystems. Therefore, it is important that the parents maintain the mutual support that characterizes the spouse subsystem.

The sibling subsystem is the first social laboratory that children use to develop peer relations. This subsystem also protects children from the adults so that they can develop their privacy and separate interests.

The family system, composed of subsystems, maintains itself with preferred patterns of interactions as long as possible. Any deviation that goes beyond the family's threshold of tolerance elicits mechanisms that will reestablish the accustomed behaviors. As the family responds to both internal and external changes, it needs to transform itself to meet the new circumstances without losing the continuity that provides a frame of reference for its members.

Family Boundaries. Minuchin believes that the clarity of boundaries within the family is a useful measure of family functioning. Families can be seen as operating along a continuum, with extremes varying from diffuse boundaries to overly rigid boundaries. When families become too close and develop their own microcosm, they reduce the distance and blur the boundaries between family members and subgroups. Such families are termed "enmeshed." At the other extreme, some families develop overly rigid boundaries, so that communication becomes more difficult and individuals and subsystems are highly differentiated. This phenomenon is labeled "disengagement." *Enmeshment* and *disengagement* are terms referring to a transactional style within the family system and are not necessarily used in describing functional or dysfunctional behaviors. Pathology is indicated only when a family operates continually at either extreme. Therefore, when examining the boundaries within a family, Minuchin looks at the degree of enmeshment or disengagement and also at whether the transactions are flexible or rigid.

Family Alignments. Another aspect of the function of boundaries concerns the manner in which the family members are aligned. The family's ability to adapt depends on its capacity to keep subsystem boundaries firm but flexible enough that realignment will occur as circumstances change. If the family responds to stressful situations by forming rigid alignments, dysfunctional patterns may occur. Whenever the boundaries separating the parental subsystem are broken, inappropriate, rigid triangles involving a child and the spouses may occur.

Minuchin describes three alignments: triangulations, detours, and coalitions. A triangulation involves each parent demanding that the child side with him or her against the other parent. An obvious example involves parents who are separated and struggling for custody of the child; however, other struggles may occur throughout a family life cycle. "Detouring" involves the spouses' focusing excessive attention on the child rather than on each other. The parents may detour affection to children rather than communicating with each other, or, rather than arguing with each other, they may detour that emotion and yell at a child. A coalition involves one parent's joining the child in a rigid alliance against the other parent. When any of these alignments is formed, it weakens the hierarchy in the family and leaves the parental subsystem less effective.

Family Functioning. Minuchin's conceptualization of the family involves three components. First, the structure of the family is an open sociocultural system in transformation. Second, the family undergoes development, moving through a number of stages that require restructuring. Third, the family adapts to changing circumstances to maintain continuity and enhancement of the psychosocial growth of each member. When the family fails to restructure and fails to adapt, dysfunction occurs.

Minuchin believes that most family dysfunction occurs when the family fails to successfully adapt to stress. He describes four categories of stress that the family may encounter. One form occurs when a family member encounters a stressful situation with an extrafamilial source—that is, a child's school problems or a parent's difficulties on the job. When one member is stressed, other family members may need to accommodate to his or her changed circumstances. The accommodation may be within a subsystem or may permeate the whole family. If the family responds with rigidity, dysfunctional transactions can occur.

A second situation involves stress in which the entire family is in conflict with an extrafamilial force such as unemployment. Once again, the family may develop a less functional transactional style that becomes rigid, rather than making continued adaptations to the situation.

A third category of stressful situations occurs at transitional points in family development. When the oldest child enters adolescence, there is a need for the family system to adjust to this transition. If the parents rigidly retain their previous style of parenting young children, the stress will affect both the youth and the parents and will frequently spill into all family transactions.

The fourth category of stress involves idiosyncratic problems. There are many types of situations that families may encounter—for example, a retarded child, a serious illness, a physical handicap, a death in the family—all of which necessitate adaptive behaviors by the family system. When facing any of these stressful situations, if a family increases the rigidity of its transactional patterns and resists exploring alternatives, it may become pathological.

Diagnosis

A family defines a problem when one of its members is behaving in ways that are stressful for the family. The family wants the counselor to change the member who is having or causing problems. The therapist, however, will focus on the whole system. One of the members may be expressing the family stress in ways that are visible, but the problem is not confined to that person. The whole family is responding to a stressful situation.

Minuchin sees diagnosis and intervention as inseparable. His interactional diagnosis changes as the therapist accommodates to the family, and it continues to change as interventions are rejected or successful in altering the family structure. Counselors evaluate the sources of stress and the support within families. They note the developmental stage of the family members and the degree of success in meeting the demands of the stages. They also observe the identified patient's symptoms and the functions they serve within the family. When using a structural approach to therapy, counselors are aware of the family structure and the transactional patterns used within that family.

Counselors are not able to understand the family unless they are part of the system and are able to observe their transactions. Minuchin draws up a diagnostic picture of the family in the form of a family map. After the initial assessment data have been accumulated, the counselor can identify the boundaries and transactional patterns and can develop hypotheses concerning the functioning of the family structure. It is important to remember that the diagnosis and intervention are inseparable and continue to change throughout the process of therapy. Therefore, the counselor should not make a rigid diagnostic map.

Minuchin presents a picture of how the family functions by using pictorial tools to describe the boundaries and transactions (see Figure 7-1). The map can describe whether the boundaries are clear, diffuse, or rigid. He also deals with the level of affiliation between persons, with two lines indicating an appropriate level of affiliation, four lines describing overinvolvement, and two slash marks through two lines indicating that there is a conflict in the transaction between those two persons. He also has symbols to describe a coalition and a detour.

After forming a map of the family's boundaries and transactions, the counselor can use this preliminary diagnosis to form hypotheses of needed changes in the family and use them as a guide for his initial intervention.

Interventions

The process goals involve getting to know the family members, forming a therapeutic system with them, exploring the areas of dysfunction, and initiating change in their transactions. Minuchin believes that the therapist must join the family and become part of its system. After the family is functioning more appropriately, the therapist once again moves outside of the system.

Counselors begin the therapeutic process by accommodating to the family and getting to know it. They track the content of the members' presentations, thereby learning about family issues. They learn the flexibility of the family's patterns by testing their limits. They may probe with certain questions or challenge some issues to determine the reaction of the family.

In order to form the therapeutic system, therapists must be accepted by the family. To join the family, they must respect the family hierarchies and join with people who are influential. They must also respect the family's values and support the subsystems. As they get to know the family, they will also make contact with individual members, giving them some positive statements as they search for each person's sense of self. Another aspect of forming the therapeutic system involves counselors' becoming the leader of that system. Minuchin believes that therapists should present themselves as an expert and establish some new rules for the system, at least while the members are in the therapy session. Therapists are able to control the flow of communication by directing people to talk to one another, establishing communication between people or within a subsystem by moving them closer together or further apart.

The advantage of having the whole family together is to see the members act out the problem in the session. This provides much clearer information for counselors than if any one person or even the members of the family describe

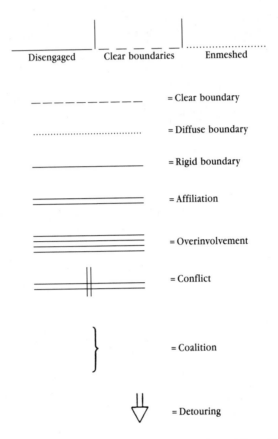

FIGURE 7-1 **Family Mapping Symbols.** (*Source*: Adapted from Minuchin, 1974)

a situation. As therapists organize the family in dyads or control its boundaries or time frames, it will enact the problems that occur outside the session. As therapists observe the family transactions, they abstract a model of the family structure. This model will serve as the first hypothesis about ways of intervening in the family.

Minuchin believes that therapists should begin intervening in the family in the first session. He believes that they should reframe the situation in a manner that challenges the family's schema. This process offers the members an alternative view and gives them encouragement that this new model will be helpful for them. Following the reframing of the situation, the therapist often sends the family home with a task to perform. The purpose of the task is to engage family members in a different transaction that will change the pattern of interaction that has maintained the dysfunctions.

Minuchin and Fishman (1981) describe three major strategies in family therapy and then identify specific techniques used with each strategy. The strategies are challenging the symptom, challenging the family structure, and challenging the family reality.

Challenging the Symptom.   Challenging the symptom refers to procedures that broaden the definition of the problem, shifting it from the identified person and onto the dysfunctional aspect of the system. The identified problem person is often only sacrificing himself or herself to defend the family's situation. The sacrifice is not attending to the problem, but the person is accepting the responsibility for the situation and providing the family with a maladaptive way to reduce the stress. The family frames its reality in such a manner that the transactional patterns reinforce and maintain the system. It is the counselor's task to challenge the context of the problem and free the family members to see the situation in a different light.

The techniques of enactment, focusing, and intensity are used in the reframing process. *Enactment* involves the family members' interacting with one another, which will illustrate the family's dysfunctional pattern. This is the best way for counselors to gain information. They are able to observe and understand the family rules. Not only will they see the problems within the system, but an enactment will also lead to possible solutions. In fact, during the enactment they can test the family's rules and begin to challenge their reality. As they gain information about the family, they need to organize it into a conceptualization that will facilitate change. They can organize the family's transactions around important themes and offer new meanings for old behavior. Actually, this *focusing* is the development of a plan that helps guide counselors through the process. It is important that they not develop tunnel vision, which would impede their sensitivity to new aspects of information. At times it may be necessary for them to increase their *intensity* to challenge the dysfunctional pattern. They use intensity to push the family members beyond the threshold of their usual pattern and to regulate the impact of the therapeutic message. Counselors can break the family rules, and once they use an enactment, they can use intensity to initiate the members' recognition. One method to increase the intensity is simple repetition. Counselors may encourage the family members to continue their transactions regardless of their habit of stopping. They may use time as a form of intensity to keep members in the interaction longer than usual, or they may use space to keep them closer to one another than has been an accepted psychological distance. The methods of intensity are used to help the family feel the challenge, because they tend to filter and distort most incoming messages and may have difficulty receiving the challenge from the counselor.

Challenging the Family Structure.   In challenging the family structure, counselors attempt to change the overaffiliation or underaffiliation exhibited in the family. They can use their position as an outsider within the system to create coalitions, conflicts, or affiliations that help in restructuring the system. Such procedures as boundary making, unbalancing, and teaching complementarity are useful.

Since boundaries define the participation of members who are excluded as well as those who are involved, therapists can use *boundary making* to control membership of family members in various subsystems. They can do this by increasing the proximity among members of a subsystem and experimenting with the exclusion of others from the subsystem. In other words, they make new boundaries for the old systems. In an effort to break a coalition between a parent and child against the other parent, they may move the parents together to discuss the resolution of an issue. This will demonstrate the parents as a subsystem, which excludes the child from the discussion.

In the method of *unbalancing,* therapists use themselves to form a disequilibrium in the family organization. They may join and support an individual or a subsystem at the expense of other family members. They can use three types of unbalancing. One is an affiliation with one side, in which they form a close relationship with a dominant person, or peripheral person, or possibly with both by alternating within the same session. Another method is to join against someone, taking the side of one member against another individual or subsystem. A third method is merely to ignore someone and focus attention only on other individuals or a subsystem. This unbalancing modifies the structure of the family interactions.

Teaching *complimentarity* involves the counselor's changing the family members' perspective from a linear causality to one in which they come to see that one person is only the symptom bearer and that the whole family is involved in the process. The idea that a child's acting-out behavior is not the fault of the child alone but a symptom of the way the parents respond to the child challenges the family's concept of blame. People and their behavior can be seen as complementary, which can increase their acceptance of everyone participating in the change of the family structure.

Challenging the Family Reality.   Not only does a change in family structure lead to a corresponding change in worldview, but a change in a family's worldview will lead to a change in its structure. Frequently families have developed a worldview that reinforces and maintains their problem areas. The use of constructions, paradoxes, and searching for strengths can influence their worldview. Usually families have a simplified version of the world on which they can act. This view often limits their behavior to the point that they do not effectively adapt to changing situations.

Counselors can influence the family's reality by introducing *constructs* that offer members more freedom in their thought and behavior. One type of construction is the universal symbol, referring to realities that are supported by an institution or a consensus larger than the family. Counselors may use such statements as ''In this society . . .'' in order to introduce concepts in a more acceptable way. They may also use family truths and emphasize things that members have previously stated but do not use. In addition, they may present their own expert advice as a way of changing a family's worldview. By relying on their own experience, wisdom, and leadership position, they may influence the family.

Paradoxes are an indirect challenge to the family reality. A paradox is designed to eliminate the symptom, which will eliminate the role for the symptom as a self-regulating mechanism for the family and therefore expose the true context of the problem. When a family does not follow the counselor's advice to try the new behaviors as prescribed, there may be some type of hidden rule in the family that is actually doing the defying. It is this hidden rule that becomes the target of the paradoxical intention. The paradox involves a redefinition of the problem so that the dysfunctional rule is prescribed. If it is made explicit, it should lose its power. The counselor regulates the pace of change by restraining the family's press for change and reaction to this prescription. Once the paradox has had the effect of challenging the family's reality, the counselor can reinforce the message so that members will continue to accept it.

Another technique in challenging the family reality is to accent and *use the family's strengths.* The counselor acknowledges the strengths of both the individual and the family and, by pointing out these strengths, challenges the family's perceived impotence to adapt and solve the problem.

Summary

Minuchin's approach to family therapy is based on systems theory. He sees the family as being composed of individuals and subsystems that maintain patterns of interaction. In assessing its structure, he focuses on family boundaries and alignments. Problems usually occur when the family fails to successfully adapt to stress. The structural approach to therapy uses a map of the family's boundaries and transactions to form hypotheses of needed change. After joining the family, the therapist uses various strategies to challenge the family's symptoms, structure, and view of reality. The goal of therapy is to change the structure of the family to permit more appropriate functioning.

Bowen's Family-of-Origin Approach

Bowen's systems theory about how families function evolved from his psychoanalytic approach to the treatment of schizophrenic patients at the Menninger Clinic. His theory provides a description of emotional illness as a relationship between and among people. He subscribes to the belief that a change in one person will create a compensatory change in every person in that emotional, interpersonal system.

Family Concepts

Bowen developed a concept of relationships formed by interlocking triangles extending over generations. He believes that a two-person relationship is not stable and that as anxiety rises, a third person is brought in to take some of the strain off the dyadic relationship. This process is called triangulation. The most uncomfortable member of the dyad initiates the new balance to achieve the outside position. The new person in the triangle gets the focus of attention, allowing the anxious person to feel outside the pressure. As a new balance is achieved, the anxiety will be reduced. When the anxiety is reduced sufficiently, the relationships will return to normal, and all members of the triangle may be able to relate as individuals. The primary goal of Bowen's therapy, then, is to help people become differentiated, by separating themselves from the family triangles and becoming a more independent person.

Bowen's concepts enter the family system on the subsystem level, focusing on an individual or the couple. His emphasis is on the differentiation of the self within the family, rather than on transactional patterns between people. But, as noted, he assumes that if one person in the system changes, the rest of the system will change in response.

Bowen has a broad concept of family systems, because he defines the family to include a multigenerational network. His theory consists of a series of interlocking concepts that account for the process of emotional functioning in the family. These principles involve triangles, the family-projection process, the multigenerational transmission process, and sibling positions.

Differentiation. Bowen describes the concept of differentiation of self as the cornerstone of his approach. He has defined differentiation as a continuum, on which the lower end of self-differentiation is a fusion between intellectual and emotional functioning that results in a lack of flexibility in responding to life situations. At this lower end of the scale, people have a confusion between a "pseudoself" and a real, or solid, self. They tend to react automatically, on the emotional level, to situations because they have not consciously worked out a set of personal operating principles and beliefs from their own life experiences that would constitute a stable, solid self. Instead, because they are controlled by the emotional system, they function as a pseudoself created by emotional pressure, unstable and unaware of the inconsistencies resulting from their attempts to conform to descrepant principles maintained by various groups in their environment. In contrast, at the other end of the continuum, well-differentiated people have constructed a set of life principles through intellectual reasoning. Because they have rationally and consciously made choices about their beliefs, they are responsible for themselves and the consequences of their behavior. The solid self of well-differentiated people can respond to others based on a personal framework of values. Well-differentiated people have a higher level of flexibility than poorly differentiated people, whose pseudoself dominates their functioning. When people fail to differentiate the emotional system from the intellectual system, they are said to be undifferentiated. When this failure occurs in a family, the family is said to have an "undifferentiated family ego mass" (Bowen, 1978).

Emotional Cutoff. Bowen established the principle of emotional cutoff as a part of the concept of differentiation. He is concerned not only with the degree to which people have differentiated themselves from their immediate family but also with their differentiation from the past. Emotional cutoff involves the way in which people differentiate themselves from their past, and it will bear on the way they live in the present generation. People who are unable to resolve their emotional attachment to their parents may separate, or cut off, from them in a variety of ways—for example, self-denial or physical running away. Individuals who run away from their family of origin, denying their unresolved emotional attachments to their parents or siblings, are setting up an artificially rigid emotional cutoff between themselves and their family of origin. Although people who are emotionally cut off from their family may appear disengaged, actually they are emotionally dependent on their family of origin, and therefore, fused to it. Bowen (1976b) wrote that "the more intense the cutoff with the past, the more likely the individual is to have an exaggerated version of his parental family problem in his own marriage, and the more likely his children to do a more intense cutoff with him in the next generation" (p. 84). An emotional cutoff should not be confused with authentic differentiation.

Triangles. Bowen (1976b) maintains that "the triangle, the three-person emotional configuration, is the molecule or the basic building block of any emotional system, whether it is the family or any other group" (p. 76). Although the ideal is to have a family of differentiated individuals, each capable of having a one-to-one relationship on a solid-self level, triangles usually develop. Parents typically bring a child into a triangle, involving the family-projection process. In this process, spousal conflicts are dealt with by forming a triangle with a child, who then becomes symptomatic. When most of the anxiety in the family is directed toward the child, the parents can remain relatively healthy and have a largely conflict-free marriage. This projection process may occur across many generations, and Bowen has labeled it the intergenerational transmission process. The child who is the object of the family-projection process matures with a lower degree of differentiation than the parents have and will do less well in life. Bowen hypothesizes that this person would seek a mate at his or her level of differentiation and would then produce a child of a still lower level of differentiation.

The nuclear family's emotional system focuses on the single-generation functioning of the family. Bowen believes that the behavior patterns between the parents and children are only re-creations of past generations and will be repeated in the following generations. The nuclear family's emotional system is a description of how the tension created by a lack of differentiation is dissipated or distributed in the family. The anxiety is expressed either in relationships or in individuals, and it appears in marital conflict or in symptoms of either spouse or a child. The mother, father, and child constitute the triangle. Relationships in the family occur in triangles or complexes of triangles, such as the brother/sister/mother triangle, the brother/sister/father triangle, the mother/father/daughter triangle, or the mother/father/son triangle.

Interventions

Bowen's point of intervention is the individual family member, preferably the most adequately functioning one. The initial interview is used to gather information about family differentiation in as many generations of the family as possible. Little attention is given to the family relations in terms of interactions.

Bowen (1976a) emphasizes that therapists must develop a capacity to stay relatively outside the family's emotional system. For this to occur, they must differentiate themselves not only from the family with which they are working but also from the emotional system of their own family of origin.

Following the initial interview, Bowen focuses attention on triangles in an attempt to dissipate anxiety. When the anxiety is reduced, treatment is aimed at creating differentiation within individual family members. A major technique involves encouraging the individual to make *I* messages. When the person uses *I* messages, the assumption is made that these are intellectual messages and promote the separation of the intellectual from the emotional aspect of the individual. The person is encouraged to express an *I* statement to the therapist, the spouse, or the extended family members. It is assumed that the impact of the individual change will create change throughout the family system.

Bowen seldom works with the whole family and prefers not to work with the children, contending that whenever children are present in the process, the attention gets focused on them. He believes that when the parents are encouraged to focus on themselves and become differentiated individuals, they will be involved in a more healthy manner with the children, and the whole system will function at a higher level. As one member of the family becomes differentiated, this change will affect all the interlocking triangles of the family system. However, he cautions that other family members will attempt to pressure the differentiating member back into his or her previous fused position.

The Genogram.   Bowen's theory has a historical perspective, and he uses a prolonged history taking to gain understanding of the family's development. He does not conduct the usual history-taking interview, however, but uses a family "genogram" to detail past family attitudes, personality habits, deaths, separations, and divorces.

The genogram consists of a chart of all the members in the genealogical tree of the extended family. Attention is given to the myths, rules, secrets, and family messages that affect the individual. As individuals develop a genogram, they may seek information from family members or their extended family of origin in an attempt to gain the details about the roles and functions of other family members. The use of the genogram is not only part of the history-taking and diagnostic component of therapy but is also a continuous basis of reference to understand the individual's behavior. Diagnosis itself involves understanding the degree of anxiety and the level of differentiation of individuals in the family system and the way a symptomatic behavior developed over time.

Carter and Orfanidis (1976) write that the differentiation process has several phases. The therapist functions as a coach, and engages the individual in the process. Next comes the teaching or planning phase, followed by the reentry, the work, and the follow-through. The reentry into the family involves establishing new relationships with family members, especially with each parent. The changing of old dysfunctional patterns with parents will vary depending on the intensity and conflict. Once the person has begun to reestablish relationships, he or she works toward having different interactions with parents or other family members. This effort could involve having the parents work out their issues face to face so the client can differentiate from a pattern of being pulled in between. The length of the work phase varies. The therapist continues to coach the person in developing individuality. During the follow-through process fewer sessions are needed, and the person talks with additional family members and continues the effort to become better differentiated.

The therapist stays outside the family system by gathering data through the genogram, rather than by encouraging the direct expression of emotions. Bowen emphasizes a matter-of-fact, objective tone and approaches the process in an intellectual, rational manner. The process involves strategy sessions in which the therapist and client discuss changes they would like to make in the family relationships, how they can go about initiating these changes, and what reactions they can expect from their family members. A Bowen therapist gives clients the tools necessary to become a co-therapist or coach for their own family.

Change. Change is evaluated according to the emotional process or degree of differentiation. There are external cues that can be indicators of change, such as the degree to which the individual makes *I* statements. These are seen as an indication of the emotional process separating from the intellectual process. The therapist also notes symptom change. Bowen (1978) acknowledges that there are patterns of changes in symptomatology that reflect one member's beginning to differentiate successfully from the family.

Although Bowen works mostly with an individual or couple, his approach is based on systems thinking. He has developed a family conceptualization based on the members forming interlocking triangles that extend over generations. Through an intergenerational transmission process, parents bring a child into family triangles that keep the child functioning at a lower degree of individuation, and this process gets passed on to the next generation. The goal of therapy is to help the individual to differentiate from the family. This is accomplished by differentiating the intellectual system from the emotional system. The individual can then respond more flexibly, based on personally examined values. As the individual changes, other family members will be affected.

Satir's Communications Approach

Virginia Satir is the proponent of a growth model of family therapy that concentrates on the communication among family members. Although much of her early training involved psychoanalytic theories, her later professional experiences led her to focus on growth, personal awareness, and Gestalt concepts. After joining the staff at the Mental Research Institute, in Palo Alto, California, in 1959, she worked with Bateson, Jackson, Haley, and Weakland. During this time she developed many of her theoretical concepts and treatment techniques. Her interest in personal growth was influenced through her experience with Fritz Perls at the Esalen Institute in California, where she worked in the mid-1960s. In recent years she has taught, practiced, and written about her model.

Family Concepts

Satir describes the families that she sees as troubled or untroubled (1972), nurturing or unnurturing, and functional or dysfunctional (1971). These descriptions are indicative of her humanistic approach to therapy. The growth model focuses not on sickness but on the interactional and transactional relationships among the family members. Satir's ideas about family functioning were influenced by the notion of homeostatis (Watzlawick et al., 1967). This view holds that a family forms a dynamic, steady-state system in which the members' interactions, including those of the identified problem person and his or her symptomatic behavior, are used to maintain the status quo of that family. Satir described open family systems as functional and closed systems as dysfunctional. The important differences between the two systems are in how they communicate.

Satir (1967) identified three *levels of communication.* The first is the denotative level, which consists of verbal communications, including words and the literal content of those words. The second level is the connotative, which has two aspects: (1) the body and sound communication, which involves facial expression, body position, muscle tone, and voice tone; and (2) meta-communication, which is a message about a message. The meta-communication usually involves the sender's attitude about the message, about himself or herself, or about the receiver. The third level of communication involves the context, which includes the time and place in which the communication occurs.

In addition to the three levels of communication, Satir (1967) identified two *patterns of communication.* The first pattern is described as incongruent, and it consists of a double-level communication. An example of an incongruent communication is a person smiling while talking about feeling sad and depressed. The second pattern is congruent, or leveling, and occurs when a person's words match his or her inner feelings, nonverbal actions, and the context in which they occur.

Style of Communication. Satir describes the five specific ways in which individuals communicate as placating, blaming, super-reasonable, irrelevant, and congruent. These five styles serve as the basis for understanding dysfunctional communication, and they are important in teaching people about their communications and improving their growth and that of the family system.

People with a *placating* style of communication are always agreeable. In the complex of self, other, and context, self is disregarded while the context and others are considered important. Such people do not consider themselves as important and try to get along by being agreeable.

People who use a *blaming* style of communication try to demonstrate power by blaming, disagreeing, and criticizing others. Other people or the context are less important, and only the self is an important consideration. Blamers self-righteously find fault and are critical of the shortcomings of others. Anything that occurs is someone else's fault, and they present themselves as being right. It is important to note that both the placater and the blamer really depend on the other person for their own survival.

People who are *super-reasonable* communicators are not acknowledging their feelings. They disregard the self and other to focus on the context of the situation. They tend to be reasonable and intellectual as well as rigid, principled, and objective. Often, by focusing on an intellectual approach, they deny their own experience and present as though their survival is controlled by things or events.

People who use an *irrelevant* communication style talk and behave in a way that appears unrelated to anything. They are highly distracting and move in an erratic, inappropriate, and purposeless manner. They do not consider self, others, or the context in communicating.

Satir believes that the person with a *congruent* communication style uses words and behaviors that relate appropriately to others and the context, and the emotional effect is congruent with the verbal message. She believes that functional families use congruent communication, whereas dysfunctional families use combinations of the four incongruent styles of communication.

Family Functioning. Satir (1972) offers an overview of the differences between the functional and dysfunctional families. In dysfunctional families, individuals have lower self-esteem, communication is indirect and vague, rules are more rigid, and their relationship with society is fearful, placating, and blaming. Because of these conditions, such families operate more at a survival level and have severe difficulty with stress. In higher-functioning families, the individual and familial self-concept is high, and communication patterns are congruent, leveling, and growth producing. These conditions permit the overt rules and role expectations to be clearly understood, and the rules are sufficiently flexible to allow the families to meet changes appropriately. Each person has sufficient privacy and is allowed to move in and out of the family system as he or she matures. The ways in which the family members relate to other people and institutions are open and hopeful.

Diagnosis

In Satir's early work she used an extensive family-life chronology. She believed that the family dysfunction was a manifestation of problems in the marital relationship and that a chronology helped change the focus from the identified patient to the marital relationship. The family-life chronology is used to gather information. It describes the whole cast of characters in the family and allows the therapist to see the old homeostatic systems that are operating in the present family. She also uses the chronology for instructive purposes. She believes that dysfunctional families do not differentiate between present and past, and this tool helps them to see the difference. The procedure of taking the chronology involves each member's expressing ideas, feelings, and memories, which allows family members to experience their difference from one another. The chronology begins with the meeting of the parents, moves to their family of origin, returns to the planning of the children, and finally focuses on the routine facts of a typical day for the family. Each member is involved in this process, discussing his or her feelings, hopes, and disappointments, as well as the facts.

In working with a family, Satir accepts the psychiatric diagnosis as an indication of the behavior manifested by the presenting problem, but she proceeds to categorize the family and individuals with her own diagnostic classification. Her classification system includes an analysis of how the family handles people being different, how they function in their family roles, how rules are set and maintained, and how people communicate with one another. By analyzing the function of communication within the family, Satir is able to have a better understanding of the members' communication problems.

Interventions

Satir's focus in therapy is on identifying and working out a rational process. For her, process implies movement. It is more a matter of "how" than of "what," and she believes that the basic process that occurs in any relationship is the encounter between persons at a particular time and place (1967). Although it is difficult for a therapist not to comment on the family's content, the process is far more important. Her growth model comes from this focus on process. Behavior changes through process, and the change is represented by transactions with others.

Satir does not focus on solving specific problems. Her therapeutic goals involve both the cognitive and emotional aspects of interactions. Her therapeutic goals are to have all members report congruently and completely what they see, hear, feel, and think about themselves and others; each person's uniqueness is recognized, so that decisions are made through negotiations rather than power, and people's differences are acknowledged and used for growth (1971).

The role of the therapist in helping the family meet these goals is to function as a leader or resource and model. Satir's idea of this leader is that of an active clinician with numerous skills and techniques. Although skills and techniques are important, they are secondary to the therapist's awareness and personhood. Her focus is on how therapists can use themselves, under certain circumstances, to help people become more personally aware (Satir, Stachowiak, & Taschman, 1975). She sees counselors as personally involved.

In recent years Satir has focused on communication techniques of the here and now of the family interaction. Believing that the identified patient is only a reflection of a well-entrenched pattern of family interaction, she tries to create a climate in which the family members can clearly see themselves. She tries to help build self-esteem through nonjudgmental communication and the reduction of emotionality. She uses limit setting in therapy to reeducate the family members about accountability. She is a master at helping family members delineate their roles and functions, at interpreting nonverbal communications, and at focusing on congruent verbal communications. She proposes that the therapist be an impartial official and model of congruent communication who serves as an experienced observer and resource person. Her interview techniques concentrate on feelings. Her strategies are verbal and nonverbal, circular and linear. They fluctuate between active and passive. She gives homework assignments called prescriptions. She also uses "ego-enhancing" statements and asks "ego-enhancing" questions. Most of her techniques involve reframing, or placing things in a positive, growth-oriented context. She uses experiential, growth-oriented exercises, as well as role-playing and sculpting techniques.

While her experiential methods are nonverbal, linear, and active, Satir clearly combines her rationale and emotive historical roots.

Satir developed a growth-oriented communication approach to family therapy. She believes that the identified patient's behaviors are used to maintain the family status quo. She focuses on the family members' style of communication and uses therapy as a change process. She does not solve specific problems but involves the family in the process of learning more congruent communication.

Summary

Family therapy is based on systems theory, which holds that the identified client is affected by and affects other members in the system. Therefore, diagnoses and interventions are focused on the system, not just the individual. Systems theory, with its belief that the family, not the individual, is the client, differs from the traditional theories used in individual and group counseling. Only recently has there been an expressed interest in integrating the concepts of individual and systems theory. The theoretical and practical applications of such an integration are still in the exploratory stage. Within the systems perspective, there are differing concepts of family functioning and therapeutic interventions. Minuchin, Bowen, and Satir are masters in the field, and their approaches serve as examples of family therapies.

Minuchin's approach contends that (1) the family is structured as an open sociocultural system in transformation, (2) the family moves through a number of stages that require family restructuring, and (3) the family adapts to changes to maintain continuity and enhance the psychosocial growth of each person. He believes most family dysfunction occurs when the family does not successfully adapt to stress. He diagnoses by observing the family subsystems, boundaries, alignments, and transactional patterns. Diagnosis involves making a tentative map of the family transactions and using it as a guide for initial interventions. Minuchin's interventions are aimed at changing the structure of the family. He works with the whole family, challenging members to reframe the problem and shift attention to the system. The process of restructuring involves the family's enacting their patterns of behavior, making new boundaries, changing alignments, unbalancing the disequilibrium in the family, and learning new patterns of behavior. When the pattern between two persons changes, the whole family system is affected.

Bowen works more with an individual or couple than with the whole family. His conceptualization of a family involves members' forming interlocking triangles that extend over generations. He focuses on two and three generations of patterns rather than just the nuclear family. Through intergenerational transmissions, parents bring children into relationships that keep them functioning at a lower level of individuation. The goal of therapy is to help the individual differentiate from the old family pattern and be able to think and behave more independently. Bowen uses a genogram to have the person examine the history of family attitudes, personality habits, deaths, and behaviors. The individual then starts to work out new relationships with his or her parents and, often, other family members. Much of this work takes place outside of counseling sessions, with the individual bringing thoughts and feelings back to discuss with the therapist.

Satir developed a growth and communication model of family therapy. She focuses on the levels, styles, and patterns of communication in the family. She believes that in dysfunctional families individuals have lower self-esteem, communication is indirect, rules are more rigid, and members' relationship with the community is fearful, placating, and blaming. She often uses a family chronology to gather information about the family history. All members express their ideas, feeling, and memories, letting them experience their differences and similarities. Satir does not have a set of techniques or focus on just solving specific problems. She works with both the cognitive and emotional aspects of behaviors. She helps people change by teaching communication techniques to the family. She builds self-esteem in members by teaching them nonjudgmental, clear communication. Her techniques involve experiential, growth-oriented exercises, role playing, and sculpting.

References

Ackerman, N. (1958). *The Psychodynamics of Family Life.* New York: Basic Books.

Bowen, M. (1960). A Family Concept of Schizophrenia. In D. Jackson (Ed.), *The Etiology of Schizophrenia* (pp. 346–372). New York: Basic Books.

Bowen, M. (1976a). Principles and Techniques of Multiple Family Therapy. In P. J. Guerin, Jr. (Ed.), *Family Therapy: Theory and Practice* (pp. 388–404). New York: Gardner Press.

Bowen, M. (1976b). Theory in the Practice of Psychotherapy. In P. J. Guerin, Jr. (Ed.), *Family Therapy: Theory and Practice* (pp. 42–90). New York: Gardner Press.

Bowen M. (1978). *Family Therapy in Clinical Practice.* New York: Aronson.

Carter, E., & Orfanidis, M. M. (1976). Family Therapy with One Person and the Family Therapist's Own Family. In P. J. Guerin, Jr. (Ed.), *Family Therapy: Theory and Practice* (pp. 193–219). New York: Gardner Press.

French, A. (1977). *Disturbed Children and Their Families: Innovations in Evaluation and Treatment.* New York: Human Sciences Press.

Guerin, P. (1976). Family Therapy: The First Twenty-Five Years. In P. J. Guerin, Jr. (Ed.), *Family Therapy: Theory and Practice* (pp. 2–22). New York: Gardner Press.

Hoffman, L. (1981). *Foundations of Family Therapy.* New York: Basic Books.

Jackson, D. (1960). *The Etiology of Schizophrenia.* New York: Basic Books.

Keeney, B. (1983). *Aesthetics of Change.* New York: Guilford Press.

Minuchin, S. (1974). *Families and Family Therapy.* Cambridge, MA: Harvard University Press.

Minuchin S., & Fishman, C. (1981). *Family Therapy Techniques.* Cambridge, MA: Harvard University Press.

Papp, P. (1983). *The Process of Change.* New York: Guilford Press.

Satir, V. (1967). *Conjoint Family Therapy* (2nd ed.). Palo Alto, CA: Science and Behavior Books.

Satir, V. (1971). The Family as a Treatment Unit. In J. Haley (Ed.), *Changing Families: A Family Therapy Reader* (pp. 127–133). New York: Grune & Stratton.

Satir, V. (1972). *Peoplemaking.* Palo Alto, CA: Science and Behavior Books.

Satir, V., Stachowiak, J., & Taschman, H. A. (1975). *Helping Families to Change.* New York: Aronson.

Watzlawick, P., Beavin, J., & Jackson, D. (1967). *Pragmatics of Human Communication.* New York: Norton.

Clinical Assessment

This chapter is not an exposition of "how to use tests." There are specialized books and courses for that purpose. Instead, this chapter covers the fundamental concepts of clinical assessment—which includes psychological and educational tests—and creates a frame of reference that the counseling psychologist can apply. As will be evident below, counseling psychologists have often felt ambivalent about assessment, but any dissonance among them has turned to harmonic convergence.

History and Evolution of Clinical Assessment in Counseling Psychology

There has long been a love/hate relationship between assessment and counseling. On the one hand, counselors recognize that they need to understand the client and that assessment methods can yield data that will help them decide on an intervention. On the other hand, they have the notion that any kind of assessment will dishonor the tenets of facilitative conditions and that the quality of therapy will suffer.

Assessment and Person-Centered Counseling

In its early days counseling psychology placed emphasis on psychological testing, but only in the restricted framework of educational and vocational appraisal. Public support of vocational guidance, such as for military personnel returning from World War II, led to occupational-preference and aptitude tests becoming standard counseling tools. This trait-and-factor approach (that is, using a test score to make an assumption about a person's characteristics) troubled some counselors. They were concerned that the approach might lead to a technical or impersonal conceptualization of the client.

About the same time the writings of Carl R. Rogers were receiving wide acclaim (Rogers, 1957, 1961). One of his core facilitative dimensions for counseling, as we have noted, was unconditional positive regard, or nonpossessive, nonevaluative, unreserved caring for the client. He concluded that diagnostic information was not essential to counseling.

Some counselors thought that Rogers's implication was that assessment might make clients feel that they were under the scrutinizing eye of a judge and that the therapist was not giving "unconditional" positive regard. Arbuckle (1965) expressed skepticism about the necessity of assessment procedures for client-centered counseling:

> The Client-centered counselor feels that in an understanding and acceptant atmosphere the client will come to see the "why" of his behavior, and any action that is taken will be *by him* on the basis of *his diagnosis* rather than that of the counselor. But, one might say, if the counselor is a student of psychology, he must have certain diagnostic understandings, and how can he avoid being diagnostic, at least in his own mind, even though he may not verbalize his conclusions to the client? This is a good question, and there seems little doubt that the Client-centered counselor does see a picture of the client as the counseling proceeds; but this picture is primarily one that is being developed by the client for himself and for the counselor. I find it extremely difficult, even if it were desirable, to be diagnostically minded toward either the client or myself during a counseling session. This is not the case, however, when one listens sometimes with a colleague to a tape of the counseling session. Under such conditions the counselor is certainly diagnostic with regard to himself, and with the client too, insofar as he is pre-planning activities with regard to where the client should go and what he should do. In the counseling session he is going to be with the client, and his intelligence and his understanding are going to be directed toward this end rather than toward the correct manner of leading or directing the client [pp. 222–223].

Part of the reticence of the client-centered counselor to embrace assessment was the wish to be nondirective. More will be said later, however, about how direction was present in interventions that were supposedly nondirective.

Before leaving the work of Rogers, it should be pointed out that he did not condemn assessment. In fact, Rogers said: "There is no intent here to maintain that diagnostic evaluation is useless. We have ourselves made heavy use of such methods in our research studies of change in personality. It is its usefulness as a precondition to psychotherapy that is questioned" (1957, pp. 102–103). Rogers seemed to hold that diagnostic information could increase the security of the therapist but was not necessary to obtain therapeutic change within the client.

As client-centered therapy progressed to person-centered therapy (with the change in terms reflecting the attempt to eliminate other-than-normal status for the "helpee"), the facilitative conditions for the counselor were revised. For example, Truax and Carkhuff (1967) held that sensing the client's inner world was not enough; "accurate empathy" involves both the therapist's *sensitivity to current feelings* and his *verbal facility to communicate this understanding* in a language attuned to the client's current feelings" (p. 46). An expectation was being placed on the therapist, and it seems that this new responsibility promoted an open-mindedness toward using assessment strategies.

Assessment and Selective Responding in Counseling

Assessment received a boost from research revealing that client-centered counseling is not nondirective. In fact, it appears that client-centered counseling involves selective responding.

In a first analysis of what was supposedly nondirective counseling, Murray (1956) studied a verbatim counseling session conducted by Rogers. He found that the categories of verbal behavior that were seemingly approved of by Rogers increased in frequency, while those categories of verbal behavior receiving disapproval decreased in frequency.

A decade later, Truax (1966a) applied a similar analysis to audio recordings of Rogers's sessions. He found that Rogers responded to certain classes of verbal responses from the client but did not respond to certain other classes of verbal responses. As learning theory would support, the classes of client responses that received a reinforcement from Rogers (for example, by a positive statement) led to the client's making a greater number of statements that would fit into the reinforced classes; and to the contrary, responses in the classes that did not receive reinforcement from Rogers decreased in frequency.

Selective responding was not confined to Rogers personally. Roberts and Renzaglia (1965) monitored counseling sessions with and without the knowledge of the counselors. They found that if the counselors knew they were being analyzed, they displayed different response styles than when they did not know they were being analyzed. Over the years numerous studies have replicated the finding that selective responding occurs in virtually every form of counseling.

None of the foregoing is intended to denigrate the importance of the work of Rogers or of the utility of the client- or person-centered approach. The message is that nondirective therapy is *not* truly nondirective and that the most efficacious (and ethical?) approach is to plan responses with an awareness of what should or should not be reinforced.

Selective responding affects counseling in several ways. Truax (1966b) describes the four modalities in which Rogerian dimensions have direct or indirect effects:

> (1) they serve to reinforce positive aspects of the patient's self-concept, modifying the existing self-concept, thus leading to changes in the patient's own self-reinforcement system; (2) they serve to reinforce self-exploratory behavior, thus eliciting self-concepts and anxiety-laden material which can then be potentially modified; (3) they serve to extinguish anxiety or fear responses associated with specific cues, both those elicited by the relationship with the therapist and those elicited by patient self-exploration; and (4) they serve to reinforce human relating, encountering or interacting and to extinguish fear or avoidance learning associated with human relating [p. 62].

This message is what helped the birth of behavioral counseling (Krumboltz, 1965). For the issue of assessment, the conclusion from research on selective responding is that the counseling process, even if "nondirective," relies on direction from the therapist. Consequently, there must be (1) an evaluation of the factors that are to be shaped, (2) a data-based plan for the therapist's intervention, and (3) a determination of what does and does not change (and why).

Staying with the facilitative dimensions for assessment, Schauble (1980) endorses rating scales for estimating the presence or absence of the facilitative dimensions in the therapeutic interactions; assessment of systems (for example, the client's family) for communication conditions; psychological tests for understanding the client's characteristics, as would be relevant to how he or she will be able to master and maintain the conditions necessary for change; and assessment of change due to treatment. There is no reason why the counseling theory, even if it is Rogerian, should preclude assessment.

How Tests Are Used in Counseling

One of the pioneer advocates of the use of tests in counseling was Leo Goldman (1961). He divided test-related data into informational and noninformational usages. We can define informational data to include diagnostic information—for example, the definition of the client's problem. Also in this category is information for the counseling process itself—for example, data that aid in making decisions about methods, approaches, tools, and techniques to be used in the treatment. Finally, there is information relating to the client's decisions after counseling—for example, the identification of possible courses of action, the evaluation of alternatives, the testing of a tentative choice, plan, or decision; and self-concept development and clarification. Noninformational test data are used to stimulate interest in areas not previously considered, lay the groundwork for later counseling, and help the client decision making (see Woody, 1972b). As we shall discuss later, assessment in counseling psychology is, of course, much broader than psychological tests per se; but tests are clearly applicable to critical counseling issues.

Counseling Psychology's Use of Assessment

In considering the relevance of clinical assessment, it is important to recognize the distinct nature of counseling psychology in contrast, for example, to clinical psychology (see Chapter 1). In pointing out the uniqueness of assessment in counseling psychology, it should be noted that in no way do we mean that there is not considerable similarity among the various psychological specialties. After years of carving our territoriality for specialties, the maturity of psychology is accommodating a present movement toward unification (Leary & Maddux, 1987; Matarazzo, 1987).

Counseling psychology has often been defined by an emphasis on health, as opposed to clinical psychology, which is defined by an emphasis on illness:

> *Clinical psychology* has typically been concerned with diagnosing the nature and extent of *psychopathology*, with the abnormalities even of normal persons, with uncovering adjustment difficulties and maladaptive tendencies, and with the acceptance and understanding of these tendencies so that they may be modified. *Counseling psychology,* on the contrary, concerns itself with *hygiology,* with the normalities even of abnormal persons, with locating

and developing personal and social resources and adaptive tendencies so
that the individual can be assisted in making more effective use of them
[Super, 1962, p. 10].

Notwithstanding the era in which this statement was made, the distinction still
prevails. The emphasis on health will continue through the contents of this chapter. For example, when an assessment strategy is selected, it will, in part, be predicated upon a "hygiological" goal, as opposed to a psychopathological goal.

Aspects of Clinical Assessment

As mentioned earlier, clinical assessment goes beyond testing: "A simple definition for an extremely complex process is that *psychological assessment is a
process of solving problems (answering questions)* in which psychological tests
are used as *one* of the methods of collecting data" (Maloney & Ward, 1976,
p. 5). Stated differently, observations of and scores for psychological behavior
are gained through systematic or standardized procedures (Kleinmuntz, 1982).

   In the realm of personality assessment, it is a matter of *"developing impressions and images, making decisions and checking hypotheses about
another person's pattern of characteristics which determine his or her behavior
in interaction with the environment"* (Sundberg, 1977, pp. 21–22). The same
principle applies to other types of assessment, such as for educational and
vocational questions. That is, clinical assessment, regardless of objective or
question, seeks to provide the counseling psychologist with a systematically
gained set of data that will clarify the characteristics of the client so as to op-
timize the benefits of the counseling intervention.

Seeking Objectivity

Clinical assessment can be formal or informal. It is important to emphasize,
however, that criticism has often been leveled at clinical assessment for being
too subjective and unsystematic. For example, to formulate a "diagnostic impression" from simply thinking about a client's characteristics, without the
benefit of standardized techniques, is to risk bias and error. Any "clinical" procedure will involve some degree of subjectivity. And the reliability and validity
of any strategy involving subjectivity is suspect. The most appropriate stance
for the counseling psychologist, therefore, is to constantly seek to minimize
subjectivity, while maximizing objectivity.

Assessment Alternatives

What are the assessment techniques? They are legion. For counseling
psychology, technical options include analysis of the client's records, interviewing of the client or significant others, observational analysis of the client in
a therapeutic milieu or rehabilitation setting, and psychological and educational
tests. When defining "assessment, evaluation, and diagnosis," the American
Psychological Association (1981b) states:

> Procedures may include, but are not limited to, behavioral observation, interviewing, and administering and interpreting instruments for the assessment of educational achievement, academic skills, aptitudes, interests, cognitive abilities, attitudes, emotions, motivations, psychoneurological status, personality characteristics, or any other aspect of human experience and behavior that may contribute to understanding and helping the user [p. 654].

Also,

> in the development, publication, and utilization of psychological assessment techniques, psychologists make every effort to promote the welfare and best interests of the client. They guard against the misuse of assessment results. They respect the client's right to know the results, the interpretations made, and the bases for their conclusions and recommendations. Psychologists make every effort to maintain the security of tests and other assessment techniques within limits of legal mandates. They strive to ensure the appropriate use of assessment techniques by others [American Psychological Association, 1981a, p. 637].

The assessment alternatives seem limitless, as evidenced by the multitude of tests that are available. The final choice of an assessment strategy must be governed by the needs of the client and the competency of the counseling psychologist. The ethical dictate is that psychologists "only provide services and only use techniques for which they are qualified by training and experience" (American Psychological Association, 1981a, p. 634).

Recall the emphasis on health. This, too, will enter into selecting an assessment strategy. If the counseling psychologist is to be true to his or her specialization, the assessment will be geared to "the normalities even of abnormal persons" (Super, 1962, p. 10). To be sure, some counseling psychologists will have the competency to shift to a clinical psychology specialization, and they should do so when the needs of the client require it. But that will be the exception.

The assessment must be tailored to fit the individual. Clients with minority backgrounds are particularly vulnerable to abuse of assessment data. For example, the standardization of psychometric instruments is infamous for failing to deal adequately with sociocultural variables. While it is obvious that the counseling relationship must be flexible enough to accept multicultural conditions, sociocultural accommodation is inconsistently attained: "Given all available evidence, there is no doubt that the counseling profession has failed to effectively meet the mental health needs of racial and ethnic minorities" (Ponterotto, 1987, p. 434). Fundamentally, this failure can be traced to the lack of multicultural competence as a training objective (Ponterotto & Casas, 1987). Even so, the counseling psychologist has an obligation to seek empirical measures of acculturation.

Subsequent sections will deal with diagnosis and with tailoring the clinical assessment to treatment interventions. These sections will focus on the needs of the client as related to the selection of an assessment strategy.

Diagnosis

The nonjudgmental nature of counseling is a major reason why counseling psychologists have tended to shy away from clinical assessment. They reason that clinical assessment, usually meaning the use of psychological tests, will lead to a diagnosis. In turn, diagnosis means branding the client with a pathological label. Pinning a label on clients is tantamount to judging them. It is reasoned, therefore, that diagnosis works against efficacy in counseling. While conceivable at first blush, such thinking is erroneous. Diagnosis is a process. It is more than determining a label or category from a psychopathological classification. It is an analysis of the client's functioning for purposes of prescribing the most helpful therapeutic intervention.

Diagnosis might readily involve the use of a term or category, as would come from the American Psychiatric Association's (1987) *Diagnostic and Statistical Manual of Mental Disorders, Third Edition-Revised* (also known as the DSM-III-R). In fact, the client's receiving reimbursement for the cost of psychotherapy from his or her health insurance carrier would probably require such a categorization.

When a client is identified by a diagnostic category, such as one from the DSM-III-R, it should be recognized that this is an identification made at a specific time. The DSM-III represented psychiatric opinion about mental disorders in 1980, whereas the DSM-III-R reflects opinions for 1987. As societal conditions change, so do psychiatric opinions. For example, Nathan and Harris (1983) trace the categorizations used through three editions of the DSM. From their analysis, it is obvious that the nature of mental illness, the number of categories, and the definitions therein are subject to change: "Unlike most medical diagnoses, which can be validated in numerous ways, psychiatric diagnoses are maintained by consensus alone" (Rosenhan, 1975, p. 464).

Diagnosis relies on the therapy relationship to produce evidence of psychological functions that can be connected to a theory for understanding the client's problems (Shevrin & Shectman, 1973). The goal is to transform observations of psychological functioning into an understanding of the client's internal experience (Shectman, 1973). There is a search for the "determination of the nature, origin, precipitation, and maintenance of ineffective abnormal modes of behavior" (Arbuckle, 1965, p. 220).

As the foregoing reveals, the objective is to move beyond labeling to a process of analysis—and the analysis is for improving the therapy. This goal is obtained through several steps: "observation, description, a delineation of causation or etiology, classification, prediction or prognosis, and control-modification or treatment plan" (Beller, 1962, p. 109).

Using the Diagnosis to Guide Treatment

The preceding discussion leads to an emphasis on using diagnosis for planning, carrying out, and evaluating treatment. That is, once a diagnosis has been made, the counseling psychologist should rely on it for sorting out the treatment track that will be followed. The diagnostic formulations should include a prognosis about the potential effectiveness of each treatment alternative.

The first application of diagnosis to treatment comes from recognizing that pathology and normality are statistical creations. The terms represent behaviors that are accepted or rejected by the society at a given time for a particular client in the context in which the client lives. Therefore, what is normal for one client in one context might be deemed pathological for another client in a different context. Further, two clients could behave in the same manner in the same community, but because of sociodemographic characteristic (such as age, gender, race, or economic level) one client could "get away" with a behavior that another client would be censured for. Notwithstanding the potential bias of accepting or rejecting behavior as normal, it is estimated that about 25% of the "normal" population has a significant degree of emotional disturbance (Goldstein, Baker, & Jamison, 1980).

What really counts, then, is not the behavior per se, but how it affects the person's daily living, both in the short run and the long run. Millon (1981) clarifies:

> When an individual displays an ability to cope with the environment in a flexible manner, and when his or her typical perceptions and behaviors foster increments in personal satisfaction, then the person may be said to possess a normal and healthy personality. Conversely, when average or everyday responsibilities are responded to inflexibly or defectively, or when the individual's perceptions and behaviors result in increments in personal discomfort or curtail opportunities to learn and to grow, then we may speak of a pathological or maladaptive pattern [p. 9].

If there are negative personal consequences, the behavior probably merits being targeted for change through therapy.

The preceding view, an emphasis on assessment of the problems in daily living, is the basis for believing that the same psychological tests should probably not be used with all (or even most) clients and that preference should be given to a problem-centered approach. For example, Sweeney, Clarkin, and Fitzgibbon (1987) recommend that assessment be matched to the client's immediate clinical problems requiring treatment: "A model focusing on the description of overt problems and symptomatology is potentially more beneficial to a patient than are the results of a comprehensive test battery" (p. 377).

There is a pragmatic benefit from focusing the assessment on the problems of living. In keeping with counseling psychology's underlying emphasis, however, the focus must also include the healthy qualities that can be activated to counteract the problems. How does the counseling psychologist recognize healthy qualities? Jahoda (1958) offers a time-honored distinction between mental disturbance and normality, emphasizing a lack of problems—that is, mental disturbances involve "clearly defined deficiencies in (1) awareness, acceptance, and correctness of self-concept; (2) continued growth and self-actualization; (3) integration and unity of personality; (4) autonomy and self-reliance; (5) perception of reality and social sensitivity; and (6) mastery of the environment and adequacy in meeting the demands of life" (pp. 26–27).

The approach of Millon (1981) to defining healthy and the unhealthy personalities requires distinguishing between personality patterns, symptom disorders, and behavior reactions. Ingrained personal traits (for example, pervasive ways of functioning) are personality patterns. Highly specific pathological responses that are precipitated by or are attributable to circumscribed external events are behavior reactions. In between these extremes are symptom disorders: "Conceived as intensifications or disruptions in a patient's characteristic style of functioning, symptom disorders are viewed as a reaction to a situation for which the individual's personality is notably vulnerable" (p. 10). Whereas personality patterns resist modification, behavior reactions change easily according to the situation. Symptom disorders, however, are more difficult to extinguish because of their tie to the ingrained personality traits.

Given this framework, the counseling psychologist should (1) pinpoint the personality patterns, which give the client inner momentum and autonomy and will be expressed regardless of stimulus-specific situations; (2) identify behavior reactions, those that lead to both health-seeking and disruptive behavior; (3) decide how to use ego-syntonic factors, which convey a sense of comfort and suitability to the client; and (4) target for therapeutic change the ego-dystonic symptom disorders, which impose discomfort and irrational or peculiar behaviors on the client. These formulations can draw from the entire array of diagnostic tools, including interviewing, observation, and psychological testing.

The final step in fitting diagnosis to the treatment strategy involves clinical hypothesis building. Since revisions in treatment will continue throughout counseling, this step is never truly final. Here the emphasis is on prognosis.

Having used assessment data to formulate classifications of functional and dysfunctional behavior, the counseling psychologist seeks "to link the current existence of a cluster of behaviors with predictable maladaptive behavior in the future" (Halleck, 1978, p. 33). The Halleck approach emphasizes causation as the means for deciding upon treatment:

> This approach requires the formulation and testing of multiple hypotheses as to the processes which cause various types of dysfunctional behavior. Given the infant state of our science, it is critical that no hypothesis or set of hypotheses should be so revered as to make us less open to other hypotheses. Being open to a variety of hypotheses will not in itself provide the clinician a precise guide for knowing which treatment to use, and when. A willingness to consider all classes of hypotheses is essential, however, if there is to be a comprehensive and systematic approach to the patient [p. 39].

The Halleck approach has four sectors. First, hypotheses of *biological dysfunctioning* are considered. Second, *past learning experiences* are inspected to estimate the influences on present behavior, recognizing that there will probably be an interrelationship of factors. Third, *informational* hypotheses (involving deficits in awareness or insight relevant to the self or the environment) are pondered. Fourth, *environmental* hypotheses point toward the stimuli from the environment that influence the patient's behavior.

The Halleck approach holds that each of these four categories of hypotheses should be systematically considered or tested clinically. Halleck cautions, however, that one cannot simply list the factors for each category and assume that the influence is additive. Rather, there may be interactive effects: "Whatever troublesome behavior is eventually defined as the patient's symptom will always be the product of complex individual-environmental interaction over a period of time" (p. 53).

Fitting the treatment to the diagnosis is the goal. The Halleck approach offers a specific intervention according to the etiology of the problem. Problems with a biological etiology can be modified through brain chemistry or physiology, such as using medications, having psychosurgery, applying electroconvulsive therapy, or using physical therapies such as yoga, relaxation, exercise, or massage. Problems with a learning etiology require behavioral interventions, such as those based on classical and operant conditioning. Problems with an informational etiology can be dealt with by insight-oriented psychotherapy. Problems with an environmental etiology can be treated by hospitalization or a therapeutic milieu. Of course, the interactional nature of etiologies may well lead to diagnosing multiple causes, and the intervention strategy will be an integration of, say, medical services and of behavioral or insight-oriented counseling.

The foregoing approach to blending diagnosis and treatment should not be discounted as being "too psychiatric" or "too psychopathological." The sources are, of course, quite clinical, but so are the problems that are dealt with in counseling psychology. The ideas in this section were selected for presentation because they exemplify (1) the *process* of diagnosis (thereby clarifying that diagnosis is more than an exercise in labeling and (2) a useful means for selecting a treatment strategy according to the diagnostic data. Moreover, careful inspection of the ideas in this section will reveal (1) a holistic approach, whereby the whole person (with all of his or her biopsychosocial qualities) is the focus of diagnosis and treatment, and (2) an endorsement of eclecticism, thereby allowing virtually all theories of therapy to find application, depending on the needs of the client. Both the holistic framework and the integration of theories and techniques are in the mainstream of counseling psychology.

Applications of Clinical Assessment to Counseling Psychology

While counseling psychology has more commonalities with other areas of professional psychology than differences, there are distinctions. Because some of these distinctions relate to the type and quality of clinical assessment—for example, the methods that will be used—this section presents practical considerations in the counseling psychologists' application of clinical assessment.

Theoretical Bias in Assessment

Earlier in this chapter we mentioned that clinical assessment, by its nature, is subjective. Also, we recommended that the counseling psychologist seek to minimize subjectivity and maximize objectivity. One of the problems with attaining objectivity comes from the theory espoused by the counseling psychologist. Bishop and Richards (1984) investigated whether the differences in theoretical orientation among counselors would be reflected in critical diagnostic judgments. They classified counseling psychologists in a university counseling center as either cognitive or humanistic. At the time of intake, it was found, the humanistically oriented counselors thought that their clients presented more severe educational problems and were more anxious than the cognitive counselors judged their clients to be.

Recalling the discussion about clinical hypothesis testing in the preceding section, it is alarming to think about how the counseling psychologist's theoretical orientation could potentially color or bias the initial assessment. This bias could, regrettably, lead to an ill-conceived determination of counseling strategy.

Preordaining a client's condition because of theoretical bias must be counteracted with every possible means of objectivity. This might include relying on objective data (such as a personality profile) for the initiation of treatment, submitting all case data to a "staffing" (a group of professional colleagues who represent differing theoretical views) to double-check clinical impressions, and requiring continual supervision for effectiveness.

Assessment Data to Guide Counseling

Theoretical bias can be avoided, in part, by letting the assessment data guide the counseling process. Of equal or greater importance, the assessment data can, in and of themselves, promote therapeutic growth and change for the client. Consider two examples. First, Ramanaiah, Heerboth, and Jinkerson (1985) used profiles of assertiveness to promote self-actualization, with the clients' recognizing the correlation between assertiveness and self-actualization (that is, the more assertive, the greater the self-actualization). Second, Dworkin and Saczynski (1984) found hedonic capacity to be important to resistance or vulnerability to schizophrenia and affective disorders; and they used diagnostic data to guide the psychotherapeutic modification of a client's hedonic capacity.

For years, test results have provided information to both the client and the counselor and have served to promote counseling interaction.

Test results can reach beyond the informational level. Giving a client feedback, such as how he or she compares with counterparts on a critical personality variable, can lead to introspection, self-assessment, and self-determined changes. For example, a youth who senses social isolation could benefit from test data that support that he or she has, in actuality, no more sense of social isolation than peers, and this awareness could allow for moving past a blockage to growth.

When clients are heavily burdened with emotional disturbance, they often have a solid defensiveness against acknowledging the severity of their problem. Again, test data that provide a comparison of their degree of, say, depression or anxiety with that of their peers could help them open up to the fact that their functioning is being impeded by emotional conditions and that these emotional conditions merit a commitment to change.

The foregoing examples involve "nomothetic" comparisons—that is, how the individual's functioning compares with the functions of groups of people (such as peers). "Idiographic" comparisons, in which the client compares one personal quality with another personal quality, can also be useful. This latter intrapersonal analysis can draw on test data in much the same way as does an interpersonal comparison.

The preceding comments specify the use of test data. The same procedures can be implemented by other types of assessment data. For example, instead of using psychological tests, a counseling psychologist could make a video recording of a group of peers engaged in a discussion of teenage dating behavior. Clients who observed that they were out of the mainstream or more socially isolated than the other teenagers could be asked to witness the videotaped interaction. Then the counseling psychologist could point out diagnostically significant behaviors (verbal or nonverbal). The counseling would proceed according to the observational analysis of the videotaped session.

In addition to using the client's self-reports (such as on psychological tests) or behaviors (such as in a videotaped interaction), the counseling psychologist can offer expert opinion. While some counseling psychologists might be alarmed with any feedback that connotes that the therapist is being judgmental (since that might tend to violate the facilitative conditions), there is reason to believe that a client can benefit from honest, well-reasoned impressions.

When therapists say in a caring fashion that they do not perceive conditions in the same way as the client and build a rationale for this discrepancy from the events and factors reported by the client, they are, in a sense, becoming a rational and logical mind for the client in an empathic manner. Therapists can also draw on their expertise to offer guidance, suggestions, recommendations, or prescriptions (and proscriptions) to the client. In both cases, clinical assessment structures therapy, and the ideal outcome is therapeutic growth for the client.

Misleading Assessment Data

Counselors must take care to avoid being misled by assessment data. To cite one example where fervor for an area of counseling research may lead to abuse of assessment data, counseling psychologists have made much ado about right-brain versus left-brain behavior. The idea is that the dominant side of the brain will determine, to a large extent, the client's functioning and behavior such as occupational preference. Robbins (1985) warns that "counselors must be careful not to use indices of cerebral specialization as generalized predictors of learnings or counseling problems with specific individuals" (p. 238). Despite extensive research (Springer & Deutsch, 1985), there is still too little known about brain-hemisphere distinctions to justify a counseling psychologist's establishing treatment from neuropsychological assessment data alone. If well-studied right-brain versus left-brain findings are inadequate for reliable and valid determination of a treatment strategy, it can almost go without saying that less-studied topics would be even more vulnerable to faulty determinations.

Being misled by assessment data can stem from blind allegiance to a psychological test. When a counseling psychologist has an apostolic zeal for a particular test, he or she is courting misuse of the test. Such abuse is often witnessed with counseling psychologists who gain expertise in a certain assessment instrument and then believe that it is virtually infallible. They illogically reason, for example, that if a major reference source, say Graham (1977), states that a certain clinical elevation on the Minnesota Multiphasic Personality Inventory (MMPI) means something and the client produces that elevation, then the resource description *must* apply *in full* to the client. Likewise, it would be illogical to assume that because research is moving forward on, say, the application of the Exner (1974) system for scoring and interpreting Rorschach inkblots, it would be acceptable to make a premature application of the research findings to clinical practice. This kind of inept reliance on clinical assessment data can be attached to any clinical assessment technique; it is certainly not limited to the MMPI and the Rorschach.

Counselors can also make the faulty assumption that when a client is placed in a given diagnostic category, there is but one treatment of choice. Again with poor reasoning, it is believed that one form of therapy is better than all other forms of therapy for a specified diagnostic grouping. There is neglect of individual differences.

While research may accumulate to support the conclusion that a client with a certain composite of assessment data would seemingly be best suited for a given intervention, there must always be a careful, idiosyncratic analysis. Counseling psychologists must maintain a constant vigil to guard against believing that every client with certain psychological characteristics is automatically a candidate for a specified treatment. Perhaps someday clinical assessment data will be precise enough that treatment can be obtained through computer matching, but today is not the day.

Assessment Methods for Counseling Psychology

As we have indicated, we make no attempt in this chapter to list all counseling tests, and neither do we try to detail what can be measured by a given test. Instead, this section offers comments about the types of clinical-assessment methods, with the emphasis on what counseling psychologists can explore to enrich the quality of their professional services.

Actuarial versus Clinical Methods

Counseling psychologists have long criticized certain clinical-assessment methods because of their inherent subjectivity. This criticism may, in part, account for the reticence of counseling psychologists to make as much use of clinical assessment as their counterparts in clinical and school psychology (although the wish to maintain the facilitative conditions, such as unconditional positive regard, is probably the primary reason).

This subjectivity came to the fore when Paul Meehl (1954) wrote a treatise on clinical versus statistical prediction. Meehl argued that psychometric data were far superior to those from other sources. Since that time some psychologists have avoided methods that are not based on an actuarial approach. The subjective, or *clinical,* approach relies on the judgments of the counseling psychologist. Unquantified observational information and opinions are used. If data are obtained by standardized tests, there is no specific formula or set of rules for reviewing and interpreting the data or for deriving conclusions and recommendations. The *actuarial,* or statistical, method emphasizes objectivity, relying on quantifiable responses and statistical comparisons. The goal is to eliminate the shortcomings of subjective judgment, such as the inconsistency of a single clinician's judgments or the lack of judgmental agreement among multiple clinicians.

The primary actuarial methods are probably the MMPI, the Sixteen Personality Factor Questionnaire (16 PF), and, more recently, the Millon Clinical Multiaxial Inventory (MCMI). Each of these instruments has extensive normative data, requires a specific type of response (such as true or false) from the client, can be objectively scored, and has a computer analysis available (which eliminates problems of interjudge reliability for the interpretation). Many other tests, of course, have incorporated these actuarially oriented principles.

The primary goal of actuarial methods is to minimize inconsistency among clinicians judging data. In other words, interjudge reliability would require two different counseling psychologists to interpret an MMPI profile in exactly the same way. Often, this does not happen. Perhaps because of different training experiences or just outright bias on the part of the counseling psychologist(s), the same test data receive varying emphases and discrepant interpretations.

Initially, this problem of interjudge reliability was counteracted by "cookbooks." That is, resource books would provide diagnostic descriptions, with the selection made according to the profile produced by the client. This approach still allowed for varying emphases.

The actuarial approach is promoted by the modern-day rush to computerization. Sampson, Shahnasarian, and Reardon (1987) describe the dramatic increase in computer assistance in counseling. In defining the relevance of the actuarial approach, Tallent (1987) writes: "Modern computer reports are based conceptually, if not totally in practice, on psychometric theory, and the conclusions they reach about the personality characteristics of the test takers are statistical (actuarial) predictions" (p. 97). Clinical assessment is particularly embraced by the current vogue for computer analysis of personality-test data.

While computerized analysis and interpretation may eliminate problems of judgmental reliability, they create the problem of lack of individuation. Also, there is a lack of standards for computerized-assessment methods (Burke & Norman, 1987). Although highly subjective, clinical-assessment processes do allow the counseling psychologist to tailor his or her judgments to the idiosyncratic features (such as unique sociocultural influences) of the client. Perhaps the solution is to blend, with as much academically based acumen as possible, the clinical and actuarial approaches. As Tallent (1987) points out: "The probabilistic statements of the computer can be used in combination with additional inputs to the assessment process" (p. 105).

Objective versus Projective Personality Methods

The foregoing discussion leads to another debate that has raged for years between psychologists—namely, the utility of objective versus projective personality methods. Applied in this dichotomy, *objective* does not refer to reliability per se:

> An objective personality test: (1) has specific stimulus items (such as ques-
> tions about the client); (2) requires the client to give a discrete response (such
> as true or false) . . . ; (3) obtains a codification (usually in writing) of the
> client's responses . . . ; (4) yields numerical measurements; and (5) has a
> standardization (such as norms to assist in the interpretation) [Woody &
> Robertson, 1988, pp. 267–268].

Projective personality methods rely on the principle of projection: what people
perceive or believe to be reality is tempered by their personality (Freud,
1911/1949). People's private world and personality processes are revealed by
their expressions, such as to a projective test (the Rorschach inkblots method
or the Thematic Apperception Test) (Frank, 1948). Lindzey (1961) provided an
often-quoted definition of a projective test:

> A projective technique is an instrument that is considered especially sen-
> sitive to covert or unconscious aspects of behavior, it permits or encourages
> a wide variety of subject responses, is highly multidimensional, and it evokes
> unusually rich or profuse response data with a minimum of subject awareness
> concerning the purpose of the test [p. 45].

In keeping with the concern about interjudge reliability, debate about objective versus projective personality methods has often focused on the skills
required of the psychologist. Graham (1977) writes: "It has been suggested that
whereas a skilled clinician is an integral part of the interpretation of projective
test protocols, objective test results can be interpreted by less skilled individuals
by reference to appropriate norms. In clinical practice, this distinction does
not exist" (p. 1). Matarazzo (1972) points out that the interpretation of both
objective and projective tests is highly subjective and requires well-trained and
experienced practitioners.

The counseling psychologist should examine the positive and negative
aspects of both objective and projective personality testing. Ethical usage of
any assessment method necessitates the practitioner's having reconciled, to some
extent, qualitative discrepancies. After all, the APA's (1981a) "Ethical Principles
of Psychologists" require: "In reporting assessment results, psychologists indicate any reservations that exist regarding validity or reliability because of the
circumstances of the assessment or the inappropriateness of the norms for the
person tested" (p. 637). Part of this mandate involves consideration of the
objective or projective nature of the method.

Professional Preference for Clinical-Assessment Methods

Historically, it has been asserted that interest and aptitude measurements are
the specific domain of counseling psychology, presumably because of the
specialty's roots in vocational guidance (Goldschmitt, Tipton, & Wiggins, 1981;
Nathan, 1977). The primary employment sites for counseling psychologists
have also created more emphasis on educationally related assessment (Tipton,
1983; Woody, 1972a). It seems likely, however, that much of the preference
relevant to clinical assessment stemmed from the counseling psychologist's
serving a normally functioning (or mildly disturbed) clientele, as opposed to

the more pathologically functioning clientele of the clinical psychologist (Tipton, 1983).

From a survey of clinical psychologists, Wade and Baker (1977) found that the foremost reason for learning to use tests was for information about personality structure and that the rank order for the six most-supported tests were (1) the Rorschach inkblot method, (2) the Thematic Apperception Test, (3) the Wechsler Adult Intelligence Scale, (4) the MMPI, (5) the Bender Visual-Motor Gestalt Test, and (6) the Wechsler Intelligence Scale for Children. They conclude: "Clinicians are probably unaffected by negative testing research because (a) there are strong needs to assess, (b) clinicians accord personal clinical experience greater weight than experimental evidence, and (c) there are few practical alternatives to tests" (p. 874).

Distinguishing between preferences of clinical psychologists and counseling psychologists, Tipton (1983) found that counseling psychologists accorded limited relevance to clinical assessment, but he thought that this decision might be due to the clientele served, as opposed to criticism or rejection of the methods. Clinical psychologists clearly supported assessment more than the counseling psychologists. Counseling psychologists did, however, give greater endorsement to interest testing.

As a follow-up to the Wade and Baker (1977) survey, Lubin, Larsen, and Matarazzo (1984) surveyed a sample of psychologists from different specialties and employment contexts; counseling psychologists, in an undetermined proportion, were included. In rank order, they found the six most frequently used tests were (1) the Wechsler Adult Intelligence Scale, (2) the MMPI, (3) the Bender Visual-Motor Gestalt Test, (4) the Rorschach inkblot method, (5) the Thematic Apperception Test, and (6) the Wechsler Intelligence Scale for Children. Two things should be noted. First, despite the passage of time, the same six tests remained most preferred. Second, despite the expanded sample of psychologists, the priority remained essentially the same.

This book repeatedly reveals how counseling psychology is moving away from its more traditional vocational-educational model. The counseling psychologist is now working with more diverse clients (in terms of pathology and counseling goals) and is employed in settings that were previously reserved for clinical psychologists. Counseling-psychology services may be made available to the criminally insane, the brain injured, and a host of other clients. For example, Lewis and Sinnett (1987) believe that it is timely for counseling psychologists to give greater emphasis to neuropsychological assessments. This diverse service framework supports the notion that counseling psychology is in transition and that one of the outcomes will be, by necessity, a greater reliance on clinical assessment by counseling psychologists in the future.

Personality assessment is especially important to counseling psychology. As evidenced by the surveys of Wade and Baker (1977) and Lubin, Larsen, and Matarazzo (1983), personality assessment already occupies a prominent place in psychological testing. Piotrowski (1985) surveyed members of the Society for Personality Assessment, of which some were counseling psychologists, and found that the following tests (with the percentage of times each was mentioned) were the most endorsed objective personality measures: the MMPI (87%), the

California Psychological Inventory (30%), the 16 PF (26%), the Edwards Personal Preference Schedule (11%), the Millon Clinical Multiaxial Inventory (10%), and the Personality Research Form (7%). For projective methods, the results were the Rorschach inkblot method (94%), the Thematic Apperception Test (91%), the Sentence Completion method (47%), the Draw-A-Person method (47%), the House-Tree-Person method (30%), the Bender Visual-Motor Gestalt Test (22%), and the Children's Apperception Test (23%).

Given the birth of projective techniques in psychoanalytic theory, it might be assumed that only psychodynamic therapists would make use of projective techniques. Or to take a different tack relevant to theory, it might be assumed that behavior therapists, with little concern about personality (as opposed to behavioral conditioning), would offer little support for personality testing at all. Piotrowski and Keller (1984) surveyed members of the Association for (the) Advancement of Behavior Therapy (AABT) and found endorsement for standard clinical-assessment methods (including projective personality methods). Granted, a substantial number (60.5%) of the AABT members thought that there would be a future decrease in projective assessments, but it seemed evident that behavior therapy did not rule out the use of clinical assessment; for example, 50% thought that objective personality assessment would increase in the future. Piotrowski and Keller posit that nonbehavioral assessment remains acceptable to behaviorists because:

> (a) Clinicians are aware of agency and third-party payment requirements. (b) Objective assessment is a means to an expeditious diagnosis of the client which at times is desirable or required. (c) Personality measures offer a way to conceptualize an individual's dynamics, traits, defenses, and cognitive strategies. (d) Objective personality instruments have gained acceptance because they have empirical and computational credibility. (e) The convenience of the recent trend toward computer scoring and interpretation has been welcomed by many clinicians despite shortcomings and criticism [p. 835].

It would seem that this five-point justification for continued endorsement of clinical assessment extends beyond advocates of behaviorism to advocates of virtually any theory of therapy.

Clinical-assessment methods can be grouped in various ways. Woody and Robertson (1988) identify seven main dimensions of clinical assessment: personal history, behavioral observations, intelligence, academic achievement, perception, neuropsychology, and personality. Under this system, certain areas of special interest to counseling psychologists, such as vocational preferences, would be classified as "personality." The evolving role of counseling psychologists certainly opens the door to use of clinical-assessment methods from each of these dimensions.

As a final point of concern, consideration should be given to self-report methods. With virtually each of the foregoing seven dimensions of clinical assessment, there is a reliance on what the client can or is willing to reveal. Many of the inventories or questionnaires used by counseling psychologists for the assessment of personality and vocational interest are self-reports.

Self-report methods are plagued by the client's potential for faking. Giving socially desirable answers is a particular problem. Social desirability is the "tendency of subjects to attribute to themselves in self-description, personality statements with socially desirable scale values and to reject those with socially undesirable scale values" (Edwards, 1957, p. vi). This means that the most prudent way of interpreting self-report data is, "The client prefers to present him-herself as being . . ." In other words, it is unwise to vest too much diagnostic power in a self-report method. This drawback contributes, no doubt, to the continued use of personal history, clinical interviewing, observational analysis, objective personality tests (especially those with lie or validity scales, like the MMPI), and projective personality tests to penetrate the client's defense system.

Summary

Contrary to popular misconception, assessment is not contradictory to the goals of counseling. In fact, any counseling approach will be complemented by astute clinical assessment. Clinical assessment involves data-based judgments for problem solving. Procedures may include behavioral observations, interviewing, and an array of psychological and educational tests. Regardless of strategy, objectivity should receive priority, and steps should be taken to safeguard against subjectivity. Diagnosis is more than "pinning a label" on a client; it is used for selecting, monitoring, and evaluating an individualized intervention plan.

References

American Psychiatric Association. (1980). *Diagnostic and Statistical Manual of Mental Disorders* (3rd ed.) Washington, DC: Author.

American Psychiatric Association. (1987). *Diagnostic and Statistical Manual of Mental Disorders* (3rd ed., revised). Washington, DC: Author.

American Psychological Association. (1981a). Ethical Principles of Psychologists. *American Psychologist, 36*, 633–638.

American Psychological Association. (1981b). Specialty Guidelines for the Delivery of Services by Counseling Psychologists. *American Psychologist, 36*, 652–663.

Arbuckle, D. S. (1965). *Counseling: Philosophy, Theory and Practice.* Boston: Allyn & Bacon.

Beller, E. K. (1962). *Clinical Process: The Assessment of Data in Childhood Personality Disorders.* New York: Free Press.

Bishop, J. B., & Richards, T. F. (1984). Counselor Theoretical Orientation as Related to Intake Judgments. *Journal of Counseling Psychology, 31*, 398–401.

Burke, M. J., & Norman, J. (1987). Computerized Psychological Testing: Overview and Critique. *Professional Psychology, 18*(1), 42–51.

Dworkin, R. H., & Saczynski, K. (1984). Individual Differences in Hedonic Capacity. *Journal of Personality Assessment, 48*, 620–626.

Edwards, A. L. (1957). *The Social Desirability Variable in Personality Assessment and Research.* New York: Dryden.

Exner, J. E., Jr. (1974). *The Rorschach: A Comprehensive System* (Vol. 1). New York: Wiley.

Frank, L. K. (1948). *Projective Methods.* Springfield, IL: Thomas.

Freud, S. (1949). Psycho-Analytic Notes upon an Autobiographical Account of a Case of Paranoia (Dementia Paranoides). In *Collected Papers* (Vol. 3). London: Hogarth Press. (Original work published 1911)

Goldman, G. (1961). *Using Tests in Counseling.* New York: Appleton-Century-Crofts.

Goldschmitt, M., Tipton, R. M., & Wiggins, R. C. (1981). Professional Identity of Counseling Psychologists. *Journal of Counseling Psychology, 28,* 158–167.

Goldstein, M. J., Baker, B. L., & Jamison, K. R. (1980). *Abnormal Psychology.* Boston: Little, Brown.

Graham, J. R. (1977). *The MMPI: A Practical Guide.* New York: Oxford University Press.

Graham, J. R. (1987). *The MMPI: A Practical Guide* (2nd ed.). New York: Oxford University Press.

Halleck, S. L. (1978). *The Treatment of Emotional Disorders.* New York: Aronson.

Hamersma, R. J. (1972). *Educational and Psychological Tests and Measurements.* Dubuque, IA: Kendall/Hunt.

Jahoda, M. (1958). *Current Concepts of Mental Health.* New York: Basic Books.

Kleinmuntz, B. (1982). *Personality and Psychological Assessment.* New York: St. Martin's Press.

Krumboltz, J. D. (1965). Behavioral Counseling: Rationale and Research. *Personnel and Guidance Journal, 44,* 383–387.

Leary, M. R., & Maddux, J. E. (1987). Progress Toward a Viable Interface Between Social and Clinical-Counseling Psychology. *American Psychologist, 42*(10), 904–911.

Lewis, L., & Sinnett, E. R. (1987). An Introduction to Neuropsychological Assessment. *Journal of Counseling and Development, 66*(3), 126–130.

Lindzey, G. (1961). *Projective Techniques and Cross-Cultural Research.* New York: Appleton-Century-Crofts.

Lubin, B., Larsen, R. M., & Matarazzo, J. D. (1984). Patterns of Psychological Test Usage in the United States: 1935–1982. *American Psychologist, 39,* 451–454.

Maloney, M. P., & Ward, M. P. (1976). *Psychological Assessment: A Conceptual Approach.* New York: Oxford University Press.

Matarazzo, J. D. (1972). *Wechsler's Measurement and Appraisal of Adult Intelligence.* Baltimore: Williams & Wilkins.

Matarazzo, J. D. (1987). There Is Only One Psychology, No Specialties, but Many Applications. *American Psychologist, 42*(10), 893–903.

Meehl, P. E. (1954). *Clinical versus Statistical Prediction: A Theoretical Analysis and a Review of the Evidence.* Minneapolis: University of Minnesota Press.

Millon, T. (1981). *Disorders of Personality. DSM-III: Axis II.* New York: Wiley.

Murray, E. J. (1956). A Content-Analysis Method for Studying Psychotherapy. *Psychological Monographs, 70*(13, Whole No. 420).

Nathan, P. E. (1977). A Clinical Psychologist Views Counseling Psychology. *Counseling Psychologist, 7,* 48–50.

Nathan, P. E., & Harris, S. L. (1983). The Diagnostic and Statistical Manual of Mental Disorders: History, Comparative Analysis, Current Status, and Appraisal. In C. E. Walker (Ed.), *The Handbook of Clinical Psychology* (Vol. 1) (pp. 303–343). Homewood, IL: Dow Jones-Irwin.

Nunnally, J. C. (1978). An Overview of Psychological Measurement. In B. B. Wolman (Ed.), *Clinical Diagnosis of Mental Disorders* (pp. 97–146). New York: Plenum.

Piotrowski, C. (1985). Clinical Assessment: Attitudes of the Society for Personality Assessment Membership. *Southern Psychologist, 2,* 80–83.

Piotrowski, C., & Keller, J. W. (1984). Attitudes Toward Clinical Assessment by Members of the AABT. *Psychological Reports, 55,* 831–838.

Ponterotto, J. G. (1987). Counseling Mexican Americans: A Multimodal Approach. *Journal of Counseling and Development, 65*(6), 308–312.

Ponterotto, J. G., & Casas, J. M. (1987). In Search of Multicultural Competence Within Counselor Education Programs. *Journal of Counseling and Development, 65*(8), 430–434.

Ramanaiah, N. V., Heerboth, J. R., & Jinkerson, D. L. (1985). Personality and Self-Actualizing Profiles of Assertive People. *Journal of Personality Assessment, 49,* 440–443.

Robbins, S. B. (1985). Left-Right Brain Research and Its Premature Generalization to the Counseling Setting. *Journal of Counseling and Development, 64,* 235–239.

Roberts, R. R., & Renzaglia, G. A. (1965). The Influence of Tape Recordings on Counseling. *Journal of Counseling Psychology, 12,* 10–16.

Rogers, C. R. (1957). The Necessary and Sufficient Conditions of Therapeutic Personality Change. *Journal of Consulting Psychology, 21,* 95–103.

Rogers, C. R. (1961). *On Becoming a Person.* Boston: Houghton Mifflin.

Rosenhan, D. L. (1975). The Contextual Nature of Psychiatric Diagnosis. *Journal of Abnormal Psychology, 84,* 462–474.

Sampson, J. P., Jr., Shahnasarian, M., & Reardon, R. C. (1987). Computer-Assisted Career Guidance: A National Perspective on the Use of DISCOVER and SIGI. *Journal of Counseling and Development, 65*(8), 416–419.

Schauble, P. G. (1980). Facilitative Conditions in Communication. In R. H. Woody (Ed.), *The Encyclopedia of Clinical Assessment* (Vol. 2) (pp. 1035–1041). San Francisco: Jossey-Bass.

Shectman, F. (1973). On Being Misinformed by Misleading Arguments. *Bulletin of the Menninger Clinic, 37,* 523–525.

Shevrin, H., & Shectman, F. (1973). The Diagnostic Process in Psychiatric Evaluations. *Bulletin of the Menninger Clinic, 37,* 451–494.

Springer, S. P., & Deutsch, G. (1985). *Left Brain, Right Brain* (rev. ed.). New York: Freeman.

Stagner, R. (1948). *Psychology of Personality.* New York: McGraw-Hill.

Sundberg, N. D. (1977). *Assessment of Persons.* Englewood Cliffs, NJ: Prentice-Hall.

Super, D. E. (1962). Transition: From Vocational Guidance to Counseling Psychology. In J. F. McGowan & L. D. Schmidt (Eds.), *Counseling: Readings in Theory and Practice* (pp. 8-26). New York: Holt, Rinehart & Winston.

Sweeney, J. A., Clarkin, J. F., & Fitzgibbon, M. L. (1987). Current Practice in Psychological Assessment. *Professional Psychology, 18*(4), 377–380.

Tallent, N. (1987). Computer-Generated Psychological Reports: A Look at the Modern Psychometric Machine. *Journal of Personality Assessment, 51*(1), 95–108.

Tipton, R. M. (1983). Clinical and Counseling Psychology: A Study of Roles and Functions. *Professional Psychology, 14,* 837–846.

Truax, C. B. (1966a). Reinforcement and Nonreinforcement in Rogerian Psychotherapy. *Journal of Abnormal Psychology, 71,* 1–9.

Truax, C. B. (1966b). Some Implications of Behavior Therapy for Psychotherapy. *Journal of Counseling Psychology, 13,* 160–170.

Truax, C. B., & Carkhuff, R. R. (1967). *Toward Effective Counseling and Psychotherapy: Training and Practice.* Chicago: Aldine.

Wade, T. C., & Baker, T. B. (1977). Opinions and Use of Psychological Tests. *American Psychologist, 32,* 874–882.

Wolman, B. B. (1978). Classification and Diagnosis of Mental Disorders. In B. B. Wolman (Ed.), *Clinical Diagnosis of Mental Disorders* (pp. 15–45). New York: Plenum.

Woody, R. H. (1972a). Clinical Assessment in Educational Facilities. In R. H. Woody & J. D. Woody (Eds.), *Clinical Assessment in Counseling and Psychotherapy* (pp. 268–312). New York: Appleton-Century-Crofts.

Woody, R. H. (1972b). The Counselor-Therapist and Clinical Assessment. In R. H. Woody & J. D. Woody (Eds.), *Clinical Assessment in Counseling and Psychotherapy* (pp. 1–29). New York: Appleton-Century-Crofts.

Woody, R. H., & Robertson, M. H. (1988). *Becoming a Clinical Psychologist.* New York: International Universities Press.

9

Consultation

During the past 20 years the development of consultation has been the major addition to the practice of a counseling psychologist. Although psychologists continue to perform traditional activities, consultation has become an increasing part of their professional role. Consultation has long been used in other professions. It generally refers to an interaction between two professionals in which one provides expertise to the other—for example, a medical specialist giving a consultation to another physician.

History of Consultation

Consultation has become an accepted role in psychology primarily as a response to human-services needs. The source of the concept is often traced to a paper by Lawrence Frank (1936) entitled "Society as the Patient." Frank wrote that many of the human problems lumped together as mental-health issues stemmed from imperfect patterns of social organization. This idea is clearly embraced today, and most mental-health professionals believe that many of their clients' problems evolve within social organizations such as the family, the school, the job, and larger societal environments.

During the 1960s the United States made a new commitment to correcting social ills, a commitment that ultimately increased the role of consultants. Social legislation focused on civil rights and services for the handicapped and disadvantaged. In the mid-'60s many of the Great Society programs of Presidents John F. Kennedy and Lyndon B. Johnson came into existence. One part of this social change was mental-health legislation that provided for community services throughout the country. The Mental Health Study Act (Public Law 84-142) led to a nationwide analysis and reevaluation of mental illness; the Joint Commission on Mental Illness and Health (1961) urged more outpatient community mental-health clinics, smaller inpatient hospitals, alternative treatment facilities, and mental-health education. The commission's message was that (1) more mental-health services were needed, (2) the services should be as mainstream as possible, (3) permitting clients to remain in the community was preferable to institutionalization, and (4) the need to prevent mental illness should be emphasized through education and consultation within the community. In 1963 Kennedy signed into law the Community Mental Health Centers Act. That act made funds available to every state to implement mental-health services at the community level. Each state was divided into "catchment areas" based on population, and federal funds were allocated for construction of facilities and hiring of staff. These programs were funded by dividing the cost among the community, state, and federal governments, with the federal share being the largest.

The Community Mental Health Centers Act required centers to provide five essential services: inpatient care, outpatient care, partial hospitalization, emergency services, and consultation and education. The community mental-health movement has had a great impact on psychology, especially in establishing new employment opportunities.

The increased demand for mental-health services was so great that consultation was used as a way of providing greater service to more people. With an insufficient number of trained professionals to staff the inpatient and outpatient centers, programs were established to prepare paraprofessionals. Psychologists consulted with other mental-health professionals and paraprofessionals who were providing direct care to the public. The model assumed that if a psychologist consulted with a teacher about a student, not only the student would profit from the new knowledge or skill of the teacher but also the other 30 students in the class. The use of a consultant with other professionals assumed that the knowledge of the consultant could be distributed through them to many other clients.

Following the heyday of the community mental-health movement came a decline in political support. Cutbacks in federal programs were made in favor of "block grants" of federal money to each state and the repeal of many federal allocations for mental health. Local communities found it necessary to pursue state funding from a federal block grant, and mental-health needs competed with other community priorities. Many community mental-health facilities have been disbanded or no longer function. But the role of the psychologist as a consultant survived.

Definition of Consultation

The psychiatrist Gerald Caplan (1970), the patriarch of mental-health consultation, defined consultation as "a process of interaction between two professional persons—the consultant, who is a specialist, and the consultee, who invokes a consultant's help in regard to a current work problem with which he is having some difficulty and which he has decided is in the other's area of specialized competence" (p. 19). MacLennan, Quinn, and Schroeder (1975) define mental-health consultation as a provision of technical assistance by an expert to individual or agency care givers. They describe it as directed to specific work-related problems and as advisory in nature. They note that consultants have no direct responsibility for the acceptance or implementation of their recommendations. They describe the consultation as being offered by a mental-health specialist to other mental-health workers with less knowledge in a specific aspect of the field or to specialists in other fields who needed assistance in the management of mental-health problems.

The definition of consultation is also influenced by its involvement with the prevention of mental illness. Parsons and Meyers (1984) identify three types of prevention. Primary prevention is focused on preventing disorders in a population, with the clientele being an entire community or a subgroup with a risk of mental-health problems. Secondary prevention focuses on problems that are beginning to emerge, with a curative goal. Tertiary prevention provides treatment for the already present symptoms of dysfunction. The connection of consultation and prevention grew from the community mental-health movement.

MacLennan and his colleagues (1975) describe how the consultation process is involved in prevention. Consultants assess an agency's need for new or modified programs. They offer advice on planning research, training, or service programs, as well as evaluating these programs. They also help others develop skills in treatment, training, research, administration, and evaluation and in preparing written and audiovisual materials.

Most people define consultation by describing what occurs in the process of consultation. According to Berger (1977), consultation is first a problem-solving process. It is not known at the initiation of consultation what changes may be needed, so the process involves a clearer definition of the problem, analysis, and development of a strategy to resolve the problem. The consultant generally does not have direct contact with the client but works instead with the consultee, who provides direct service to the client. Consultation involves a collegial relationship because the consultant has no authority over the consultee. This process between two equals differentiates consulting from a treatment situation with a superior and supervisee or from teaching, in which the expert is teaching the novice.

After a review of the literature, Lounsbury, Roisium, Pakarney, Sills, & Meissen (1979) aptly concluded that *consultation* was a term used to describe a wide variety of activities and relationships. It describes not only the relationship between two professionals working on a case but also the interaction between agencies or professionals concerned with linking resources, training, or developing new programs. Human services specialists have also modified the concept of consultation to include a relationship between a professional and parents or teachers. Consultation has been used to refer to nearly any type of meeting between professionals or agencies directed toward improving the quality of service.

Models of Consultation

The concepts and practices of consultation have not reached a sufficiently sophisticated level to be termed theories. The practice of consultation has not been systematically integrated into general formulations; therefore we talk about models of consultation rather than theories.

Schein's Models

Schein (1969) described three prevalent models of consultation.

The Purchase Model.   The most common model, according to Schein, is called the purchase model, because the consultee purchases expert knowledge or service. In this model the buyers, or consultees, define something they want to know or have done that they or their agency cannot do, so a consultant is hired. Schein points out that consultees frequently express dissatisfaction about the quality of consultation they receive. Such problems are understandable when all the variables involved in successful consultation are considered. First, consultees must have correctly diagnosed their own needs. Schein points out that consultees frequently do not know specifically what they need but know only that there is a problem. A consultant who does what is asked but does not meet the specific need of the consultee or that organization will be evaluated as ineffective. Secondly, success is dependent on the consultee's ability to correctly communicate diagnosed needs to the consultant. Again, consultants who accept at face value what is asked may not meet the actual needs of the consultee. A third requirement for success with the purchase model involves the consultee's accurately assessing the consultant's ability to provide the right service. If the consultee hires someone who does not have the specific expertise but does the job anyway, the consultation will be less effective. A fourth requirement for effectiveness in this model involves consultees' thinking through the consequences of having a consultant do the job. If they have not examined the consequences of implementing the recommendation and changes of the consultant, they may only discard the report or change what the consultant has helped devise.

The Doctor/Patient Model.   Another popular model of consultation identified by Schein is termed the doctor/patient model. This model is frequently used when an evaluation of a program is requested. The object of this model is to have the consultant determine what is wrong with a program and then recommend strategies to make the improvement. Although this model is frequently used, there are some concerns for the consultant. First, many members of the consultee's organization may be reluctant to reveal information. Individuals worried about job security may hide information, which would make a correct diagnosis difficult. On the other hand, some individuals may use the consultation interview as a gripe session and exaggerate the problems in areas of dissatisfaction. All this suggests that it may be difficult for the consultant to get an accurate picture of the consultee's system. Another difficulty involves the consultee's being unwilling to believe the diagnosis or accept the consultant's recommendation. Many reports of consultants' evaluations are merely filed away. A third difficulty with this model occurs when the consultant does the evaluation and then leaves. The consultee may have difficulty implementing the recommendations. Consultations are often considered to be ineffective only because the organization does not have the expertise to carry out the recommended plan.

The Process Model. Schein described the process model as the set of procedures most likely to lead to success. Because the consultee often does not know exactly what the problem is, the consultant needs to have the consultee involved in the diagnostic process. The cooperative diagnostic endeavor will lead not only to a clearer statement of the problem but also to a more probable acceptance of the final outcome. The consultee may also not know the kinds of help the consultant can provide, so one of the early consulting roles is to determine whether the consultant can provide the right expertise. If not, the consultant helps the consultee find the right person. This model stresses that consultees have a constructive intent to improve things and that when they are given help in identifying the problems and carrying out the recommendation, success is likely. Most consultees, whether persons or organizations, can be effective when they learn to diagnose their own strengths and weaknesses. Consultants cannot by themselves learn enough about the client system to make good recommendations; therefore they need to have a joint working relationship with the consultees, who really know the situation. Following a shared diagnosis, the consultees can be active in suggesting remedies.

The process model has two versions, the catalyst model and the facilitator model (Schein, 1978). The catalyst model is used when consultants do not know the solution but have skills in helping clients establish their own solutions. The facilitator model occurs when consultants have ideas or possible solutions but decide that a better solution or better implementation of that solution will occur if they withhold suggestions and concentrate on helping the consultee solve the problem.

The major role of the consultant is to provide new and challenging alternatives for the consultee to consider. The decision of what to do always remains with the consultee. This model puts emphasis on the consultant's being an expert in the diagnostic process and establishing working relationships with the consultee. Interpersonal skills form the major area of expertise. Even so, it seems important to have expert knowledge in the areas that need attention.

Caplan's Models

Caplan (1963) described four types of consultation in mental health, focusing on a client, a consultee, a program, or a program administrator.

Client-Centered Consulting. In the client-centered case consultation, the consultant's main emphasis is on a specific problem the consultee is encountering in a work situation with a client. The consultee may be a teacher working with a student and seeking a means of handling the immediate problem. The client then becomes the target of the consultant's attention. Assessment of the actual problematic condition is needed, and this task is done by whatever method the consultant finds useful, usually involving a discussion with the consultee and possibly the client, as well as observations and study of previous data and related information. Based on this information, strategies for working with the client are agreed on by the consultant and consultee. The actual implementation of the method is left to the consultee. Success or failure depends on the consultee, who can either accept or reject the suggestions.

Consultee-Centered Consulting.   As the name suggests, consultee-centered consultation focuses on the consultee rather than the particular client with whom the consultee is having difficulty. In working with the client certain problems may arise with the consultee that hinder the performance of work. Consultee-centered consultation would occur, for example, when the consultant found that the teacher's attitude or behavior was stimulating the student's classroom condition. The consultant helps the consultee come to a better understanding of the nature of the problem and a method of coping with it. Being outside the usual consultee/client situation, consultants bring a certain objectivity that consultees may be lacking. Through the consultation process the consultees may bring to the fore previously overlooked material, so that they can gain a better understanding of their part in the problem and develop knowledge of themselves and how to handle the problem at hand. Obviously this approach borders on counseling with the consultee, and each consultant will have to deal with that as an issue in this form of consultation.

Program-Centered Consulting.   In program-centered administrative consultation, the consultants help with current problems in the administration of programs. Their focus is on making a specialized assessment of the program and then recommending a plan of action. They usually interview staff and administration, review program goals, and examine the operational procedures. Then, after meeting with the staff administration, they make recommendations for short- and long-term development. A written report is then usually submitted.

Adminstrator-Centered Consulting.   Administrator-centered consultation is similar to program-centered consultation insofar as it looks at the administrative aspect of a particular program. The major difference is that the focus is on those persons in charge of a program, rather than the effectiveness of the program itself. Concentration may be not on one individual but on a group of administrators. The goals are to assess their performance level and, based on substantiated findings, to make recommendations on how they can function better.

Parsons' and Meyers' Models

Based on Caplan's four types, Parsons and Meyers (1984) describe four similar categories of consultation: direct service to the client, indirect service to the client, service to the consultee, and service to the system. Their service model of consultation is used as four levels on a continuum from direct to indirect service. Direct service to the client involves assessment of the client by the consultant and is considered level one because the consultant has the most direct contact with the client. Service to the larger system involves techniques in which the consultant is further removed from the client. Therefore, this service approach is labeled level four. This model is based on the principle that services should be provided in the most parsimonious manner, and it emphasizes the approach that includes the least direct client contact. The model also provides a decision tree to determine which category of service to provide. It is recommended that the consultant first determine if the organizational system accounts for the problem. If so, the consultant would work at a systems level. If this is not the problem source, the consultant would consider whether the consultee was a significant factor and, if so, provide service at that level. If it is determined that the client is the primary target for consultation, the consultant would consider having the consultee gather the data and provide this service. If necessary, the consultant would work most directly by gathering the information about the client personally in order to modify the client's behavior, attitudes, or feelings.

Hodges' and Cooper's Models

Hodges and Cooper (1983) propose three basic models of consultation: educational, individual-process, and system-process.

The *educational* model focuses the consultant's attention on solving a mental-health-related problem that is primarily due to lack of skill or knowledge. The consultant intervenes by modeling or providing information. The consultant may help the staff members develop the knowledge or assist them in gaining skills through in-service instruction.

Individual-process consultation focuses on the consultee's attitudes, motivation, intrapsychic conflicts, or personal style. The consultant's intervention is aimed at eliminating defensiveness, resolving interferences with personal goals, and facilitating personal development. This model is similar to Caplan's administrator-centered and consultee-centered models.

System-process consultants perceive a problem as related to the characteristics of the organization of the consultee. Their intervention is directed toward improving the communication processes among people and units of the organization.

Triadic Model

Tharp and Wetzel (1969) described consultation in a triadic model involving a consultant, a consultee, and a client. In their model the consultant works only with the consultee, which could be a parent, teacher, or employer, but not with a client. If the consultee is a significant person in the life situation of the client, he or she can effectively change the variables in the actual living situation, which will help the client change. Tharp and Wetzel also note that other significant people may provide reinforcement for the client and also for the consultee. The consultant's role is to provide expertise in the problem area and help the consultee work through the procedures to solve the problem. Their relationship is voluntary, temporary, and egalitarian in nature, which leaves the responsibility with the consultee. Following the consultation meeting, the consultee carries out the program with the client. It is clear that this particular triadic model is based on a social-learning theory.

Behavioral Model

Behavioral consultation comes close to qualifying as a formal theoretical approach, in that it implements learning-theory principles in the consultation process. It uses applied behavioral analyses to help the consultee understand and change the behavior of the client. It is assumed that the causes of the client's behavior are in the setting in which the behavior problem occurs. Therefore, changes in that setting can lead to new behaviors. Berger (1977) describes the steps in behavioral consultation as identifying the problem, analyzing the problem, carrying out a plan, and evaluating the program. The consultation begins by stating the problem in terms of the client's behavior, and the consultant and consultee agree on a method for obtaining baseline data on the behavior. After they analyze the problem behavior and the environmental factors, they establish specific objectives. The consultant and consultee develop a plan that will change the client's behavior. The consultee implements that plan and then evaluates the client's change in behaviors to determine if the consultation program was effective.

A Meta-Theory

Gallessich (1985) asserts that the practice of consultation is generally atheoretical and intuitive. Although several consultation models have been developed, theory and research lag far behind the practices. To overcome this problem, she proposed a consultation meta-theory to unify scattered and heterogeneous concepts by identifying their fundamental similarities and differences and to present a guide to practice, research, and training in the field of consultation.

In developing her paradigm, Gallessich identified five common elements of models of consultation: (1) the consultant's body of knowledge, (2) goals, (3) rules of the relationship between the consultant and consultee, (4) a set of processes through which the consultant works to achieve the goals, and (5) an ideology, or value system, determined by the consultant.

Following the five common parameters in previous models, Gallessich suggests three new configurations. The differences in these three approaches to consultation are found in their value systems, or ideologies.

The *scientific/technological* consultation model is based on a belief in the scientific method. Problems are seen as knowledge deficits, and the goal is to provide appropriate information. The consultant's role is to provide technological expertise, and goals are achieved by using cognitive processes in applying the knowledge and techniques.

In the *human-development* consultation model, problems are seen as the consultee's personal and professional developmental needs. There are two assumptions in this approach, each leading to different roles and procedures. In the therapeutic approach, the consultant takes responsibility for assessment and intervention to enhance the development of both the consultee and client's organization. In a collaborative approach, the consultant and consultee assess the problem and evolve solutions together. The consultant's role is primarily educational and facilitative with both approaches and involves affective and cognitive processes.

The *social/political* consultation model is involved with the ideological perspective of the consultee's work and organization. Problems are seen in terms of partisan biases, and the goal is to change organizations to make them more consistent with particular values. The role of the consultant is to assume a partisan position.

Consultation Procedures

There appears to be agreement on a set of procedures that are generally recommended for consultants. Numerous writers have described essentially the same steps, or stages, in the process. Kurpius (1978) describes nine stages in the consulting process: (1) preentry, (2) entry, (3) information gathering, (4) problem definition, (5) identifying and selecting alternative solutions, (6) stating objectives, (7) implementing the plan, (8) evaluation, and (9) termination. Schein (1969) presented a seven-stage process: (1) initial contact; (2) defining the relationship, formal contract, and psychological contract; (3) selecting a setting and method of work; (4) data gathering and diagnosis; (5) intervention; (6) reducing involvement; and (7) termination. We have consolidated these conceptualizations of the consulting process into five stages: (1) preentry, (2) initial contact and establishment of a relationship, (3) assessment and diagnosis, (4) intervention, and (5) termination.

Preentry

The preentry stage is used by the consultant before accepting a consultation. Consultants need to define their own values, needs, and assumptions about people and organizations. These values will certainly influence their practices in solving problems. Since they are in an influencing position, it is important that they be aware of their biases and not press them on the consultee. Specific training in consultation is clearly beneficial. Brown (1985) proposes modalities of training to develop specific competencies. Gibbs (1985) calls for specific training with a cross-cultural perspective. She would include didactic information about the impact of sociocultural factors in consultation, culturally appropriate intervention strategies, and placement experiences with diverse groups.

Initial Contact

The first contact is usually made by the person soliciting help for a problem. The consultant can thus usually presuppose readiness to work toward finding a solution to the problem. The success of the process will depend to a large extent on the degree of openness the consultee exhibits. In the initial discussion, the consultant will be seeking answers to two questions: Is the consultee willing to explore why situations or problems exist? More importantly, is the consultee willing to change if change is necessary? The attitude of the consultee needs to be thoroughly examined by the consultant. Beyond making a mental note, the consultant should openly discuss readiness for change with the consultees so that they are clearly aware of the part they will play in the process.

The consultant has two goals in the initial meeting: to develop a working relationship and to develop an understanding of the consultee's situation. The reason for the consultee's seeking consultation should be clearly examined and given as sharp a focus as possible. The consultee should be clear in his or her own mind what the program is and what is expected of the consultant.

This definition of roles is of extreme importance if the consultant is to function effectively. During this initial discussion, the consultant has to listen carefully to what is said and what, if any, hidden meanings are behind what is said. For example, if the consultee is asking for a program evaluation, is there an assumption that the consultant will also report on individual employee effectiveness? In other words, is the consultant evaluating the program, or will information be given about individual employees that may be used for their dismissal? Kurpius writes that the consultant needs to (1) determine what the consultee has already done to solve the problem, (2) identify the forces that may be barriers as well as aids in solving the problem, (3) identify resources that can be used in solving the problem, (4) avoid offering solutions in the initial meetings, and (5) seek relevant information and have the consultee clarify the problem areas.

After becoming aware of the consultee's purpose in securing this relationship and identifying the role he or she needs to play, consultants should step back momentarily and ask in utter honest objectivity whether they believe they can be of assistance in this situation. If the decision is affirmative, they can then move on with the process.

Most consultants concur that after the decision to enter into the relationship is made, there is a need to form some type of contract so that each participant is aware of the ground rules. Although it is not always necessary to have a written contract, it is advantageous to do so. The contract itself is based on mutual collaboration. It should specify the purpose of the consultation, role of consultant and consultee, and work setting. With the basics understood, the actual means of exploring the problem become easier, and the process tends to function more smoothly.

In the initial stage, consultants show appreciation and respect for what the consultee has provided. They should not begin with an obviously diagnostic stance but reveal themselves as appreciative visitors, acknowledging the strengths and tasks of the consultee and the organization. Consultants can make an effort to understand the long- and short-term goals of the consultee. It is important that they demonstrate that they are seeking a collegial relationship.

What pitfalls do the consultants face in this initial stage? They may be caught in an exploration of the organization's problems as a primary focus. They may get involved in the personality problems of the consultee or subtly transmit the feeling that the consultee is incompetent. They may subtly or perhaps unconsciously accept the consultee's feelings that they should assume responsibility for dealing with the problem presented. Sometimes it is as though an unspoken agreement has been entered into, and later consultants become aware that the whole problem has been dumped in their lap.

Assessment and Diagnosis

The assessment stage involves three processes: continuing development of the relationship between the consultant and the consultee, data gathering, and diagnosis. The development of a relationship is a vital element if there is to be a sense of shared responsibility for resolving target problems. In solving more complex problems involving larger numbers of people, it may be necessary for the consultant to establish a working relationship with many individuals or subgroups within an organization. Without mutual trust and confidence, little progress is made in diagnosing or intervening in the problem.

The actual process of diagnosis has to be carefully determined. The original conceptualization of the problem lies in the mind of the consultee. Blake and Mouton (1978) emphasize that the consultant focuses on the issues that affect the client's present problem, and they offer four major focal issues. The consultee's issue may be any one of the four or a combination of them. The consultant focuses attention on what he or she thinks the issue is, even though other issues may, in some way, be linked to it. The first issue involves the exercise of power and authority; the second is related to morale and cohesion; the third involves problems that arise from standards or norms of conduct; and the fourth concerns any issue in the goals or objectives area. The type of intervention used may be dictated by what the focal issue is thought to be. Therefore, it is important to determine what information is needed, where that information is located, and who will collect it and how and to analyze and synthesize the information for decision making. The methods for data collection are usually chosen by the consultant and consultee. This may be done through discussion with the consultee alone, observation of the situation, interviewing, or survey questionnaires. The essential point is that there must be some basis on which to form a diagnosis and, hence, make recommendations. It is all too easy for a consultant to intervene before enough data have been collected and explored. The result might be inappropriate recommendations or suggestions. It should be noted that misperceptions may often occur; before going further, these differences must be examined and discussed so there is a mutual understanding of the information and its significance.

The process of goal setting and planning is often a continuation of the diagnostic stage. The task involves the final clarification and definition of the problem. It is at this point that the problem statement is translated into a goal statement. This transition is actually the most important part of reaching a solution. The consultant and consultee explore the many facets of the problems, all possible sides are considered, and feasible courses of action are explored. Ideally, the consultee gains new insights so that, in the end, there is a clear course of action. In this stage the emphasis is on mutuality and a collaborative approach to the work. The goal is to facilitate exploration and insight by the consultee, so that he or she can formulate the best plan of action.

Intervention

The process of intervention includes the consultant's work with the consultee as well as the activities and procedures the consultee and client will engage in to solve the problem. There should be an appropriate deadline for each step in the problem-solving process and a statement of the criteria to be used in determining the success of the intervention.

An intervention occurs whenever the consultant helps the consultee in problem solving. Blake and Mouton (1978) outline five basic interventions: acceptance, catalysis, confrontation, prescription, and theory and principle. The consultant's *acceptance* of the consultee is used to give him or her a sense of personal security, which is necessary in establishing a working relationship. The consultee will feel free to express personal thoughts as well as specific information without concern for the consultant's judgment or rejection. The *catalytic* intervention involves the cooperative collection of information so the consultee is able to achieve a clearer statement of the problem and possible solutions. A *confrontational* intervention challenges the consultee to examine his or her present thinking or perceptions. Confrontation of the consultee's selective perception or value-laden assumptions will provide a more accurate picture of the situation. The consultant may give a *prescription* or tell the client what to do to resolve a situation. In this intervention the consultant takes responsibility for formulating a resolution and recommends the specific action. Finally, the consultant may teach *theories* or *principles* that are pertinent to the problem so the client can learn systematic and empirically tested ways of understanding the situation and rectifying it. Consultants may use one of these forms of intervention to the exclusion of others; however, most consultants use several in each consultation situation.

The final responsibility for carrying out the plan rests with the consultees. If they have had a part in its conceptualization, they will be more likely to carry it through.

Termination

Many consultation situations are terminated after the selection of an intervention, leaving the consultee to carry out the plan and evaluate it. In other situations the consultant may remain involved in the process while the consultee implements the plan, and both may participate in the evaluation. When the problem has been solved or a mode of handling the situation has been decided on, there needs to be preparation for ending the relationship. A final meeting date can be set up and a decision made about whether there will be any follow-up. The consultee often expresses some anxiety at the thought of closure, and the consultant should make it clear that he or she is always available. However, consultation is focused on the solution to a specific problem, and it should not be continued beyond the problem area. If the consultees have learned enough to approach the problem with greater effectiveness, they will be able in time to replace their sense of reliance on the consultant with a realistic increased sense of personal confidence.

What problems may be found in terminating consultation? If the consultant does not allow enough time for closure, the process may not come to a full and natural end. Consultees are then left with many problems explored but few decisions made that could help them toward more effective work. A second concern involves personal gratification. Because of personal satisfactions, the consultant or the consultees may prolong the consultation beyond the time when it is actually productive in solving problems. A different problem occurs when the consultant tends to slip into the role of a supervisor, appearing to evaluate and direct the consultees' work and to hold them accountable to the consultant for their performance (Beisser & Green, 1972).

Research on Consultation

The effectiveness of consultation in bringing about change or attaining goals has relatively little documentation. Several reviews of the research in this area report inconclusive findings at best. Mannino and Shore (1975) reviewed 35 outcome studies reported between 1958 and 1972. They concluded that in 70% of the cases some evidence of change in the consultee, client, or system was evident. Later analysis of these studies provides a less optimistic view of the evidence (Cooper & Hodges, 1983; Dustin & Blocker, 1984). The wide variety of activities described as consultation, the inadequacies of specified outcome criteria, the great variability in results, and the lack of rigorous designs make it difficult to draw conclusions from the early studies.

Medway (1979, 1982) reviewed the research done in the area of consultation during the 1970s. Of 145 articles reviewed, 34 reported empirical findings, and nearly 20 of those focused on the effectiveness of consultation. Dustin and Blocker's (1984) analysis of these reviews reports little improvement over earlier studies either in the rigor of methodology or the appropriateness of outcome criteria. They do report some improvement in the research designs of systematic case studies, intensive case studies, consultation analog designs, and consumer satisfaction surveys. Although each has its limitations, they do constitute a direction for future research. It is difficult to draw a conclusion about the effectiveness of consultation. Although previous studies report evidence of success, the lack of rigor leaves our belief up to a matter of faith. Practitioners have faith that it is effective, but it is imperative that quality research methods be applied to verify that belief.

Summary

The role of consultant has become a part of a psychologist's position as an outgrowth of the community mental-health movement. Consultation is pragmatic but not based on specific theories. Instead, several models of practice have been developed to guide the consultant in helping an individual or organization assess a problem and then in offering ideas to resolve the situation. All models place some reliance on the consultant's having an area of expertise, either in assessment, the specific problem area, or human relations. Among the more prominent models are the purchase model; the doctor/patient model; the process model; models focusing on the client, the consultee, the program, or the program administrator; the behavioral model; and Gallessich's meta-theory.

Although each model has assumptions that would suggest some variability in methods, most writers describe similar stages in the process. The five most common stages are preentry, initial contact, assessment and diagnosis, intervention, and termination. The practice of consultation has progressed more rapidly than either process or outcome research. As a result, the practice remains atheoretical and tends to follow descriptive models.

References

Beisser, A., & Green, R. (1972). *Mental Health Consultation and Education.* Palo Alto, CA: National Press Books.

Berger, J. (1977). *Behavioral Consultation.* Columbus, OH: Merrill.

Blake, R., & Mouton, J. (1978). Toward a General Theory of Consultation. *Personnel and Guidance Journal, 56,* 328–330.

Brown, D. (1985). The Preservice Training and Supervision of Consultants. *The Counseling Psychologist, 13,* 410–473.

Caplan, G. (1963). Types of Mental Health Consultation. *American Journal of Orthopsychiatry, 33,* 470–481.

Caplan, G. (1970). *The Theory and Practice of Mental Health Consultation.* New York: Basic Books.

Cooper, S., & Hodges, W. (1983). *The Mental Health Consultation Field.* New York: Human Sciences Press.

Dustin, D., & Blocker, D. (1984). Theories and Models of Consultation. In S. Brown & R. Lent (Eds.), *Handbook of Counseling Psychology.* New York: Wiley.

Frank, L. (1936). Society as the Patient. *American Journal of Sociology, 42,* 335–344.

Gallessich, J. (1985). Toward a Meta-Theory of Consultation. *The Counseling Psychologist, 13,* 336–362.

Gibbs, J. (1985). Can We Continue to Be Color-Blind and Class-Bound? *The Counseling Psychologist, 13,* 426–435.

Hodges, W., & Cooper, S. (1983). Models of Consultation. In S. Cooper & W. Hodges (Eds.), *The Mental Health Consultation Field* (pp. 29–38). New York: Human Sciences Press.

Joint Commission on Mental Illness and Health. (1961). *Action for Mental Health.* New York: Basic Books.

Kurpius, D. (1978). Consultation Theory and Process: An Integrated Model. *Personnel and Guidance Journal, 56,* 335–338.

Lounsbury, J., Roisium, K., Pakarney, L., Sills, A., & Meissen, G. (1979). An Analysis of Topic Areas and Topic Trends in the *Community Mental Health Journal* from 1965 Through 1977. *Community Mental Health Journal, 15,* 267–276.

MacLennan, B., Quinn, R., & Schroeder, D. (1975). The Scope of Community Mental Health Consultation. In F. Mannino, B. MacLennan, & M. Shore (Eds.), *The Practice of Mental Health Consultation* (DHEW Publication No. ADM 74-112) (pp. 3–24). Washington, DC: U.S. Government Printing Office.

Mannino, F., & Shore, M. (1975). The Effects of Consultation: A Review of Empirical Studies. *American Journal of Community Psychology, 3,* 1–21.

Medway, F. (1979). How Effective Is School Consultation?: A Review of Recent Research. *Journal of School Psychology, 17,* 275–282.

Medway, F. (1982). School Consultation Research: Past Trends and Future Directions. *Professional Psychology, 13,* 422–443.

Parsons, R., & Meyers, J. (1984). *Developing Consultation Skills.* San Francisco: Jossey-Bass.

Schein, E. (1969). *Process Consultation: Its Role in Organization Development.* Reading, MA: Addison-Wesley.

Schein, E. (1978). The Role of the Consultant: Content Expert or Process Facilitator? *Personnel and Guidance Journal, 56,* 339–343.

Tharp, R., & Wetzel, R. (1969). *Behavioral Modification in the Natural Environment.* New York: Academic Press.

10

Forensic Psychology

American society is in a litigious era. Lawsuits can be filed for an ever-expanding number of reasons. As we point out in Chapter 12 and elsewhere (Woody, 1988a, 1988b), this increase in litigation includes an escalation of legal actions against mental-health professionals (for a discussion of the increased liability for counselors, see Thiers, 1987). Legal actions are intended to be in the best interests of justice, but some critics believe that the rash of suits has led to unjust rewards. In fact, the right to legal action and the damages awarded are products of public policy: U.S. society is gravely concerned about safeguarding the rights of all individuals, and the judicial system is the source of protection.

Counseling psychologists have a mandate to be involved in the judicial system; that is, the legal system is seeking unprecedented involvement from "experts." In the courtroom there are legal facts that can be defined, understood, and weighed by the judge or jury only through academically or experientially based testimony. Experts are relied on to offer the benefit of their special knowledge and skills.

At one point expert testimony was essentially restricted to physicians. This was particularly the case when physical injury and mental condition were at issue. In 1908 there was a turning point for involvement of nonphysicians in legal cases. In *Muller v. Oregon* (1908), Supreme Court Justice Louis D. Brandeis acknowledged the usefulness of research-based information for determining legal issues (which led to the so-called "Brandeis Brief," a research-oriented legal brief).

Over the years courts have come to recognize that many types of professionals (with academic training) or even nonprofessionals (with relevant experiences) can provide testimony. While a state statute may specify limits on expert testimony, the general view is that

> if scientific, technical, or other specialized knowledge will assist the trier of fact in understanding the evidence or in determining a fact in issue, a witness qualified as an expert by knowledge, skill, experience, training, or education may testify about it in the form of an opinion; however, the opinion is admissible only if it can be applied to evidence at trial [Florida Statutes, 1985b, p. 367].

Today, courts are generally open to virtually any psychologist's involvement in a legal matter.

We do not mean that the sole or even primary function of a counseling psychologist in a legal case is giving expert testimony. In fact, there are many and diverse functions for the forensic counseling psychologist. The American Board of Forensic Psychology (1981) indicates that forensic psychology includes, but is not limited to, the following functions:

A. Consultation
   1. providing consultation and training to attorneys, law students, and paralegals
   2. providing consultation to lawmakers
   3. providing service to the judiciary as *amicus curiae* and in related capacities
   4. providing consultation to criminal justice and correctional systems
   5. providing consultation to mental health systems and practitioners on forensic issues
   6. providing consultation and training to law enforcement personnel

B. Diagnosis, treatment, and recommendations
   7. diagnosing, prognosticating, and treating criminal and juvenile justice populations, at all stages of the justice process
   8. diagnosing, treating, and/or making recommendations including, but not limited to, mental status, children's interests, test validity, litigation, testamentary capacity, and incapacities related to tort liability
   9. analysis of problems and/or making recommendations pertaining to human performance, product liability, mental health, and safety in matters involving, but not limited to, effects of ingested substances; ambient environment; design, layout, and operation of artifacts and man/machine systems; and organizational variables
   10. serving as expert witness in civil, criminal, and administrative law cases
   11. screening, evaluating, and/or treating law enforcement and other criminal justice personnel

C. Other functions
   12. serving as a special master in administrative and judicial tribunals
   13. conducting behavioral science research and analysis pertaining to the understanding of legal issues and to the development and evaluation of legal processes, statutes, and regulations
   14. engaging in policy and program development in the psychology-law arena
   15. teaching, training, and supervising others in forensic psychology

These 15 functions offer a vast array of opportunities for counseling psychologists. Each one can be dissected to reveal many day-to-day services.

Because of forensic psychology's relatively recent inclusion in the legal system, its quality continues to be questioned:

The quality of psychologists' forensic assessments should be of some concern to all psychologists who have an interest in psychology's social image and its impact on society, because (a) the legal system has an enormous impact on human lives, (b) a very large number of forensic clinical psychologists provide assessments to courts for use in their legal decisions about citizens in a wide variety of circumstances, and (c) these practitioners may represent psychology's greatest influence on the legal process [Grisso, 1987, p. 832].

As a psychological specialty, counseling psychology must be an influential component of forensic mental-health services.

Entering the Legal System

The legal system has conditions that are quite different from those that most counseling psychologists have experienced. It gives priority to society's interest and welfare. An individual's rights, as established by the U.S. Constitution, are certainly protected and ever-present, but public policy—as set forth in statutory laws (federal, state, or local) and case laws (as derived from judgments in specific cases)—supersedes catering to individual needs (as would be the situation in counseling).

The Adversarial Arena: Rules and Procedures

Mental-health and educational services are developmental in nature; legal services are adversarial in nature. Whether it is the state versus an alleged criminal or a husband versus a wife in a divorce matter, two parties are locked in combat to prove that one party should be accorded approval over the other.

The "combat" is accomplished by specific rules, known as the "rules of evidence." They are enforced according to highly restrictive procedures of criminal or civil law. This means, for example, that a counseling psychologist usually cannot determine what he or she will say in a legal proceeding. The rules or procedures prescribe and proscribe what is allowed.

The wresting away of the control of communication offends the sensibilities of some counseling psychologists. After all, it is reasoned, "if I am a professional, I can best determine what will express the full and accurate story." The court may allow this sort of professionally determined information flow. More often than not, however, the flow of professional information is impeded by the rules and procedures.

When counseling psychologists provide testimony they must address the legal issues, and they must rely on facts. They may offer opinions and make inferences, but there has to be a knowledge base. They may respond to hypothetical questions (at least in some jurisdictions), but only if they have specialized training to justify an answer that deserves to be admissible as evidence.

Expert testimony must be "so distinctively related to some science, profession, business, or occupation as to be beyond the ken of the average layman"

(Cleary, 1972, p. 9). Sometimes the professional view goes beyond what has, in fact, been accepted by the profession; and such a view, even if firmly held by the expert, will be deemed inadmissible. For example, a psychiatrist attempted to give expert testimony that asserted that an alleged criminal did not have the psychological traits of a rapist. The court ruled that the testimony was inadmissible because the psychiatrist could not show that the scientific community generally accepted identifiable character traits to be common to rapists or that psychiatrists had a special ability to determine that an individual was *likely* to be a rapist (*State v. Cavallo,* 1985).

It may seem that the adversarial nature of the courtroom is counter to the nature of counseling. To the contrary, Dorn (1984) contends that giving testimony in a legal proceeding is "the essence of counselor advocacy" (p. 120). Of course, the advocacy of a client may be defused by other considerations. For example, the verve of advocacy might foster a tendency to go beyond the bounds of established scientific thought (as in the previously mentioned *Cavallo* case). When this happens, it is unethical to maintain that the testimony is "expert." In fact, it is "personal," and apostolic zeal must not be allowed to draw from professional stature.

The forensic expert must deal with the matter of allegiance. Consider the situation of a counseling psychologist's being employed by the father in a child-custody dispute. Due to the commitment to advocacy, the inclination might be to accentuate the positive and to eliminate the negative about the father. It might be reasoned that "after all, he is paying the bills." To be a forensic expert, the overriding commitment must be to public policy. In a child-custody case, for example, there can be no absolute allegiance to the client "paying the bills"; the expert testimony must be committed to honesty, justice, and the *best interests of the children.* The point is simply that client advocacy is consonant with counseling, as Dorn notes, but in legal cases the definition of advocacy is more complex than in counseling.

The Relationship Between the Counseling Psychologist and the Attorney

The counseling psychologist and the attorney sometimes make for the proverbial strange bedfellows. The most honest and well-meaning attorney will logically want to extract the maximum advocacy for the client that the counseling psychologist will allow. Often the counseling psychologist will have to tactfully, but firmly, set the limits for the relationship.

It is common to encounter situations in which the mental-health needs of the client would be best accommodated by a legal outcome other than the one the attorney is pursuing. For example, some parents will seek custody of a child not because it is in the best interests of the child or because they will be in a good mental state, but to inflict punishment on the divorcing spouse. Even though the counseling psychologist may recognize the negative psychological effects that the parent/client is likely to suffer if awarded custody, the task is to advocate that client's preference. This situation becomes compounded further when that parent does, in fact, seem the more capable of meeting the best interests of the child, albeit that he or she will personally suffer.

The foregoing dilemma may lead to the counseling psychologist's informing the attorney about what the client's mental status will be as the result of a particular legal outcome and how the attorney can help the client make adjustments. Often the counseling psychologist and the attorney counsel the client together (Sutton, Seibel, & Redfield, 1985).

The counseling psychologist must constantly be aware that a legal case is always under the control of the attorney. If it were a mental-health case, it would be otherwise; but when the counseling psychologist is recruited into a legal case, the care of the client (read: the legal interest of the client) always remains for the attorney to dictate.

To avoid a conflict with the attorney, the counseling psychologist should never enter a case with a predetermined opinion about what will or will not be offered as expert testimony. Rather, the attorney should specify the legal issues and how psychological testimony could be used. In turn, the counseling psychologist should specify what would be the most appropriate options for garnering the psychological data to contribute to the legal issues, with the provision that it will be after the data-collection phase that specific services or statements are set forth:

> There must be acceptance for the approach that would involve: (1) the psychologist conducts the assessment; (2) the psychologist tells the attorney what can and cannot be said; and (3) if the attorney believes it is not in the best interest of the client to have the testimony, the psychologist should bow out of the case with no hard feelings [Woody, 1983b, p. 1424].

The foregoing, obviously, applies to legal cases that are aligned with clinically oriented services, as opposed, say, to consulting with an attorney about other nonclinical issues—for example, selecting a jury according to psychological characteristics. Another exception would be when the counseling psychologist is appointed by the court. In that instance other rules apply, and the counseling psychologist has the court as a client.

A problem exists when the counseling psychologist has information that would seemingly be in the best interest of justice (and perhaps of the client as well), yet the attorney does not want it to be provided to the court. For example an attorney might prefer that the testimony be avoided for the purpose of legal strategy in order to win the case. The counseling psychologist is bound by ethics to preserve the client's right to confidentiality and, quite possibly, by law to preserve the client's right to privileged communication. Yet the counseling psychologist believes that the court should have access to the information. There is no simple answer, but there are two exceptions that should be considered:

> (1) if the psychologist legitimately assesses that the party in question poses a significant threat of violence and dangerousness to self or others, it could be appropriate to warn the relevant persons (thereby opening the door to being called into court regardless of an attorney's preferences); and (2) if the psychologist senses that the best interests and welfare of a child will

be endangered unless he/she offers professional information (such as about admitted child abuse), it could be appropriate to notify the authorities (again making it likely that his/her testimony would be solicited despite objections from one of the attorneys) [Woody, 1983b, pp. 1424–1425].

In almost every instance of this nature, the counseling psychologist can expect the attorney to be responsive to a straightforward explanation of the position a psychologist should assume. Generally, the attorney, relying on his or her legal acumen, will want and be able to accommodate what the counseling psychologist believes *should* be presented to the court. It is the rare attorney who doggedly pursues advocacy for a client that will lead to a disservice to justice or to harm to another person. Overall, the legal profession is prepared to honor both the individual's legal rights and public policy.

Courtroom Behavior

As reflected in earlier comments, the counseling psychologist is an invitee to the legal system. Being a guest, he or she must approach the courtroom recognizing that entry is under the control of the legal system, with the judge as gatekeeper. No courtroom behavior can be according to individual preference. The "guests," such as the counseling psychologist, sit in a designated place, they rise as the judge enters and leaves, and they remain silent unless spoken to: any response must be to the question, and no questions can be asked by the counseling psychologist.

All aspects of the legal proceeding are under the control of the court. Personal appearance and mannerisms must conform to the expectations of the court. Court rules may test the limits for some busy counseling psychologists. For example, when an appearance is scheduled by the court, it is common for the counseling psychologist to have to show deference. That is, while most courts will try to accommodate everyone's schedule as much as possible, when the chips are down and the schedule is set, the forensic expert must adhere to it. Often there will be frustrations.

In one child-custody case, the judge instructed the attorneys to have the pediatrician, social worker, and counseling psychologist in the courtroom for the entire day. Each professional cleared his or her schedule. Upon arriving in court, the judge noted a bit of information that had not previously come to his attention, and he promptly continued the case until a later date. This left all three professionals without income for the day.

Theoretically, the parties (the parents in the preceding case) should be responsible for the experts' lost income, but many clients can ill afford such a financial burden; and many judges would, in fact, frown on efforts to charge the parties under these circumstances. While this example may be an exception and a bit extreme, it is very common to be scheduled to appear in court at a certain time and then to have to wait far beyond the designated hour.

Once in court the professional, counseling psychologist or otherwise, does not receive unlimited acceptance. Indeed, the opposing counsel (the attorney whose client seems to be benefiting the least from the testimony) is obliged to "impeach" the testimony of the expert. This is accomplished by, frankly, trying to make the expert look bad.

Impeachment is accomplished in several ways. Qualifications are picked apart. Tactics are used to get the professional to make contradicting, confusing, or erroneous comments. Statements may be made during the cross-examination that are designed to provoke inappropriate emotional responses (such as defensiveness, anger, uncertainty, and so on) from the professional.

Notwithstanding their professional training, many psychologists have been known to defeat their attempted contribution by responding ineptly or inappropriately during cross-examination. Of course, the other attorney (whose client stands to benefit the most from the testimony) can attempt to "rehabilitate" the testimony of the counseling psychologist, but the dread foot-in-mouth disease with which the counseling psychologist has been infected by the opposing counsel has long-lasting debilitating effects.

Of pragmatic concern, the disruptions to schedules and the less-than-friendly demands placed on the expert during cross-examination lead many professionals to charge more for involvement in legal cases than for other kinds of cases. Further, it is certainly wise to have a written agreement that spells out the service and financial arrangements. It is also a good idea to require payment in advance; a client's motivation to pay for professional services can dissipate rapidly when the legal pressure is over. Counseling psychologists seem reluctant to be firm about financial matters. This tendency is unwise and unnecessary:

> There should be a reasonable estimate of time made at the onset and a payment arrangement formalized. The nature of legal decisions often means dissatisfaction by the loser, and even though the psychologist gave high-quality service, there may be less willingness to pay after the legal proceedings than there was before they got underway. As attorneys routinely do, the psychologist would be well advised to require an up-front retainer for the majority or total amount of time estimated for the case [Woody, 1983b, p. 1425].

If there is a problem with collecting one's fee, the counseling psychologist should have no hesitation in asking the court for an order of payment or implementing other collection methods.

Being Prepared

The Boy Scout motto "Be prepared" could have been written for counseling psychologists who appear in the courtroom. With the exception, perhaps, of computing a statistical formula, there is probably no other psychological function that requires as much precision and exactitude as providing psychological expertise in legal cases.

Failure to be adequately prepared can result in denigration of professional stature. The counseling psychologist's testimony may be given little or no weight in the legal determination. Or if the counseling psychologist performs with gross incompetency, there may be the basis for a malpractice action by a dissatisfied client.

Consider the following example. In one child-custody case, the psychologist was giving testimony about a mother's personality characteristics. Upon cross-examination, the opposing counsel asked the basis for the professional opinion. The psychologist acknowledged that he was relying heavily on the Minnesota Multiphasic Personality Inventory (MMPI). The opposing counsel (having had another psychologist review the test data for errors or weak points) asked about the importance of the validity scales. The psychologist said that the clinical interpretation was, by necessity, predicated on the three validity scales. When asked to read the three scores, the psychologist, with great chagrin and embarrassment, realized for the first time and for some unknown reason that the K Scale had not been scored. The opposing counsel then asked if he was "familiar with a text titled *The MMPI: A Practical Guide* by John R. Graham, Ph.D.," and would he "consider it an authoritative scientific treatise on the MMPI?" The psychologist answered yes to both parts of the question. The opposing counsel then read that, according to Graham (1977), "the K scale was developed as a more subtle and more effective index of attempts by the examinee to deny psychopathology and to present himself in a favorable light or, conversely, to exaggerate psychopathology and to try to appear in a very unfavorable light" (pp. 22–23). He asked the psychologist, "Would not that be highly valuable, perhaps even essential, data for you to have to make your assessment of Ms. X's personality characteristics?" From there on out, the psychologist became defensive and basically defeated himself.

Similar impeachable performances by psychologists have been witnessed in a variety of courtroom situations. Recounting a few of these situations will help clarify the qualitative problems faced by the forensic counseling psychologist.

In one case testimony was given about data from certain tests, but the psychologist had to admit never having received formal training in the tests. In another case the psychologist cited credentials as qualifications for expertise, but it was revealed that the "certification" had involved only making application and paying a fee; that is, there was no examination (caveat: beware of vanity credentials—they do more harm than good!).

Errors in judgment are not confined to inexperienced psychologists. One "Diplomate" presented records to the court revealing that only a few of the Wechsler subtests had been given, and the opposing attorney was prepared with the research that contradicted the reliability and validity of short-form Wechsler testing. The protocol for the Rorschach inkblot method was not scored and was, therefore, of dubious reliability and validity. Cards for the Thematic Apperception Test were randomly selected and were, thus, interpreted without even the most tenuous of standardized frameworks. Again, doubt was cast on the reliability and validity of the opinion.

Sometimes the fault is more with the service-delivery system than with the professional per se. In one case it was revealed that the psychologist had had an assistant administer the tests, and both the client and the psychologist admitted that they had never had a face-to-face meeting. As might be expected, this lessened the weight attributed to the testimony.

Often the problem is brought about by failure to do one's "homework" in preparation for the courtroom appearance. One psychologist could not define certain psychological terms used in the testimony. In another case, the psychologist's diagnosis of a client did not conform to the criteria of the American Psychiatric Association's (1980) *Diagnostic and Statistical Manual of Mental Disorders,* even though the psychologist said it had been relied on in choosing the diagnosis. One senior psychologist made an ethical assertion during testimony and was impeached by an attorney who knew that the ethical principles had been changed since the set to which the psychologist referred. In numerous cases psychologists have been unable to effectively explain their approaches to counseling or to justify their interventions by research or academically based reasoning.

The foregoing are but a few of the faux pas that have been witnessed. The message is simple. Forensic applications of counseling psychology require adherence to an academically based standard of care, meticulous practice, and scholarly preparation. Nothing can be taken for granted. There must be a professional basis for all services.

Effective Testimony

Obviously the most effective testimony is honest and scholarly testimony. Professional opinions are buttressed when they are objective and based on psychological data, and they should have a clear-cut academic rationale.

Persuasion is the goal. Testimony will be most persuasive when it is vivid—that is, interesting emotionally, concrete, image provoking, and proximate in a sensory, temporal, or spatial manner (Nisbett & Ross, 1980). Bell and Loftus (1985) point out that vividness receives more weight in judgments: "Relative to pallid information, vivid information presented at trials may garner more attention, recruit more additional information from memory, be perceived as having a more credible source, and have a greater affective impact" (p. 663).

The foregoing academic view must be tempered by the harsh reality of the legal proceedings. While a certain homage to persuasion is appropriate, it must be recognized that juries and judges are not psychologists, and what would be persuasive content to psychologists might not be persuasive to the laypersons on a jury or even a judge (albeit that he or she, in this day and age, is likely to have a reasonable understanding of psychology). It is best to (1) keep testimony in simple, everyday terms; (2) strive for objectivity; (3) explain all statements; and (4) avoid pretentious behavior or language. The legal determination is made by the judge or jury (depending on the nature of the case), not the psychologist.

In the remainder of this chapter, we shall focus on the major legal areas in which the counseling psychologist can participate. In no way do these areas constitute an exhaustive list of entry points, but they do exemplify the more important avenues for input to the judicial system.

Criminal Justice

For a crime to exist, there must be at least three prerequisites. First, a legislative definition must make the act criminal. Such definitions can vary from time to time, as dictated by public policy. Second, the accused person must commit the necessary act, known as the *actus reus* (or wrongful act), that has been proscribed by law. Third, the accused person must have a culpable state of mind, known as the *mens rea* (or guilty mind), at the time that the criminal act was committed (Porter, 1984a).

Criminal laws are a reflection of public morality and represent an effort to construct an orderly and safe society. Those members of society who are accused of violating a criminal law are subjected to a trial by peers. Roche (1958) provides a psychiatric description of the criminal trial:

> The criminal trial is an operation having a religious meaning essential as a public exercise in which the prevailing moral ideals are dramatized and reaffirmed. The religious meaning is the adjusting of tensional moral conflict within the law-abiding. The conflict is materialized in the actions of the criminal and dissipated in the ritual of guilt fastening, condemnation, and punishment. The ritual is the homologue of the child-parent interaction containing the same motivational mechanisms and rationalizations. In this view, the criminal trial has the function of the public edification rather than that of welfare of the individual wrong-doers who pass over its stage in an endless process. In fixed formula and procedure, the trial reiterates the moral parables of our child-rearing and, in the person of the judge, brings to the transgressor a power and punitive enforcement once exercised by the parent. Both judge and parent act as agents of an order defined by the prevailing ethical system [p. 245].

The emphases in this definition are satisfying the public and continuing the parent/child relationship through laws.

When an accused person is convicted of a crime, the result is usually punishment. Slovenko (1973) writes:

> Seething passions are unleashed by a wrong, be it real or fancied, and some means are needed to channel and control them. The law, of course, is one of the major institutions designed by man to control his impulses. There is a compelling need for the imposition of punishment, either when there is a strong reason to believe that the behavior in question can be deterred or when noncompliance with a particular norm is generally felt to be so serious that doing nothing will be unacceptable in individuals or groups in the society [p. 13].

Society uses punitive enforcement for various objectives, such as retribution, general deterrence (keeping others from doing what was done by the convicted person), specific deterrence (teaching the convicted person a lesson so that he or she will never commit a crime again), and rehabilitation.

Since there are mixed motives for punishment, counseling psychologists, because of their professional philosophy, may experience a conflict with the societal decision. For example, a man with a law-abiding record was arrested for being a member of a religious paramilitary group that had killed one of its members and stolen thousands of dollars worth of property to finance its operations "in the name of the Lord and democracy." When the members were arrested, this man offered to plead *nolo contendere* (meaning he would not contest the criminal allegations) and would cooperate with the prosecution as a witness against the other alleged criminals. In the ensuing months he made good his promise. He single-handedly helped the law-enforcement officers recover well over $100,000 worth of stolen goods, and he testified for the state in several trials to help obtain the convictions of persons who were much more central to the criminal activity. He was evaluated by a counseling psychologist, who drew up a presentencing report that concluded that the man was not dangerous or violent (based on his psychological test data and his personal history), that he could be self-supporting (he had held the same job for 12 years before getting involved with the group), and that he would not benefit from (nor did he need) incarceration. A rehabilitation plan was set forth to the court. Notwithstanding the psychologist's report and testimony at the sentencing hearing (as well as the man's total cooperation with the legal authorities), the judge proceeded to impose the maximum penalty, which included several decades of imprisonment and hard labor and a large fine, and no provision was made for rehabilitation.

In this era there is a philosophical conflict between the mental-health professions and society. From the vantage point of a counseling psychologist, rehabilitation is logical. From the vantage point of society (through its judges), retribution and deterrence are often more logical than rehabilitation. The counseling psychologist might reason, "Let's see, it costs $90 a day to house a prisoner, that's $32,850 per year, and it only costs $90 a week for outpatient psychotherapy, that's $4,680. Surely a saving of $28,170 per year and the humanitarian commitment to rehabilitation will justify alternatives to prison." Not necessarily! Society might reason, "If we don't teach them a lesson, crime will become an epidemic. Stiff sentences and capital punishment, that's what we need."

The Insanity Defense

Some alleged criminals will wish to defend themselves by contending that they did not possess the *mens rea* at the time of the act and that, therefore, they are not guilty. Most commonly, this is thought of as the "insanity defense." The actual definition of *insanity* for legal-defense purposes is set forth in each state's criminal code. Essentially there are two definitions for insanity that come into play. Each deserves detailed consideration.

The first definition is the so-called *M'Naghten rule*. This rule was named after Daniel M'Naghten, who tried to kill the prime minister of England in 1843 but shot and killed his secretary. M'Naghten defended his murderous action by arguing that he had had delusions that overpowered his sense of right and wrong. Under this rule, the accused person must have labored under a defect of reason, from "disease of the mind," to the point that he or she did not know the nature and quality of the act done or, if he or she did know the nature of the act, was unable know that it was wrong (Spring, 1979).

The second definition comes from a prototype scholarly position on criminal law. Specifically, the American Law Institute created the Model Penal Code, whose Section 4.01 states:

(1) A person is not responsible for criminal conduct if at the time of such conduct as a result of mental disease or defect he lacks substantial capacity either to appreciate the criminality (wrongfulness) of his conduct or to conform his conduct to the requirements of law. (2) As used in this Article, the terms "mental disease or defect" do not include an abnormality manifested only by repeated criminal or otherwise antisocial conduct. [pp. 490–491].

The foregoing "incorporates a so-called volitional approach to insanity, thus adding as an independent criterion for insanity the defendant's ability (or inability) to control his actions" (American Psychiatric Association, 1983, p. 682).

As mentioned, the insanity defense is defined by statutory law for each jurisdiction. While the two foregoing definitions are prominent, each state legislature adopts a definition to meet its unique public policy priorities.

Expert testimony, such as from a counseling psychologist, is used to prove the existence of *mens rea,* or sanity, at the time of the crime. Stated differently, it must be established that the alleged criminal was not insane at the time he or she committed the wrongful act.

Just as crime is created and defined by society, so too are the defenses created and defined by society. There have long been reservations about the insanity defense, and its successful use by John Hinckley after he shot President Ronald Reagan and three others led to a public outcry against it. State legislatures began considering alternatives, such as "(1) abolishing the insanity defense altogether; (2) defining the term 'insanity' more strictly; (3) shifting the burden of proving insanity to the defense; (4) creating a new verdict of guilty but mentally ill" (Porter, 1984a, p. 48). Each of these options has been tried in one way or another.

The notion of "guilty but mentally ill" struck a responsive chord for many moderates on the issue. This verdict would allow finding the defendant guilty of the crime, providing him or her with treatment for the mental illness, and reserving the right of the court to impose further punishment for the criminal act after a "cure." The American Psychiatric Association (1983) cautions:

> The "guilty but mentally ill" approach may become the easy way out. Juries may avoid grappling with the difficult moral issues inherent in adjudicating guilt or innocence, jurors instead settling conveniently on "guilty but mentally ill." The deliberations of jurors in deciding cases are, however, vital to set societal standards and to give meaning to societal ideas about responsibility and nonresponsibility. An important symbolic function of the criminal law is lost through the "guilty but mentally ill" approach [p. 684].

Such an adjudication would also require treatment being available, and history has revealed that treatment in correctional facilities had often been less than effective, not to mention the present reluctance in society to fund mental-health treatment services.

Competency and Waiver of Rights

A criminal trial cannot be held unless the alleged criminal is competent at the time of the proceedings. According to Schwitzgebel and Schwitzgebel (1980), three criteria must be established: "(1) the accused's ability to cooperate with an attorney in the preparation of his defense, (2) his awareness and understanding of the nature and object of the proceedings, and (3) his understanding of the consequences of the proceedings" (p. 64).

Similar to competency to stand trial, an accused person must have an understanding of his or her *Miranda* rights—that is, rights at the time of detainment and when making a statement. In New York they include:

a. You have the right to remain silent and refuse to answer questions.
b. Anything you do say may be used against you in a court of law.
c. You have the right to consult an attorney before speaking to the police, and to have an attorney present during any questioning now or in the future.
d. If you cannot afford an attorney, one will be provided for you without cost.
e. If you do not have an attorney available, you have the right to remain silent until you have an opportunity to consult one.
f. Now that I have advised you of your rights, are you willing to answer questions without an attorney present? [Stricker, 1985, p. 656].

Stricker believes that a psychological assessment is needed to ascertain whether an offender's waiver of rights was both competent and voluntary. With adult defendants, this would involve assessment of cognitive capacity and motivational state. While intelligence is usually rather stable, the passage of time from the waiver of rights until the time of the assessment makes estimation of the motivational state difficult. Stricker asserts that expert testimony "will turn on the specific ability to comprehend the letter of the rights, rather than the abstract concept of rights" (p. 658).

The Counseling Psychologist's Roles

Counseling psychologists can provide important services to criminal cases. Among other things, they can assess an alleged criminal for *mens rea,* such as for the insanity defense, or for competency to stand trial. They can provide testimony about these two states of mind. The stress of the legal proceedings could justify the provision of counseling to the alleged criminal (and his or her family). If the defendant is found guilty, the counseling psychologist could contribute information to the presentencing investigation and could subsequently provide follow-up treatment. Counseling psychologists should also attempt to constructively influence public policy. Among many efforts, they have assisted in developing position statements on and legislation for the insanity defense, treatment facilities for offenders, and probation/parole/rehabilitation planning.

The enactment of U. S. Public Law 98-473, the Comprehensive Crime Control Act of 1984, has thrust psychologists into an unsurpassed role: "A review of the new provisions of the federal criminal justice code [18 U.S.C. Sections 4241–4247], now entitled Offenders with Mental Disease or Defect, makes it quite clear that there is to be complete parity between the professions of psychology and psychiatry" (DeLeon & Kraut, 1986, p. 2). Geis (1983) provides an overview of the criminal justice system and addresses how counseling psychology is relevant to pretrial phases, different types of defenses, preliminary hearing and grand juries, plea bargains, and the correctional system.

Even before an arrest is made, the counseling psychologist can be integral to law enforcement. Klyver and Reiser (1983) describe how the counseling psychologist can work alongside police officers, such as assisting in crisis intervention (for example, a family dispute that threatens violent behavior) or training officers to "deal with people's problems in uncontrolled and often hostile settings" (p. 49).

The very nature of police work may be contrary to that of the counseling psychologist: "Psychologists may often encounter difficulties with police organizations because they: (a) harbor unfavorable prejudices and stereotypes about police, (b) lack sensitivity in communicating and selling their programs, and (c) lack support from political sources" (p. 511). In turn, the psychologist may find resistance from the police: "Resistances from within the police organization may block the acceptance of psychological knowledge because of: (a) the history and quasi-military character of police organizations, (b) police training and peer pressure, (c) prejudices and stereotypes about psychologists by police, and (d) lack of support by police administrators" (p. 51). Counseling psychologists can work directly and indirectly with the citizen drawn into the police system or with the police themselves; police are under great stress, and special therapeutic help is often needed (Alkus & Padesky, 1983).

Given the overload of cases, prosecutors often seek alternative means for dealing with an alleged criminal. Relying on a governmental analysis, Porter (1984a) states:

> For one hundred cases reported, twenty-six arrests are made, six of which result in sentencing. Only about 2% of the original one hundred cases end with the perpetrator sent to prison [p. 52].

To justify dismissal of charges or acquittal at trial, reliance on mental-health professionals is commonplace. Gottheil and Ghosh (1983) describe how the counseling psychologist can participate in "diversion programs—that is, help the system and the alleged offender by diverting the person" out of the criminal justice system, suspending further criminal justice processing and providing alternative programs and services" (p. 17). This approach is designed to reduce the burden on the criminal-justice system, provide needed service to the individual (as might justify dismissal of the charges or reduce recidivism), and increase the cost-effectiveness of the system.

Whatever the intervention provided by the counseling psychologist, assessment is usually a pivotal point. That is, assessment data are used to justify recommendations for correction or rehabilitation actions. Davis (1985) has analyzed those persons subjected to the trauma of arrest and conviction for a crime and the later imprisonment and has found a direct parallel with the stages of dying. This finding leads him to urge that assessment be developmental--that is, be longitudinal and consider the "life-space" of the person, as opposed to simply collecting data for "static formulations."

If the person has been sentenced to incarceration, the counseling psychologist may have to try to provide a humanistic service in an environment that is rather antithetical. Whiteley and Hosford (1983) assert that correctional counseling, although designed to be therapeutic, also casts the counseling psychologist into the role of being a security officer, which raises barriers to the traditional counseling procedure. The correctional counseling psychologist has a complex role, yet Whiteley and Hosford say: "Perhaps no other area or specialty in psychology presents to the professional helper more opportunities for challenge, confirmation, frustration, and pure physical risk" (p. 32). Scharf, Dindinger, and Vogel (1983) add further clarity to the complexities and difficulties of correctional counseling, such as in a prison. For example, they mention that confidentiality in the prison context is perplexing, as when an inmate confides to the counselor that he or she has been involved with unprosecuted crimes or intends to commit further offenses. They note that correctional counselors are rarely free of the administrative connections and loyalties that prevent them from having free dialogue and relationship of trust with inmates.

When it is time for parole from a correctional facility, the counseling psychologist again enters the picture. Reentry into society has not been obtained simply by leaving prison. There is usually parole, wherein the correctional system continues to monitor the person's behavior. Carny (1983) believes that counseling during parole is essential, although the counseling psychologist is not serving solely the parolee. The "clients" are both society and the former convict, and professional allegiance must be both to helping the person reenter society in a positive fashion and to promoting social order.

Juvenile Justice

The juvenile court commonly has jurisdiction over dependent or neglected children, status offenders (runaways, incorrigibles, truants), and juveniles who have committed criminal offenses (Binder, 1983). Juveniles who are alleged to have committed a crime receive far different treatment than their adult counterparts.

Public policy requires the state to have a *parens patriae* philosophy. That is, the youth of today are the adult resources of tomorrow for the state. Consequently, the state protects young people by becoming, in a sense, their parents. If natural parents neglect or abuse a child, the *parens patriae* doctrine allows the state to supersede parental rights, with certain constitutional protections assured for the parents.

Society accepts that "trouble-making kids" will grow out of or can be rehabilitated from delinquency or problem behavior. In creating a juvenile-justice system, "The goals were to investigate, diagnose, and prescribe treatment, not to adjudicate guilt or fix blame" (President's Commission on Law Enforcement and Administration of Justice, 1967, p. 3).

Even the choice of terms used in the juvenile court is based on destigmatizing the process. As Binder (1983) writes:

> To symbolize the change in philosophy, the legal vocabulary was altered
> to reflect the new spirit; there was a petition on behalf of the child rather

than a complaint against him, there were hearings not trials, there was a finding of involvement instead of a conviction, dispositional treatments rather than sentencing followed adjudication [p. 67].

The philosophical "decriminalizing" framework of the juvenile-justice system readily allows for a counseling approach. As Porter (1984b) describes the process of disposition:

> The usual disposition of a case involving juvenile law violation is to put the youth on probation under court-ordered conditions. Both adult and juvenile probation orders carry conditions forbidding future law violations and requiring that a person live in a specific place and either obtain employment or attend school. In addition, juvenile judges also attempt to reinforce parental authority over youth by specifying such conditions as completing certain regular chores, complying with a curfew, and minding parents. Since most juvenile cases are not appealed, juvenile court judges are rarely challenged about their almost unlimited discretion in fashioning probation conditions [p. 88].

The "almost unlimited discretion" can be a double-edged sword. It can, of course, allow a judge to be quite insensitive to the needs of the youth, or it can give an almost carte blanche mandate for counseling and other rehabilitation services.

Institutionalized Mental Patients

American society provides treatment for mentally ill patients, although there is far less commitment of resources for mental health in this era than was true in certain earlier periods. The shift in emphasis is partially philosophical. It is reasoned that patients should have the least restrictive alternative, which may mean being at home or in the community as opposed to being in a residential facility.

There is also reason to believe that fiscal priorities have shifted away from mental health, with the result that many people in need of residential treatment are being denied the opportunity for essential health services and left to the harsh reality of coping with an unsupportive system. The "street people" syndrome, with sleeping in doorways and "dumpster diving" for food, is common for people who, in another era, would have received institutionalized health care.

For those who do find placement in a hospital or another mental-health facility, there is a constitutionally mandated right to treatment, expecially for the involuntary patient. The hallmark ruling in *Wyatt v. Stickney* (1971) declared, "To deprive any citizen of his or her liberty upon the altruistic theory that the confinement is for humane therapeutic reasons and then fail to provide adequate treatment violates the very fundamental right of due process" (p. 785). This case led to a court declaration of the services that were required, right down to the ratio of psychologists (and other personnel) to patients. Savitsky and Karras (1984) provide a detailed history of the right-to-treatment cases.

Once in a hospital, the patient has certain legal protections regarding treatment decisions. In *Covington v. Harris* (1969), the esteemed Judge Bazelon stated, "It makes little sense to guard jealously against the possibility of unwarranted deprivations prior to hospitalization only to abandon the watch once the patient disappears behind hospital doors" (pp. 623–624). Thus, legislation commonly prescribes procedures for establishing a treatment plan, as could be reviewed by a court.

Protecting the rights of hospital patients would seemingly be honored by a respectable professional. Brakel (1981) studied the legal services available in five hospitals. He found blatant efforts by professional and nonprofessional staff members to circumvent the legal rights of patients, going so far as to create barriers to the patients' consulting with attorneys. Woody (1982) analyzed Brakel's findings and made recommendations for being prepared to deal with organizational resistance to ensuring patients their legal rights. It is recommended that "(1) priority be given to the advocacy approach, (2) adversarial actions be carefully controlled (because they are capable of penetrating defenses through logical, rational, and intellectual authority), and (3) there be a blend of individual representation (of the client), professional consultation (through offering information), and a striving toward general therapeutic growth" (p. 241).

Each state typically specifies the criteria for involuntary commitment of a mental patient. In general, it is a twofold test: (1) the person must be mentally ill; and (2) the person must be dangerous to self or others. Case law usually translates the criteria into operational guidelines. As an example, consider the Florida statute:

394.467 Involuntary Placement
(1) Criteria. A person may be involuntarily placed for treatment upon a finding of the court by clear and convincing evidence that:
(a) He is mentally ill and because of his mental illness,
    1.a. He has refused voluntary placement for treatment after sufficient and conscientious explanation and disclosure of the purpose of placement for treatment; or
    b. He is unable to determine for himself whether placement is necessary; and
    2.a. He is manifestly incapable of surviving alone or with the help of willing and responsible family or friends, including available alternative services, and without treatment, he is likely to suffer from neglect or refuse to care for himself, and such neglect or refusal poses a real and present threat of substantial harm to his well-being; or
    b. There is a substantial likelihood that in the near future he will inflict serious bodily harm on himself or another person, as evidenced by recent behavior causing, attempting, or threatening such harm; and
    c. All available less restrictive treatment alternatives which would offer an opportunity for improvement of his condition have been judged to be inappropriate [Florida Statutes, 1985c, p. 719].

As mentioned, the criteria vary according to a state's preferences and emphases. The Florida statute seems to exemplify most of the elements found in the statutes of other states.

Each state has an administrative legal system to carry out the statutory mandates. Mental-health commitments are often under the auspices of a mental-health board. Again there are differences among states, but typically the board has members from medicine or psychology, law, and the public. It hears evidence for involuntary commitment, such as a petition filed by a family member who believes a person is mentally ill and dangerous. Professional testimony, such as from a counseling psychologist who has assessed or treated the person, will be considered, and if the evidence of mental illness and dangerousness meets the burden (in Florida it is "clear and convincing" evidence, which is more than the "preponderance" of the evidence but less than evidence "beyond a reasonable doubt"), the person will be committed regardless of his or her wishes. Subsequently, the board will usually be charged with monitoring the treatment of the patient, such as by periodically reviewing treatment plans.

One of the more troubling aspects of involuntary commitment is the prediction of dangerousness to self or others. The Florida statute contains a provision that "there is a substantial likelihood that in the near future he will inflict serious bodily harm on himself or another person, as evidenced by recent behavior causing, attempting, or threatening such harm" (p. 719). Often whether "recent behavior" was a reliable and valid index of violence remains a subject for conjecture.

From an analysis of prediction studies, Haddad (1985) notes that dangerousness is overpredicted, with accurate predictions of potential dangerousness being from 35% to, with controlled conditions, 60% to 70%. Whatever the level of predictive accuracy, courts expect mental-health professionals to make predictions of dangerousness (Knapp & VandeCreek, 1982). Moreover, Haddad (1985) asserts that the supreme court of a state is apt to be "lenient in admitting psychiatric testimony" (p. 244) and to allow error-prone expert testimony on dangerousness because "psychiatric expertise is greater than that of non-clinicians, as well as a necessary element in certain legal proceedings" (pp. 243). "To eliminate all non-scientifically proven psychiatric evidence would deprive the legal system of potentially valuable observations, opinions and judgments" (p. 244). Note that in this context, the term *psychiatric* applies to all mental-health testimony, regardless of the expert's professional discipline.

There is no sure-fire formula for calculating a prediction of dangerousness. Walters (1980) and Hall (1984) offer helpful ideas. Nonetheless, the counseling psychologist must go ahead and make predictions of dangerousness; to do otherwise is to be vulnerable to malpractice actions (J. D. Woody & R. H. Woody, 1988; R. H. Woody, 1983a, 1985, 1988a, 1988b).

Counseling psychologists can be part of the mental-health board's proceedings. In addition to testifying about assessment data or treatment information, they can be the source of a petition for commitment proceedings. They also may be eligible to serve as members of a mental-health board.

Family Law

Marriage and family therapy has become a mainstay of counseling psychology. Often the therapeutic exploration and development of a marriage turns into pre- or postdivorce counseling. What was intended to be family therapy becomes counseling the reconstituted family or stepfamily.

When a divorce occurs between a couple with children, legal determinations of custody and visitation must be made. These decisions are not for the natural parents to make but are up to the court. However, if the parents are not in dispute over custody or visitation and if there has been no allegation of detriment to the child (such as neglect or abuse), the court will probably affirm the preferences of the parents.

The Best Interests of the Child

If a dispute over custody or visitation does occur, the court is concerned about the child's welfare. Given the *parens patriae* doctrine and the wish of the state to protect its resources (that is, the children), statutes set forth criteria for how the court will decide what is in the best interests of the children. Consider the following from the Michigan statutes:

> "Best interests of the child" means the sum total of the following factors to be considered, evaluated, and determined by the court:
>
> a. The love, affection, and other emotional ties existing between the parties involved and the child.
> b. The capacity and disposition of the parties involved to give the child love, affection, and guidance and continuation of the educating and raising of the child in its religion or creed, if any.
> c. The capacity and disposition of the parties involved to provide the child with food, clothing, medical care or other remedial care recognized and permitted under the laws of this state. . . .
> d. The length of time the child has lived in a stable, satisfactory environment, and the desirability of maintaining continuity.
> e. The permanence, as a family unit, of the existing or proposed custodial home or homes.
> f. The moral fitness of the parties involved.
> g. The mental and physical health of the parties involved.
> h. The home, school, and community record of the child.
> i. The reasonable preference of the child, if the court deems the child to be of sufficient age to express preference.
> j. The willingness and ability of each of the parents to facilitate and encourage a close and continuing parent-child relationship between the child and the other parent.
> k. Any other factor considered by the court to be relevant to a particular child custody dispute [Michigan Statutes Annotated, 1980, p. 74].

In Michigan (and most other states), the court relies on expert testimony in a custody dispute. The counseling psychologist would, therefore, evaluate the child's needs and the respective parents' qualities and then apply them to the criteria maintained in the particular state, in order to protect the best interests of the child.

The criteria specified in a statute are not always clear-cut. They may be translated by mental-health professionals, attorneys, and judges in different ways. Woody (1977a) collected data from psychiatrists, psychologists, social workers, and attorneys who worked in child custody and found that: (1) there were disciplinary distinctions (including by sex of the practitioner); (2) there was general agreement among disciplines about the most important criteria; and (3) demographic variables (age, marital/divorce history) influenced their preferences for criteria as applied to the mother or the father. The latter finding led Woody (1977b) to conclude that even professionals who deal regularly with child-custody legal determinations are not assuredly free from sexism in their endorsement of criteria that are supposedly in service to the best interests of the child. He recommends:

> In other words, care should be taken to determine that a professional participant in a child custody decision has: (1) developed a professional stature that will allow involvement without personal ego needs dictating actions; (2) worked through any personal experience (such as possible a divorce and custody dispute within his/her personal life) that could potentially shape opinions; (3) established an academic rationale for criteria deemed to be important; and (4) the capability of utilizing evaluation methods that are reasonably objective [Woody, 1977a, p. 17].

Based on this research, Woody (1978) offers guidelines for divorcing parents.

Joint Custody and Shared Parental Responsibility

Mental-health professionals tend to advocate joint custody. From the perspective of mental health, it is in the best interests of the child to have continuing care from and contact with both parents, even though they have divorced. Some states have placed formal weight on a parent's willingness to promote continuing contact; from the Michigan statute, recall: "(j) The willingness and ability of each of the parents to facilitate and encourage a close and continuing parent-child relationship between the child and the other parent."

Joint custody is not necessarily joint possession. Possession refers to where the child resides. Few judges would approve a living arrangement that required a child to live, say, three and one-half days with the father and three and one-half days with the mother. Children of divorce are disrupted enough without being subjected to residential instability. Also, joint custody is not relevant directly to alimony or child support.

Joint custody is joint decision making. Derdeyn and Scott (1984) report that about half of the states have some form of joint custody. While joint custody may cut down the number of custody cases brought back to court for possible modification and may benefit children by affording them continued contact with both parents, Derdeyn and Scott believe that it remains unproven whether joint custody actually brings about cooperation between the divorced parents.

Resistance to joint custody seems to be emerging, especially among legalists. Legalists and mental-health professionals alike support trying to benefit the children of divorce in any way possible, but the legal vantage point reveals that joint custody may create other problems that lead to detrimental effects for the children. Smith (1984) surveyed Michigan judges and found that joint custody was growing in popularity, but that there were substantial criticisms of it.

Joint custody has been revised a bit to become "shared parental responsibility." In Florida, "The court shall order that the parental responsibility for a minor child be shared by both parents unless it finds that shared parental responsibility would be detrimental to the child" (Florida Statute, 1985a, p. 277). The statute continues:

> "Shared parental responsibility" means that both parents retain full parental rights and responsibilities with respect to their child and requires both parents to confer so that major decisions affecting the welfare of the child will be determined jointly.
>
> In ordering shared parental responsibility, the court may consider the expressed desires of the parents and may grant to one party the ultimate responsibility over specific aspects of the child's welfare, or the court may divide those aspects between the parties based on the best interests of the child. When it appears to the court to be in the best interests of the child, the court may order or the parties may agree how any such responsibility will be divided. Such areas of responsibility may include primary physical residence, education, medical and dental care, and any other responsibilities which the court finds unique to a particular family and/or in the best interests of the child [Florida Statutes, 1985a, p. 278].

The statutes do allow for "sole parental responsibility" and even allow grandparents (with several limitations) to seek visitation rights.

The test of the best interests of the child and the objectives of joint custody or shared parental responsibility depend on mental-health professionals. The counseling psychologist must establish contact with family-law practitioners to provide assessment and counseling services to divorcing parents. Incidentally, similar counseling should be extended to persons adopting children, terminating their parental rights, or accepting foster placements.

Divorce Mediation

The doctrine of the best interests of the child has led mental-health practitioners to support mediation as an alternative to litigation. That is, it is believed that divorcing parents can best establish healthy communication and co-parenting if they avoid the proverbial knock-down, drag-out battle over custody and visitation in the courtroom:

> Proponents of mediation claim it avoids the adversarial relationship and concomitant hostility that often characterizes the traditional divorce process. Also, returning responsibility and autonomy to the parties in reaching their own settlement of marital disputes will likely mean that agreements will be adhered to. Finally, it is generally thought that mediation will be more expeditious and less expensive than traditional adversarial negotiations or litigation [Silberman, 1982, p. 108].

The alternative is for a mediator to work with the parents toward a solution to the issues affecting the child. The mediator does not make the decision. Rather, he or she helps the parents draw their own conclusion, which is supposed to make the outcome more palatable to them and motivate them to cooperate more than if the arrangement is determined by a court after litigation.

Counseling psychologists seem to endorse mediation. Perhaps it is because of the benefits that they believe will be derived by their clients, or perhaps it is, in part, because of the benefits that they expect to derive for themselves: increased referrals, a new kind of service, or an entrée into the legal arena. The latter self-serving notion comes from actual statements made by counseling psychologists.

Benefits to the practitioner are more limited than is often realized. In fact, the guidelines for divorce mediators state:

> A mediator who is a mental health person, shall not provide counseling or therapy to either party or both during or after the mediation process. If the mediator has provided marriage counseling to the participants, or therapy to either of them beforehand, the mediator shall not undertake the mediation [American Bar Association, 1984a, p. 457].

Further, all mediated agreements, even if done by a lawyer/mediator, should be reviewed by the attorneys handling the divorce: "Any memo of understanding or proposed agreement which is prepared in the mediation process should be separately reviewed by independent counsel for each participant before it is signed" (American Bar Association, 1984b, p. 367). Thus, the notion that legal fees can be reduced or eliminated may not prove to be true; the parties still need legal counsel.

While the mental-health rationale for mediation is logical, reservations have been expressed by the legal profession (Crouch, 1982). One of these reservations may stem from a fear of "losing business" (at least that is often alleged by mental-health professionals). Another, seemingly more plausible, reason for resistance to mediation is that nonattorneys could venture into conflict areas for which they lack adequate training. Consider the statement by Gornbein and Bookholder (1984):

> Some therapists seek to exclude attorneys from divorce mediation, or propose to involve attorneys only after mediation has begun or is completed. That is a grave mistake, fraught with legal and possible malpractice implications. Some therapists take the attitude that when mediation is commenced, everything can be handled by a mediators who is not an attorney. Once the "agreement" has been reached between the parties, then an attorney should be brought into the case to review the agreement and reduce it to legal form and then take the parties through the courts for a divorce. This is dangerous and totally inadequate [p. 1137].

At the risk of sounding like heretics from counseling psychology, we feel that this statement by Gornbein and Bookholder is well founded: mediation is highly complex and involves legal and financial issues (for example, tax consequences) that few counseling psychologists are qualified to handle. On the other hand, if the counseling psychologist can adhere strictly to the psychological aspects of custody and visitation, mediation can be helpful. Remember that statutes proscribe the practice of law without admission to the bar of the state, so criminal and legal actions against the errant mediator/psychologist are possible. Likewise, well-meaning but legally unwise counseling could lead a client to later bring a malpractice action against the mediator/psychologist.

Personal-Injury Law

The notion that American society is infatuated with litigation comes, for the most part, from the number of suits involving personal-injury law. Public policy now upholds a person's right to access to the court whenever an injury is inflicted on person or property. Personal injuries are under the rubric of tort law: "tort refers to a civil wrong wherein one person's behavior causes a compensable injury to the person, property, or recognized interest of another and for which a civil remedy is sought" (Palagi & Springer, 1984, p. 155).

Many behaviors can be the cause of action in a legal case. A few of the more important ones will be described. Intentional torts include assault (an act intended to and causing apprehension of hurtful contact with another person), battery (a harmful or offensive contact with another person), false imprisonment (by act or omission, a person is confined against his or her will in a bounded area), and intentional infliction of mental distress (acts of an extreme and outrageous manner that are intended to and do cause severe mental distress).

Negligence that produces harm or injury to another person or property creates liability. More will be said about negligence theory shortly within the framework of malpractice, but for now it should be noted that negligent behavior, such as when driving an automobile recklessly, that produces injury to person or property may justify a financial remedy. Premises liability is incurred when land or buildings are allowed to contain dangers and someone is injured because of the existing dangerous conditions. Products liability is applied to manufacturers and their agents (such as retailers, under certain circumstances) when the product being marketed contains flaws, defective materials, or unnecessarily dangerous properties and injury to someone results. Some torts, such as assault and battery, may be pursued legally as both a crime and a tort (that is, the defendant may be prosecuted criminally, sued for civil damages, or both).

Our society provides that the governmental system should be responsible under tort law. While at one time governmental entities were granted immunity from lawsuits, that has been changed, and governmental facilities, such as the U.S. Veterans Administration hospitals (to name just one source that employs counseling psychologists), can be sued for personal injuries, such as malpractice by hospital personnel. Public policy has led states to establish workers' compensation programs, whereby employees receive income and medical benefits after suffering accidents at work; Merrikin, Overcast, and Sales (1987) describe the role of psychologists in workers' compensation cases. For example, the counseling psychologist can formulate a rehabilitation counseling plan for a claimant, thereby assisting the court in determining the degree of disability and/or amount of damages due to the work-related injury.

Negligence

Although it may seem that any person can sue for any injury, it is not that simple. In fact, personal-injury law in general, and negligence-based cases in specific, are complex and have numerous threshold tests that must be satisfied before the case can enter the courtroom.

To adequately understand the theory of negligence, consider the following definition:

> Negligence . . . is simply one kind of conduct. But a cause of action founded upon negligence, from which liability will follow, requires more than conduct. The traditional formula for the elements necessary to such a cause of action can be stated briefly as follows:
>
> 1. A duty, or obligation, recognized by the law, requiring the person to conform to a certain standard of conduct, for the protection of others against unreasonable risks.
>
> 2. A failure on the person's part to conform to the standard required: a breach of the duty. These two elements go to make up what the courts usually have called negligence; but the term quite frequently is applied to the second alone. Thus it may be said that the defendant was negligent, but is not liable because he was under no duty to the plaintiff not to be.
>
> 3. A reasonably close causal connection between the conduct and the resulting injury. This is what is commonly known as "legal cause," or "proximate cause," and which includes the notion of cause in fact.
>
> 4. Actual loss or damage resulting to the interests of another. . . . Nominal damages, to vindicate a technical right, cannot be recovered in a negligence action, where no actual loss has occurred. The threat of future harm, not yet realized, is not enough. Negligent conduct in itself is not such an interference with the interests of the world at large that there is any right to complain about it, or to be free from it, except in the case of some individual whose interests have suffered [Keeton, Dobbs, Keeton, & Owen, 1984, pp. 164–165].

It is important to underscore that all four of these criteria must be fulfilled. For example, it is fairly common to hear complaints that clearly establish the duty, a breach of the duty, and a causal connection between the conduct and the resulting "injury," but the injury produced no clear-cut damage or the damage was so slight that it would be foolish to go to the expense of a legal action.

There are several defenses against a legal action based on negligence theory. Among others, if the plaintiff contributed to the negligence or if he or she entered willingly into an activity that produced injury (known as "assumption of risk"), a legal action might be discounted or dismissed. Even in these instances, however, there may be extenuating circumstances, and it is essential that any potential cause of action be evaluated carefully by an attorney.

A legal action based on negligence may be barred unless it is filed in a timely fashion. The so-called "statute of limitations" usually does not start to run against a negligence action until damage has occurred or the plaintiff knows or should have known about the injury. The duration applied by a statute of limitations varies according to the type of case and the state in which the action would be brought.

Damages

As the fourth criterion specifies, there must be actual loss or damages, and it must be compensable. Kionka (1977) sets forth three rules for damages: (1) the plaintiff must have the right to be restored to his or her preinjury condition through financial compensation; (2) noneconomic losses must be translated into monetary damages; and (3) all damages claimed by the plaintiff from a particular tort must be obtained in a single lawsuit and judgment.

The purpose of damages is compensation. While punitive damages (to teach a lesson) may be allowed in some states, damages are not intended to be punitive per se. Rather, the plaintiff is supposed to be restored insofar as possible to the preinjury state.

Damages take on different forms. General damages allow for recovery for the inherent qualities of the injury, such as pain and suffering, disfigurement, and disability, but they must be attributable to the injury. Special damages allow for recovery of all losses and expenses resulting from the injury. This would include medical bills, lost wages or business profits, special assistance (such as household help), and so on. Expenses already incurred or reasonably expected to be incurred in the future may be recovered. As mentioned, punitive damages may be imposed to teach the defendant or others in society (such as, in malpractice, members of the same profession). Punitive damages are restricted and are usually not awarded for negligence. For punitive damages to emerge from a negligence case, there must be, for example, outrageous and gross conduct associated with the negligence.

The Counseling Psychologist in Personal-Injury Cases

The counseling psychologist has received ready acceptance into personal-injury cases. The involvement of a counseling psychologist can continue from moments after the injury (crisis intervention) to long after the trial has been completed (rehabilitation and treatment).

The awarding of damages is commonly in the hands of a jury. Attorneys recognize that the personal characteristics of the men and women seated on the jury can influence the jury's deliberations and verdict. Therefore, each attorney carefully formulates *voir dire* questions for every potential member of the jury, in hopes that the persons selected will be supportive of the attorney's party in the case. Covington (1985) points out that "the techniques available to the modern litigator are: (1) Community attitudinal analysis, (2) Investigation of prospective jurors, (3) Juror questionnaire for voir dire, (4) Design of voir dire questions which are tailored to the case, (5) In-courtroom assessment, (6) Focus group, (7) Mirror jury, (8) Witness review, (9) Demonstrative evidence, and (10) Power positions" (p. 20). Without going into definitions of each of these techniques, it is easy to recognize how psychological expertise could complement legal strategies, and psychologists are being used more and more in these activities. Frederick (1984) describes four ways to use a "litigation psychologist" in jury trials: (1) preparing opinion polls about important issues or problems that will be faced in the trial; (2) pretrying the case before a mock jury; (3) developing *voir dire* questions for jury selection; and (4) observing for psychological factors (for example, how well the jury responds to a certain legal strategy) during the trial.

Psychological research is replete with data revealing that witnesses' accounts are susceptible to error and bias (Loftus, 1979). Abney (1986) acknowledges the distortion created for the eyewitness by being under stress at the time of the occurrence, the group pressure that alters the recollection of the events or actors, and the memory errors that are part of human nature. As for the ability of the eyewitness to recall or retrieve information, Abney writes:

> This function can easily be affected by the expectations or suggestibility of the witness. Retrieval of information is also influenced by language and cultural differences between the witness and the questioner, by the phrasing of the questions asked, and even by the size and type of pictures used at a photo line-up. The self-induced pressure to cooperate with investigators leads witnesses to identify at least one of those persons placed before them, with repeated exposure to the "criminal" merely reinforcing the initial identification. This is a form of "unconscious transference," in which the witness confuses a person seen in one context with a person seen in an entirely different situation [p. 28].

He recognizes that "the courts of this country have historically disfavored expert testimony on eyewitness identification" (p. 37) but predicts: "As the research affirming the worth of the psychological theories in this field mounts, judicial recalcitrance will diminish" (p. 37). Already attorneys are relying on counseling psychologists for help with impeaching the credibility of eyewitnesses. Incidentally, these uses of counseling psychologists for jury, trial, and eyewitness matters are not confined to personal-injury cases; they apply to virtually any sort of trial.

Returning to the issue of damages, when there is a physical injury, there can be permanent damage, such as to the brain. Neuropsychology allows for psychologist/attorney teamwork to aid the brain-injured plaintiff (Galski, 1985). If there is a physical handicap, assessment and rehabilitation can be done by the counseling psychologist. Injury often produces pain and suffering, and behavioral interventions for pain control might be useful. When there is disability or disfigurement, the plaintiff is likely to suffer adverse emotional states, and counseling will be essential for postinjury adjustment.

As emphasized previously, damages must be established. Special damages include past, present, and future professional services required by the injury. The cost of psychotherapy provided by the counseling psychologist would be deemed special damages. Moreover, the counseling psychologist who is treating the plaintiff is apt to be asked to testify about how long therapy should continue. While this determination may be a bit speculative, public policy supports that a prevailing plaintiff is entitled to future damages and that a treating professional should make such an evaluation and prognosis.

The counseling psychologist's familiarity with educational and vocational matters is particularly important to personal-injury cases. For example, when a person is physically or mentally impaired from an accident, it is necessary to establish what resources will be needed to restore him or her, as much as possible, to the preaccident status. This might well involve education or training or some form of vocational rehabilitation.

Throughout the subsequent restoration period, the person will, in all likelihood, be losing income. Lees-Haley (1985) believes that psychologists can provide this sort of information to the court through an earnings-capacity evaluation:

> The evaluator must provide answers to several key questions:
> 1. What is the nature and extent of the psychological disability?
> 2. Did this disability occur as a result of the litigated event?
> 3. What evidence can be offered to prove that the disabling condition existed or did not exist prior to the litigated event?
> 4. How much money would the plaintiff have been able to earn if not for the injury, and how much can the plaintiff earn now? [p. 34].

The training in vocational psychology received by the counseling psychologist should not neglect the financial dimension.

As stated before, public policy supports that the prevailing plaintiff is entitled to damages to cover education, training, and rehabilitation needs. The counseling psychologist can provide the assessments and the rehabilitation counseling, as well as the testimony that will guide the court toward a fair, just, and reasonable award of damages, such as for lost income.

Professional Negligence

Professional negligence translates into malpractice. While malpractice may produce injury, this topic has been held for presentation in a final section in order to give it special emphasis—and deservedly so.

Chapter 12 provides a detailed analysis of malpractice (see also Woody, 1988a, 1988b). Reiteration is unnecessary. What is essential is to recognize how malpractice constitutes negligence and to posit how a counseling psychologist can and should be prepared to participate in a malpractice action against another practitioner.

On negligence, public policy holds that any professional service carries an elevated duty to the recipients. This is definitely true for the psychotherapeutic relationship.

The counseling psychologist must fulfill a duty to safeguard the interests and welfare of the client. This means meeting a reasonable standard of care, as is imposed upon the profession. The issues of duty and standard of care are addressed in Chapter 12. When a breach of the standard of care occurs and the client experiences damages, the four criteria for negligence have been met.

In order to prove malpractice, it is necessary to have testimony from other practitioners of the same profession. The medical profession has often been accused of maintaining a protective cloak around its members when a malpractice action occurs—namely, by refusing to testify against a medical brother or sister. Whether this has occurred within medicine is beside the point. What is important is that counseling psychologists recognize their commitment to the betterment of society by being willing to provide testimony about the standard of care and about whether a particular act was malpractice to best of their professional knowledge.

Testifying against another counseling psychologist might create some personal feelings, such as uneasiness, but they must be set aside in favor of promoting social order. In the long run, this will benefit every honorable counseling psychologist. To testify against another practitioner is not a personal vendetta, it is a matter of providing academically based information to the court, which is much like providing academically based information in a classroom to students.

Summary

Counseling psychologists have a mandate to be involved in the judicial system, namely by allowing their expertise to assist the trier-of-fact (judge or jury) and the parties to litigation. However, the courtroom is considerably different from the therapy room, The counseling psychologist must remember that the courtroom is under the public aegis of the judicial system and is not subject to the same social philosophy of rules for practice that apply to the therapy room. The counseling psychologist is invited into the courtroom for the purpose of assisting the trier-of-fact. To be of maximum usefulness, the counseling psychologist must manifest only role-appropriate behavior.

The counseling psychologist can work within the criminal justice system— for example, testify about the relevance of the client's mental condition to the crime (for instance, the insanity defense) and competency to stand trial, counsel those who attend trials, and shape public policy. Similar contributions can be made to the juvenile justice system.

Institutionalized patients have legal rights that deserve protection by counselors. Family law, especially laws protecting the interests of children (for example, in custody disputes and abuse cases), can benefit from counseling psychology services. With its connection to rehabilitation, counseling psychology is essential in personal injury cases, such as those involving clients injured on the job and seeking worker's compensation.

References

Abney, D. L. (1986). Expert Testimony and Eyewitness Identification. *Case and Comment, 91*(2), 26–31, 34–37.

Alkus, S., & Padesky, C. (1983). Special Problems of Police Officers: Stress-Related Issues and Interventions. *The Counseling Psychologist, 11*(2), 55–64.

American Bar Association, Family Law Section. (1984a). Standards of Practice for Family Mediators. *Family Law Quarterly, 17,* 455–460.

American Bar Association, Family Law Section. (1984b). Standards of Practice for Lawyer Mediators in Family Disputes. *Family Law Quarterly, 18,* 363–368.

American Board of Forensic Psychology. (1981). *Summary Brochure.* Ann Arbor, MI: Author.

American Law Institute. (1974). *Uniform Laws Annotated, 10,* Section 4.01, pp. 490–491.

American Psychiatric Association. (1980). *Diagnostic and Statistical Manual of Mental Disorders* (3rd ed.). Washington, DC: Author.

American Psychiatric Association, Insanity Defense Work Group. (1983). American Psychiatric Association Statement on the Insanity Defense. *American Journal of Psychiatry, 140,* 681–688.

Bell, B. E., & Loftus, E. F. (1985). Vivid Persuasion in the Courtroom. *Journal of Personality Assessment, 49,* 659–664.

Binder, A. (1983). Juvenile Justice and Juvenile Offenders: An Overview. *The Counseling Psychologist, 11*(2), 65–67.

Brakel, S. J. (1981). Legal Aid in Mental Hospitals. *American Bar Foundation Research Journal, 1,* 21–93.

Carny, L. P. (1983). The Counseling Perspective in Parole. *The Counseling Psychologist, 11*(2), 41–47.

Cleary, E. W. (Ed.). (1972). *McCormick's Handbook of the Law of Evidence* (2nd ed.). St. Paul, MN: West.

Covington, M. (1985). Use of Expert Assistance in Jury Selection. *Case and Comment, 90*(4), 20, 22–24, 26.

Covington v. Harris, 419 F.2d 617 (D.C. Circ. 1969).

Crouch R. E. (1982). Divorce Mediation and Legal Ethics. *Family Law Quarterly, 16,* 219–250.

Davis, R. W. (1985). Assessing Offenders: Dying for Reprieve. *Journal of Personality Assessment, 49,* 605–612.

DeLeon, P. H., & Kraut, A. (1986). Psychology's Entree into the Criminal Justice System. *American Psychology-Law Society Newsletter, 6*(1), 2–3.

Derdeyn, A. P., & Scott, E. (1984). Joint Custody: A Critical Analysis and Appraisal. *American Journal of Orthopsychiatry, 54,* 199–209.

Dorn, F. J. (1984). The Counselor Goes to Court. *Journal of Counseling and Development, 63,* 119–120.

Florida Statutes. (1985a). *Title VI. Civil Practice and Procedure.* Chapter 61. Dissolution of Marriage; Support; Custody, *1,* 274–285.

Florida Statutes. (1985b). *Title VII. Evidence.* Chapter 90. Evidence Code, *1,* 358–372.

Florida Statutes. (1985c). *Title XXIX. Public Health.* Chapter 394, Mental Health, *2,* 709–739.

Frederick, J. T. (1984). Four Ways to Use a Litigation Psychologist in Jury Trials. *Florida Bar Journal, 58,* 633–637.

Galski, T. (1985). The Neuropsychologist: Key Member of the Doctor-Lawyer Team. *Case and Comment, 90*(4), 10, 12–14.

Geis, G. (1983). Criminal Justice and Adult Offenders: An Overview. *The Counseling Psychologist, 11*(2), 11–16.

Gorbein, H. S., & Bookholder, R. M. (1984). Divorce Mediation: What Are The Options? Where Is It Heading? *Michigan Bar Journal, 63,* 1136–1141.

Gottheil, D., & Ghosh, S. A. (1983). Pretrial Intervention: Counseling in Adult Diversion Programs. *The Counseling Psychologist, 11*(2), 17–25.

Graham, J. R. (1977). *The MMPI: A Practical Guide.* New York: Oxford University Press.

Grisso, T. (1987). The Economic and Scientific Future of Forensic Psychological Assessment. *American Psychologist, 42*(9), 831–839.

Haddad, L. K. (1985). Predicting the Supreme Court's Response to the Criticism of Psychiatric Predictions of Dangerousness in Civil Commitment Proceedings. *Nebraska Law Review, 64,* 215–247.

Hall, H. V. (1984). Predicting Dangerousness for the Courts. *American Journal of Forensic Psychology, 11,* 5–21.

Keeton, W. P., Dobbs, D. B., Keeton, R. E., & Owen, D. G. (1984). *Prosser and Keeton on Torts* (5th ed.). St. Paul, MN: West.

Kionka, E. J. (1977). *Torts: Injuries to Person and Property.* St. Paul, MN: West.

Klyver, N., & Reiser, M. (1983). Crisis Intervention in Law Enforcement. *The Counseling Psychologist, 11*(2), 49–54.

Knapp, S., & VandeCreek, L. (1982). *Tarasoff:* Five Years Later. *Professional Psychology, 13,* 511–516.

Lees-Haley, P. R. (1985). Psychological Personal Injuries and Earnings Loss. *Case and Comment, 90*(4), 34–35, 38.

Loftus, E. F. (1979). *Eyewitness Testimony.* Cambridge, MA: Harvard University Press.

Merrikin, K. J., Overcast, T. D., & Sales, B. D. (1987). Recognition of Psychologists in Workers' Compensation Law. *Professional Psychology, 18*(3), 260–264.

Michigan Statutes Annotated. (1980). *Best Interests of the Child.* Section 25.312(3), 74.

Muller v. Oregon, 208 U.S. 412 (1908).

Nisbett, R. E., & Ross, L. (1980). *Human Inference: Strategies and Shortcomings of Social Judgment.* Englewood Cliffs, NJ: Prentice-Hall.

Palagi, R. J., & Springer, J. R. (1984). Personal Injury Law. In R. H. Woody (Ed.), *The Law and the Practice of Human Services* (pp. 155–198). San Francisco: Jossey-Bass.

Porter, J. B. (1984a). Criminal Law. In R. H. Woody (Ed.), *The Law and the Practice of Human Services* (pp. 39–81). San Francisco: Jossey-Bass.

Porter, J. B. (1984b). Juvenile Law. In R. H. Woody (Ed.), *The Law and the Practice of Human Services* (pp. 83–112). San Francisco: Jossey-Bass.

President's Commission on Law Enforcement and Administration of Justice, Task Force on Juvenile Delinquency. (1967). *Report: Juvenile Delinquency and Youth Crime.* Washington, DC: U.S. Government Printing Office.

Roche, P. Q. (1958). *The Criminal Mind.* New York: Farrar, Straus, & Cudahy.

Savitsky, J. C., & Karras, D. A. (1984). Rights of Institutionalized Patients. In R. H. Woody (Ed.), *The Law and the Practice of Human Services* (pp. 289–339). San Francisco: Jossey-Bass.

Scharf, P., Dindinger, M., & Vogel, R. (1983). Keeping Faith: Roles and Problems of Counselors in Prison Settings. *The Counseling Psychologist, 11*(2), 35–40.

Schwitzgebel, R. L., & Schwitzgebel, R. K. (1980). *Law and Psychological Practice.* New York: Wiley.

Silberman, L. J. (1982). Professional Responsibility Problems of Divorce Mediation. *Family Law Quarterly, 16,* 107–145.

Slovenko, R. (1973). *Psychiatry and Law.* Boston: Little, Brown.

Smith, E. C. (1984). Joint Custody: The View from the Bench. *Michigan Bar Journal, 63,* 1151–1156.

Spring, R. L. (1979). The End of Insanity. *Washburn Law Journal, 19,* 23–37.

State v. Cavallo, 88 NJ 508, 443 A2d 1020, 42 ALR4th 919 (1985).

Stricker, G. (1985). Psychological Assessment and Miranda Rights. *Journal of Personality Assessment, 49,* 656–658.

Sutton, J. M., Jr., Seibel, R. F., & Redfield, W. C. (1985). A Joint Internship Program for Law and Counseling Students. *Journal of Counseling and Development, 64,* 143–144.

Thiers, N. (1987). Counselors Keep Wary Eye on Liability Developments. *AACD Guidepost, 30*(7), 1, 16.

Walters, H. A. (1980). Dangerousness. In R. H. Woody (Ed.), *The Encyclopedia of Clinical Assessment* (Vol. 2) (pp. 1104–1111). San Francisco: Jossey-Bass.

Whiteley, S. M., & Hosford, R. E. (1983). Counseling in Prisons. *The Counseling Psychologist, 11*(2), 27–34.

Woody, J. D., & Woody, R. H. (1988). Public Policy in Life-Threatening Situations. *Journal of Marital and Family Therapy, 14, 2,* 133–137..

Woody, R. H. (1977a). Behavioral Science Criteria in Child Custody Determinations. *Journal of Marriage and Family Counseling, 3,* 11–18.

Woody, R. H. (1977b). Sexism in Child Custody Decisions. *Personnel and Guidance Journal, 56,* 168–170.

Woody, R. H. (1978). *Getting custody: Winning the Last Battle of the Marital War.* New York: Macmillan.

Woody, R. H. (1982). Public Policy and Legal Aid in Mental Hospitals: The Dimensions of the Problem and Their Implications for Legal Education and Practice. *American Bar Foundation Research Journal, 1,* 237–243.

Woody, R. H. (1983a). Avoiding Malpractice in Psychotherapy. In P. A. Keller & L. G. Ritt (Eds.), *Innovations in Clinical Practice: A Source Book* (Vol. 2) (pp. 205–216). Sarasota, FL: Professional Resource Exchange.

Woody, R. H. (1983b). Techniques for Handling Psycholegal Cases. In C. E. Walker (Ed.), *The Handbook of Clinical Psychology* (Vol. 2) (pp. 1420–1439). Homewood, IL: Dow Jones-Irwin.

Woody, R. H. (1985). Public Policy, Malpractice Law, and the Mental Health Professional: Some Legal and Clinical Guidelines. In C. P. Ewing (Ed.), *Psychology, Psychiatry, and the Law* (pp. 509–525). Sarasota, FL: Professional Resource Exchange.

Woody, R. H. (1988a). *Fifty Ways to Avoid Malpractice.* Sarasota, FL: Professional Resource Exchange.

Woody, R. H. (1988b). *Protecting Your Mental Health Practice.* San Francisco: Jossey-Bass.

Wyatt v. Stickney, 325 F. Supp. 781 (M.D. Ala. 1971).

Zelig, M. (1987). Clinical and Demographic Characteristics of Police Psychologists. *Professional Psychology, 18*(3), 269–275.

Health Psychology

In the early days of their specialty, counseling psychologists met resistance to their efforts to treat problem behaviors or mental disorders. The simplistic notion was that counseling psychologists were really educational-guidance personnel and that their use of the title "psychologist" was unjustified.

Doubt about the counseling psychologist's expanded role was exacerbated by certain educationally oriented professionals who did not believe it necessary to conform to existing training for psychologists (such as taking courses in the behavioral sciences, psychopathology, experimental methods, and psychodiagnosis). They asserted that counseling was distinctly different from psychology. Unfortunately, many of these same people sought to be licensed, certified, or titled under the rubric of psychology. Their opponents from traditional psychology, particularly from clinical psychology, challenged their attempted entry. They were accused of wanting the benefits of being deemed a psychologist without having fulfilled the rigorous academic standards, of wanting to enter professional psychology by the back door.

Rapprochement required the traditional clinical psychologist and the traditional educational-guidance specialist to create a hybrid training model, and today's counseling-psychology training program represents the justification for expanding practice beyond the previously accepted educational and vocational guidance into diagnosis and treatment of behavior problems and mental disorders. Dealing with behavior problems and mental disorders allowed counseling psychologists to move further into the mind, figuratively and literally, such as by unabashedly providing in-depth psychotherapy (as opposed to "guidance for superficial problems").

By entering the far recesses of mind, counseling psychologists barged into the complex mind/body system. As they wandered (therapeutically) through the maze of mind/body interfaces, it became apparent that they were confronting both mental disorders and physical disorders. This meant that counseling psychologists had to be prepared to accommodate their clients' physical needs, ailments, and illnesses.

The question became whether the counseling psychologist should totally avoid any client with a manifest physical concern, refer clients for every physically defined issue to a physician, or treat by counseling-psychology methods some of the physical difficulties. The answer that has emerged would probably surprise the founders of counseling psychology, because it clearly establishes that many of the clients' physical concerns are within the professional province of counseling psychology—under the rubric of "health psychology."

The rationale for involving counseling psychologists in matters of physical health is straightforward. Pelletier (1977) presents extensive evidence that mental and physical disorders are "created out of a complex interaction of social forces, physical and psychological stress, the personality of the person subjected to these influences, and the inability of the person to adapt adequately to pressures" (p. 13). From such an etiological matrix, the adaptation process reaches the accepted definition of counseling psychology.

Then there is the pragmatic concern about health. Contemporary American society has placed a premium on health. High priority is given to allowing every person to live happier, longer, and with better health. Economic reality enters the picture and frames the health-seeking goal with escalating costs. When the premium on health and the high cost of health services combine, the result is a willingness to recognize that "psychological services reduce medical costs because 60% of all doctor visits are made by patients who have no physical illness and who are somaticizing emotional problems" (Cummings, 1986, p. 431). Alternative models of health-service delivery are being developed that rely heavily on counseling psychologists.

Health psychology might be called a specialization, but it seems more accurate to consider it as a conceptual framework for developing the whole person—physically, mentally, and spiritually—that can be used by numerous psychological specialties. For example, professionals from counseling psychology, clinical psychology, school psychology, or industrial psychology—and various other specialties as well—can practice health psychology within their established specializations.

In moving toward a definition of health psychology, it is important to keep specialization in a correct frame of reference. Bakal (1979) has said:

> Although specialization is necessary, it is important to remember that each specialty has a particular way of viewing things. Thus a biochemist will view illness from a molecular level while a psychologist will see the same illness from a behavioral perspective. There is nothing inherently wrong with specialization. The problem begins when the specialists attempt to generalize from their particular model to include all aspects of human functioning [p. 5].

For counseling psychology, this means that counseling theory and techniques must not be allowed to define the nature of health. To the contrary, the bio/psycho/social nature of health must define counseling theory and techniques.

The holistic approach to treating the person is centuries old, and the treatment of somatic problems was a prominent part of the early days of psychoanalysis (Bromberg, 1975). The conceptual framework for health psychology was, at least in modern times, put forth in the Yale Conference on Behavioral Medicine's definition of behavioral medicine:

> Behavioral medicine is the field concerned with the development of behavioral-science knowledge and techniques relevant to the understanding

of physical health and illness and the application of this knowledge and these techniques to prevention, diagnosis, treatment and rehabilitation. Psychosis, neurosis, and substance abuse are included only insofar as they contribute to physical disorders as an end point [Schwartz & Weiss, 1977, p. 4].

One of the first, and most often quoted, definitions of health psychology created by and for the psychologist was offered by Matarazzo (1982):

Health psychology is the aggregate of the specific educational, scientific, and professional contributions of the discipline of psychology to the promotion and maintenance of health, the prevention and treatment of illness, the identification of etiologic and diagnostic correlates of health, illness, and related dysfunction, and the analysis and improvement of the health care system and health policy formation [p. 4].

Klippel and DeJoy (1984) compare these two definitions, and say: "the single most important difference appears to be the emphasis that health psychology places on intervention strategies based on educational, not medical, models to facilitate changes in health behavior" (p. 220).

One of the most recent of the American Psychological Association's 42 divisions is the Division of Health Psychology. The *Directory* of the APA (1985) shows that the division has 101 fellows and 2,275 members (of which 73.3% are men and 26.7% are women). The division was "established to bring together psychologists interested in the psychological and behavioral aspects of physical health" (APA, undated, p. 1). For example:

Some of the many clinical activities of health psychologists are participation in programs of smoking prevention and cessation, stress management, exercise and fitness, accident prevention, rehabilitation, and consultation on medical specialty services. Some of the many research activities are evaluation of the foregoing clinical activities, investigation of behavioral factors involved in the prevention of physical disease, and compliance with medical regimens and basic laboratory investigation of mechanisms linking behavior and disease risk [p. 1].

Two objectives should be underscored. Health psychology is dedicated to *preventing illness* and *promoting health*. As we shall show in this chapter, these two cornerstones of health psychology are the foundation on which counseling psychologists can structure their involvement with the health needs of their clients.

Reflecting back of the stated definitions, it would seem that the traditional orientation of counseling psychology toward health has found a home. Klippel and DeJoy (1984) say:

Counseling psychology appears to be made for such research efforts given its historical commitment to qualitative assessment and its recognition of the importance of personal and cultural context to implementing healthy change. . . . The opportunity is at hand for counseling psychology to move away from conventional medical approaches and to move toward broad-based quality of life approaches to the health concerns of individuals, families, and communities [p. 225].

The Goal of Health

Attaining and maintaining health is a challenge. The challenge is not met without effort and responsibility. Consequently, many people can benefit from counseling in their search for health.

Health is more than the absence of disease. It is a system of maintaining life, fueled by the body, the mind, and the spirit. Thoresen and Eagleston (1985) assert:

> Good health is as much a state of mind as a condition of the body. How the body functions is intimately connected to how a person thinks and feels, that is, to cognitive and emotional processes. The ongoing complex relationships among thinking, feeling, and behaving are the prime determinants of health [p. 15].

According to Knowles (1977), "The health of human beings is determined by their behavior, their food, and the nature of their environment. Over 99% of us are born healthy and suffer premature death and disability only as a result of personal misbehavior and environmental conditions" (p. 79). While every person can and, as a contributing member of society, should work to improve environmental conditions (for example, eliminating pollution, promoting medical research, and supporting laws to provide for safe living conditions), the primary task remains a personal one: to adopt a healthy lifestyle.

Unfortunately, many people enter into self-destructive behaviors such as adverse emotional states (depression, anxiety, anger, guilt), substance abuse, over- or undereating, illogical obsessions (being a "workaholic"), and so on. One of the sources of being unhealthy is lacking control over one's functioning. Control over life's events has been recognized as integral to a person's overall state, as exemplified by the critical importance attributed to helplessness (Seligman, 1975) and locus of control (Rotter, 1966). Seeman and Seeman (1983) assert: "A sense of low control is shown to be significantly associated with (1) less self-initiated preventive care; (2) less optimism concerning the efficacy of early treatment; (3) poorer self-rated health; and (4) more illness episodes, more bed confinement, and greater dependence upon the physician" (p. 144). They conclude:

> The sense of helplessness may well be the 'disease' that it is claimed to be, for we find that those who believe their health can be effectively influenced by their own behavior act in more positive ways with apparently positive results. . . . Our evidence shows that the sense of control is associated with: (1) practicing preventive health measures, e.g., diet, exercise, alcohol moderation; (2) making an effort to avoid the harm in smoking (by quitting, trying to quit, or simply not smoking); (3) being more sanguine about early medical treatment for cancer; (4) achieving higher self-ratings on general health status; (5) reporting fewer episodes of both chronic and acute illness; (6) evidencing a more vigorous management style with respect to illness, e.g., staying in bed less once a bed-confinement occasion has occurred; and (7) showing less dependence on the use of the physician—and perhaps, less dependence so far as medical compliance is concerned [p. 155].

Surely these areas of personal responsibility are within the purview of counseling psychology.

Achieving a Healthy Lifestyle

Being responsible for one's own body is fundamental to achieving a healthy lifestyle. People who rely on an external locus of control—that is, attributing outcomes to the acts of other people, bad luck, and so on—as opposed to those with an internal locus of control are at the highest risk for continuation of unhealthy behavior (Clarke, MacPherson, & Holmes, 1982).

Self-actualization, closely related to locus of control, is a mainstream objective of counseling psychology. Through self-actualizing efforts, the client gains more self-understanding, appreciation of his or her uniquenesses, a set of healthier lifestyle practices, and a commitment to healthful growth and development (Petosa, 1984a).

A healthy lifestyle must evolve. It is inevitably influenced by the person's heredity, be it in the form of the capabilities and limitations for activities or the predispositions of the organism. Influences also come, of course, from development, socialization, learning experiences, critical events (such as accidents), special familial circumstances (financial status, emotional conditions), and chance alone. While the utmost determinant remains personal choice and responsibility, a person-oriented lifestyle becomes manifest through a system:

> (1) your life-style must be acceptable to society; if it is not, your existence will be subject to negative complications; (2) your life-style must be tailored to give and receive emotional support and to meet your material needs and the needs of those for whom you are responsible—there must be a mutual need fulfillment; (3) when there is a change in your "group," such as the birth of a baby or the taking of a spouse, there must be changes to accommodate the new system and its needs; and (4) the people in your lifespace must be committed to harmonious interaction [Woody, 1980a, p. 12].

This is a tall order for most people, and a less than optimal living system often ensues, to the detriment of health.

Resistance to Changing Unhealthy Behaviors

In keeping with an educational orientation, a counseling psychologist can provide information about illness and health and can reinforce healthy behavior. This effort may, however, meet with substantial resistance: "There is abundant evidence that no matter how much people know about the benefits of dieting, exercising, fastening seat belts, or moderating their use of drugs, alcohol, and tobacco, this knowledge has had little effect on habits in most cases" (Parcell, 1985, p. 21).

There are, of course, many reasons why a client will discount logical and well-reasoned health information and continue a seemingly self-destructive lifestyle. Many of these sources of resistance are psychological in nature. Consequently a counseling-psychology intervention is often the prescription. Let us consider just a few of the psychological sources of resistance.

Resistance to health-related behavior changes can have many causes. It may stem from a lack of information about health, the sociodemographic framework (including the sex-role stereotypes that are inflicted on men and women), the basic character structure that a person develops, the emotions that are shaped (such as by stress), and day-to-day obstacles. Of course other forms of resistance may reflect such classic ego-defense mechanisms as denial, regression, projection, displacement, and so on. In any case, the counseling psychologist's first steps toward helping the client are to identify the presence of resistance and then to select helping strategies that will promote health.

Dealing with Stress

Stress is a disruption in the organism, conveyed by the autonomic nervous system, as might be associated with psychosomatic disorders. Tension and anxiety, whatever the source, lead to stressful conditions.

How one handles stress is of the highest priority in health-related counseling. In a study of female patients in a neighborhood health-care center, Gortmaker, Eckenrode, and Gore (1982) found that the presence of stress on a given day increased the probability of a woman's seeking treatment. Similarly, Pilisuk, Boylan, and Acredolo (1987) found that "stress contributes to an increased rate of medical care unless buffered by the effects of social support" (p. 284).

Often stress is manifested in emotions. For example, the frustration/ aggression hypothesis holds that frustrations in one's daily life will lead to aggressive behavior. Not only can aggressive behavior create interpersonal problems, it can have implications for health. In helping the client deal more effectively with stress, the counseling psychologist should introduce healthful handling of anger and other potentially deleterious emotions. Alschuler and Alschuler (1984) point out that anger (which originates in the hypothalamus with a release of noradrenalin) has distinct physical effects (for example, elevated blood pressure), and they urge that the client be helped to communicate, clarify, express, or redirect anger.

The basic character of the person is linked to emotions. There is always the "chicken or the egg" question: did emotions (caused, perhaps, by stressful events) create the character, or vice versa? For example, O'Neill (1984) found that obstinacy and contrariness (the hallmarks of the "anal personality") were linked to stress-related behavior patterns and created a substantial obstacle to treatment (such as with the coronary-prone client). Regardless, the counseling psychologist should be in tune with the reciprocal effects of character and emotions.

Environmental Sources of Stress

Environmental influences may aid or plague the effort to achieve a healthy lifestyle. In other words, notwithstanding the importance of being self-determining, there may be outside conditions that are related to illness and health. Some can be altered, others not.

The past years have brought difficult economic conditions to the American scene. Through a longitudinal analysis, Catalano and Dooley (1983) found that economic contraction increased the incidence of unemployment and financial difficulties, which in turn led to an increase in the incidence of illness and injury. Counseling psychologists should be readily available to the unemployed or anyone else (including the underemployed) who experiences stress as a result of the press of the economy.

Beyond societal conditions, such as an economic climate that leads to a bleak employment forecast, a person's overall composite of sociodemographic factors can relate to health. Of special relevance to the objectives of counseling psychology, employment and marital status are connected with health. Cleary and Mechanic (1983) found: "Employed married women experienced slightly less distress than housewives, but having minor children in the household was especially stressful for these women and counteracted the advantage of employment. . . . The strain of working and doing the majority of the work associated with raising children increases distress among married women" (p. 111). For both men and women, Verbrugge (1983) found that "employed married parents tend to have the best health profile, while people with none of these roles tend to have the worst profile" (p. 16). She summarizes:

> (1) Employment, marriage, and parenthood are related to good health status and infrequent health behavior. (2) Of the three roles, employment has the strongest relationship. In other words, the health differences between employed and nonemployed people are larger than between marital or parenthood groups. Both full-time and part-time employed people have the health advantage. (3) The combination of job and family roles has no special effect, positive or negative, on health. People with multiple roles do tend to have the best health, but this is due to straightforward effects of each role, not to any special effect of combining roles. (4) Employment has a more pronounced effect on men's health than on women's. But marriage has similar effects on men and women; the same holds for parenthood [p. 25].

Since counseling psychology places a special emphasis on vocational development and individual self-actualization (as would relate to fully functioning, constructive, and healthy involvement in marriage and parenthood), it is apparent that there must be an interface of these issues with health considerations.

The Physiology of Stress

Anxiety is the emotion and/or maladaptive avoidance response that creates a negative stressful condition within the organism. From the beginning of modern-day mental-health services, anxiety has been recognized as a destructive condition. Its deleterious effects permeate mind and body and harm the functioning of the entire organism. (Recall the previous comments about the relationship between stress and the need for medical or health-care service.)

The birth process may be the infant's first encounter with tension or anxiety. As Fenichel (1945) describes it: "This flooding with excitation without an adequate defense apparatus is . . . the model for all later anxiety" (p. 34). Anxiety becomes a deep-seated part of the person: "Anxiety is a painful emotional experience which is produced by excitations in the internal organs of the body. These excitations result from internal or external stimulation and are governed by the autonomic nervous system" (Hall, 1954, p. 61). Parents contribute to the increase or decrease of anxiety in early life, such as through nurturance or rejection. Society comes into play by imposing values and morals. For example, Horney (1937) describes how females may experience "tortured conscience or social disgrace" (p. 62) because of natural instincts (for example, their sexuality), with the result being anxiety.

Anxiety reactions have physiological effects, which include increased or rapid heart rate, rapid or irregular breathing, and dizziness. The negative changes can be affective or behavioral:

> The person may experience numerous negative feelings, particularly apprehension, some kind of anticipation of a problem arising or of impending doom, and fears of going crazy or losing control. There can be pronounced irritability and depression. Behaviorally, there can be sleeping and eating problems. There can be uncontrolled restlessness. The mind may wander and have faulty concentration and poor recall. There can be physical fatigue for no real reason (the reason, of course, is mental, namely the exhaustive expenditure of energy required to counteract the insecurity). There can be a breakdown in efficiency, such as at work or in school [Woody, 1980a, p. 17].

Anxiety may be based on a logical awareness of danger in the external world, or it may be neurotic—that is, illogical and instinct-based (but exaggerated due to unresolved emotional conflicts). Neurotic anxiety may be (1) free-floating, with anxiety being attached to virtually any condition or object; (2) phobic, as a reaction of fear to a specific stimulus; (3) obsessive/compulsive, with illogical repetition of thoughts or acts; (4) hysterical, body symptoms due to conversion hysteria or departure from normal consciousness due to dissociation hysteria; (5) depressive, such as self-depreciation or unresolved grief; or (6) panicky, involving a sudden emotional and behavioral upheaval with irrational provocation (Hall, 1954; Martin, 1971).

Anxiety emanates from the autonomic nervous system, which is part of the central nervous system, and is located within the spinal cord and the brain stem. The autonomic nervous system regulates bodily processes and contributes to emotional reactions. It controls the vascular, respiratory, gastrointestinal, and reproductive functions. This is the neurological source of psychosomatic disorders (that is, physical conditions with a psychological etiology) and ushers in the stress to the person's lifestyle, thereby making health psychology an issue for counseling psychology.

The Results of Stress

Stress brings on all sorts of harmful conditions. Pelletier (1977) asserts that "stress-induced disorders have long since replaced epidemics of infectious disease as the major medical problem of the post-industrial nations" (p. 6). He believes that 30% to 50% of all patients who go to a physician are "worried well," meaning that stress connected to their body condition leads them to seek medical attention. Often, he says, this is for good cause:

Even the most conservative sources classify the following illnesses as psychosomatic: peptic ulcer, mucous colitis, ulcerative colitis, bronchial asthma, atopic dermatitis, urticaria and angioneurotic edema, hay fever, arthritis, Raynaud's disease, hypertension, hyperthyroidism, amenorrhea, enuresis, paroxysmal tachycardia, migraine headache, impotence, general sexual dysfunctions, sleep-onset insomnia, alcoholism, and the whole range of neurotic and psychotic disorders [p. 7].

Indeed, Pelletier believes that 50% to 80% of all diseases are psychosomatic or stress-related conditions.

When inspecting psychosomatic or stress-related conditions for treatment by counseling psychology, it is helpful to look at the causes of death and the risk factors associated with them. According to the U.S. Public Health Service (1981), the causes of death (with their respective percentage of all deaths and risk factors) are as follows: heart or cardiovascular disease (37.8%; smoking, hypertension, elevated serum cholesterol, diet, lack of exercise, diabetes, stress, family history); cancer or malignant neoplasms (20.4%; smoking, work-site carcinogens, environmental carcinogens, alcohol, diet); stroke or cerebrovascular disease (9.6%; hypertension, smoking, elevated cholesterol, stress); accidents, other than motor accidents (2.8%; alcohol, drug abuse, smoking and fires, product design, handguns); influenza and pneumonia (2.7%; smoking, vaccination status); motor-vehicle accidents (2.6%; alcohol, no seat belts, speed, roadway design, vehicle engineering); diabetes mellitus (1.7%; obesity); cirrhosis of the liver (1.6%; alcohol abuse); arteriosclerosis (1.5%; elevated serum cholesterol); and suicide (1.5%; stress, alcohol and drug abuse, guns). Since life-threatening and life-sustaining conditions change with time, the percentages are not indelibly written, and the risk factors are not associated with major causes of death. In turn, it is readily apparent that many, if not all, of these factors are potentially subject to modification and control by counseling psychology.

Stress can destroy the person through illness. Conversely, the person can avoid illness (and stress) by his or her health practices. Behavioral and environmental conditions for health effects were studied longitudinally by Belloc and Breslow (1972). Over 5-1/2 years, 6928 California adults were scrutinized for seven behaviors: (1) ate breakfast almost every day; (2) rarely or never ate between meals; (3) slept 7 to 8 hours daily; (4) maintained normal weight adjusted for height, age, and sex; (5) never smoked cigarettes; (6) avoided alcohol or used alcohol moderately; and (7) had regular physical activity. Thoresen and Eagleston (1985) summarize the results:

Those who engaged in all or almost all of these behaviors were much less likely to die during the study period than those who engaged in none or only a few. For example, males at age 45 who followed six or seven of these health practices had an average life span eleven years longer than males at 45 who followed three or fewer. From another perspective the data revealed, for example, that men ages 55–64 who failed to engage in these practices (none, one, or two) had a death rate of slightly more than 30%, compared to a rate of 5% for men regularly involved in six or seven health practices—a sixfold difference. For women of the same ages, the differences were less pronounced: 4% versus 2%. However, in the next decade of life (65–74), the differences among women were dramatic: over 30% versus only 4%—almost an eightfold difference. This relationship between higher number of health practices and lower death rates remained, even when socioeconomic level and physical health status of subjects at the beginning of the study were considered [pp. 25–26].

Nine and one-half years later, Breslow and Enstrom (1980) did a follow-up on almost 5000 of the original subjects, and the significant differences were basically replicated. In addition to the health behaviors cited previously, social support appears to be an important variable for maintaining life (Berkman & Syme, 1979).

One of the best-known unhealthy syndromes is the so-called Type A behavior pattern. Friedman (1969) identifies a coronary-prone behavior pattern:

a characteristic action-emotion complex which is exhibited by those individuals who are engaged in a relatively *chronic struggle* to obtain an *unlimited* number of *poorly defined* things from their environment in the *shortest period of time* and, if necessary, against the opposing efforts of other things or persons in this same environment [p. 84].

People with this behavior pattern are termed Type A, while those who are relatively unhurried, relaxed, satisfied, and have a serene style of life are termed Type B.

As for the connection of the Type A behavior pattern to illness and health, Burish (1980) states:

The primary dimension along which Type A and Type B individuals vary is their "coronary proneness": Type A individuals are more likely to develop angina pectoris (a disorder involving a distinct type of chest pain), myocardial infarction (a disorder involving necrosis of heart tissue, commonly called heart attack), and other coronary heart diseases (CHD) than are Type B individuals. In addition, Type A individuals show relatively extreme degrees of impatience; mental and physical alertness; deep commitment to their occupation or profession; tenseness of facial musculature; rapid and animated speech, with frequent bursts of increased volume; hurried eating habits; feelings of being under almost continuous time pressure; and a vague guilt or uneasiness about relaxing or slowing down [pp. 244–245].

To be sure, the preceding are generalities, and the Type A syndrome may be manifest in idiosyncratic fashion.

While there are critics of the notion of a Type A syndrome, research findings continue to support its conceptual usefulness. It may, however, prove to be that the symptoms associated with the Type A syndrome will vary with age or the assessment measures used, which will mean that the behaviors targeted for counseling intervention will differ for children, adolescents, and adults (Jackson & Levine, 1987).

To summarize, the Type A behavior pattern reflects chronic stress on the organism. In addition to lessening enjoyment of life, the symptoms of the Type A behavior pattern can literally kill the person. Needless to say, the kinds of behavior associated with the Type A behavior pattern are essential issues for health education and counseling.

The next section will deal with the healthy body/mind, including strategies for stress reduction. At this point, it should be noted that stress management should not be distorted into being merely symptom reduction without lifestyle changes. Hillenberg and Di Lorenzo (1987) believe that a focus on symptom reduction can lead to a lack of attention on etiological factors. Using a transactional definition of stress—"stress occurs when an individual appraises the situation as one in which he or she is unable to cope adequately when confronted with specific valued or significant demands" (p. 403)—they advocate that stress-management techniques be "cohesively tied" to treatment: "In summary, the principal goal of stress management interventions should be to go beyond just the control of symptoms of psychological distress and to equip individuals and possible significant others with the central conflicts contributing to the stress in their lives" (p. 403). Changes in lifestyle are necessary to perpetuate improvements in maintenance of health. This is the subject of the next section.

Body/Mind Liberation

The body and mind combine to accommodate health or to produce illness. This body/mind unity should be the focus of counseling-psychology interventions. In this section we set forth a frame of reference that can be adopted by the counseling psychologist, as described in detail by Woody (1980a).

The philosophical framework for body/mind counseling is captured by Lowen (1975):

> Life itself is a process of growth that starts with the growth of the body and its organs, moves through the development of motor skills, the acquisition of knowledge, the extension of relationships, and ends in the summation of experience that we call wisdom. These aspects of growth overlap, since life and growth take place in a natural, cultural and social environment. And though the growth process is continuous, it is never even. There are periods of leveling-off when the assimilation of experience occurs preparing the organism for a new ascent. Each ascent leads to a new high or summit and creates what we call a peak experience. Each peak experience, in turn, must be integrated into the personality for new growth to occur and for the individual to end in a state of wisdom [p. 33].

While heredity and socialization have significant contributions to make, be they positive or negative, to the organism's health status, self-determination can have equal or greater (more likely the latter for most people) significance for determining a health-promoting lifestyle.

Tenets of Body/Mind Health

Basic guidelines for body/mind health include: (1) avoiding unnecessary reliance on ego-defense mechanisms, as they thwart positive movement and sap much-needed energy; (2) reaching for personal power; "There is in every organism, at whatever level, an underlying flow of movement toward constructive fulfillment of its inherent possibilities" (Rogers, 1977, p. 7); (3) striving to be self-actualizing or fully functioning; (4) recognizing self-worth—for example, acknowledging accomplishments and taking responsibility for outcomes; and (5) eliminating faulty, illogical beliefs and values and replacing them with rational reasoning and actions. Each of these tenets is clearly accessible through counseling psychology.

In keeping with the notion that health requires an effective social-support system, the body/mind framework emphasizes that interpersonal relationships are important. Self-acceptance requires (1) minimizing any self-defeating behaviors and (2) using self-assertion for reciprocal benefits in human relationships. Need fulfillment is an acceptable outcome of interpersonal relations. While care should be taken to have a healthy balance between dependence on and independence from others, the person gains from trusting, caring, and sharing. Helpful communications, drawing on facilitative conditions, are essential:

> Communication is helpful and hurtless when words are congruent with feelings and when feelings are congruent with actions. Helpful and hurtless communication does not blame, does not placate, does not compute, and does not distract. It does not put down or put up. It does not deceive, distort, or deny one's feelings and those of others [L'Abate, 1973, p. 137].

Reinforcement is purposefully given and sought, to bring about healthful conditions. Reinforcement combines with cognitive restructuring to eliminate irrational emotions (anxiety, guilt, depression, anger/hostility).

Counseling psychology can rely on six strategies to promote and maintain body/mind health. They are (1) breathing (Lowen, 1975; Lowen & Lowen, 1977), (2) nutrition and diet, (3) weight control, (4) relaxation (Benson, 1976), (5) countering maladaptive habits (destructive behaviors like smoking and substance abuse), and (6) physical fitness. The client can also be guided to healthful touching, body awareness, and sexual expression (Woody, 1979). Woody (1980a, 1980b) describes specific techniques for each of the foregoing strategies. In addition to mental fitness, counseling psychology should promote physical fitness. Doan and Scherman (1987) review research on the therapeutic effects of physical fitness and offer guidelines for counseling psychologists.

The SCORE Formula

The client's commitment to health can be promoted by the SCORE Formula (Woody, 1984). Everyone has an inherent propensity for pleasure, achievement, and richness in living. Naturally, this tendency embraces a healthy lifestyle.

SCORE is an acronym for five strategies that the counseling psychologist can teach to the client for coping with the problems of life: S = self-concept development; C = control, or responsibility; O = originality, or creativity; R = relaxation; and E = energy.

S = Self: The self-concept is cultivated to (1) allow for fulfillment of needs (2) avoid punitive self-judgments, (3) live in the here and now, and (4) adopt a commitment to self-actualization. It is recommended that clients (1) always try to be authentic, (2) trust in themselves to allow others to experience their transparency, (3) avoid ego-defense mechanisms, (4) accept responsibility for themselves and their actions, and (5) maintain helpful communications with others.

C = Control: Behavior is goal directed, and the person must be responsible for its outcomes. Reinforcement contingencies are selected. Motivation toward achievement is maintained. The locus of control is internal. There is personal responsibility for one's life in total.

O = Originality: Creativity is essential to mental health. It is tied to the achievement motive and the need for mastery. Creativity is used to counteract tension in and demands on the organism.

R = Relaxation: The healthy organism is free from destructive anxiety and tension. Body/mind techniques can be used to regulate breathing, muscular tension, and anxiety-related responses. The person should strive to deprogram the self from anxiety-causing messages and to reprogram the self with health-promoting messages. This task is followed by continual day-to-day practice of activities (mental and physical) that replace anxiety with a relaxed state.

E = Energy: Effective nutrition and diet, weight control, physical fitness, and elimination of maladaptive habits can prepare the organism for the movement toward self-actualization and a fully functioning state. Energy must not be wasted, such as on neurotic defenses and self-destructive behaviors. Energy is interrelated with the self, control, originality, and relaxation and is the fuel that can propel the person to a healthy and happy existence.

The Healthy Counseling Psychologist

Health promotion is more than an academic knowledge of principles of physical and mental health. This is one area in which the counseling psychologist must, by necessity, be a role model. The cigarette smoker has often been heard to ask, in effect, "Why should I quit smoking just because my doctor said it might be harmful. Why, my doctor's a chain smoker."

It appears that the deep-seated nature of a person's health attitudes and habits issues a special mandate for maximum impact from the therapist. This means that counselors must draw on every available option for persuasion. It is unlikely that clients will accept messages about health from therapists who do not practice what they preach. Unless counseling psychologists are prepared to live a commitment to health—controlling nutrition, weight, physical fitness, and maladaptive habits, among other things—their effectiveness as health psychologists will be restricted.

The counseling psychologist's attitudes about health are likely to have a significant influence on the client's resistance or willingness to seek further health services. Part of this attitudinal posture is the time-honored "bedside manner":

> When a physician is sensitive to a client as a social and psychological being, listens to and respects the client, and has an open, give-and-take relationship with the client (a constellation of interpersonal behaviors that we call good psychosocial care), then the client is not discouraged from returning to the doctor. When a physician is insensitive, ignores questions, and treats the client as a disease entity rather than as a person to be respected

(a constellation of interpersonal behaviors that we call poor psychosocial care), then the client is reluctant to return to the doctor. In sum, good experiences with the interpersonal aspects of care increase subsequent utilization; poor experiences decrease subsequent utilization [Ross & Duff, 1982, p. 128].

Before the counseling psychologist defensively asserts, "I *always* provide good psychosocial care," it should be recognized that dealing with illness (such as with a terminal cancer patient) can bring out atypical responses from even well-trained professionals. Therefore, part of developing a constructive attitudinal stance toward health involves the counseling psychologist's resolving personal conflicts about illness and death.

Beyond the Individual Client

The health of the client is the primary goal of health psychology. To obtain this goal, it is necessary to go beyond the client. There are two reasons. First, many individuals will be unable to adopt a healthful lifestyle if left to their own resourcefulness. They will need the support and reinforcement of others, particularly family members. Second, the society must endorse healthful living. An individual struggling for personal health will be hindered or aided by the community's views about health and resources for promoting it.

Working with the Family

Every person operates within a system. Each member of the system influences and is influenced by others. Therefore, health efforts are under the shaping power of those with whom the person interacts, directly or indirectly:

> The family is viewed not as a collection of individuals, but as a naturally interacting system of individual members in which each member affects all other members and is affected by the family as a whole. A change in one member of the system produces change in other members, since all react to restore equilibrium. In addition, family functioning is influenced by its interrelationships with the cultural or community system of which it is a part. [Logan, 1985, p. 24].

In earlier days, counseling psychology emphasized helping the individual. Today, health psychology recognizes that there are systemic effects.

The counseling psychologist must constantly assess the family system in which the client exists. Woody and Springer (1985) suggest that family therapy be used to identify a client's (1) use of stress-related words; (2) tales of anxious moments; (3) preoccupation with body frailties or organ weakness; (4) storytelling about the illnesses of others; (5) attempts to gain sympathy; (6) emphasis on the negative; (7) orientation toward the past, while excluding the positive of the present or hopes for the future; and (8) references to death and related issues.

From the family analysis, the counseling psychologist can implement a tailor-made intervention. Woody and Springer (1985) recommend that the counseling psychologist (1) help each family member attain the universal goals of pleasure, achievement, and richness of living; (2) help each member develop a positive self-concept; (3) emphasize healthful communication within the family; (4) contradict irrational and unhealthy behaviors; (5) guide the family toward healthy emotional and physical intimacy; (6) facilitate healthy sexual expression among family members; (7) reveal the unhealthy implications of any individual or family actions and present healthy alternatives; (8) distribute health-education materials to the family members; (9) establish referral connections to health specialists; and (10) help the individual and the family in their quest for spiritual consonance.

A health-psychology intervention goes beyond family. The individual client and his or her family are part of a community. The community manifests its views about health and illness through public policy, as established by legislative bodies and governmental agencies. Regrettably, health is often given a negative connotation; that is, it is grouped with "welfare" services and is viewed ambivalently by the public (AuClaire, 1984). What is interesting is how many citizens frown on governmentally supported health services yet want health services for themselves that exceed their personal ability to pay: "The psychology of illness, and the importance that consumers give to their own medical care, make policy formulation particularly difficult. . . .There is agreement that frivolous utilization and expenditures should be discouraged, but few patients ever think their own problems frivolous or unworthy of the best care available" (Mechanic, 1981, p. 82). American society is in an era when President Lyndon B. Johnson's dream of a Great Society that would serve all in need has been replaced by a fiscal conservatism that imposes stringent cutbacks on virtually all health-related services (as well as social and educational services). This mandate for cost containment is often accomplished by a decrease in both the quality and quantity of health services (Bice, 1981).

A society that seems uncaring about the health of its members must be helped to recognize that short-term benefits may create long-term liabilities (Woody, 1985). This antihealth movement within the American government is a call to arms for counseling psychologists and all other health-care professionals.

In a sense, the counseling psychologist should help society accept responsibility for its health-related public policies. Such an effort should start with community involvement. This commitment is consonant with the locus-of-control principle: people should internalize responsibility for the quality of life in a society. It cannot be rationalized away; that would be an external locus of control, which is well proven to be unhealthy.

The counseling psychologist can deal with a myriad of health-policy issues (Lum, 1982). Important issues include (1) attacking economic and organizational barriers to accessibility to health care; (2) countering the inflationary costs of care; (3) trying to attain a reasonable service-delivery system, either by extending health services to relatively isolated clients or having adequate numbers of well-trained professionals; (4) ensuring the availability of primary, secondary, and tertiary services; (5) maximizing the standard and quality of care; (6) improving governmental regulations; and (7) encouraging consumer participation in health-care planning.

In order to be effective in the community, the counseling psychologist must adopt a systemic perspective:

> Family therapists need to change their focus from problem-focused direct service to enhancement of family health through "macro" linkages with community supports and resources. As an advocate and "broker," the professional can establish new networks within the community, not only to meet immediate and long-term client needs, but also to join previously unrelated networks of services and resources in the community to better serve common family needs. Family life issues should be considered in the context of the community environment; for example, the traditions, status, interests, and characteristics of the family group should be examined in the context of other subgroups or specific, unique cultures. The economic, political, and social supports of the community should be considered in relationship to these systemic factors so that the sociocultural basic functions of family life are preserved [Burch, 1985, p. 18].

The systemic approach can become multisystemic. Thus, networking becomes an important part of the family and community intervention.

The counseling psychologist has a professional duty to promote health. To reach the community, so as to benefit the individual client (and his or her family), the counseling psychologist should (1) stay informed about public policy concerning health, (2) seek to sensitize clients and families to voice their opinions and preferences to policymakers, (3) actively communicate professional views to policymakers, (4) urge professional colleagues into public-policy actions, and (5) maintain a futuristic perspective and an active stance (Woody, 1985).

Many of these community-level goals can be promoted by one-to-one encounters, such as letters to or meetings with legislators. They can also be encouraged through health education, either in counseling sessions with individuals or families or in public-service efforts (for example, letters to the editor about critical local health issues) (Petosa, 1984b). Mass-communications media can be especially powerful in shaping community and societal public policies. Given its purpose, educational radio and television should be readily available, and they are certainly suitable for conveying health messages (Woody, 1974). Snegroff (1983) offers guidelines for conducting health education through the media and links the approach to counseling psychologists by this assertion: "Mass media are most effective when combined with more personal programs and sources to promote the trial and adoption of positive health behaviors" (p. 11).

Toward Being a Health-Oriented Counseling Psychologist

The public has supported the psychologist's being a health-care provider and, thus, the specialty of health psychology. As exemplified by the definitions for health psychology provided earlier in this chapter, there is no clear-cut boundary for professional roles yet. It seems likely, however, that the evolution of health psychology, like that of so many other psychological specialties heretofore, will bring very specific training and practice requirements. Such specificity is needed and justified to ensure a standard of care adequate to safeguard the consumer and society.

We have previously underscored the importance of the counseling psychologist's being a role model for health and working through personal conflicts about illness and death. These are prerequisites for effective helping. Moreover, many areas of academic knowledge about health and illness are not yet common to counseling-psychology training programs. Among many topics, the health psychologist needs familiarity with epidemiology, chronic diseases, rehabilitation, health conditions for special populations (infants, children, the elderly), family planning, health-care delivery systems, public-health policy, and innumerable techniques tailored to alter unhealthy behavior.

The practice framework for health psychology needs to be preventive, therapeutic, and remedial/rehabilitative. There must be an integration of research and practice. Self-ordainment as a "health psychologist" is unacceptable. To be a health psychologist, the counseling psychologist must acquire specialized health-related training and attain a unification of personal attitudes and practices with professional competencies to promote and maintain health. There is, as we have said, a pronounced public mandate for improved health services and an endorsement for psychologists to be health-care providers. Counseling psychology is destined to promote health.

Summary

This is an era in which our American society has a strong commitment to health. Consequently, health psychology is a rapidly growing specialty that offers a context for counseling psychology. Long endorsed by counseling psychologists, interventions are directed at enhancing the holistic person (mind, body, and spirit) for optimal health. Unfortunately, human nature offers resistance to changing health-related attitudes and behaviors. Stress has deleterious effects but can be countered with counseling strategies.

The body and mind combine to accommodate health or to produce illness—the counseling psychologist seeks "bodymind liberation" to replace illness-producing behavior with healthful behavior. The acronym *SCORE* can serve as a reminder of five strategies: S = self-concept development; C = control, or responsibility; O = originality, or creativity; R = relaxation (freedom from stress); and E = energy for enriched living.

References

Alschuler, C. F., & Alschuler, A. S. (1984). Developing Healthy Responses to Anger: The Counselor's Role. *Journal of Counseling and Development, 63,* 26–29.
American Psychological Association. (1985). *Directory.* Washington, DC: Author.
American Psychological Association. (Undated). *Health Psychology: New Perspectives* (brochure). Washington, DC: Author.

AuClaire, P. A. (1984). Public Attitudes Toward Social Welfare Expenditures. *Social Work, 29,* 139–144.

Bakal, D. A. (1979). *Psychology and Medicine: Psychological Dimensions of Health and Illness.* New York: Springer.

Belloc, N. B., & Breslow, L. (1972). Relationship of Physical Health Status and Health Practices. *Preventive Medicine, 1,* 409–421.

Benson, H. (1976). *The Relaxation Response.* New York: Avon.

Berkman, L., & Syme, E. L. (1979). Social Networks, Host Resistance and Mortality: A Nine Year Follow-Up Study of Alameda County Residents. *American Journal of Epidemiology, 109,* 186–203.

Bice, T. W. (1981). Social Science and Health Services: Contributions to Public Policy. In J. B. McKinlay (Ed.), *Issues in Health Care Policy* (pp. 1–28). Cambridge, MA: MIT Press.

Breslow, L., & Engstrom, J. E. (1980). Persistence of Health Habits and Their Relationship to Mortality. *Preventive Medicine, 9,* 469–483.

Bromberg, W. (1975). *From Shaman to Psychotherapist: A History of the Treatment of Mental Illness.* Chicago: Regnery.

Burch, G. K. W. (1985). Influencing the Community and Its Agencies Toward Family Health. In J. R. Springer & R. H. Woody (Eds.), *Health Promotion in Family Therapy* (pp. 13–21). Rockville, MD: Aspen Systems.

Burish, T. G. (1980). Type A/B Behavior Patterns. In R. H. Woody (Ed.), The Encyclopedia of Clinical Assessment (Vol. 1) (pp. 244–256). San Francisco: Jossey-Bass.

Catalano, R., & Dooley, D. (1983). Health Effects of Economic Instability: A Test of Economic Stress Hypothesis. *Journal of Health and Social Behavior, 24,* 46–60.

Clarke, J. H., MacPherson, B. V., & Holmes, D. R. (1982). Cigarette Smoking and External Locus of Control Among Young Adolescents. *Journal of Health and Social Behavior, 23,* 253–259.

Cleary, P. D., & Mechanic, D. (1983). Sex Differences in Psychological Distress Among Married People. *Journal of Health and Social Behavior, 24,* 111–121.

Cummings, N. A. (1986). The Dismantling of Our Health System: Strategies for the Survival of Psychological Practice. *American Psychologist, 41,* 426–431.

Doan, R. E., & Scherman, A. (1987). The Therapeutic Effect of Physical Fitness on Measures of Personality: A Literature Review. *Journal of Counseling and Development, 66*(1), 28–36.

Fenichel, O. (1945). *The Psychoanalytic Theory of Neurosis.* New York: Norton.

Friedman, M. (1969). *Pathogenesis of Coronary Artery Disease.* New York: McGraw-Hill.

Gortmaker, S. L, Eckenrode, J., & Gore, S. (1982). Stress and the Utilization of Health Services: A Time Series and Cross-Sectional Analysis. *Journal of Health and Social Behavior, 23,* 25–38.

Hall, C. S. (1954). *A Primer on Freudian Psychology.* New York: World.

Hillenberg, J. B., & Di Lorenzo, T. M. (1987). Stress Management Training in Health Psychology Practice: Critical Clinical Issues. *Professional Psychology, 18*(4), 402–404.

Horney, K. (1937). *The Neurotic Personality of Our Time.* New York: Norton.

Jackson, C., & Levine, D. W. (1987). Comparison of the Matthews Youth Test for Health and the Hunter-Wolfe A-B Rating Scale: Measures of Type A Behavior in Children. *Health Psychology, 6*(3), 255–267.

Klippel, J. A., & DeJoy, D. M. (1984). Counseling Psychology in Behavioral Medicine and Health Psychology. *Journal of Counseling Psychology, 31,* 219–227.

Knowles, J. H. (1977). *Doing Better and Feeling Worse: Health in the United States.* New York: Norton.

L'Abate, L. (1973). Psychodynamic Interventions: A Personal Statement. In R. H. Woody & J. D. Woody (Eds.), *Sexual, Marital, and Familial Relations: Therapeutic Interventions for professional helping.* (pp. 122–180). Springfield, IL: Thomas.

Logan, D. (1985). Health in Family Therapy Theories. In J. R. Springer & R. H. Woody (Eds.), *Health Promotion in Family Therapy* (pp. 22–35). Rockville, MD: Aspen Systems.

Lowen, A. (1975). *Bioenergetics.* New York: Penguin.

Lowen, A., & Lowen, L. (1977). *The Way to Vibrant Health: A Manual of Bioenergetic Exercises.* New York: Harper & Row.

Lum, D. (1982). Problem Context of Health Care Policy. In D. Lum (Ed.), *Social Work and Health Care Policy* (pp. 3–13). Totowa, NJ: Allanheld, Osmun.

Martin, B. (1971). *Anxiety and Neurotic Disorders.* New York: Wiley.

Matarazzo, J. D. (1982). Behavioral Health and Behavioral Medicine: Frontiers for a New Health Psychology. *American Psychologist, 37,* 1–14.

Mechanic, D. (1981). Some Dilemmas in Health Care Policy. In J. B. McKinlay (Ed.), *Issues in Health Care Policy* (pp. 80–94). Cambridge, MA: MIT Press.

O'Neill, R. M. (1984). Anality and Type A Coronary-Prone Behavior Pattern. *Journal of Personality Assessment, 48,* 627–628.

Parcell, C. L. (1985). Wellness vs. Illness: Which Road Are We Taking? *Employee Assistance Programs Digest, 5*(3), 18–25.

Pelletier, K. R. (1977). Mind as Healer, Mind as Slayer: A Holistic Approach to Preventing Stress Disorders. New York: Dell.

Petosa, R. (1984a). Self-Actualization and Health-Related Practices. *Health Education, 15*(3), 9–12.

Petosa, R. (1984b). Wellness: An Emerging Opportunity for Health Education. *Health Education, 15*(6), 37–39.

Pilisuk, M., Boylan, R., & Acredolo, C. (1987). Social Support, Life Stress, and Subsequent Medical Care Utilization. *Health Psychology, 6*(4), 273–288.

Rogers, C. R. (1977). *Carl Rogers on Personal Power.* New York: Delacorte.

Ross, C. E., & Duff, R. S. (1982). Returning to the Doctor: The Effect of Client Characteristics, Type of Practice, and Experiences With Care. *Journal of Health and Social Behavior, 23,* 119–131.

Rotter, J. B. (1966). Generalized Expectancies for Internal Versus External Control of Reinforcement. *Psychological Monographs, 80*(1 Whole No. 609).

Schwartz, G. E., & Weiss, S. M. (1977). *Proceedings of the Yale Conference on Behavioral Medicine* (DHEW Publication No. NIH 78-1424). Washington, DC: U.S. Government Printing Office.

Seeman, M., & Seeman, T. A. (1983). Health Behavior and Personal Autonomy: A Longitudinal Study of the Sense of Control in Illness. *Journal of Health and Social Behavior, 24,* 144–160.

Seligman, M. E. P. (1975). *Helplessness: On Depression, Development and Death.* San Francisco: Freeman.

Snegroff, S. (1983). Health Education and Mass Communication. *Health Education,* (3), 8–11.

Springer, J. R., & Woody, R. H. (Eds.). (1985). *Health Promotion in Family Therapy.* Rockville, MD: Aspen Systems.

Thoresen, C. E., & Eagleston, J. R. (1985). Counseling for Health. *The Counseling Psychologist, 13,* 15–87.

U.S. Public Health Service. (1981). *Health—United States, 1981* (DHHS Publication PHS 82-1232). Washington, DC: U.S. Government Printing Office.

Verbrugge, L. M. (1983). Multiple Roles and Physical Health of Women and Men. *Journal of Health and Social Behavior, 24,* 16–30.

Woody, R. H. (1974). Educational Television Programming and School Health. *Journal of School Health, 44,* 246–249.

Woody, R. H. (1979). Intimacy-Related Anxiety and Massage. *Voices: The Art and Science of Psychotherapy, 15*(1), 36–42.

Woody, R. H. (1980a). *Bodymind Liberation: Achieving Holistic Health.* Springfield, IL: Thomas.

Woody, R. H. (1980b). *The Use of Massage in Facilitating Holistic Health.* Springfield, IL: Thomas.

Woody, R. H. (1984). *Practical Mental Health.* Springfield, IL: Thomas.

Woody, R. H. (1985). Shaping Public Policy for Family Health. In J. R. Springer & R. H. Woody (Eds.), *Health Promotion in Family Therapy* (pp. 1–12). Rockville, MD: Aspen Systems.

Woody, R. H., & Springer, J. R. (1985). A Holistic Health Model for Family Therapy. In J. R. Springer & R. H. Woody (Eds.), *Health Promotion in Family Therapy* (pp. 36–45). Rockville, MD: Aspen Systems.

Ethics and Law

Academic training of counseling psychologists has to be enriched with a mixture of ethics and the law. Trainees must recognize that society requires all ideas, skills, and services to be judged, at least in part, by their ethical and legal qualities. Many trainees probably assume that there are highly specific and permanent ethical and legal dictates and that the only challenge is to commit the list of proscriptions and prescriptions to memory and then, forevermore, operate accordingly. Such is not the case.

Ethics and law, as relevant to professionalism, are never fixed but are continually evolving. Consequently, counseling psychologists must internalize principles and create their own guidelines, using always-changing information from sometimes ambiguous sources. That is, while professional organizations commonly offer position statements, the implications for ethics and the law are often not succinctly stated. These implications must be detected and interpreted by the individual professional.

In this chapter we define and analyze ethics and law to help the counseling psychologist develop such a self-monitoring ability. Since ethics and law are not one and the same, we make the distinction. An inadequate or improper grounding in ethics and the law could cast a long-term pall over the counseling psychologist's career, so we consider training issues. We identify specific pitfalls or problem areas and offer ideas for avoiding negative consequences. Throughout, the emphasis is on pragmatics. Ethics and law can be quite abstract. While abstraction may be fine for purely academic study, we are seeking to provide both academic and practical values.

Professional Ethics

Professionalism is a product of society. Society recognizes that it needs services of a prescribed quality and cannot tolerate behaviors of a certain type. To attain these ends, it uses university degrees and licenses to anoint certain persons with "professional" status. This status, however, is neither fixed in definition nor permanent to the holder. Professionals must maintain standards promulgated by public policy. The cornerstone is ethics.

Today's counseling psychologist operates with an ethical set quite different from ours when we entered the profession several decades ago. The infancy of counseling psychology was marked by the profession's carrying the burden of creating and monitoring ethics. Among other influences, professional organizations—such as the American Personnel and Guidance Association (now the American Association for Counseling and Development) and the American Psychological Association—brought practitioners of the same discipline together to caucus about what should and should not occur in training and practice. The result would commonly be a position statement for the individual professional to rely on.

In this era counseling psychology has matured as a profession, and society is more concerned with monitoring professionalism. Kitchener (1984) declares that "nationally and internationally, there has been a great revival in applied ethics in an attempt to better define what it means for professionals to act in an ethical manner towards their patients or clients" (p. 15). She cites medical practices as spawning the interest in ethics that has now spread into other disciplines, including counseling psychology. This interest is evidenced by the plethora of governmental policy efforts, court cases, and continually modified codes of professional ethics.

The legal and ethical waters are turbulent. Society would like to entrust self-regulation to the ethics committees but is now hesitant to do so, probably, in part, because there is a belief that professional associations have been too self-serving and have failed to adequately protect clients. Consequently, state regulation (such as through licensing boards) and civil legal remedies (such as malpractice actions) have increased.

Despite this surge in governmental regulation and litigation, the number of ethical complaints against psychologists has continued to increase:

> One of the reasons for this increase in complaints is that at least eight state associations have disbanded their ethics committees or are using those committees solely for educative and referral purposes in order to protect themselves from potential legal liability. This issue is confounded by state associations either having difficulty obtaining liability insurance or not being able to afford adequate coverage [American Psychological Association (APA), 1987b].

It seems that there is a clear-cut diminution of reliance on ethics committees, and the increase in legal liability reflects a societal demand for accountability that surpasses the authority of a professional discipline. One means for rectifying the situation (that is, recovering self-regulation by the profession) is for each practitioner to maintain a stronger allegiance to ethics than has been the case in the past. This chapter is geared toward cultivating such an allegiance.

Defining "ethics" for professionalism is not simple and certainly is not always readily practical. There is an interweaving of abstract concepts, which must be translated into concrete behaviors. This effort will be our goal as our analysis moves from definition to behavioral examples.

Morality and Ethics

Morality is fundamental to ethics. Taylor (1978) defines ethics as the "philosophical study of morality" (p. 3). For DeGeorge (1982),

Morality is a term used to cover those practices and activities that are considered importantly right and wrong, the rules which govern those activities, and the values that are imbedded, fostered, or pursued by those activities and practices. The morality of a society is related to its mores or the customs accepted by a society or group as being the right and wrong ways to act, as well as to the laws of a society which add legal prohibitions and sanctions to many activities considered to be immoral [p. 12].

Note that mores or customs lead to morality, which leads to values and rules; they, in turn, produce ethics, and there is legal surveillance and enforcement. Certainly society wants professionals to manifest moral behavior. The intimate nature of the therapist/client relationship in counseling psychology fosters a special requirement for moral behavior.

As is true with so many aspects of ethics, moral behavior is not a firm set of conditions. Moral behavior comes from the individual's interpretation of society's mores and values and represents a blending of the personal and the social.

Behaving morally involves psychological processes. Rest (1984, p. 19) describes the processes this way:

1. The person must interpret the particular situation in terms of who is involved, what lines of action are possible for the actor, and how each of these lines of action would affect the welfare of each party involved.
2. The person must judge which of the alternative lines of action is more just or fair, or morally right.
3. A person is usually also aware that other values besides *moral* goals can be served by alternative courses of action.
4. The person must have actually carried through on the decision to do the moral action, persisting and not wandering from the goal, and must have been able to implement that intention.

Rest asserts that many counseling-psychology trainees complete their programs with an inclination to avoid moral issues in employment; are poorly prepared to deal with a moral problem; and fail to recognize moral issues in a way that would preclude blunders in practice.

Going beyond morality per se, Kitchener (1984) analyzes ethics in counseling psychology:

Traditionally, ethics has been a branch of study in philosophy concerning how people ought to act toward each other, pronouncing judgments of value about those actions, e.g., deciding whether in a just society people ought to act in a certain way, and developing rules of ethical justification (e.g., asking how we can justify holding one set of values over another) [p. 16].

This "oughtness" is expressed in public policy. Professionals play a major role in shaping public policy, such as through research, press releases, political lobbying, and public information. But in the end the society, whether at the individual level or through a governing body (such as a state legislature that passes a statute on the licensing and regulation of professional practice), makes the final decision of what *ought* to be ethical behavior.

We do not mean that professionals must abstain from shaping public policy. To the contrary, an essential ingredient of professionalism is educating the public and, in the process, influencing public policy. For example, psychologists are important to the legal system, such as when they inform the courts and legislatures about useful scientific knowledge. This function is to be executed in a manner "(a) that preserves the integrity of the data, (b) that is comprehensible to educated persons not trained in the social sciences, and (c) that is consonant with procedural and evidentiary rules for consideration of scientific evidence" (Melton, 1987, p. 489).

Public policy must provide definition to ethical behavior. The "oughtness" has to be systematic. DeGeorge (1982) offers a useful definition:

> *Ethics* in general can be defined as a systematic attempt through the use of reason to make sense of our individual and social moral experience in such a way as to determine the rules which ought to govern human conduct and the values worth pursuing in life. The attempt is systematic and hence goes beyond what each reflective person tends to do in his daily life in making sense of his moral experience, organizing it, and attempting to make it coherent and unified. Since it uses reason and does not use revelation, it can be distinguished from a religious or theological approach to morality. Insofar as it attempts to ascertain what rules and *values* ought to be followed and pursued, it can be distinguished from anthropology, psychology, and sociology. Those disciplines describe how people behave but usually do not prescribe how they should or ought to behave. Ethics concerns itself with human conduct, taken here to mean human activity which is done knowingly and, to a large extent, willingly. It does not concern itself with automatic responses, actions done in one's sleep or under hypnosis, and so on [p. 12].

This definition provides an important emphasis on the components of ethics. There must be a system, one that is predicated on moral reason. There must be an evaluation of behavioral alternatives for the benefit of people. And human conduct in a profession, like counseling psychology, occurs knowingly and with a sense of personal responsibility, duty, and control.

In professional practice, "ethics is usually concerned with *justifying* controlling practices rather than merely describing them" (Skinner, 1953, p. 328). Consequently, professional organizations are interested in determining the justification for their members' practices, thereby allowing a degree of institutional control. This control is commonly obtained through a "code of ethics," which we shall discuss later. At this point, suffice it to say that a professional code of ethics provides guidance, governance, and control of professional behavior (Mappes, Robb, & Engels, 1985).

Implicit to ethics, whether applied to the person or the profession, is the notion of self-regulation. Even though a professional organization may maintain a code of ethics that applies to its members and even though a state statute may implicitly or explicitly endorse a code of ethics, the individual practitioner is, for the most part, left to his or her own regulation.

There can never be (nor should there be) an "ethics enforcer" at the elbow of the practitioner. Welfel and Lipsitz (1984) indicate that

Thus it appears that effective self-regulation entails more than clearly written, widely disseminated, frequently taught, and strictly enforced ethical codes. What appears to be necessary is a membership capable of making sophisticated judgments about which course of action may be ethical in situations in which no one behavior seems entirely ethical or unethical. Moreover, members must be able to self-monitor impulses and strong feelings that may threaten to overwhelm their better judgment [p. 31].

Analysis of published accounts indicates that there may be a helplessness to resist even those behaviors recognized as improper or unethical, such as sexual intimacies between therapists and patients (Butler & Zelen, 1977).

Ethical Standards

Counseling psychology, with its vocational, educational, and psychological blend, has used ethical position statements from at least two sources—namely, the American Psychological Association (1981a) and the American Association for Counseling and Development (1988). Each of these organizational documents sets forth proscriptions and prescriptions for the members of the association. These codes are included as Appendixes A and B.

It should be noted that a code of ethics applies only to those who hold membership in the particular association. If a counseling psychologist is not a member of the association, it has no jurisdiction, so to speak. There is an exception, as when a state statute sets a licensing standard for professional conduct that has an implicit or explicit link to the ethical guidelines of a discipline; more will be said on this matter later.

There are also numerous documents from professional associations that create standards for specialized services. For example, specialized documents that the counseling psychologist should consider include "General Guidelines for Providers of Psychological Services" (APA, 1987a), "Speciality Guidelines for the Delivery of Services by Counseling Psychologists" (APA, 1981b), *Guidelines for Psychologists Conducting Growth Groups* (APA, 1973), *Standards for Educational and Psychological Tests* (APA, 1985), and *Ethical Principles in the Conduct of Research with Human Participants* (APA, 1983)—and there are others.

Also, as the counseling psychologist becomes specialized, the ethical umbrella may expand beyond professional psychology, such as to marriage and family therapy (American Association for Marriage and Family Therapy, 1985) or sex education, counseling, and therapy (American Association of Sex Educators, Counselors, and Therapists, 1978).

Some courts will determine the standard of care that should have been maintained by a practitioner who claims specialization by citing what the foremost professional organization supports, regardless of whether the practitioner is a member. Therefore, in a malpractice action against a counseling psychologist who professed to be (or whose client had a reasonable basis for believing him or her to be) a specialist in, say, sex therapy, it is quite possible that the counseling psychologist's conduct would be compared to the standard for certified sex therapists (as certified by the American Association for Sex

Educators, Counselors, and Therapists), even though he or she was not certified by that organization.

The APA's guidelines for counseling psychologists (1981b) include sections for clinical, counseling, industrial/organizational, and school psychologists. Since a psychologist could potentially function professionally in each of these four specialties, depending upon the skills, services, and contexts, it is best to be familiar with the guidelines for all of the specialties. While there are more similarities than differences among them, there are distinctions.

The specialty guidelines are prefaced by a statement of their voluntary nature:

> Traditionally, all learned disciplines have treated the designation of specialty practice as a reflection of preparation in greater depth in a particular subject matter, together with a voluntary limiting of focus to a more restricted area of practice by the professional. Lack of specialty designation does not preclude general providers of psychological services from using the methods or dealing with the populations of any specialty, except insofar as psychologists voluntarily refrain from providing services they are not trained to render. . . . Therefore, these Guidelines are meant to apply only to those psychologists who voluntarily wish to be designated as *counseling psychologists* [APA, 1981b, p. 652].

While neither ethics nor law per se, the specialty guidelines have taken on both statuses. For example, one state psychological association recommended to the state board of psychological examiners that the guidelines be used to judge alleged violators of the state statute for licensing psychologists. Further, it seems quite likely that the widespread professional endorsement accorded to the specialty guidelines will lead to their being the standard of care applied to a malpractice action against a counseling psychologist, regardless of his or her "voluntary wish to be designated" as a counseling psychologist under the auspices of the APA.

Distinguishing Ethics and the Law

The preceding discussion illustrates how ethics and the law are often intertwined, but the two can and should be distinguished. Kitchener (1984) notes that "the law and ethics are not necessarily co-extensive" (p. 16), and she adds: "They can probably be best conceptualized as two over-lapping circles which share a common intersection" (p. 16).

Ethics can proscribe a behavior; for example, "Sexual intimacies with clients are unethical" (APA, 1981a, p. 636). Yet sexual intimacies between therapists and clients occur. Pope, Keith-Spiegel, and Tabachnick (1986) surveyed psychotherapists and found that 95% of the male and 76% of the female respondents had been sexually attracted to their clients. Of these respondents, 9.4% of the male and 2.5% of the female psychotherapists had acted out such feelings. Indeed, a report by the APA's Ethics Committee (1987b) reveals a continuing increase in the number of cases involving "sexual intimacy, dual relationship, or exploitation and/or sexual harassment" (p. 732).

Ethical proceedings within a professional organization can lead to the overlap with the law. Wisconsin makes it a misdemeanor for a psychotherapist to engage in sexual contact with a client. Of greater impact, civil tort law applies as well, allowing for personal injury (and related) claims for what amounts to professional malpractice. While malpractice will be discussed in detail later, it should be noted that this example of the overlap between ethics and the law is timely and profound. This one type of wrongful behavior has resulted in the greatest increase in lawsuits against psychologists.

The overlap between ethics and the law is evidenced in licensing statutes. At one time there was a move toward having a state statute cite, say, the APA's (1981a) "Ethical Principles of Psychologists," thereby transforming ethics into law. This approach, however, was fraught with problems of antitrust and conflict-of-interest violations, and it has essentially been abandoned in favor of a more subtle (but equally effective) form of legal support. For example, the Office of the Attorney General for Florida responded in this way when asked for clarification of how a violation of APA ethics would overlap with the state licensing statute:

> The APA *Ethical Principles of Psychologists* are not a part of Florida law, and as such are not enforceable by the Board of Psychological Examiners. However, a violation of the ethical principles would likely be a violation of Section 490.009(2)(s) which reads as follows: Failing to *meet the minimum standards of performance and professional activities when measured against generally prevailing peer performance,* including the undertaking of activities for which the licensee is not qualified by training or experience. The APA ethical principles are very likely the best indication of prevailing peer performance standards, and violation of such standards may result in discipline by the Board [Florida Psychological Association, 1986, p. 16].

Keep in mind that a psychologist who is licensed by the State of Florida but is not a member of the APA is, nonetheless, very much under the influence of the association for the definition of ethical behavior.

The Law

For most counseling psychologists, the foremost legal source is the state licensing law. In addition to specifying training and examination prerequisites for licensed practice, the statute commonly indicates the behaviors that will potentially lead to discipline under the law. For example, Florida Chapter 490: Psychological Services states that any applicant or licensee who commits any of 23 acts set forth may receive one or more of the following penalties:

   a. Denial of an application for licensure, either temporarily or permanently.
   b. Revocation of an application for licensure, either temporarily or permanently.
   c. Suspension, after hearing, of a license for a period of up to 5 years.

    d. Immediate suspension of a license. . . .

    e. Imposition of an administrative fine not to exceed $1,000.

    f. Issuance of a public reprimand [Florida Statutes, 1985, p. 1512].

Beyond penalties under the licensing law, an errant counseling psychologist could potentially be legally liable under civil law for damages to a client, such as through a malpractice action.

The far-reaching coverage of penalties from the licensure law should be recognized. Although each state has its own statute, the Florida law is exemplary in listing the following violations:

    a. Attempting to obtain, obtaining, or renewing a license under this chapter by bribery or fraudulent misrepresentation or through an error of the board or department.

    b. Having a license to practice a comparable profession revoked, suspended, or otherwise acted against, including the denial of certification or licensure by another state, territory, or country.

    c. Being convicted or found guilty, regardless of adjudication, of a crime in any jurisdiction which directly relates to the practice of his profession or the ability to practice his profession.

    d. False, deceptive, or misleading advertising or obtaining a fee or other thing of value on the representation that beneficial results from any treatment will be guaranteed.

    e. Advertising, practicing, or attempting to practice under a name other than one's own.

    f. Maintaining a professional association with any person whom the applicant or licensee knows, or has reason to believe, is in violation of this chapter or of a rule of the department or, in the case of psychologists, of the department or the board.

    g. Knowingly aiding, assisting, procuring, or advising any non-licensed person to hold himself out as licensed under this chapter.

    h. Failing to perform any statutory or legal obligation placed upon a person licensed under this chapter.

    i. Willfully making or filing a false report or record; failing to file a report or record required by state or federal law; willfully impeding or obstructing the filing of a report or record; or inducing another person to make or file a false report or record or to impede or obstruct the filing of a report or record.

    j. Paying or receiving a kickback, rebate, bonus, or other remuneration for receiving a patient or client or referring a patient or client to another provider of mental health care services or to a provider of health care services or goods.

    k. Committing any act upon a patient or client, other than the spouse of the actor, which would constitute sexual battery or which would constitute sexual misconduct. . . .

    l. Making misleading, deceptive, untrue, or fraudulent representations in the practice of any profession licensed under this chapter.

    m. Soliciting patients or clients personally, or through an agent, through the use of fraud, intimidation, undue influence, or a form of overreaching or vexatious conduct.

n. Failing to make available to a patient or client, upon written request, copies of tests, reports, or documents in the possession or under the control of the licensee which have been prepared for and paid for by the patient or client.

o. Failing to respond within 30 days to a written communication from the department concerning any investigation by the department or to make available any relevant records with respect to any investigation about the licensee's conduct or background.

p. Being unable to practice the profession for which he is licensed under this chapter with reasonable skill and competence as a result of any mental or physical condition or by reason of illness; drunkenness; or excessive use of drugs, narcotics, chemicals, or any other substance.

q. Violating provisions of this chapter . . . or any rules adopted pursuant thereto.

r. Performing any treatment or prescribing any therapy which, by the prevailing standards of the mental health professions in the community, would constitute experimentation on human subjects, without first obtaining full, informed, and written consent.

s. Failing to meet the minimum standards of performance in professional activities when measured against generally prevailing peer performance, including the undertaking of activities for which the licensee is not qualified by training or experience.

t. Delegating professional responsibilities to a person whom the licensee knows or has reason to know is not qualified by training or experience to perform such responsibilities.

u. Violating a rule relating to the regulation of the profession or a lawful order of the department previously entered in a disciplinary hearing.

v. Failure of the licensee to maintain in confidence a communication made by a patient or client in the context of such services, except by written permission or in the face of a clear and immediate probability of bodily harm to the patient or client or to others.

w. Making public statements which are derived from test data, client contacts, or behavioral research and which identify or damage research subjects or clients [Florida Statutes, 1985, pp. 1512–1513].

Clearly the "long arm of the law" reaches beyond the license on the wall and well into professional practices and conduct in one's personal life (for example, substance use).

Licensure or certification by state statute represents a form of professional regulation. Society has concluded that self-regulation by the practitioner and member regulation by professional organizations should be supplemented by legal regulation. The basic premise is, of course, that the public welfare is safeguarded by governmental approval of competency by licensure or certification.

Selected Problem Areas in Ethics and the Law

There are numerous problems in maintaining an ethical and lawful practice in counseling psychology. In this section we consider advocacy versus objectivity, recognizing an ethical or legal problem, working for an organization, the helping relationship, confidentiality and privileged communication, misrepresentation, and malpractice.

Advocacy versus Objectivity

One of the dilemmas facing the counseling psychologist is how to honor sociophilosophical ideals while meeting business objectives. As a business-oriented professional, the counseling psychologist should retain objectivity, but as a professional committed to bettering society, he or she has need for advocacy.

Championing human rights is a problem area. Refusal to condone discrimination should surely be part of professional practice, as should pursuit of civil rights for all people. Our culturally pluralistic society must ensure dignity and worth to all, without regard to age, social class, handicap, race, or gender. Ibrahim (1985) asserts that "counselors need to attend to the human rights concerns that are still unresolved (economic and political equality, equity, deprivation, poverty, and violence)" (p. 134). We take up this challenge now to underscore that (1) advocacy may be necessary, (2) action is often a wise strategy, and (3) the counseling psychologist should approach the areas of ethics and law as an agent for change, one who dares to promote advances for the benefit of others.

Ethics and law are not always in accord. Mappes and his colleagues (1985) acknowledge that professional ethical preferences may be in conflict with the judicial process—for example, in the realm of confidentiality. (More will be said on confidentiality and privileged communication later.) They maintain that "state and national ethics committees can become more proactive in working with bar associations, legislatures, and the judiciary to achieve laws that best represent both the public's right to protection and the profession's need to take calculated risks in providing responsible service to the public" (p. 251).

Although there are several groups whose rights are jeopardized, children should receive special mention. The educational roots of the counseling psychologist offer a connection to schools and other children's concerns. The jeopardy to children who are thrust into litigation by adults compels involvement by all mental-health professionals (Melton, 1986).

Notwithstanding the *parens patriae* doctrine (which gives society certain protective rights over children), there are many deficits in the U.S. legal system when it comes to protecting the rights of children. C. M. Glenn (1980) points out that there have been many proponents of legal rights for children but that public policy is responding slowly. Parents still control the relationship between a counselor and a child. For example, the minor child has no legal right to privacy per se. Glenn asserts:

> The role of the traditional child psychotherapist must be modified to include the role of information provider to the children, so as to provide the children with informed consent. In addition, the child therapist must be able to function as child advocate . . . and must also function as a social/political/legal change agent [pp. 617–618].

While this child advocacy seems unimpeachable, it does, in fact, run counter to laws that protect the sanctity of the family.

Child abuse has carved out some inroads in public policy, such as the statutory mandates that require professionals (among others) to report abuse and that grant them immunity from any possible legal action for doing so. Children still, however, have very limited legal rights exclusive of their parents. For example, one state-level committee on mental-health law opposed parents' being able to usurp an adolescent child's right to an attorney in an involuntary-commitment proceeding. That is, if the parents wanted their son or daughter committed to a mental hospital, the child would have no right to legal counsel at a hearing of the mental-health board. When this committee sent forward a draft of legislation that would afford legal counsel to minor children, there was strong opposition from both health and legal sources, and the effort was dropped. Child advocacy is a difficult subject. There is no simple solution.

Recognizing a Problem: A Deficit in Training and Research?

Counseling psychologists do not consistently recognize legal or ethical problems, apparently because of a lack of knowledge. Hinkeldey and Spokane (1985) found that mental-health counselors relied very little on legal guidelines and needed more familiarity with legal and ethical issues in counseling. Tymchuk and his colleagues (1982) studied ethical decision making, and concluded that "consistency in ethical decision making exists in some situations, but not in others" (p. 420). Apparently the type of ethical question was important. The researchers found the greatest consensus on issues involving sexual behavior, confidentiality, and client dangerousness, whereas there was weakened consensus on issues involving advertising, research precaution, test security and interpretation, and fees for service. This inconsistency has led Welfel and Lipsitz (1983) to assert that counseling psychology's interest in ethics has, to date, received an inadequate translation into systematic study of the dynamics of unethical behavior. They call for a "comprehensive approach to ethics research and education" and assert: "Failing to emphasize and study this area through rigorous research designs is not only a disservice to the public and our students, but also inconsistent with the principles of professional conduct to which we say we adhere" (p. 329).

Even with training, there is reason to doubt whether practitioners have enough ethical information to handle everyday problems. Green and Hansen (1986) surveyed family therapists and found that they encountered dilemmas that were not included in their code of ethics. They also report that

Family therapists who were trained at workshops reported facing significantly more dilemmas in the area of professional development than those trained through formal education, supervision, or any combination of the three. . . . One wonders if therapists can get enough out of workshops to be able to competently do family therapy [p. 227].

(Wilcoxon, 1987, provides a helpful review of Green and Hansen's study.)

Working for an Organization

An organization, even one committed to human service, may have an aim that is divergent from an individual's needs. As an institution, the organization is predicated on preserving itself. The counseling psychologist is faced with reconciling any divergence between organizational and individual needs.

As an example, every service organization has to be mindful of its budget. The administrators establish priorities. While it might be assumed that the welfare of the client would always be foremost, the definition of how this priority is translated into operations can lead to alternatives. As an example, should a certain amount of money be allocated to increase the travel budget for administrators to "establish a presence" at national conferences (thereby presumably promoting the status of the organization)? Or should the money be used to employ an additional counseling psychologist (thereby increasing the availability of direct service)? There is not one answer for this sort of question. The APA's specialty guidelines (1981b) state: "A counseling psychological service unit includes sufficient numbers of professional and support personnel to achieve its goals, objectives, and purposes" (p. 657). What if the organization chooses to make budget allocations that result in a failure to include "sufficient numbers" of personnel? The implication is that the counseling psychologist would be a party to a substandard operation and that it would be unethical, therefore, to remain employed there.

Does this mean that when an organization seems, in the opinion of the counseling psychologist, to be offering substandard care, he or she should resign? It could be! After all, the specialty guidelines state: "The promotion of human welfare is the primary principle guiding the professional activity of the counseling psychologist and the counseling psychological unit" (p. 659). It would seem unlikely that substandard care would be fulfilling the "promotion of human welfare." Of course, it could be argued that some professional care, albeit substandard, is better than no professional care. Likewise, it could be argued that the counseling psychologist, rather than resigning, should "stand and fight"—that is, stay employed and try to upgrade the quality of the service.

In addition to ethical problems, the organization can create legal liability. As we shall elaborate on in the malpractice section later in this chapter, professional services must meet a certain standard of care, derived from what is reasonable and prudent under the circumstances. Failure to meet this standard results in liability for any damage that a client experiences.

Sometimes administrative practices exacerbate the liability. For example, if a counseling psychologist were assigned supervisory duties for practicum and internship students from a university, if the administrator would not allow adequate time for supervision, and if a student behaved negligently or wrongfully to the detriment of a client, the counseling psychologist could still be held liable. it would probably be of little defense to say, "Don't blame me. If I had been allowed more time to supervise, it wouldn't have happened."

A certain type of counseling-psychological service may, by its nature, have expectations that contradict client rights. Nowhere is the possible dissonance between the profession and the law as evident as in the criminal-justice system. Binder (1983) notes that most of the psychologists involved with the system provide assessment and treatment directly to offenders. The system expects the psychologist to predict the dangerousness of the offender, yet the psychologist knows that such predictions have an infamously low level of accuracy. Rogers (1987) indicates that forensic evaluations are fertile ground for ethical problems such as implicit coercion (forcing the offender to submit to psychological assessment), which negates informed consent.

The criminal-justice system expects the psychologist to support law-enforcement and correctional goals, which may make it difficult to protect the offender/clients' right to privacy and confidentiality. Although the specialty guidelines state that "the counseling psychologist does not release confidential information, except with the written consent of the user directly involved (APA, 1981b, p. 659), there are exceptions if there is "clear and imminent danger to, or involving, the user" or if the psychologist is "directed otherwise by statute or regulations with the force of law or by court order" (p. 659). But when the latter occurs, "the psychologist seeks a resolution to the conflict that is both ethically and legally feasible and appropriate" (p. 659).

The problem in any organization/client conflict is that it may be impossible to protect each party's preferences and rights. Although it would be "feasible" to derive a solution that is ethical *or* that is legal from the point of view of *either* societal rights *or* individual rights, it is likely that there will have to be a compromise of one of the party's rights. In criminal cases, the counseling psychologist employed in a correctional facility is expected (by public policy) to be a servant of societal rights. That is, the counseling psychologist is to give highest priority to societal rights. The rights of the individual are diminished because of his or her status as an offender.

As alluded to earlier with regard to an organization that expects the counseling psychologist to continue to work with a substandard level of care, there will be many situations in which the counseling psychologist struggles with the question "How can I be both ethical and legal? How can I do what is expected of me by my boss and what I believe is best for the client? I'm damned if I do and damned if I don't." That is the nature of providing human services in contemporary society.

The solution calls for the counseling psychologist to (1) be familiar with the prescriptions and proscriptions of relevant ethical and legal sources; (2) be able to analyze conflicts between organizations and individuals with astute ethical and legal acumen; and (3) be prepared to take a responsible action. Unfortunately, the responsible action will not always be fully satisfying.

Yes, there may be some employment situations in which the most responsible action is to resign, and there will be negative consequences (for example, unemployment). And yes, there may be some employment situations that are confused and unpleasant but in which the most responsible action is to stay in the fray and try to bring about positive change.

The Helping Relationship

Perhaps one of the most hallowed dimensions of counseling psychology is the relationship that is established with the client. As we have noted, relationship is generally viewed as the essence of change, regardless of the theory that is espoused.

The APA's ethical principles (1981a) hold that "psychologists respect the integrity and protect the welfare of the people and groups with whom they work" (p. 636). In more specific terms:

> Psychologists are continually cognizant of there own needs and of their potentially influential position vis-à-vis persons such as clients, students, and subordinates. They avoid exploiting the trust and dependency of such persons. Psychologists make every effort to avoid dual relationships that could impair their professional judgment or increase the risk of exploitation. Examples of such dual relationships include, but are not limited to, research with and treatment of employees, students, supervisees, close friends, or relatives. Sexual intimacies with clients are unethical [p. 636].

In other words, the nature of the therapeutic relationship creates a special importance for the counseling psychologist in the mind of the client.

Examination of the relationship is of great ethical and legal importance. Ethically, it is clear that a faulty or wrongful relationship denigrates the quality of professional service. Legally, negligence may be created by a faulty or wrongful relationship, with the outcome being damage to the client and malpractice by the counseling psychologist.

The predictors of doom, both ethically and legally, are counseling psychologists who are unable to be, as the APA ethical principles prescribe, "continually cognizant of their own needs and of their potentially influential position" (p. 636) in a manner helpful to the client.

> The most basic relationship term to consider is 'transference': Transference is the experiencing of feelings, drives, attitudes, fantasies, and defenses toward a person in the present which do not befit that person but are a repetition of reactions originating in regard to significant persons of early childhood, unconsciously displaced onto figures of the present [1967, p. 155].

Transference occurs in all psychotherapy. The client may or may not be aware of the reactions' being present, excessive, or strange; and is commonly unknowing of the meaning. Transference reactions, such as reacting to the counseling psychologist as though he or she has qualities or characteristics that are not actually evident in the session, provide rich material for psychodynamically oriented analysis and progress in self understanding for the client.

> The follow-up to transference is countertransference: Countertransference is based, as is transference, on unconscious unresolved issues with inter-

nalized objects from the therapist's past that are to some degree inappropriate to the current reality of the therapeutic relationship [Cerny, 1985, p. 362].

Grey and Fiscalini (1987) prefer the term "parallel process," saying: "The participants do not become alike; that is identify or imitate, one another, as is commonly asserted; rather, they are like one another, at least in some crucial way" (p. 141). Whatever term is preferred, be it countertransference or parallel process, Grey and Fiscalin support that the professional should guard against getting stuck in the empathic process; with proper handling of the countertransference, wrongful acts can be precluded and the professional need not cease to treat the client.

Many abuses of clients can be traced to inept handling of transference or countertransference. Watkins (1983) has investigated acting out by counselors and believes that it is frequently rooted in countertransference. Watkins (1985) asserts:

> Destructive countertransference patterns can have a significant and pervasive effect on the counseling relationship. They can erode any sense of trust or rapport that may have developed between counselor and clients. They also can result in a counseling interaction that is unidirectional; that is, when countertransference behaviors become prominent, it frequently happens that counseling serves the needs of the counselor more so than those of the client [p. 359].

The counseling psychologist's professional training must include preparation to recognize and use countertransference reactions to benefit the client, not to fulfill the needs of the counseling psychologist.

Greenson (1967) illustrates the ethical and legal problems that can arise out of faulty handling of transference and countertransference:

> Very often fantasies of childhood are experienced as having actually taken place. Patients will experience feelings toward the analyst that can be construed as a sexual seduction by the father, which are later revealed to be a repetition of a wish that occurred originally as a childhood fantasy. Transference feelings that are acted out usually turn out to be such attempts at wish fulfillment [p. 153].

With that as a backdrop, let us assume that the client has a sexually oriented transference reaction to the counseling psychologist. This can, of course, be analyzed in counseling for the benefit of the client—namely, for its psychodynamic significance.

Staying with this illustration, consider what would happen if the counseling psychologist did not properly deal with the transference reaction. Marmor (1976) says: "When a therapist lends reality to a patient's erotized fantasies of transference love, he fosters a serious state of confusion between reality and fantasy in the patient, with inevitably antitherapeutic results" (p. 322). The need to keep fantasy from becoming reality underlies, in part, the APA ethical principles' requirement that "psychologists make every effort to avoid dual relationships" (p. 636).

The safeguard for the client (and for society) is for the counseling psychologist to have adequate self-understanding to maintain a proper and helpful relationship, which would include therapeutic use of transference and countertransference reactions. Although it may not be part of the counseling-psychology curriculum per se, this self-understanding must be part of professional preparation (Woody, 1971). Ulanov (1979) writes of the counselor: "Having been analyzed himself and introduced in his training to the textures and guises of the unconscious, he can be clear about when his own personal complexes are being touched by a patient's transference" (p. 109). To safeguard against negative consequences form countertransference, Watkins (1985) recommends that counselor preparation include "(a) self-analysis, (b) personal counseling, (c) supervision, (d) genuineness and self-disclosure, and (e) referral" (p. 359).

Any failure to deal effectively and appropriately with a client's transference reactions must be directly attributed to the incompetence of the counseling psychologist. The client is not responsible. In legal language, there is no "informed consent" for, say, a dual relationship. Hare-Mustin, Marecek, Kaplan, and Liss-Levinson (1979) point out that the ethical principles "place the responsibility for clients' rights on the therapist" (p. 4). Misuse of transference is unethical and can be the basis for malpractice (Stone, 1976).

A counseling psychologist might defensively contend: "Well, those quotes were about psychoanalysts, and that wouldn't apply to a counseling psychologist" or "Transference may occur in psychodynamic therapy, but I'm a humanist." In reality, transference and countertransference reactions occur in virtually any professional helping relationship, regardless of discipline or theory (Serban, 1981). Moreover, R. D. Glenn (1974) concluded that a claim to being a member of a unique "school" of therapy would be discounted in a malpractice case and that deference would be given to a traditional standard of care, even for those practitioners who identified with a nontraditional theory. Woody (1984) concludes:

> Stated differently, it seems doubtful that a human services practitioner, especially one licensed as a general practitioner in a particular discipline, could find legal refuge in the confines of a theoretical school, since other theoretical views would enter into the legal analysis of whether the standard of care had been achieved [pp. 394–395].

The inevitable point of view is that ethical responsibility and legal liability must be accommodated in all elements of the relationship between the counseling psychologist and the client. There is no immunity.

Confidentiality and Privileged Communication

The field of counseling psychology has an unrelenting commitment to the sanctity of confidentiality and, if allowed by state statute, privileged communication. *Confidentiality* is a form of secrecy and is derived from ethics, but it is commonly recognized in both statutory and case law. *Privileged communication* is a right granted by law, usually specified in a state's rules of evidence and in the relevant professional licensure law. Slovenko (1973) makes the distinction:

> The legal duty of professional confidentiality or secrecy refers to the obligation not to release information about a client or patient without his permis-

sion, except when divulgence is required by law. The concept of privileged communication . . . involves the right to withhold information in a legal proceeding. The duty of professional confidentiality or secrecy is in essence a restriction on the volunteering of information outside the courtroom. A professional person is bound, legally as well as ethically, to hold in confidence all information that is revealed to him or discovered as a result of his relationship with his client or patient [p. 434].

While neither confidentiality nor privileged communication is a constitutional right per se, each has an element of the right to privacy and is created by society to further human welfare.

There is an ethical mandate for confidentiality in the APA's (1981a) ethical principles:

Psychologists have a primary obligation to respect the confidentiality of information obtained from persons in the course of their work as psychologists. They reveal such information to others only with the consent of the person or the person's legal representative, except in those unusual circumstances in which not to do so would result in clear danger to the person or to others. Where appropriate, psychologists inform their clients of the legal limits of confidentiality [pp. 635–636].

Information from the counseling relationship may be shared only with those professionals who are "clearly concerned with the case" (p. 636), and the storage and disposal of records are protected. Although the wordings and specific contents may differ, the code of ethics for virtually every professional human-service organization follows the aforementioned general notion of confidentiality.

The APA's (1981b) specialty guidelines also deal with confidentiality: "Providers of counseling psychological services maintain a system to protect confidentiality of their records" (p. 659). Access to the records is controlled, and written consent of the client is required for release (unless a legal order is issued to the contrary, such as a *subpoena duces tecum*).

It is important to recognize that neither confidentiality nor privileged communication is absolute. Wigmore (1940), a noted legalist, indicates the criteria for confidentiality:

(1) the communications must originate in confidence that they will not be disclosed; (2) this element of confidentiality must be essential to the full and satisfactory maintenance of the relation between the parties; (3) the relation must be one which in the opinion of the community must be sedulously fostered; and (4) the injury that would inure to the relation by disclosure of the communications must be greater than the benefit thereby gained for the correct disposal of the litigation [p. 531].

Herlihy and Sheeley (1987) write: "Providers of counseling services need to be aware that privileged communication statutes, even when they do exist, do not represent absolute guarantees. Even when clients' communications are privileged under law, there are circumstances in which counselors are ethically or legally obligated to breach confidence" (p. 483). In other words, there are circumstances under which confidentiality, although perhaps preferred by the client, will not receive endorsement by public policy. These exceptions to confidentiality and privileged communication may be unique to each given state, and counseling psychologists should be well versed in their state statutes on this matter.

Even if specified in a state statute, privileged communication may be denied in deference to justice. *Privilege* means "a freedom from compulsion to give evidence or to discover-up material, or a right to prevent or bar information from other sources, during or with a view of litigation, but on grounds extrinsic to the goals of litigation" (Rothstein, 1970, p. 303). Society believes that justice is best served by having all the evidence (as qualified by the rules of evidence applied to a particular court), and this means that there should be a right to discover evidence.

If a party prefers to keep certain information out of the legal proceeding, such as the testimony of the treating counseling psychologist, the court may determine whether confidentiality or privileged communication should be applied to the information. For example, if a party's attorney sent a subpoena to a counseling psychologist (whose clients received privileged communication by the state's licensing law) and the client did not want him or her to have to testify, the attorney for the client could file a motion to quash the subpoena, and the court would have the option of issuing a protective order or denying the motion. (Note that the nuances of this process will vary among states.)

There are exceptions to legal protections of confidentiality and privileged communication. To name three: (1) when the counseling psychologist gets involved in the case by court order, such as to perform a psychological examination; (2) when professional testimony about the client's mental or emotional problems is necessary to accommodate justice; and (3) when the client bases a legal claim or defense on an emotional condition (R. M. Fisher, 1964). Herlihy and Sheeley (1987) cite three exceptions to privileged communications: "(a) when the client requests it, (b) when the client brings charges against the counselor, and (c) when the counselor believes that the client poses a clear and imminent danger to others and that revealing confidential information may avert the danger" (p. 483). Also, if there is a legitimate involuntary-commitment proceeding under way, the client may not be able to invoke either confidentiality or privileged communication. Finally, there are state laws that mandate the reporting of certain types of information, even if it is obtained under what would normally be the protection of confidentiality or privileged communication, such as child abuse, gunshot wounds, communicable diseases, and threats of physical harm to self and others.

Mandatory reporting of child abuse has special relevance to counseling psychology. All 51 jurisdictions in the United States have some sort of legal requirement for reporting suspected child abuse (Miller & Weinstock, 1987). In meeting the legal mandate to report sexual child abuse, Wagner (1987) recognizes that "some mental health professionals may hesitate to initiate investigative procedures for fear that such discovery may damage the therapeutic relationship with the client" but cautions that "clinicians must remember that failure to report is both legally and ethically improper" (p. 437). Miller and Weinstock (1987) believe that criminal prosecution is ineffective for preventing child abuse, and they favor changing statutory requirements to allow mental-health professionals to treat suspected abusers. This may well prove to be the best tack; therapeutic change for the abuser could potentially benefit the victim and society. Even so, society has, thus far, given preference to prosecution over treatment of child abusers, and counseling psychologists must honor the mandatory reporting law of their jurisdiction. (At the same time, they can seek to influence changes in public policy justified by behavioral science.)

The failure of a counseling psychologist to make an appropriate exception to confidentiality and privileged communication can result in legal liability. For example, a counseling psychologist failed to warn an intended victim of a client's intention to harm her. Upon her murder, the counseling psychologist was held to be legally liable for failing to uphold his duty to warn. The confidential nature of his counseling relationship did not negate the duty to warn the intended victim (*Tarasoff v. Regents*, 1976). It should be noted that the court has ruled against the defense that violation of confidentiality would destroy the tenets of psychotherapy (*McIntosh v. Milano,* 1979). The psychotherapist has the duty to initiate whatever precautions are necessary to protect potential victims of his or her client (*Lipari v. Sears, Roebuck,* 1980). At this time, the duty to warn is well established and has been found by most courts to be applicable (Knapp & VandeCreek, 1982). Writing for counselors, Henderson (1987) describes the principles of negligence and the duties to predict harm, refer, and warn of violence. Unfortunately, the counseling psychologist must fulfill the duty to warn, even though "the role of the mental health professional in dealing with violence is ambiguous at best" (Gross & Robinson, 1987). J. D. Woody and R. H. Woody (1988) provide a review of public policy issues and critical cases and offer guidelines for dealing with life-threatening situations.

Informed consent has both ethical and legal importance. In the context of this section, informed consent could be applied to whether to release confidential or privileged communications, or it could be applied to allowing a certain intervention strategy to be applied. More will be said on this matter in the later section on malpractice.

Knowing when confidentiality and privileged communication do or do not apply is ambiguous and complex. For example, it is feasible that a counseling psychologist not licensed as a psychologist in the state and who uses the title "mental-health counselor" or "professional counselor" might have an ethical obligation, but not a legal right, to privileged communication with clients, but if he or she was licensed as a psychologist, privileged communication would apply.

As pointed out by *Tarasoff* and other legal cases, failure to correctly fulfill the duty to warn could result in liability. Conversely, an incorrect breech of confidentiality, such as warning someone about a danger that proved nonexistent, could result in a legal action from the client against the counseling psychologist. The conclusion must be that the counseling psychologist should have legal counsel readily available.

Misrepresentation

As we have underscored, the counseling psychologist of today functions in a litigious society. Avoiding a legal action requires caution and prudence in every aspect of professional practice. One problem area is misrepresentation. The APA's (1981a) ethical principles provide that "psychologists recognize the boundaries of their competence and the limitations of their techniques. They only provide services and techniques for which they are qualified by training and experience" (p. 634). Similarly, the association's specialty guidelines (1981b) state: "Counseling psychologists limit their practice to their demonstrated areas of professional competence" (p. 656).

From this foundation of competence, the ethical principles continue: "Psychologists accurately represent their competence, education, training, and experience. They claim as evidence of education qualifications only those degrees obtained from institutions acceptable under the Bylaws and Rules of Council of the American Psychological Association" (p. 634). In the realm of public statements, the ethical principles require: "Psychologists represent accurately and objectively their professional qualifications, affiliations, and functions, as well as those of the institutions or organizations with which they or the statements may be associated" (p. 634).

Stated simply, it is unethical to communicate a false impression. It does not have to be an explicit communication; it is equally wrong to allow the client to misinterpret a professional qualification. Incidentally, a client's misinterpretation, if founded on a reasonable basis for belief (such as a counseling psychologist's not correcting it), can apply to a malpractice action.

Perhaps because of the press of economic conditions, some counseling psychologists are prone to seek a status by less-than-honorable means. For example, one counseling psychologist, with a doctoral degree in educational psychology from a major university, states in his brochure that his training was in "pediatric psychology." The university has no such major! He also professes to have received training in behavioral medicine at a highly prestigious university. The training was received, but it was only a brief workshop.

"Degree mills" exist, and a goodly number of them are known to offer "doctorates" to persons interested in being counseling psychologists. Such diploma sources may advertise that they are licensed by the state, but that does not mean that they attain the stature prescribed by the Bylaws and Rules of Council of the APA. The "license" they mention is a business license that allows the state to collect fees. Some diploma mills, however, may have no license, no campus, no faculty, and no requirements—except payment of a tuition fee. To claim such a credential for purposes of being a counseling psychologist could potentially be both unethical and illegal and could be the subject of both criminal charges and civil actions.

Specialized credentials are valuable for employment. Consequently, some counseling psychologists seek all sorts of certificates, even those that reflect no legitimate peer review.

The awarding of Diplomate status by the American Board of Professional Psychology (with specialties in counseling psychology, clinical psychology, school psychology, clinical neuropsychology, forensic psychology, and industrial/organizational psychology) is especially time honored. To emulate the American Board of Professional Psychology, a number of organizations have been established to award "Diplomate" status in given specialties. Sechrest (1985) indicates that "there are now about 30 different groups proposing themselves as specialties" (p. 1); and he asserts that, beyond the motive to make more money by claiming to be a specialist,

> One suspects also that just sheer ego has something to do with the problem of specialization. Most diplomas, at least in psychology, are probably of very little material value; they may serve no greater purpose than persuading their possessors that they are in some way special. Presumably some warm feeling flows from the practitioner who can gaze upon the large array of neatly framed documents decorating his or her office wall. One of my colleagues has suggested that we go into business manufacturing diploma wallpaper that could simplify the whole thing [p. 1].

Unfortunately, some of the "specialty credential" boards or organizations generate money for the creators but do not, in fact, connote any true professional qualification. It could be argued, therefore, that to display such a "credential" is to be unethical. Indeed the problem is severe enough that a federal law-enforcement agency closed down a number of diploma mills and "specialty credential" boards or organizations. In addition to ethical concerns, there are all sorts of legal ramifications. Woody and Robertson (1988) provide details about developing acceptable specialization credentials.

The ethical, prudent, and legitimate counseling psychologist should studiously avoid even the appearance of impropriety, much less the actual conveyance of misinformation. There is no shortcut to competency or professional stature. The route must be traditional and qualified by professional standards.

Malpractice

Malpractice lawsuits against health-care professionals are great in number (for details on the escalation of liability and malpractice actions, see Woody, 1988a). This is an era when every practitioner is subject to liability and, potentially, a lawsuit that alleges damages to a client because of failure to maintain an adequate standard of care. In no way can counseling psychologists believe that, because of their discipline, they have any more insulation from malpractice than any other health-care professional.

To illustrate the increase in malpractice liability, K. Fisher (1985) points out that APA members (insured by the association-endorsed carrier) had no claims from 1955 to 1965; from 1976 to 1981 there were 266 claims, or an average of 44 claims per year; and from 1982 to 1984 the number more than tripled, with an average of 155 claims a year. Moreover, Fisher says, "the number of claims against psychologists have risen faster in the past three years than for any other mental health profession" (p. 6). Why are psychologists being sued so readily? There are three primary reasons.

The first reason is that U.S. society believes that everyone, including health-care providers, should be accountable for their actions. This means that professionals, to justify professional status under public policy, must maintain a reasonable standard of care and that any damages that ensue from a failure to maintain acceptable services must be compensated for by the professional.

Professionals are often quick to assert, "All this malpractice hoopla is because of the lawyers' wanting to make a fast buck." The attorneys, in turn, are often quick to assert, "There would be no malpractice if health-care professionals were better trained and would exercise caution and quality, instead of trying to earn a fast buck." The fast-buck explanation is faulty. In fact, the prevalence of malpractice actions stems from society's wanting better health care and assurance that practitioners will seek such an objective. The award of a damage judgment in a malpractice case is made by a jury of laypersons, not by a lawyer.

A second reason for so many suits, according to K. Fisher (1985), is that psychologists have been successful. Success brings increased exposure and vulnerability. Certainly psychologists are much more prominent in society and accepted by the public today than they were a very few years ago. Being a well-established profession with all the accoutrements of success (social responsibility, status, authority, income), psychology should not be treated any differently from the other health-care professions.

A third reason is that psychologists are working in more diverse settings than in previous years and are providing new kinds of service. As reflected throughout this book, counseling psychologists have moved far beyond the traditional vocational/educational orientation. To take one example, counseling psychologists are commonly employed in health-care facilities. Knapp and VandeCreek (1981) interpret this entry as an introduction to a new legal liability. They point out that the mystique of therapy is eliminated, and the psychologist working in the medical context deals with clients who are not hesitant to acknowledge publicly that they have seen a psychologist.

Mental-health professionals can be sued for many offenses. Hogan (1979) analyzed malpractice actions against psychotherapists and found that "more than twenty-five types of actions were brought including involuntary servitude, false arrest, trespass, malicious infliction of emotional distress, abuse of process, loss of liberty, misrepresentation, libel, assault and battery, malicious prosecution and false imprisonment" (p. 7). Wilkinson (1982) details an array of areas that carry malpractice liability for mental-health professionals: (1) liability for client-inflicted injuries and suicide; (2) harm by the client to third persons; (3) errors in judgment, such as when making custodial arrangements or releasing information; (4) treatment methods; (5) drug-related liability; and (6) sexual misconduct. From analyzing malpractice claims against social workers (which would probably apply to counseling psychologists as well), Besharov (1985) lists (in decreasing frequency): sexual impropriety; incorrect treatment; improper child placement; breach of confidentiality; improper death of a patient or others; child placement removal (including custody disputes); violation of civil rights; bodily injury to a client; defamation (libel/slander); failure to supervise a client properly; causing injury to a client or others; the suicide of a patient; failure to diagnose or improper diagnosis; a countersuit due to fee collection; false imprisonment (improper hospitalization); breach of contract; assault and battery; failure to warn of a client's dangerousness; abandonment of a client; failure to cure or poor results; failure to refer; accident on premises; licensing or peer review; and undue influence (and there was a miscellaneous category).

A major legal problem arises from abuse of the therapist/client relationship. Although it is unethical to engage in sexual contact with a client, some therapists violate this proscription. Consequently, K. Fisher (1985) says: "In the past two years, the number of sexual malpractice suits against psychologists have multiplied by five, so they represent 20 to 30 percent of all suits, and cost insurers twice as much as all other causes combined" (p. 7). This type of problem alone is contributing to the rising cost of malpractice insurance. While the preponderance of cases involve a male therapist, Turkington (1984) points out that women therapists are not immune to suits over sexual involvement.

According to Prosser (1971), the standard of care does not require a warranty of a successful outcome. An honest mistake of judgment, if predicated on a reasonable rationale, may be exempt from legal liability. The counseling psychologist must, however, possess the skill and learning common to other members of the profession who are in good standing. Further, if the counseling psychologist professes to be a "specialist," the standard of care is elevated. For example, if counseling psychologists profess or allow a client to reasonably believe that they are specialists, and if there is a recognized professional association that sets standards, it is feasible that they will be held legally to those standards, even though they may have no affiliation with the association (Woody, 1984, 1988a).

It is not enough for the counseling psychologist to fail to maintain the appropriate standard of care. There are four criteria, all of which must be met before a lawsuit is viable:

> Ordinarily, a plaintiff must demonstrate that: (1) a legal duty existed between the practitioner and the injured party; (2) the practitioner was derelict in that duty (either through action or through an omission); (3) [there was] harm or injury of some sort; and (4) the harm or injury was directly and proximately caused by the professional's dereliction of duty [Hogan, 1979, p. 8].

The confines of this chapter preclude a detailed system for avoiding malpractice. Knapp (1980) offers a "primer of malpractice," wherein he recommends achieving good rapport, documenting informed consent and aspects of treatment, inviting consultation, and acting cautiously with life-endangering clients. Blending legal, ethical, and business principles, Woody (1988b) sets forth a system for "protecting your mental-health practice." Also, Woody (1988a) offers "50 ways to avoid malpractice." In an abbreviated version, Woody (1983) gives 11 guidelines; since they have special relevance to counseling psychology, each should be considered.

First: "When a complaint arises, revert to a defensive posture" (p. 206). Therapists are prone to think, by training and professional orientation, that any conflict can be resolved. Indeed it can, but when it is a legal conflict, it is best to turn the situation over to the legal process, not the therapeutic process.

Second: "Know your standard of care and communicate it to the client" (p. 207). By knowing one's professional competencies and having established that they are consonant with the standard of the profession, self-monitoring can be successful. Moreover, the client's knowing what is and is not part of the counseling psychology services will eliminate any misunderstandings that could lead to legal allegations.

Third: "Maintain a supervisory relationship" (p. 209). Having an outside review of one's practice is a safeguard, and in the event that an allegation of malpractice is made, being able to counter with the testimony of a supervisor that he or she, as a representative of the profession, deemed the practice reasonable would be an important legal defense. For malpractice purposes (and other purposes as well), a counseling psychologist never outgrows the need for supervision. While it may be relatively informal and periodic, it is a valuable asset for assuring quality in practice. (Newman, 1981, discusses the ethical issues in the supervision of psychotherapy.)

Fourth: "Have the client assume the responsibility for all communications" (p. 209). For example, it is a preferred practice to return all health-insurance forms to the client for submission to the carrier, as opposed to the therapist's by-passing the client. The client can receive therapeutic benefits from being fully informed, and this practice avoids any allegations that the counseling psychologist has released information to a third party without the client's permission.

Fifth: "Establish a diagnostic system" (p. 210). In addition to facilitating treatment, a diagnostic system documents that the counseling psychologist has studiously evaluated the client's circumstances, used standardized procedures, and based interventions on relevant psychological data. It is also helpful for countering any allegation that the therapist should have, for example, taken steps to prevent suicide by a client (Wilkinson, 1982). This guideline is in keeping with the duty to warn, and it is definitely part of the standard of care for counseling psychologists. For example, Fusimura, Weis, and Cochran (1985) point out that both ethics and law require the counseling psychologist to be prepared to recognize, assess, prevent, and treat suicide. They recommend that the counseling psychologist "(a) recognize the importance of knowing how, when, and where to appropriately refer clients whose concerns fall beyond the counselor's area of expertise; (b) undergo training for suicide prevention and intervention skills; and (c) obtain adequate supervision" (p. 615). This is the sort of standard-setting opinion that a plaintiff's attorney would rely on in a case against a counseling psychologist who had allegedly failed to take reasonable steps to prevent a client's suicide.

Sixth: "Base all psychotherapeutic interventions on a well-established theory" (p. 211). A comment was made earlier about nontraditional therapies being held to standards consonant with more traditional approaches (R. D. Glenn, 1974). Experimentation and innovation are encouraged by public policy, but any translation into service to a client must have passed professional scrutiny.

Seventh: "Serve strictly as a psychotherapist to your clients" (p. 213). Ethics precludes dual roles with clients. It is easy to recognize how changing a therapeutic relationship into a sexual relationship would be subject to both ethical and legal censure. It goes further. For example, while the counseling psychologist may care about a client and, in the process of therapeutic accepting, "like" the client, social or business relations are precluded. How long does this prohibition apply after the therapeutic relationship is over? There is no single answer, but it would seem that the prudent position is "always."

Eighth: "Do not allow clients to accrue a deficit in payments" (p. 214). It is well established that efforts to collect money due for professional services often lead the client to try to find justification for avoiding payment, and what better reason could there by than to allege that he or she had suffered injury from the service (Wright, 1981). When a counseling psychologist says, "I'll let the client owe me for treatment," the possibility of nonpayment or a malpractice action has been elevated. Rather than seeking to justify credit systems as "being nice to the client," it is suggested that the granting of credit is an effort to get all the income possible. Recall the adage "Greed destroys!"

Ninth: "Learn to rely upon an attorney" (p. 214). As mentioned in the first guideline, a legal dispute is usually beyond the capability of the counseling psychologist to resolve. Calling on an attorney is essential—and it is a tax-deductible business expense.

Tenth: "Carry malpractice insurance" (p. 214). A caveat should be added: read your policy. Some malpractice-insurance policies exclude coverage for activities that would seemingly be included, and some cover the judgment awarded by the court but do not cover the cost of the attorney.

Eleventh: "If you work for an agency or institution, have a contract that specifies the employers' legal liability for your professional functioning" (p. 215). At one time, certain types of employers, such as charitable agencies or governmental units (for example, a state mental-health clinic), were immune from suit; this is now seldom. Further, it is often assumed that an employee is always covered by the liability insurance of the employer and is immune from personal liability; this is not necessarily true.

We have touched on a number of problem areas, such as dual relationship (for example, sexual contact with a client). Given the nature of counseling psychology, one area that deserves elaboration is informed consent.

Clients have rights, and one of the most basic rights is to be fully informed about and to consent to any treatment intervention. Margolin (1982) gives seven elements to be explained by the counselor who is obtaining informed consent:

> (a) an explanation of the procedures and their purpose, (b) the role of the person who is providing therapy and his or her professional qualifications, (c) discomforts or risks reasonably to be expected, (d) benefits reasonably to be expected, (e) alternatives to treatment that might be of similar benefit, (f) a statement that any question about the procedures will be answered at any time, and (g) a statement that the person can withdraw his or her consent and discontinue participation in therapy or testing at any time [p. 794].

Covering the foregoing seven points in a written document is a good idea, as is having the client sign an "informed-consent" endorsement for the specific service. Just because a client agrees to an intervention, however, does not provide total insurance against a legal action:

> In some instances it may be necessary to write out the issues and have the client give written approval. These "contracts," however, may be vulnerable

in the event of a legal action. That is, if there is any evidence that the powerful influence wielded by the professional was inappropriately used to misinform a client or to coercively extract acceptance from the client, such evidence will certainly be used against the professional. For example, if the therapist fully informed the client of a therapeutic intervention—and if that intervention was "unconscionable" in the eyes of the court, as deduced from public policy—the client's written informed consent might be set aside as a way of shaping the professional's conduct and safeguarding the public against similar unconscionable activities by professionals [Woody, 1984, pp. 378–379].

The logical route to legally safe informed consent is to (1) take the time to explain all interventions to the client; (2) be sure that the client senses being informed and expresses approval; (3) document the approval; and (4) be traditional and mainstream in style, theory, and technique.

Summary

This chapter has presented a contemporary frame of reference for the relevance of ethics and law to the practice of counseling psychology. It is an understatement to assert that no counseling psychologist can function free from the regulations of professional ethics and of statutory and common law. Since public policy has given great acceptance to professional psychology and since psychological practice is clearly a commercial endeavor (regardless of contest), legal accountability is certain, be it through licensure or malpractice actions.

In no way should these regulations be viewed as harmful. To the contrary, they should be viewed as promoting success. The challenge, of course, is to be professionally and personally prepared to make adaptations to accommodate the expectations of society.

Disciplinary ethics offer important guidance to the counseling psychologist. Governmental regulation, such as through licensing, and the law, such as through malpractice complaints, now control the standards for practice. Specialty guidelines prescribe and proscribe how counseling psychology services should be provided. Special concern is necessary to honor clients' rights, such as to confidentiality and privileged communication. Counseling psychologists face the "malpractice crisis," but proactive strategies can minimize risks.

References

American Association for Counseling and Development (1988). *Ethical Standards.* Washington, DC: Author.

American Association for Marriage and Family Therapy. (1985). *Code of Ethical Principles for Marriage and Family Therapists.* Washington, DC: Author.

American Association of Sex Educators, Counselors, Therapists. (1978). *Code of Ethics.* Washington, D.C.: Author.

American Psychological Association. (1973). *Guidelines for Psychologists Conducting Growth Groups.* Washington, DC: Author.

American Psychological Association. (1981a). Ethical Principles of Psychologists. *American Psychologist, 36,* 633–638.

American Psychological Association. (1981b). Speciality Guidelines for the Delivery of Services by Counseling Psychologists. *American Psychologist, 36,* 652–663.

American Psychological Association. (1983). *Ethical Principles in the Conduct of Research with Human Participants.* Washington, DC: Author.

American Psychological Association. (1985). *Standards for Educational and Psychological Tests.* Washington, DC: Author.

American Psychological Association. (1987a). General Guidelines for Providers of Psychological Services. *American Psychologist, 42,* 712–723.

American Psychological Association. (1987b). Report of the Ethics Committee: 1986. *American Psychologist, 42,* 730–734.

Besharov, D. J. (1985). *The Vulnerable Social Worker.* Silver Spring, MD: National Association of Social Workers.

Binder, V. L. (1983). Ethical and Legal Issues in Criminal Justice Counseling. *The Counseling Psychologist, 11*(2), 85–89.

Breslow, L., & Enstrone, J. E. (1980). Persistence of Health Habits and Their Relationship to Mortality. *Preventive Medicine, 9,* pp. 469–483.

Butler, S., & Zelen, S. L. (1977). Sexual Intimacies Between Therapists and Patients. *Psychotherapy: Theory, Research, and Practice, 14,* 139–145.

Cerny, M. S. (1985). Countertransference Revisited. *Journal of Counseling and Development, 63,* 362–364.

DeGeorge, R. T. (1982). *Business Ethics.* New York: Macmillan.

Fisher, K. (1985). Charges Catch Clinicians in Cycle of Shame, Slip-Ups. *APA Monitor, 16*(5), 6–7.

Fisher, R. M. (1964). The Psychotherapeutic Professions and the Law of Privileged Communications. *Wayne Law Review, 10,* 609–654.

Florida Psychological Association. (1986). Ethics. *Florida Psychologist, 36*(1), 16.

Florida Statutes. (1985). Title XXXII Chapter 490. Psychological Services, 1509–1514.

Fusimura, L. E., Weis, D. M., & Cochran, J. R. (1985). Suicide: Dynamics and Implications for Counseling. *Journal of Counseling Psychology, 63,* 612–615.

Glen, C. M. (1980). Ethical Issues in the Practice of Child Psychotherapy. *Professional Psychology, 11,* 613–619.

Glenn, R. D. (1974). Standard of Care in Administering Non-Traditional Psychotherapy. *University of California, Davis Law Review, 7,* 56–83.

Green, S. L., & Hansen, J. C. (1986). Ethical Dilemmas in Family Therapy. *Journal of Marital and Family Therapy, 12,* 225–230.

Greenson, R. R. (1967). *The Technique and Practice of Psychoanalysis* (Vol. 1). New York: International Universities Press.

Grey, A., & Fiscalini, J. (1987). Process as Transference-Countertransference Interaction. *Psychoanalytic Psychology, 42,* 131–144.

Gross, D. R., & Robinson, S. E. (1987). Ethics, Violence, and Counseling: Hear No Evil, See No Evil, Speak No Evil? *Journal of Counseling and Development, 65,* 340–344.

Hare-Mustin, R. T., Marecek, J., Kaplan, A. G., & Liss-Levinson, N. (1979). Rights of Clients, Responsibilities of Therapists. *American Psychologist, 34,* 3–16.

Henderson, D. H. (1987). Negligent Liability and the Foreseeability Factor: A Critical Issue for School Counselors. *Journal of Counseling and Development, 66,* 86–89.

Herlihy, B., & Sheeley, V. L. (1987). Privileged Communication in Selected Helping Professions: A Comparison Among Statutes. *Journal of Counseling and Development, 65,* 479–483.

Hinkeldey, N. W., & Spokane, A. R. (1985). Effects of Pressure and Legal Guideline Clarity on Counselor Decision Making in Legal and Ethical Conflict Situations. *Journal of Counseling and Development, 64,* 240–245.

Hogan, D. B. (1979). *The Regulation of Psychotherapists: Vol. 3. A Review of Malpractice Suits in the United States.* Cambridge, MA: Ballinger.

Ibrahim, F. A. (1985). Human Rights and Ethical Issues in the Use of Advanced Technology. *Journal of Counseling and Development, 64,* 134–135.

Kitchener, K. S. (1984). Ethics and Counseling Psychology: Distinctions and Directions. *The Counseling Psychologist, 12*(3), 15–18.

Knapp, S. (1980). A Primer on Malpractice for Psychologists. *Professional Psychology, 11,* 606–612.

Knapp, S., & VandeCreek, L. (1981). Behavioral Medicine: Its Malpractice Risks for Psychologists. *Professional Psychology, 12,* 677–683.

Knapp, S., & VandeCreek, L. (1982). *Tarasoff:* Five Years Later. *Professional Psychology, 13,* 511–516.

Lipari v. Sears, Roebuck, 497 F. Supp. 185 (D. Neb. 1980).

Mappes, D. C., Robb, G. P., & Engels, D. W. (1985). Conflicts Between Ethics and Law in Counseling Psychology. *Journal of Counseling and Development, 64,* 246–252.

Margolin, G. (1982). Ethical and Legal Considerations in Marital and Family Therapy. *American Psychologist, 37,* 788–801.

Marmor, J. (1976). Some Psychodynamic Aspects of the Seduction of Patients in Psychotherapy. *American Journal of Psychoanalysis, 36,* 319–323.

McIntosh v. Milano, 403 A. 2d 500 (N.J. Super. Ct. 1979).

Melton, G. B. (1986). Litigation *In the Interest of Children:* Does Anybody Win? *Law and Human Behavior, 10,* 337–353.

Melton, G. B. (1987). Bringing Psychology to the Legal System. *American Psychologist, 42,* 488–495.

Miller, R. D., & Weinstock, R. (1987). Conflict of Interest Between Therapist-Patient Confidentiality and the Duty to Report Sexual Abuse of Children. *Behavioral Sciences and the Law, 5,* 161–174.

Newman, A. S. (1981). Ethical Issues in the Supervision of Psychotherapy. *Professional Psychology, 12,* 690–695.

Pope, K. S., Keith-Spiegel, P. C., & Tabachnick, B. G. (1986). Sexual Attraction to Clients: The Human Therapist and the (Sometimes) Inhuman Training System. *American Psychologist, 41,* 147–158.

Prosser, W. L. (1971). *Handbook of the Law of Torts* (4th ed.). St. Paul: West.

Rest, J. R. (1984). Research on Moral Development: Implications for Training Counseling Psychologists. *The Counseling Psychologist, 12*(3), 19–29.

Rogers, R. (1987). Ethical Dilemmas in Forensic Evaluations. *Behavioral Sciences and the Law, 5,* 149–160.

Rothstein, P. F. (1970). *Evidence.* St. Paul: West.

Sechrest, L. B. (1985). Specialization? Who Needs It? *The Clinical Psychologist, 38,* 1, 3.

Serban, G. (1981). Sexual Activity in Therapy: Legal and Ethical Issues. *American Journal of Psychotherapy, 35,* 76–85.

Skinner, B. F. (1953). *Science and Human Behavior.* New York: Free Press.

Slovenko, R. (1973). *Psychiatry and Law.* Boston: Little, Brown.

Stone, A. A. (1976). The Legal Implications of Sexual Activity Between Psychiatrist and Patient. *American Journal of Psychiatry, 133,* 1138–1141.

Tarasoff v. Regents of the University of California, 17 Cal. 3d 425,551 P.2d 334, 131 Cal. Rptr. 14 (1976).

Taylor, P. W. (1978). *Problems of Moral Philosophy.* Belmont, CA: Wadsworth.

Turkington, C. (1984). Women Therapists Not Immune to Sexual Involvement Suits. *APA Monitor, 15,* 12, 15.

Tymchuk, A. J., Drapkin, R., Major-Kingsley, L., Ackerman, A. B., Coffman, E. W., & Baum, M. S. (1982). Ethical Decision Making and Psychologists' Attitudes Toward Training in Ethics. *Professional Psychology, 13,* 412–421.

Ulanov, A. B. (1979). Follow-Up Treatment in Cases of Patient/Therapist Sex. *Journal of the American Academy of Psychoanalysis, 7,* 101–110.

Wagner, W. G. (1987). Child Sexual Abuse: A Multidisciplinary Approach to Case Management. *Journal of Counseling and Development, 65,* 435–439.

Watkins, C. E., Jr. (1983). Counselor Acting Out in the Counseling Process: An Exploratory Analysis. *Personnel and Guidance Journal, 61,* 417–423.

Watkins, C. E., Jr. (1985). Coutertransference: Its Impact on the Counseling Situation. *Journal of Counseling and Development, 63,* 356–359.

Welfel, E. R., & Lipsitz, N. E. (1983). Wanted: A Comprehensive Approach to Ethics Research and Education. *Counselor Education and Supervision, 22,* 320–332.

Welfel, E. R., & Lipsitz, N. E. (1984). The Ethical Behavior of Professional Psychologists: A Critical Analysis of the Research. *The Counseling Psychologist, 12*(3), 31–42.

Wigmore, J. H. (1940). *Evidence* (3rd ed.) (10 vols.). Boston: Little, Brown.

Wilcoxon, S. A. (1987). Ethical Standards: A Study of Application and Utility. *Journal of Counseling and Development, 65,* 510–511.

Wilkinson, A. P. (1982). Psychiatric Malpractice: Identifying Areas of Liability. *Trial 18*(12), 73–77, 89–90.

Woody, J. D., & Woody, R. H. (in press). Public Policy in Life-Threatening Situations. *Journal of Marital and Family Therapy, 14,* 2, 133–137.

Woody, R. H. (1971). *Psychobehavioral Counseling and Therapy: Integrating Behavioral and Insight Techniques.* New York: Appleton-Century-Crofts.

Woody, R. H. (1983). Avoiding Malpractice in Psychotherapy. In P. A. Keller & L. G. Ritt (Eds.), *Innovations in Clinical Practice: A Source Book* (Vol. 2) (pp. 205–216). Sarasota, FL: Professional Resource Exchange.

Woody, R. H. (1984). *The Law and the Practice of Human Services.* San Francisco: Jossey-Bass.

Woody, R. H. (1988a). *Fifty Ways to Avoid Malpractice: A Guidebook for Mental Health Professionals.* Sarasota, FL: Professional Resource Exchange.

Woody, R. H. (1988b). *Protecting Your Mental Health Practice.* San Francisco: Jossey-Bass.

Woody, R. H., & Robertson, M. H. (1988). *Becoming a Clinical Psychologist.* New York: International Universities Press.

Wright, R. H. (1981). What to Do Until the Malpractice Lawyer Comes: A Survivor's Manual. *American Psychologist, 36,* 1535–1541.

Appendix A

Ethical Principles of Psychologists

American Psychological Association

PREAMBLE

Psychologists respect the dignity and worth of the individual and strive for the preservation and protection of fundamental human rights. They are committed to increasing knowledge of human behavior and of people's understanding of themselves and others and to the utilization of such knowledge for the promotion of human welfare. While pursuing these objectives, they make every effort to protect the welfare of those who seek their services and of the research participants that may be the objects of study. They use their skills only for purposes consistent with these values and do not knowingly permit their misuse by others. While demanding for themselves free-dom of inquiry and communication, psychologists accept the responsibility this freedom requires: competence, objectivity in the application of skills, and concern for the best interests of clients, colleagues, students, research participants, and society. In the pursuit of these ideals, psychologists subscribe to principles in the following areas: 1. Responsibility, 2. Competence, 3. Moral and Legal Standards, 4. Public Statements, 5. Confidentiality, 6. Welfare of the Consumer, 7. Professional Relationships, 8. Assessment Techniques, 9. Research with Human Participants, and 10. Care and Use of Animals.

Acceptance of membership in the American Psychological Association commits the member to adherence to these principles.

Ethical Principles of Psychologists (revised edition), by the American Psychological Association. Copyright 1981 by the American Psychological Association. Reprinted by permission of the publisher.

This version of the *Ethical Principles of Psychologists* (formerly entitled *Ethical Standards of Psychologists*) was adopted by the American Psychological Association's Council of Representatives on January 24, 1981. The revised *Ethical Principles* contain both substantive and grammatical changes in each of the nine ethical principles constituting the *Ethical Standards of Psychologists* previously adopted by the Council of Representatives in 1979, plus a new tenth principle entitled "Care and Use of Animals." Inquiries concerning the *Ethical Principles of Psychologists* should be addressed to the Administrative Officer for Ethics, American Psychological Association, 1200 Seventeenth Street, N.W., Washington, D.C., 20036.

These revised *Ethical Principles* apply to psychologists, to students of psychology, and to others who do work of a psychological nature under the supervision of a psychologist. They are also intended for the guidance of nonmembers of the Association who are engaged in psychological research or practice.

Any complaints of unethical conduct filed after January 24, 1981, shall be governed by this 1981 revision. However, conduct (a) complained about after January 24, 1981, but which occurred prior to that date, and (b) not considered unethical under prior versions of the principles but considered unethical under the 1981 revision, shall not be deemed a violation of ethical principles. Any complaints pending as of January 24, 1981, shall be governed either by the 1979 or by the 1981 version of the *Ethical Principles,* at the sound discretion of the Committee on Scientific and Professional Ethics and Conduct.

Psychologists cooperate with duly constituted committees of the American Psychological Association, in particular, the Committee on Scientific and Professional Ethics and Conduct, by responding to inquiries promptly and completely. Members also respond promptly and completely to inquiries from duly constituted state association ethics committees and professional standards review committees.

Principle 1: Responsibility

In providing services, psychologists maintain the highest standards of their profession. They accept responsibility for the consequences of their acts and make every effort to ensure that their services are used appropriately.

a. As scientists, psychologists accept responsibility for the selection of their research topics and the methods used in investigation, analysis, and reporting, They plan their research in ways to minimize the possibility that their findings will be misleading. They provide thorough discussion of the limitations of their data, especially where their work touches on social policy or might be construed to the detriment of persons in specific age, sex, ethnic, socioeconomic, or other social groups. In publishing reports of their work, they never suppress disconfirming data, and they acknowledge the existence of alternative hypotheses and explanations of their findings. Psychologists take credit only for work they have actually done.

b. Psychologists clarify in advance with all appropriate persons and agencies the expectations for sharing and utilizing research data. They avoid relationships that may limit their objectivity or create a conflict of interest. Interference with the milieu in which data are collected is kept to a minimum.

c. Psychologists have the responsibility to attempt to prevent distortion, misuse, or suppression of psychological findings by the institution or agency of which they are employees.

d. As members of governmental or other organizational bodies, psychologists remain accountable as individuals to the highest standards of their profession.

e. As teachers, psychologists recognize their primary obligation to help others acquire knowledge and skill, They maintain high standards of scholarship by presenting psychological information objectively, fully, and accurately.

f. As practitioners, psychologists know that they bear a heavy social responsibility because their recommendations and professional actions may alter the lives of others. They are alert to personal, social, organizational, financial, or political situations and pressures that might lead to misuse of their influence.

Principle 2: Competence

The maintenance of high standards of competence is a responsibility shared by all psychologists in the interest of the public and the profession as a whole. Psychologists recognize the boundaries of their competence and the limitatons of their techniques. They only provide services and only use techniques for which they are qualified by training and experience. In those areas in which recognized standards do not yet exist, psychologists take whatever precautions are necessary to protect the welfare of their clients. They maintain knowledge of current scientific and professional information related to the services they render.

a. Psychologists accurately represent their competence, education, training, and experience. They claim as evidence of educational qualifications only those degrees obtained from institutions acceptable under the Bylaws and Rules of Council of the American Psychological Association.

b. As teachers, psychologists perform their duties on the basis of careful preparation so that their instruction is accurate, current, and scholarly.

c. Psychologists recognize the need for continuing education and are open to new procedures and changes in expectations and values over time.

d. Psychologists recognize differences among people, such as those that may be associated with age, sex, socioeconomic, and ethnic backgrounds. When necessary, they obtain training, experience, or counsel to assure competent service or research relating to such persons.

e. Psychologists responsible for decisions involving individuals or policies based on test results have an understanding of psychological or educational measurement, validation problems, and test research.

f. Psychologists recognize that personal problems and conflicts may interfere with professional effectiveness. Accordingly, they refrain from undertaking any activity in which their personal problems are likely to lead to inadequate performance or harm to a client, colleague, student, or research participant. If engaged in such activity when they become aware of their personal problems, they seek competent professional assistance to determine whether they should suspend, terminate, or limit the scope of their professional and/or scientific activities.

Principle 3: Moral and legal standards

Psychologists' moral and ethical standards of behavior are a personal matter to the same degree as they are for any other citizen, except as these may compromise the fulfillment of their professional responsibilities or reduce the public trust in psychology and psychologists. Regarding their own behavior, psychologists are sensitive to prevailing community standards and to the possible impact that conformity to or deviation from these standards may have upon the quality of their performance as psychologists. Psychologists are also aware of the possible impact of their public behavior upon the ability of colleagues to perform their professional duties.

a. As teachers, psychologists are aware of the fact that their personal values may affect the selection and presentation of instructional materials. When dealing with topics that may give offense, they recognize and respect the diverse attitudes that students may have toward such materials.

b. As employees or employers, psychologists do not engage in or condone practices that are inhumane or that result in illegal or unjustifiable actions. Such practices include, but are not limited to, those based on considerations of race, handicap, age, gender, sexual preference, religion, or national origin in hiring, promotion, or training.

c. In their professional roles, psychologists avoid any action that will violate or diminish the legal and civil rights of clients or of others who may be affected by their actions.

d. As practitioners and researchers, psychologists act in accord with Association standards and guidelines related to practice and to the conduct of research with human beings and animals. In the ordinary course of events, psychologists adhere to relevant governmental laws and institutional regulations. When federal, state, provincial, organizational, or institutional laws, regulations, or practices are in conflict with Associaiton standards and guidelines, psychologists make known their commitment to Association standards and guidelines and, wherever possible, work toward a resolution of the conflict. Both practitioners and researchers are concerned with the development of such legal and quasi-legal regulations as best serve the public interest, and they work toward changing existing regulations that are not beneficial to the public interest.

Principle 4: Public statements

Public statements, announcements of services, advertising, and promotional activities of psychologists serve the purpose of helping the public make informed judgments and choices. Psychologists represent accurately and objectively their professional qualifications, affiliations, and functions, as well as those of the institutions or organizations with which they or the statements may be associated. In public statements providing psychological information of professional opinions or providing information about the availability of psychological products, publications, and services, psychologists base their statements on scientifically acceptable psychological findings and techniques with full recognition of the limits and uncertainties of such evidence.

a. When announcing or advertising professional services, psychologists may list the following information to describe the provider and services provided: name, highest relevant academic degree earned from a regionally accredited institution, date, type, and level of certification or licensure, diplomate status, APA membership status, address, telephone number, office hours, a brief listing of the type of psychological services offered, an appropriate presentation of fee information, foreign languages spoken, and policy with regard to third-party payments. Additional relevant or important consumer information may be included if not prohibited by other sections of these Ethical Principles.

b. In announcing or advertising the availability of psychological products, publications, or services, psychologists do not present their affiliation with any organization in a manner that falsely implies sponsorship or certification by that organization. In particular and for example, psychologists do not state APA membership or fellow status in a way to suggest that such status implies specialized professional competence or qualifications. Public statements include, but are not limited to, communication by means of periodical, book, list, directory, television, radio, or motion picture. They do not contain (i) a false, fraudulent, misleading, deceptive, or unfair statement; (ii) a misinterpretation of fact or a statement likely to mislead or deceive because in context it makes only a partial disclosure of relevant facts; (iii) a testimonial from a patient regarding the quality of a psychol-

ogist's services or products; (iv) a statement intended or likely to create false or unjustified expectations of favorable results; (v) a statement implying unusual, unique, or one-of-a-kind abilities; (vi) a statement intended or likely to appeal to a client's fears, anxieties, or emotions concerning the possible results of failure to obtain the offered services; (vii) a statement concerning the comparative desirability of offered services; (viii) a statement of direct solicitation of individual clients.

c. Psychologists do not compensate or give anything of value to a representative of the press, radio, television, or other communication medium in anticipation of or in return for professional publicity in a news item. A paid advertisement must be identified as such, unless it is apparent from the context that it is a paid advertisement. If communicated to the public by use of radio or television, an advertisement is prerecorded and approved for broadcast by the psychologist, and a recording of the actual transmission is retained by the psychologist.

d. Announcements or advertisements of "personal growth groups," clinics, and agencies give a clear statement of purpose and a clear description of the experiences to be provided. The education, training, and experience of the staff members are appropriately specified.

e. Psychologists associated with the development or promotion of psychological devices, books, or other products offered for commercial sale make reasonable efforts to ensure that announcements and advertisements are presented in a professional, scientifically acceptable, and factually informative manner.

f. Psychologists do not participate for personal gain in commercial announcements or advertisments recommending to the public the purchase or use of proprietary or single-source products or services when that participation is based solely upon their identification as psychologists.

g. Psychologists present the science of psychology and offer their services, products, and publications fairly and accurately, avoiding misrepresentation through sensationalism, exaggeration, or superficiality. Psychologists are guided by the primary obligation to aid the public in developing informed judgments, opinions, and choices.

h. As teachers, psychologists ensure that statements in catalogs and course outlines are accurate and not misleading, particularly in terms of subject matter to be covered, bases for evaluating progress, and the nature of course experiences. Announcements, brochures, or advertisements describing workshops, seminars, or other educational programs accurately describe the audience for which the program is intended as well as eligibility requirements, educational objectives, and nature of the materials to be covered. These announcements also accurately represent the education, training, and experience of the psychologists presenting the programs and any fees involved.

i. Public announcements or advertisements soliciting research participants in which clinical services or other professional services are offered as an inducement make clear the nature of the services as well as the costs and other obligations to be accepted by participants in the research.

j. A psychologist accepts the obligation to correct other who represent the psychologist's professional qualifications, or associations with products or services, in a manner incompatible with these guidelines.

k. Individual diagnostic and therapeutic services are provided only in the context of a professional psychological relationship. When personal advice is given by means of public lectures or demonstrations, newspaper or magazine articles, radio or television programs, mail, or similar media, the psychologist utilizes the most current relevant data and exercises the highest level of professional judgment.

l. Products that are described or presented by means of public lectures or demonstrations, newspaper or magazine articles, radio or television programs, or similar media meet the same recognized standards as exist for products used in the context of a professional relationship.

Principle 5: Confidentiality

Psychologists have a primary obligation to respect the confidentiality of information obtained from persons in the course of their work as psychologists. They reveal such information to others only with the consent of the person or the person's legal representative, except in those unusual circumstances in which not to do so would result in clear danger to the person or to others. Where appropriate, psychologists inform their clients of the legal limits of confidentiality.

a. Information obtained in clinical or consulting relationships, or evaluative data concerning children, students, employees, and others, is discussed only for professional purposes and only with persons clearly concerned with the case. Written and oral reports present only data germane to the purposes of the evaluation, and every effort is made to avoid undue invasion of privacy.

b. Psychologists who present personal information obtained during the course of professional work in writings, lectures, or other public forums either obtain adequate prior consent to do so or adequately disguise all identifying information.

c. Psychologists make provisions for maintaining confidentiality in the storage and disposal of records.

d. When working with minors or other persons who are unable to give voluntary, informed consent, psychologists take special care to protect these persons' best interests.

Principle 6: Welfare of the consumer

Psychologists respect the integrity and protect the welfare of the people and groups with whom they work. When conflicts of interest arise between clients and psychologists' employing institutions, psychologists clarify the nature and direction of their loyalties and responsibilities and keep all parties informed of their commitments. Psychologists fully inform consumers as to the purpose and nature of an evaluative, treatment, educational, or training procedure, and they freely acknowledge that clients, students, or participants in research have freedom of choice with regard to participation.

a. Psychologists are continually cognizant of their own needs and of their potentially influential position vis-à-vis persons such as clients, students, and subordinates. They avoid exploiting the trust and dependency of such persons. Psychologists make every effort to avoid dual relationships that could impair their professional judgment or increase the risk of exploitation. Examples of such dual relationships include, but are not limited to, research with and treatment of employees, students, supervisees, close friends, or relatives. Sexual intimacies with clients are unethical.

b. When a psychologist agrees to provide services to a client at the request of a third party, the psychologist assumes the responsibility of clarifying the nature of the relationships to all parties concerned.

c. Where the demands of an organization require psychologists to violate these Ethical Principles, psychologists clarify the nature of the conflict between the demands and these principles. They inform all parties of psychologists' ethical responsibilities and take appropriate action.

d. Psychologists make advance financial arrangements that safeguard the best interests of and are clearly understood by their clients. They neither give nor receive any remuneration for referring clients for professional services. They contribute a portion of their services to work for which they receive little or no financial return.

e. Psychologists terminate a clinical or consulting relationship when it is reasonably clear that the consumer is not benefiting from it. They offer to help the consumer locate alternative sources of assistance.

Principle 7: Professional relationships

Psychologists act with due regard for the needs, special competencies, and obligations of their colleagues in psychology and other professions. They respect the prerogatives and obligations of the institutions or organizations with which these other colleagues are associated.

a. Psychologists understand the areas of competence of related professions. They make full use of all the professional, technical, and administrative resources that serve the best interests of consumers. The absence of formal relationships with other professional workers does not relieve psychologists of the responsibility of securing for their clients the best possible professional service, nor does it relieve them of the obligation to exercise foresight, diligence, and tact in obtaining the complementary or alternative assistance needed by clients.

b. Psychologists know and take into account the traditions and practices of other professional groups with whom they work and cooperate fully with such groups. If a person is receiving similar services from another professional, psychologists do not offer their own services directly to such a person. If a psychologist is contacted by a person who is already receiving similar services from another professional, the psychologist carefully considers that professional relationship and proceeds with caution and sensitivity to the therapeutic issues as well as the client's welfare. The psychologist discusses these issues with the client so as to minimize the risk of confusion and conflict.

c. Psychologists who employ or supervise other professionals or professionals in training accept the obligation to facilitate the further professional development of these individuals. They provide appropriate working conditions, timely evaluations, constructive consultation, and experience opportunities.

d. Psychologists to not exploit their professional relationships with clients, supervisees, students, employees, or research participants sexually or otherwise. Psychologists do not condone or engage in sexual harassment. Sex ual harassment is defined as deliberate or repeated comments, gestures, or physical contacts of a sexual nature that are unwanted by the recipient.

e. In conducting research in institutions or organizations, psychologists secure appropriate authorization to conduct such research. They are aware of their obligations to future research workers and ensure that host institutions receive adequate information about the research and proper acknowledgment of their contributions.

f. Publication credit is assigned to those who have contributed to a publication in proportion to their professional contributions. Major contributions of a professional character made by several persons to a common project are recognized by joint authorship, with the individual who made the principal contribution listed first. Minor contributions of a professional character and extensive clerical or similar nonprofessional assistance may be acknowledged in footnotes or in an introductory statement. Acknowledgment through specific citations is made for unpublished as well as published material that has directly influenced the research or writing. Psychologists who compile and edit material of others for publication publish the material in the name of the originating group, if appropriate, with their own name appearing as chairperson or editor. All contributors are to be acknowledged and named.

g. When psychologists know of an ethical violation by another psychologist, and it seems appropriate, they informally attempt to resolve the issue by bringing the behavior to the attention of the psychologist. If the misconduct is of a minor nature and/or appears to be due to lack of sensitivity, knowledge, or experience, such an informal solution is usually appropriate. Such informal corrective efforts are made with sensitivity to any rights to confidentiality involved. If the violation does not seem amenable to an informal solution, or is of a more serious nature, psychologists bring it to the attention of the appropriate local, state, and/or national committee on professional ethics and conduct.

Principle 8: Assessment techniques

In the development, publication, and utilization of psychological assessment techniques, psychologists make every effort to promote the welfare and best interests of the client. They guard against the misuse of assessment results. They respect the client's right to know the results, the interpretations made, and the bases for their conclusions and recommendations. Psychologists make every effort to maintain the security of tests and other assessment techniques within limits of legal mandates. They strive to ensure the appropriate use of assessment techniques by others.

a. In using assessment techniques, psychologists respect the right of clients to have full explanations of the nature and purpose of the techniques in language the client can understand, unless an explicit exception to this right has been agreed upon in advance. When the explanations are to be provided by others, psychologists establish procedures for ensuring the adequacy of these explanations.

b. Psychologists responsible for the development and standardization of psychological tests and other assessment techniques utilize established scientific procedures and observe the relevant APA standards.

c. In reporting assessment results, psychologists indicate any reservations that exist regarding validity or reliability because of the circumstances of the assessment or the inappropriateness of the norms for the person tested. Psychologists strive to ensure that the results of assessments and their interpretations are not misused by others.

d. Psychologists recognize that assessment results may become obsolete. They make every effort to avoid and prevent the misuse of obsolete measures.

e. Psychologists offering scoring and interpretation services are able to produce appropriate evidence for the validity of the programs and procedures used in arriving at interpretations. The public offering of an automated interpretation service is considered a professional-to-professional consultation. Psychologists make every effort to avoid misuse of assessment reports.

f. Psychologists do not encourage or promote the use of psychological assessment techniques by inappropriately trained or otherwise unqualified persons through teaching, sponsorship, or supervision.

Principle 9: Research with human participants

The decision to undertake research rests upon a considered judgment by the individual psychologist about how best to contribute to psychological science and human welfare. Having made the decision to conduct research, the psychologist considers alternative directions in which research energies and resources might be invested. On the basis of this consideration, the psychologist carries out the investigation with respect and concern for the dignity and welfare of the people who participate and with cognizance of federal and state regulations and professional standards governing the conduct of research with human participants.

a. In planning a study, the investigator has the responsibility to make a careful evaluation of its ethical acceptability. To the extent that the weighing of scientific and human values suggests a compromise of any principle, the investigator incurs a correspondingly serious obligation to seek ethical advice and to oberve stringent safeguards to protect the rights of human participants.

b. Considering whether a participant in a planned study will be a "subject at risk" or a "subject at minimal risk," according to recognized standards, is of primary ethical concern to the investigator.

c. The investigator always retains the responsibility for ensuring ethical practice in research. The investigator is also responsible for the ethical treatment of research participants by col-laborators, assistants, students, and employees, all of whom, however, incur similar obligations.

d. Except in minimal-risk research, the investigator establishes a clear and fair agreement with research participants, prior to their participation, that clarifies the obligations and responsibilities of each. The investigator has the obligation to honor all promises and commitments included in that agreement. The investigator informs the participants of all aspects of the research that might reasonably be expected to influence willingness to participate and explains all other aspectsd of the research about which the participants inquire. Failure to make full disclosure prior to obtaining informed consent requires additional safeguards to protect the welfare and dignity of the research participants. Research with children or with participants who have impairments that would limit understanding and/or communication requires special safeguarding procedures.

e. Methodological requirements of a study may make the use of concealment or deception necessary. Before conducting such a study, the investigator has a special responsibility to (i) determine whether the use of such techniques is justified by the study's prospective scientific, educational, or applied value; (ii) determine whether alternative procedures are available that do not use concealment or deception; and (iii) ensure that the participants are provided with sufficient explanation as soon as possible.

f. The investigator respects the individual's freedom to decline to participate in or to withdraw from the research at any time. The obligation to protect this freedom requires careful thought and consideration when the investigator is in a position of authority or influence over the participant. Such positions of authority include, but are not limited to, situations in which research participation is required as part of employment or in which the participant is a student, client, or employee of the investigator.

g. The investigator protects the participant from physical and mental discomfort, harm, and danger that may arise from research procedures. If risks of such consequences exist, the investigator informs the participant of that fact. Research procedures likely to cause serious or lasting harm to a participant are not used unless the failure to use these procedures might expose the participant to risk of greater harm, or unless the research has great potential benefit and fully informed and voluntary consent is obtained from each participant. The participant should be informed of procedures for contacting the investigator within a reasonable time period following participation should stress, potential harm, or related questions or concerns arise.

h. After the data are collected, the investigator provides the participant with information about the nature of the study and attempts to remove any misconceptions that may have arisen. Where scientific or humane values justify delaying or withholding this information, the investigator incurs a special responsibility to monitor the research and to ensure that there are no damaging consequences for the participant.

i. Where research procedures result in undesirable consequences for the individual participant, the investigator has the responsibility to detect and remove or correct these consequences, including long-term effects.

j. Information obtained about a research participant during the course of an investigation is confidential unless otherwise agreed upon in advance. When the possibility exists that others may obtain access to such information, this possibility, together with the plans for protecting confidentiality, is explained to the participant as part of the procedure for obtaining informed consent.

Principle 10: Care and use of animals

An investigator of animal behavior strives to advance understanding of basic behavioral principles and/or to contribute to the improvement of human health and welfare. In seeking these ends, the investigator ensures the welfare of animals and treats them humanely. Laws and regulations notwithstanding, an animal's immediate protection depends upon the scientist's own conscience.

a. The acquisition, care, use, and disposal of all animals are in compliance with current federal, state or provincial, and local laws and regulations.

b. A psychologist trained in research methods and experienced in the care of laboratory animals closely supervises all procedures involving animals and is responsible for ensuring appropriate consideration of their comfort, health, and humane treatment.

c. Psychologists ensure that all individuals using animals under their supervision have received explicit instruction in experimental methods and in the care, maintenance, and handling of the species being used. Responsibilities and activities of individuals participating in a research project are consistent with their respective competencies.

d. Psychologists make every effort to minimize discomfort, illness, and pain of animals. A procedure subjecting animals to pain, stress, or privation is used only when an alternative procedure is unavailable and the goal is justified by its prospective scientific, educational, or applied value. Surgical procedures are performed under appropriate anesthesia; techniques to avoid infection and minimize pain are followed during and after surgery.

e. When it is appropriate that the animal's life be terminated, it is done rapidly and painlessly.

B

Appendix B

Ethical Standards

American Association for Counseling and Development

(Approved by AACD Governing Council, March 1988.)

PREAMBLE

The Association is an educational, scientific, and professional organization whose members are dedicated to the enhancement of the worth, dignity, potential, and uniqueness of each individual and thus to the service of society.

The Association recognizes that the role definitions and work settings of its members include a wide variety of academic disciplines, levels of academic preparation, and agency services. This diversity reflects the breadth of the Association's interest and influence. It also poses challenging complexities in efforts to set standards for the performance of members, desired requisite preparation or practice, and supporting social, legal, and ethical controls.

The specification of ethical standards enables the Association to clarify to present and future members and to those served by members the nature of ethical responsibilities held in common by its members.

The existence of such standards serves to stimulate greater concern by members for their own professional functioning and for the conduct of fellow professionals such as counselors, guidance and student personnel workers, and others in the helping professions. As the ethical code of the Association, this document establishes principles that define the ethical behavior of Association members. Additional ethical guidelines developed by the Association's Divisions for their specialty areas may further define a member's ethical behavior.

Section A: General

1. The member influences the development of the profession by continuous efforts to improve professional practices, teaching, services, and research. Professional growth is continuous throughout the member's career and is exemplified by the development of a philosophy that explains why and how a member functions in the helping relationship. Members must gather data on their effectiveness and be guided by the findings. Members recognize the need for continuing education to ensure competent service.

2. The member has a responsibility both to the individual who is served and to the institution within which the service is performed to maintain high standards of professional conduct. The member strives to maintain the highest levels of professional services offered to the individuals to be served. The member also strives to assist the agency, organization, or institution in providing the highest caliber of professional services. The acceptance of employment in an institution implies that the member is in agreement with the general

policies and principles of the institution. Therefore the professional activities of the member are also in accord with the objectives of the institution. If, despite concerted efforts, the member cannot reach agreement with the employer as to acceptable standards of conduct that allow for changes in institutional policy conducive to the positive growth and development of clients, then terminating the affiliation should be seriously considered.

3. Ethical behavior among professional associates, both members and nonmembers, must be expected at all times. When information is possessed that raises doubt as to the ethical behavior of professional colleagues, whether Association members or not, the member must take action to attempt to rectify such a condition. Such action shall use the institution's channels first and then use procedures established by the Association.

4. The member neither claims nor implies professional qualifications exceeding those possessed and is responsible for correcting any misrepresentations of these qualifications by others.

5. In establishing fees for professional counseling services, members must consider the financial status of clients and locality. In the event that the established fee structure is inappropriate for a client, assistance must be provided in finding comparable services of acceptable cost.

6. When members provide information to the public or to subordinates, peers, or supervisors, they have a responsibility to ensure that the content is general, unidentified client information that is accurate, unbiased, and consists of objective, factual data.

7. Members recognize their boundaries of competence and provide only those services and use only those techniques for which they are qualified by training or experience. Members should only accept those positions for which they are professionally qualified.

8. In the counseling relationship, the counselor is aware of the intimacy of the relationship and maintains respect for the client and avoids engaging in activities that seek to meet the counselor's personal needs at the expense of that client.

9. Members do not condone or engage in sexual harassment which is defined as deliberate or repeated comments, gestures, or physical contacts of a sexual nature.

10. The member avoids bringing personal issues into the counseling relationship, especially if the potential for harm is present. Through awareness for the negative impact of both racial and sexual stereotyping and discrimination, the counselor guards the individual rights and personal dignity of the client in the counseling relationship.

11. Products or services provided by the member by means of classroom instruction, public lectures, demonstrations, written articles, radio or television programs, or other types of media must meet the criteria cited in these Standards.

Section B: Counseling Relationship

This section refers to practices and procedures of individual and/or group counseling relationships.

The member must recognize the need for client freedom of choice. Under those circumstances where this is not possible, the member must apprise clients of restrictions that may limit their freedom of choice.

1. The member's primary obligation is to respect the integrity and promote the welfare of the client(s), whether the client(s) is (are) assisted individually or in a group relationship. In a group setting, the member is also responsible for taking reasonable precautions to protect individuals from physical and/or psychological trauma resulting from interaction within the group.

2. Members make provisions for maintaining confidentiality in the storage and disposal of records and follow

an established record retention and disposition policy. The counseling relationship and information resulting therefrom must be kept confidential, consistent with the obligations of the member as a professional person. In a group counseling setting, the counselor must set a norm of confidentiality regarding all group participants' disclosures.

3. If an individual is already in a counseling relationship with another professional person, the member does not enter into a counseling relationship without first contacting and receiving the approval of that other professional. If the member discovers that the client is in another counseling relationship after the counseling relationship begins, the member must gain the consent of the other professional or terminate the relationship, unless the client elects to terminate the other relationship.

4. When the client's condition indicates that there is clear and imminent danger to the client or others, the member must take reasonable personal action or inform responsible authorities. Consultation with other professionals must be used where possible. The assumption of responsibility for the client's(s') behavior must be taken only after careful deliberation. The client must be involved in the resumption of responsibility as quickly as possible.

5. Records of the counseling relationship, including interview notes, test data, correspondence, tape recordings, electronic data storage, and other documents are to be considered professional information for use in counseling, and they should not be considered as part of the records of the institution or agency in which the counselor is employed unless specified by state statute or regulation. Revelation to others of counseling material must occur only upon the expressed consent of the client.

6. In view of the extensive data storage and processing capacities of the computer, the member must ensure that data maintained on a computer is: (a) limited to information that is appropriate and necessary for the services being provided; (b) destroyed after it is determined that the information is no longer of any value in providing services; and (c) restricted in terms of access to appropriate staff members involved in the provision of services by using the best computer security methods available.

7. Use of data derived from a counseling relationship for purposes of counselor training or research shall be confined to content that can be disguised to ensure full protection of the identity of the subject client.

8. The member must inform the client of the purposes, goals, techniques, rules of procedure, and limitations that may affect the relationship at or before the time that the counseling relationship is entered. When working with minors or persons who are unable to give consent, the member protects these clients' best interests.

9. In view of common misconceptions related to the perceived inherent validity of computer generated data and narrative reports, the member must ensure that the client is provided with information as part of the counseling relationship that adequately explains the limitations of computer technology.

10. The member must screen prospective group participants, especially when the emphasis is on self-understanding and growth through self-disclosure. The member must maintain an awareness of the group participants' compatibility throughout the life of the group.

11. The member may choose to consult with any other professionally competent person about a client. In choosing a consultant, the member must avoid placing the consultant in a conflict of interest situation that would preclude the consultant's being a proper party to the member's efforts to help the client.

12. If the member determines an inability to be of professional assistance to the client, the member must either avoid initiating the counseling reltionship or immediately terminate

that relationship. In either event, the member must suggest appropriate alternatives. (The member must be knowledgeable about referral resources so that a satisfactory referral can be initiated.) In the event the client declines the suggested referral, the member is not obligated to continue the relationship.

13. When the member has other relationships, particularly of an administrative, supervisory, and/or evaluative nature with an individual seeking counseling services, the member must not serve as the counselor but should refer the individual to another professional. Only in instances where such an alternative is unavailable and where the individual's situation warrants counseling intervention should the member enter into and/or maintain a counseling relationship. Dual relationships with clients that might impair the member's objectivity and professional judgment (e.g., as with close friends or relatives) must be avoided and/or the counseling relationship terminated through referral to another competent professional.

14. The member will avoid any type of sexual intimacies with clients. Sexual relationships with clients are unethical.

15. All experimental methods of treatment must be clearly indicated to prospective recipients, and safety precautions are to be adhered to by the member.

16. When computer applications are used as a component of counseling services, the member must ensure that: (a) the client is intellectually, emotionally, and physically capable of using the computer application; (b) the computer application is appropriate for the needs of the client; (c) the client understands the purpose and operation of the computer application; and (d) that a follow-up of client use of a computer application is provided to both correct possible problems (misconceptions or inappropriate use) and assess subsequent needs.

17. When the member is engaged in short-term group treatment/training programs (e.g., marathons and other encounter-type or growth groups), the member ensures that there is professional assistance available during and following the group experience.

18. Should the member be engaged in a work setting that calls for any variation from the above statements, the member is obligated to consult with other professionals whenever possible to consider justifiable alternatives.

19. The member must ensure that members of various ethnic, racial, religious, disability, and socio-economic groups have equal access to computer applications used to support counseling services and that the content of available computer applications does not discriminate against the groups described above.

20. When computer applications are developed by the member for use by the general public as self-help/stand-alone computer software, the member must ensure that: (a) self-help computer applications are designed from the beginning to function in a stand-alone manner, as opposed to modifying software that was originally designed to require support from a counselor; (b) self-help computer applications will include within the program statements regarding intended user outcomes, suggestions for using the software, a description of the conditions under which self-help computer applications might not be appropriate, and a description of when and how counseling services might be beneficial; and (c) the manual for such applications will include the qualifications of the developer, the development process, validation data, and operating procedures.

Section C: Measurement and Evaluation

The primary purpose of educational and psychological testing is to provide descriptive measures that are objective and interpretable in either comparative or absolute terms. The member must recognize the need to interpret the statements that follow as applying to the whole range of appraisal techniques including test and nontest data. Test results constitute only one of a variety of pertinent sources of information for personnel, guidance, and counseling decisions.

1. The member must provide specific orientation or information to the examinee(s) prior to and following the test administration so that the results of testing may be placed in proper perspective with other relevant factors. In so doing, the member must recognize the effects of socioeconomic, ethnic, and cultural factors on test scores. It is the member's professional responsibility to use additional unvalidated information carefully in modifying interpretation of the test results.

2. In selecting tests for use in a given situation or with a particular client, the member must consider carefully the specific validity, reliability, and appropriateness of the test(s). General validity, reliability, and related issues may be questioned legally as well as ethically when tests are used for vocational and educational selection, placement, or counseling.

3. When making any statements to the public about tests and testing, the member must give accurate information and avoid false claims or misconceptions. Special efforts are often required to avoid unwarranted connotations of such terms as IQ and grade equivalent scores.

4. Different tests demand different levels of competence for administration, scoring, and interpretation. Members must recognize the limits of their competence and perform only those functions for which they are prepared. In particular, members using computer-based test interpretations must be trained in the construct being measured and the specific instrument being used prior to using this type of computer application.

5. In situations where a computer is used for test administration and scoring, the member is responsible for ensuring that administration and scoring programs function properly to provide clients with accurate test results.

6. Tests must be administered under the same conditions that were established in their standardization. When tests are not administered under standard conditions or when unusual behavior or irregularities occur during the testing session, those conditions must be noted and the results designated as invalid or of questionable validity. Unsupervised or inadequately supervised test-taking, such as the use of tests through the mails, is considered unethical. On the other hand, the use of instruments that are so designed or standardized to be self-administered and self-scored, such as interest inventories, is to be encouraged.

7. The meaningfulness of test results used in personnel, guidance, and counseling functions generally depends on the examinee's unfamiliarity with the specific items on the test. Any prior coaching or dissemination of the test materials can invalidate test results. Therefore, test security is one of the professional obligations of the member. Conditions that produce most favorable test results must be made known to the examinee.

8. The purpose of testing and the explicit use of the results must be made known to the examinee prior to testing. The counselor must ensure that instrument limitations are not exceeded and that periodic review and/or retesting are made to prevent client stereotyping.

9. The examinee's welfare and explicit prior understanding must be the criteria for determining the recipients of the test results. The member must see that specific interpretation accompanies any release of individual or group test data. The interpretation of test data must be related to the examinee's particular concerns.

10. Members responsible for making decisions based on test results have an understanding of educational and psychological measurement, validation criteria, and test research.

11. The member must be cautious when interpreting the results of research

instrument possessing insufficient technical data. The specific purposes for the use of such instruments must be stated explicitly to examinees.

12. The member must proceed with caution when attempting to evaluate and interpret the performance of minority group members or other persons who are not represented in the norm group on which the instrument was standardized.

13. When computer-based test interpretations are developed by the member to support the assessment process, the member must ensure that the validity of such interpretations is established prior to the commercial distribution of such a computer application.

14. The member recognizes that test results may become obsolete. The member will avoid and prevent the misuse of obsolete test results.

15. The member must guard against the appropriation, reproduction, or modification of published tests or parts thereof without acknowledgment and permission from the previous publisher.

Section D: Research and Publication

1. Guidelines on research with human subjects shall be adhered to, such as:
   a. Ethical Principles in the Conduct of Research with Human Participants, Washington, D.C.: American Psychological Association, Inc., 1982.
   b. Code of Federal Regulations, Title 45, Subtitle A, Part 46, as currently issued.
   c. *Ethical Principles of Psychologists,* American Psychological Association, Principle #9: Research with Human Participants.
   d. Family Educational Rights and Privacy Act (the "Buckley Amendment").
   e. Current federal regulations and various state rights privacy acts.

2. In planning any research activity dealing with human subjects, the member must be aware of and responsive to all pertinent ethical principles and ensure that the research problem, design, and execution are in full compliance with them.

3. Responsibility for ethical research practice lies with the principal researcher, while others involved in the research activities share ethical obligation and full responsibility for their own actions.

4. In research with human subjects, researchers are responsible for the subjects' welfare throughout the experiment, and they must take all reasonable precautions to avoid causing injurious psychological, physical, or social effects on their subjects.

5. All research subjects must be informed of the purpose of the study except when withholding information or providing misinformation to them is essential to the investigation. In such research the member must be responsible for corrective action as soon as possible following completion of the research.

6. Participation in research must be voluntary. Involuntary participation is appropriate only when it can be demonstrated that participation will have no harmful effects on subjects and is essential to the investigation.

7. When reporting research results, explicit mention must be made of all variables and conditions known to the investigator that might affect the outcome of the investigation or the interpretation of the data.

8. The member must be responsible for conducting and reporting investigations in a manner that minimizes the possibility that results will be misleading.

9. The member has an obligation to make available sufficient original research data to qualified others who may wish to replicate the study.

10. When supplying data, aiding in the research of another person, reporting research results, or in making original data available, due care must be taken to disguise the identity of the subjects in the absence of specific authorization from such subjects to do otherwise.

11. When conducting and reporting research, the member must be famil-

iar with and give recognition to previous work on the topic, as well as to observe all copyright laws and follow the principles of giving full credit to all to whom credit is due.

12. The member must give due credit through joint authorship, acknowledgment, footnote statements, or other appropriate means to those who have contributed significantly to the research and/or publication, in accordance with such contributions.

13. The member must communicate to other members the results of any research judged to be of professional or scientific value. Results reflecting unfavorably on institutions, programs, services, or vested interests must not be withheld for such reasons.

14. If members agree to cooperate with another individual in research and/or publication, they incur an obligation to cooperate as promised in terms of punctuality of performance and with full regard to the completeness and accuracy of the information required.

15. Ethical practice requires that authors not submit the same manuscript or one essentially similar in content for simultaneous publication consideration by two or more journals. In addition, manuscripts published in whole or in substantial part in another journal or published work should not be submitted for publication without acknowledgment and permission from the previous publication.

Section E: Consulting

Consultation refers to a voluntary relationship between a professional helper and help-needing individual, group, or social unit in which the consultant is providing help to the client(s) in defining and solving a work-related problem or potential problem with a client or client system.

1. The member acting as consultant must have a high degree of self-awareness of his/her own values, knowledge, skills, limitations, and needs in entering a helping relationship that involves human and/or organizational change and that the focus of the relationship be on the issues to be resolved and not on the person(s) presenting the problem.

2. There must be understanding and agreement between member and client for the problem definition, change of goals, and prediction of consequences of interventions selected.

3. The member must be reasonably certain that she/he or the organization represented has the necessary competencies and resources for giving the kind of help that is needed now or may be needed later and that appropriate referral resources are available to the consultant.

4. The consulting relationship must be one in which client adaptability and growth toward self-direction are encouraged and cultivated. The member must maintain this role consistently and not become a decision maker for the client or create a future dependency on the consultant.

5. When announcing consultant availability for services, the member conscientiously adheres to the Association's Ethical Standards.

6. The member must refuse a private fee or other remuneration for consultation with persons who are entitled to these services through the member's employing institution or agency. The policies of a particular agency may make explicit provisions for private practice with agency clients by members of its staff. In such instances, the clients must be apprised of other options open to them should they seek private counseling services.

Section F: Private Practice

1. The member should assist the profession by facilitating the availability of counseling services in private as well as public settings.

2. In advertising services as a private practitioner, the member must advertise the services in a manner that accurately informs the public of professional services, expertise, and

techniques of counseling available. A member who assumes an executive leadership role in the organization shall not permit his/her name to be used in professional notices during periods when he/she is not actively engaged in the private practice of counseling.

3. The member may list the following: highest relevant degree, type and level of certification and/or license, address, telephone number, office hours, type and/or description of services, and other relevant information. Such information must not contain false, inaccurate, misleading, partial, out-of-context, or deceptive material or statements.

4. Members do not present their affiliation with any organization in such a way that would imply inaccurate sponsorship or certification by that organization.

5. Members may join in partnership/ corporation with other members and/or other professionals provided that each member of the partnership or corporation makes clear the separate specialties by name in compliance with the regulations of the locality.

6. A member has an obligation to withdraw from a counseling relationship if it is believed that employment will result in violation of the Ethical Standards. If the mental or physical condition of the member renders it difficult to carry out an effective professional relationship or if the member is discharged by the client because the counseling relationship is no longer productive for the client, then the member is obligated to terminate the counseling relationship.

7. A member must adhere to the regulations for private practice of the locality where the services are offered.

8. It is unethical to use one's institutional affiliation to recruit clients for one's private practice.

Section G: Personnel Administration

It is recognized that most members are employed in public or quasi-public institutions. The functioning of a member within an institution must contribute to the goals of the institution and vice versa if either is to accomplish their respective goals or objectives. It is therefore essential that the member and the institution function in ways to: (a) make the institution's goals explicit and public; (b) make the member's contribution to institutional goals specific; and (c) foster mutual accountability for goal achievement.

To accomplish these objectives, it is recognized that the member and the employer must share responsbilities in the formulation and implementation of personnel policies.

1. Members must define and describe the parameters and levels of their professional competency.

2. Members must establish interpersonal relations and working agreements with supervisors and subordinates regarding counseling or clinical relationships, confidentiality, distinction between public and private material, maintenance and dissemination of recorded information, work load, and accountability. Working agreements in each instance must be specified and made known to those concerned.

3. Members must alert their employers to conditions that may be potentially disruptive or damaging.

4. Members must inform employers of conditions that may limit their effectiveness.

5. Members must submit regularly to professional review and evaluation.

6. Members must be responsible for inservice development of self and/or staff.

7. Members must inform their staff of goals and programs.

8. Members must provide personnel practices that guarantee and enhance the rights and welfare of each recipient of their service.

9. Members must select competent persons and assign responsibilities compatible with their skills and experiences.

10. The member, at the onset of a counseling relationship, will inform the client of the member's intended use

22. of supervisors regarding the disclosure of information concerning this case. The member will clearly inform the client of the limits of confidentiality in the relationship.
11. Members, as either employers or employees, do not engage in or condone practices that are inhumane, illegal, or unjustifiable (such as considerations based on sex, handicap, age, race) in hiring, promotion, or training.

Section H: Preparation Standards

Members who are responsible for training others must be guided by the preparation standards of the Association and relevant Division(s). The member who functions in the capacity of trainer assumes unique ethical responsibilities that frequently go beyond that of the member who does not function in a training capacity. These ethical responsibilities are outlined as follows:

1. Members must orient students to program expectations, basic skills development, and employment prospects prior to admission to the program.
2. Members in charge of learning experiences must establish programs that integrate academic study and supervised practice.
3. Members must establish a program directed toward developing students' skills, knowledge, and self-understanding, stated whenever possible in competency or performance terms.
4. Members must identify the levels of competencies of their students in complicance with relevant Division standards. These competencies must accommodate the paraprofessional as well as the professional.
5. Members, through continual student evaluation and appraisal, must be aware of the personal limitations of the learner that might impede future performance. The instructor must not only assist the learner in securing remedial assistance but also screen from the program those individuals who are unable to provide competent services.
6. Members must provide a program that includes training in research commensurate with levels of role functioning. Paraprofessional and technician-level personnel must be trained as consumers of research. In addition, personnel must learn how to evaluate their own and their program's effectiveness. Graduate training, especially at the doctoral level, would include preparation for original research by the member.
7. Members must make students aware of the ethical responsibilities and standards of the profession.
8. Preparatory programs must encourage students to value the ideal of service to individuals and to society. In this regard, direct financial remuneration or lack thereof must not influence the quality of service rendered. Monetary considerations must not be allowed to overshadow professional and humanitarian needs.
9. Members responsible for educational programs must be skilled as teachers and practitioners.
10. Members must present thoroughly varied theoretical positions so that students may make comparisons and have the opportunity to select a position.
11. Members must develop clear policies within their educational institutions regarding field placement and the roles of the student and the instructor in such placement.
12. Members must ensure that forms of learning focusing on self-understanding or growth are voluntary, or if required as part of the educational program, are made known to prospective students prior to entering the program. When the educational program offers a growth experience with an emphasis on self-disclosure or other relatively intimate or personal involvement, the member must have no administrative, supervisory, or evaluating authority regarding the participant.
13. The member will at all times provide students with clear and equally acceptable alternatives for self-understanding or growth experiences. The

member will assure students that they have a right to accept these alternatives without prejudice or penalty.

14. Members must conduct an educational program in keeping with the current relevant guidelines of the Association.

Name Index

Abney, D. L., 211
Ackerman, A. B., 247
Ackerman, N., 128, 129
Acredolo, C., 222
Adler, A., 41–49, 108
Alkus, S., 199
Allport, G., 37, 38, 44, 46
Alschuler, A. S., 222
Alschuler, C. F., 222
Anastasi, A., 4
Apanaitis, B. E., 28
Arbuckle, D. S., 151, 156
Arif, A., 26
AuClaire, P. A., 231

Bakal, D. A., 219
Baker, B. L., 157
Baker, T. B., 165
Bales, R. R., 112, 113
Band, L., 1, 3
Bandura, A., 41, 44, 47
Barclay, J. R., 41, 42, 45
Barker, C., 70
Barnett, R. C., 75
Baruch, G. K., 75
Barzun, J., 1, 2
Bateson, G., 128, 129, 143
Baum, M. S., 247
Bazelon, J., 202
Beavin, J., 129
Beck, A., 115, 119, 121
Bednar, R., 110, 118
Bell, H., 8
Beller, E. K., 156
Belloc, N. B., 225
Benne, K. C., 112, 113
Benrett, G., 8
Benson, H., 228
Berger, J., 173, 178

Berger, M., 114
Berkman, L., 226
Bernier, J. E., 92
Besharov, D. J., 258
Betz, N. E., 64, 101
Bice, T. W., 231
Biener, L., 75
Binder, A., 200, 200–201
Binder, V. L., 249
Binet, A., 10
Bishop, J. B., 159–160
Blake, R., 181, 182
Blocher, D., 183
Boll, T. L., 16
Bonney, W., 115
Bookholder, R. M., 207
Bordin, E., 57, 59, 63
Borgen, F. N., 95
Borow, H., 20, 22, 23, 24
Bowen, M., 129, 131, 132, 139, 140,
    141, 142, 143, 147, 148
Boylan, R., 222
Bozwarth, J., 62
Brabender, V., 115
Brakel, S. J., 202
Brammer, L., 55, 65, 66
Brandeis, L. D., 186
Brenson, B., 68
Breslow, L., 225, 226
Brodsky, A., 75
Bromberg, W., 218
Brooks, D. K., 23
Brown, D., 179
Brown, J. C., 49, 50
Buczek, T., 75, 76
Buhler, C., 86
Burch, G. K. W., 232
Burish, T. G., 226
Burke, M. J., 163

Butler, S., 241
Byhler, C., 44, 45

Caplan, G., 172, 175–176
Carder, C. E., 99, 100, 104
Carkhuff, R., 61, 151
Carney, L. P., 200
Carney, M., 65, 66
Carter, E., 142
Carter, J., 56, 57, 60, 62, 65
Cartwright, D., 107, 109
Casas, J. M., 155
Caskey, N., 70
Catalano, R., 222
Cerney, M., 66
Chein, I., 36, 37, 38
Childers, W. C., 23
Claiborn, C., 71, 72
Clarke, J. H., 221
Clarkin, J. F., 157
Clearly, P. D., 223
Cleary, E. W., 189
Cochron, J. R., 260
Coffman, E. W., 247
Cognetta, P., 92
Cohen, I., 40
Collins, W. A., 92
Cook, E. P., 76
Cooney, E. W., 92
Cooper, R., 71
Cooper, S., 177, 183
Corazzini, J., 110
Corey, G., 108, 109
Corey, M., 108, 109
Cornfeld, J. L., 92
Corzzini, J. G., 16
Covington, M., 210
Cowley, W. H., 5
Cramer, S., 87, 92, 93, 95, 96, 97, 98, 101
Crouch, R. E., 207
Crowley, M., 72
Curran, W. J., 26

D'Augelli, A., 64
Dagley, J, 107, 113
Danish ,S. J., 30, 64
Darley, J., 8
Davies, D., 123, 124
Davis, R. U., 14
Davis, R. W., 199
DeForest, D., 64
DeGeorge, R. T., 238–239, 240
DeJoy, D. M., 219
DeLeon, P. H., 198–199

Delworth, U., 16
Derdeyn, A. P., 205
Deutch, G., 161
Di Lorenzo, T. M., 227
Dickerman, W., 115
Dies, R. R., 64
Dillard, J. M., 77, 78
Dindinger, M., 200
Dinges, N., 64
Dixon, D., 72
Doan, R. E., 228
Dobbs, D. B., 209
Dooley, D., 222
Dorn, F. J., 189
Drapkin, R., 247
Dreese, M., 8
Duff, R. S., 229–230
Dugo, J., 115, 119, 121
Dunphy, D., 115
Dustin, D., 183
Dworkin, R. H., 160
Dyer, R., 64

Eagleston, J. R., 225–226
Eckenrode, J., 222
Edinger, L., 71, 72
Edwards, A. L., 167
Egan, G., 69, 73, 74
Ehrenwald, J., 32
Elliot, R., 70
Engels, D. W., 240
England, G. W., 14
Enstrom, J. E., 226
Erikson, E., 44, 50, 86, 87
Exner, J. E., 162
Eysenck, H., 41

Feldstein, J. C., 76
Fenichel, O., 223
Ference, C. M., 28
Fiedler, F. E., 40
Fiscalin, J., 257
Fisher, C., 64
Fisher, K., 257–258, 259
Fisher, R. M., 254
Fishman, C., 136
Fitzgerald, L., 101
Fitzgerald, L. F., 16
Fitzgibbon, M. L., 157
Fix, A. J., 113
Flanagan, J., 10
Fletcher, F., 8
Ford, D. H., 44
Frank, J., 33
Frank, L., 171
Frank, L. K., 164

Frederick, J. T., 211
French, A., 130
Fretz, B. R., 28
Freud, A., 49, 50
Freud, S., 3, 12, 41, 43, 44, 48, 49,
    50, 51, 86, 164
Friedman, M., 226
Fromm, E., 42, 49, 50
Fryer, D., 10
Fusimura, L. E., 260

Gallessich, J., 178, 183
Galshi, T., 211
Garetz, C., 113
Gary, A. L., 64
Gazda, G., 108
Gazda, G. M., 23, 24, 25, 26
Gazda, L. M., 107, 113, 115
Geis, G., 199
Gelatt, H. B., 96
Gelso, C., 38, 56, 57, 60, 62, 65, 66
Gershenfeld, M., 110
Ghosh, S. A., 199
Gibbs, J., 179
Gilbert, W., 8
Glenn, C. M., 246–247
Glenn, R. D., 252, 260
Glover, J., 72
Goldman, L., 153
Goldschmitt, T., 164
Goldstein, A. P., 72, 73, 74, 75
Goldstein, K., 42
Goldstein, M. J., 157
Gordon, E. V., 103
Gore, S., 222
Gornbein, H. S., 207
Gortmaker, S. L., 222
Gottheil, D., 199
Graff, R. W., 64
Graham, J. R., 161–162, 164, 193
Green, S. L., 247–248
Greenson, R., 56, 251
Grey, A., 251
Grisso, T., 188
Gross, D. R., 255
Guerin, P., 128

Haddad, L. K., 203
Hagen, E., 10
Hahn, M., 5, 8
Halberg, E., 72
Haley, J., 128, 129, 131, 143
Hall, C. S., 224
Hall, H. V., 203
Halleck, S. L., 158–159
Halmos, P., 1, 2

Halpern, T., 40
Hammond, R., 64
Hansen, J. C., 247–248
Hare-Mustin, R. T., 75, 252
Harrell, T., 10
Harris, S. L., 156
Harrison, K. H., 92
Hauer, A., 64
Heck, E., 75
Heckel, R. V., 115
Heerboth, J. R., 160
Henderson, D. H., 255
Herlihy, B., 253–254
Herr, E. L., 20, 21, 27, 87–90, 91, 92,
    93, 95, 96–97, 98
Hershenson, D. B., 102, 103
Hill, D. 70
Hill, W., 116
Hillenberg, J. B., 227
Hinckley, J., 197
Hinkeldy, N. W., 247
Hitt, W. D., 36–37, 38
Hodges, W., 177, 183
Hoffman, L., 129, 130
Hogan, D. B., 258, 259
Holland, J. L., 10, 13, 91
Holmes, D. R., 221
Holmes, G. R., 115
Hoover, N., 22
Horney, K., 41, 49, 50, 224
Horwitz, L., 57, 58
Hosford, R. E., 200
Houts, A. C., 34
Howard, G. F., 55
Huber, J. T., 47, 52
Huebener, L. A., 16
Hull, C., 3, 4
Hunt, C., 92

Ibrahim, F. A., 246
Immergluck, L., 38
Isaacson, L. E., 89, 93, 95
Ivey, A. E., 28, 29

Jackson, C., 226
Jackson, D., 128, 129, 143
Jaques, M. E., 10, 11, 25, 102
Jahoda, M., 157
Jamison, K. R., 157
Jennings, J. F., 26
Jinkerson, D. L., 160
Johnson, D. W., 74
Johnson, L. B., 171, 231
Jones, E. J., 76
Jourard, S. M., 63, 64
Jung, C. G., 44, 49

Kanter, S., 116
Kaplan, A. G., 252
Kaplan, M., 75
Karras, D. A., 201
Kaul, T., 67, 110
Kauppi, D. R., 10, 11, 25, 102
Keeney, B., 131
Keeton, R. E., 209
Keeton, W. P., 209
Keitel, M. A., 101
Keith-Speigel, P. C., 242
Keller, J. W., 166
Kelman, H. C., 122, 123
Kennedy, J. F., 171, 172
Kimble, G. A., 33, 34
Kionka, E. J., 210
Kitchner, K. S., 238, 239, 242
Kivlinghan, D., 110
Klein, M., 49
Kleinmuntz, J. D., 154
Klippel, J. A., 219
Klyver, N., 199
Knapp, S., 203, 255, 258, 259
Knowles, H., 109
Knowles, J. H., 220
Knowles, M., 109
Koch, S., 33
Krasner, L., 34, 47
Krauft, C., 62
Kraut, A., 198–199
Krumboltz, J. D., 41, 47, 152–153
Kunin, C. C., 76
Kurpius, D., 179, 180
Kuypers, B., 123, 124
Kwawer, J., 66

L'Abate, L., 228
Lacoursier, R., 115
Langer, J., 43, 44, 47
Larsen, R. M., 165
Leaman, D., 68, 69
Leary, M. R., 153–154
Lee, D., 72
Lees-Haley, P. R., 212
Lerner, H., 67
Lerner, S., 67
Levenstein, A., 85, 86
Levine, A., 19, 20
Levine, D. W., 226
Levine, M., 19, 20
Lewis, L., 165
Lichtenberg, J., 75
Lieberman, M. A., 114, 115, 116
Lindzey, G., 164
Lipsitz, N. E., 240–241, 247
Liss-Levinson, N., 252

Livesley, W., 116, 118, 120, 122, 124
Lloyd, A. P., 78
Loevinger, J., 44
Lofquist, L. H., 13
Loftus, E. F., 194, 211
Logan, D., 230
London, P. C., 39, 45
Loonsbury, J., 173
Lopez, F., 71
Lowe, C. M., 40, 41, 42, 43
Lowen, A., 227, 228
Lowen, L., 228
Lubin, B., 165
Luft, J., 110, 114
Lum, D., 231
Luria, A. R., 44

M'Naghten, D., 196
MacKenzie, K., 116, 118, 120, 122, 124
Maclean, M. S., 55
MacLennan, B., 172, 173
MacPherson, B. V., 221
Maddux, J. E., 153–154
Mahler, C., 116
Major-Kingsley, L,. 247
Maloney, M. P., 154
Mann, R. D., 115, 116
Mannino, F., 183
Mappes, D. C., 240, 246
Marecek, J., 252
Margolin, J., 261
Marmor, J., 251
Martin, B., 224
Martin, E., 116
Masling, J., 40
Maslow, A., 51, 91
Matarazzo, J. D., 153–154, 164–165, 219
May, R., 52
McCabe, J., 26
McCarthy, P., 64
McClellend, D. C., 2
McGee, T., 124
McGovern, T., 110
Meara, N. M., 27, 28
Mechanic, D., 223, 231
Medway, F., 183
Meehl, P. E., 162
Meissen, G., 173
Melnick, J., 110, 117
Melton, G. B., 240, 246
Mendelsohn, R., 65
Merrikin, K. J., 208
Meyer, J., 173, 176–177
Miles, M. D., 114, 115
Miller, C. H., 2

Miller, R. D., 254–255
Millman, H. M., 47, 52
Millon, T., 157–158
Mills, D. H., 28
Mills, T., 115
Minuchin, S., 129, 131, 132, 133, 134, 135, 136, 139, 147
Mitcheu, K., 62
Moreland, R., 117
Moreno, J. L., 108
Moursand, J., 45
Mouton, J., 181, 182
Murray, E. J., 152
Musserick, F., 44
Myers, P., 55

Nance, D. W., 55
Napier, R., 110
Naroll, R., 32
Nathan, P. E., 156, 164
Neff, W., 84, 85
Newman, A. S., 260
Nisbet, R. E., 194
Norcross, J., 55
Norman, J., 163
Nye, R. D., 46, 47, 48, 50, 52

O'Neil, R. M., 222
Orfanidis, M. M., 142
Osipow, S. H, 16, 17
Otis, A., 10
Overcast, T. D., 208
Owen, D. G., 209

Padesky, C., 199
Pakarney, L., 173
Palagi, R. J., 208
Papp, P., 130, 131
Pappas, J. P., 8, 9
Parcell, C. L., 221
Parloff, M., 62, 76
Parloff, R., 45
Parsons, F., 3, 4, 19, 88
Parsons, R., 173, 176–177
Patterson, M., 71, 72
Peabody, S., 66
Pedersen, P., 78
Pelletier, C. L., 218
Pelletier, K. R., 224–225
Pepinsky, H., 13
Perls, F., 143
Peterson, J. A., 39, 43
Petosa, R., 221, 232
Phillips, J., 39
Piaget, J., 44
Pilisuk, M., 222

Pinson, N. M., 20, 21, 27
Piotrowski, C., 165–166
Pistole, M., 107, 113
Pistrang, N., 70
Ponterotto, J. G., 155
Pope, K. S., 242
Porter, J. B., 195, 197, 199, 201
Porter, L., 26
Pratt, J. A., 107
Prediger, D. J., 94
Prosser, W. L., 259
Prothaska, J., 55

Quinn, R., 172

Racusen, F., 124
Ramanaiah, N. V., 160
Rappl, L., 72
Reagan, R., 197
Reardon, R. C., 163
Redfield, W. C., 190
Reiser, M., 199
Renzaglia, G. A., 152
Rest, J. R., 239
Reynolds, C., 64
Richards, T. F., 159–160
Robb, G. P., 240
Robbins, S. B., 161
Roberts, R. R., 152
Robertson, M. H., 164, 166, 257
Robinson, F., 8, 41
Robinson, R., 55, 69
Robinson, S. E., 255
Roche, P. Q., 195
Rodin, E., 8
Rodin, M. J., 76
Roe, A., 10, 13, 91
Rogers, C. R., 5, 12, 42, 51–52, 60, 61, 62, 65, 150–151, 152, 153, 227
Rogers, R., 249
Roisium, K., 173
Roll, S., 72
Roosevelt, F. D., 22
Rose, G., 110
Rosecrans, C. J., 115
Rosenhan, D. L., 156
Rosenthal, D., 40
Ross, C. E., 229–230
Ross, L., 194
Rossberg, R. H., 1, 3, 101
Rothstein, P. F., 254
Rotter, J. B., 220
Rotter, J. B., 73, 74, 220
Royce, J., 33–34, 34, 35
Ruiz, R. A., 77

Ruppel, G., 67
Rustad, K., 92

Saczynski, K., 160
Sales, B. D., 208
Samler, J., 8
Sampson, J. P., 163
Satir, V., 128, 129, 132, 143, 144, 145, 146, 147, 148
Savitshu, J. C., 201
Scharf, P., 200
Schauble, P. G., 153
Schein, E., 174–175, 179
Scherman, A., 228
Schmidt, L. D., 27, 28, 73
Schroeder, D., 172
Schuman, B., 125
Schwartz, S. M., 218–219
Schwebel, M., 6
Schwitzgebel, R. L., 197
Scott, E., 205
Scott, W., 8
Seaman, M., 220
Seaman, T. A., 220
Seashore, H., 8
Seibel, R. F., 190
Seligmen, M. E. P., 220
Selman, R. L., 92
Serban, G., 252
Shahnasarian, M., 163
Shambaugh, P., 116
Sheats, P., 112, 113
Shectman, F., 156
Sheeley, V. L., 253–254
Shevrin, H., 156
Shore, M., 183
Shostrom, E., 65, 66
Shullman, S. L., 99, 100, 104
Silberman, L. J., 207
Sills, A., 173
Sinnett, E. R., 165
Skinner, B. F., 12, 41, 44, 46–47, 51, 240
Slavson, S., 108
Slovenko, R., 195, 252–253
Smaby, M., 68
Smith, D., 55
Smith, E. C., 206
Smith, E. J., 77, 78
Smith, M., 75
Snegroff, S., 232
Spokane, A. R., 247
Spring, R. L., 196
Springer, J. R., 208, 230, 231
Springer, S. P., 161
Staats, W., 33

Stachowiak, J., 146
Stephenson, B. W., 92
Stone, A. A., 252
Stone, G., 64
Straumfjord, A. A., 64
Stricker, G., 198
Strong, E. K., 10
Strong, S., 71, 73, 74
Strong, S. R., 71, 72, 73
Stuit, D., 8, 10
Sturgis, D. K., 28
Sue, D. W., 77, 78
Sue, S., 78
Sullivan, H. S., 41, 49, 50
Sundberg, N. D., 154
Super, D., 3, 4, 8, 9, 10, 12, 13, 84, 86, 87, 104
Super, D. E., 153–154, 155
Sutton, J. M., Jr., 190
Sweeney, J. A., 157
Syme, E. L., 226
Szasz, T., 20, 22

Tabachnick, B. G., 242
Tallent, N., 163
Tamminen, A., 68
Taschman, H. A., 146
Taylor, P. W., 238
Terman, L., 10
Tharp, R., 177
Thelen, H., 115
Thiers, N., 186
Thompson, A. A., 17
Thoresen, C., 47
Thoresen, C. E., 220, 225–226
Tipton, R. M., 16, 164–165
Torbet, D., 39
Touchton, J. G., 92
Truak, C. B., 151–152
Truax, C., 62
Turkington, C., 259
Tyler, L., 17
Tymchuk, A. J., 247
Tyson, J., 72

Ulanov, A. B., 252
Urban, H. B., 44

VandeCreek, L., 203, 255, 257
Verbrugge, L. M., 223
Vilman, L. P., 47
Vogel, R., 200
Vygotsky, L. S., 44

Wade, T. C., 165
Wagner, W. G., 254
Wakefield, J. C., 75

Waldrop, R., 8
Wall, S., 72
Walters, H. A., 203
Wambach, C., 71
Ward, M. P., 154
Ward, S. R., 71
Warner, D. E., 44
Waskow, I., 62, 76
Watkins, C. E., 66, 67, 104, 119
Watkins, C., Jr., 251, 252
Watzlawick, P., 129, 144
Weakland, J., 128, 129, 143
Weigel, R. G., 64
Weinstock, R., 254–255
Weis, D. M., 260
Weiss, G. E., 218–219
Welfel, E. R., 240–241, 247
Werner, H., 44
Wertheimer, L. G., 92
Wetzel, R., 177
Whitaker, C., 129
Whitaker, D., 116
Whiteley, S. M., 200
Whiteley, J. M., 2, 3, 6, 7, 8, 11, 12, 13, 14, 15
Widick, C., 92
Wiggins, R. C., 164

Wigmore, J. H., 253
Wilcoxon, S. A., 248
Wilkinson, A. P., 258, 260
Williamson, E. G., 4–5, 8, 41
Witmer, L., 19
Wolfe, B., 62, 76
Wolpe, J., 41, 47
Woods, M., 117
Woody, J. D., 203, 255
Woody, R. H., 153, 163–164, 166, 186, 190, 191, 192, 202, 203, 205, 212, 221, 224, 227, 228, 230, 231, 232, 252, 255, 257, 259, 261–262
Worthy, G., 64
Wrenn, G., 8
Wright, R. H., 261

Yalom, I. D., 114, 117, 124
Yerkes, R., 10

Zander, A., 107, 109
Zane, N., 78
Zelen, S. L., 241
Zoppel, C. L., 76
Zytowski, D. G., 17, 95

Subject Index

accreditation, 16
acts(s) of law:
  Barden-LaFollette, 24
  civil rights, 26
  community mental health centers, 25, 172
  Comprehensive Crime Control (1984), 198–199
  disabled veterans rehabilitation, 25
  elementary and secondary education, 24
  George-Barden, 22
  George-Dean, 22
  George-Reed, 22
  manpower development and training, 24
  mental health, 25
  mental health study, 171
  mental health system, 26
  National Defense Education (1958), 13, 23, 24
  Smith-Fess, 24
  Smith-Hughs, 22
  Smith-Sears, 24
  Vocational Rehabilitation 1954, 13, 24
  Wagner-Peyser, 23
actuarial methods of assessment, 162–163
administrator-centered consulting (Caplan), 126
advocacy, 246–247
altruism and career development, 86
ambiguity, use of, 63
American Association for Counseling and Development (AACD):
  ethical standards, 277–286
  ethics, 241
  training, 238

American Association for Marriage and Family Therapy (AAMFT), 241
American Association of Sex Educators, Counselors, and Therapists (AASECT), 241–242
American Bar Association (ABA), 207
American Board of Examiners in Professional Psychology, 14
American Board of Forensic Psychology, 107
American Board of Professional Psychology, 27, 256
American College Personnel Association, 8
American Group Psychotherapy Association, 108
American Law Institute, 196
American Personnel and Guidance Association (APGA), 8, 13 (see also American Association for Counseling and Development [AACD])
American Psychiatric Association (APA), 197
American Psychological Association (APA), 6, 7–8, 12, 16, 26, 27, 28, 29, 154–155, 156, 164
  confidentiality, 249, 253
  divisions (see divisions of American Psychological Association)
  educational training, 238
  Education and Training Board, 13, 16
  ethical principles, 250, 251, 253, 267–275
  ethical training, 241
  ethics committee report, 242
  guidelines for counseling psychologists, 242, 248, 267–275

American Psychological Association
   (*continued*):
  malpractice insurance claims, 257
  misrepresentation, 256
  publications, 241
American Rehabilitation Counselors
   Association, 11
American Society of Group Therapy,
   108
anthropology, 12, 13
anxiety, 223–224
aptitude tests, in career development,
   95
assessment, 3, 4, 10, 23, 198–199
  actuarial methods, 162–163
  alternatives to, 154–155, 161
  bias in, 155, 159–160
  in career development, 94–95
  clinical aspects, 154–155
  definition, 154, 155
  ethics, 155
  history of, 150–151
  methods, 162–167
  minority issues, 155, 163
  misleading data, 161–162
  misuse of test data 160–162
  person centered, 150–153
  selective responding, 152–153
  techniques of, 154–155
  theoretical bias, 159–160
  tools, 158 (*see also* tests)
  use in counseling, 153–154,
   160–161
  use in treatment, 155
  vocational, 150
assessment and diagnosis stage, consultation, procedures of, 181
Association for Advancement of
   Behavior Therapy (AABT), 166
autonomic nervous system, 224

behavioral attitude toward testing, 166
behavioral model of consultation, 178
behaviorism, 37, 41, 46–47
  origin of, 152
Bender Visual-Motor Gestalt Test, 165,
   166
bias:
  assessment/testing 155, 159–160
  diagnosis, 156–157
body/mind unity, 227–230
  counseling, 227
  counseling psychologist as a role
   model, 229–230
  health, 227–228
  score formula, the, 228–229

Boulder Conference, 16
"Brandeis Brief," 186
Bureau of Labor Statistics, 23

California Psychological Inventory, 166
career:
  maturity, 95
  plateauing, 100
  shifts, 100
  system, 100
career development:
  achievement tests, 95
  assessment in, 94–95
  in community, 99
  decision making in, 93, 94, 99
  disabled and, 101–103
  group intervention, 96–97
  individual intervention, 95–96
  in industry, 99–100
  interventions, 93–97
  minorities and, 103
  in schools, 92, 97–99
  settings, 97–100
  special populations, 100–103
  stages of, 86–88
  theoretical approaches, 86–91
  values and, 93, 98
  women and, 101
  work, role of, 84–86
career development, theoretical approaches, 86–91
  decision theories, 89–90
  developmental theories, 86–88, 92
  personality theories, 90–91
  sociological theories, 90
  trait and factor theories, 88–89
career psychology (*see* vocational
   psychology)
certification, 27
child abuse:
  confidentiality issues, 254–255
  public policy, 247
child advocacy, 247
children, legal rights of, 246–247
Children's Apperception Test (CAT),
   166
client rights, 202, 261–262
  in contrast to societal, 249
clinical assessment:
  aspects of, 154–155
  methods, 162–167
  minority issues, 155, 183
  use in therapy, 160–161
  (*see also* assessment)
clinical psychology, 3, 13, 153, 217,
   218

cohesiveness in group counseling, 111, 121–122
  commitment to process, 122
collective unconscious, 44, 49
Commission on Mental Illness, 25
communication (*see* privileged communication)
communication in families:
  blaming, 144
  congruent, 145
  irrelevant, 145
  levels, 144
  patterns, 144
  placating, 144
  super-reasonable, 144–145
communications approach, family therapy:
  diagnosis, 145–146
  family concepts, 143–145
  family functioning, 145
  interventions, 146–147
  style of communication, 144–145
communication techniques:
  degree of lead, 69–70
  nonverbal, 71–72
  response types, 70–71
community:
  and career development, 99
  role in health psychology, 231–232
competency to stand trial, 197–198
confidentiality, 252–255
  APA ethical mandate, 253
  child abuse and, 254–255
  circumstances for breaching, 253
  in the criminal justice system, 190–191, 200
  criteria for, 253
  defined, 252
  exceptions to, 254–255
  parameters of, 219
conflict and confrontation stage, group counseling, 120–121
  members' leadership roles, 120–121
  resistance, 121
confrontation:
  in group therapy, 120–121
  in therapy, 61, 68–69
consultation:
  definition of, 172–173
  forensic, 187, 190
  history of, 171–172
  models of, 173–179
  procedural stages of, 179–183
  (*see also* consultation models; consultation, procedural stages)

consultation, procedural stages, 179–183
  assessment and diagnosis, 181
  initial contact, 179–181
  intervention, 181–182
  pre-entry, 179
  termination, 182–183
consultation models, 173–179
  behavioral model, 178
  Caplan's models, 175–176
    administrator-centered, 176
    client-centered, 175–176
    consultee-centered, 176
  Hodges' and Cooper's, 177
    educational model, 177
    individual-process model, 177
  Kurpius model, 179
  meta-theory model, 178–179
    human development model, 178
    scientific technological model, 178
    social/political model, 179
  Parson's and Meyer's models, 176–177
  program-centered, 176
  Schein's models, 174–175, 179
    doctor/patient, 174
    process model, 175
    purchase model, 174
  triadic model, 177
correctional counseling, 200
corrective emotional experience, 58
  in group therapy, 123–124
counseling:
  guidelines, 5
  historical roots, 2–6, 7, 20, 33
  and mental health, 3
  special populations, 9
  test use in, 153–154, 160–161
  (*see also* groups; history; minority issues; relationship, therapeutic; techniques; theory)
counseling psychologist:
  health-policy issues, 231
  interactions with police, 199
  relationship with attorney, 189–191
  role in the commuity, 231–232
  role in the criminal justice system, 198–200
  role model of health, 229–230
  roles and functions, 5, 14
  training, 29
  (*see also* counselor; training)
Counseling Psychologist, The, 14
counseling psychology:
  challenges facing, 15, 26–27

counseling psychology (*continued*):
  computer use, 163
  concerns of, 153–154
  confidentiality parameters, 219
  definitional issues, 12
  development of, 217, 232, 233
  as distinct from clinical psychology,
    165, 217
  ethical training, 237, 247–248
  founders, 7–8
  future public policy, 26
  generic education for applied
    psychology, 16
  historical development, 11–15,
    23–24
  historical roots, 2–6, 7, 20, 33, 217
  professional identity, 4–5, 7–8, 14,
    16, 33
  trends in, 165
  use of assessment, 153–154
  (*see also* ethical issues; history;
    training)
counseling skills (*see* therapeutic skills)
counseling theories, critical three,
    45–52
  behaviorism, 46–47
  humanism, 50–52
  psychodynamic, 48–50
counselor(s):
  eclectic, 55, 56
  educator, 98
  gender roles, 75, 76
  liability, 248–250, 254–255, 258
  malpractice, 192, 208, 208–213,
    257–262
  moral position of, 39, 43
  qualities, 72–75
  (*see also* privileged communication;
    training)
counselor qualities:
  expertness, 72–73
  interpersonal attractiveness, 74–75
  trustworthiness, 73–74
countertransference, 57, 65–67,
    250–252
court cases:
  Covington v. Harris, 202
  Lipari v. Sears, Roebuck, 255
  McIntosh v. Milano, 255
  Muller v. Oregon, 186
  State v. Cavallo, 189
  Tarasoff v. Regents, 255
  Wyatt v. Stickney, 201
courtroom:
  behavior, 191–192
  preparation, 192–194

  problems faced by psychologists,
    193
  rules and procedures, 188
credentialing, 27, 28–29
  specialization, 256–257
  (*see also* licensing statutes)
criminal justice system, 194–201
  counseling psychologists' roles,
    198–199
  diversion programs, 199
cross-cultural counseling, 76, 77, 78,
    79, 101–103 (*see also* minority
    issues; special populations)

dangerousness, determination of, 203
deceleration, 88
decision making, career, 93, 94, 99
decision theory and career develop-
    ment, 89–90, 96
decline stage of career development,
    88
decriminalizing, juvenile justice
    system, 201
defense mechanisms, 37, 50, 222
Department of Health, Education, and
    Welfare, 25
Department of Labor, 22
depth psychology, 37
determinism, 38–39, 48
developmental theories and career
    development, 86–88, 92, 98
diagnosis, 151, 153, 155–159
  client-centered, 150, 151
  factors in, 158
  family systems, 134–135, 145–146
  forensic, 187
  history, 150–151
  holistic approaches, 159
  minority issues, 156–157
  process, 159
  tools, 158
  use in treatment, 155–159
*Diagnostic and Statistical Manual of
    Mental Disorders,* third edition-
    revised (DSM III-R), 156, 194
Dictionary of Occupational Titles, 23
differential psychology, 10, 12, 23, 88,
    94
directive counseling, 5
  and assessment, 151–153
disabled and career development,
    101–103
disengagement, 88, 91
Division of Counseling and Guidance
    (*see* Division of Counseling
    Psychology)

Division of Counseling Psychology, 6, 7, 11, 12, 16, 28

Division of Personnel Psychologists (*see* Division of Counseling Psychology)

Division 17, 6, 7, 11, 12, 16, 28

divisions of American Psychological Association:
  Division of Clinical Psychology, 6
  Division of Counseling Psychology, 6, 7, 11, 12, 16, 28
  Division of Educational Psychology, 6
  Division of Health Psychology, 219
  Division of Industrial Psychology, 6
  Division of Military Psychology, 6
  Division of Psychologists in Public Service, 6
  Division of School Psychology, 6

divorce mediation, 206–208

Draw-A-Person, 166

DSM-III-R, 156, 194

dual-career families, 101

Dynamics, group, 109

eclecticism, 55–56

ecological ignorance, 131

economic sources of stress, 223

educational model, Hodges' and Cooper's model of consultation, 177

educational psychology, 3

Edwards Personal Preference Schedule, 166

ego psychology, 44, 50

epistemic differential, 34–36

establishment stage of career development, 88

ethical issues:
  codes, 267–286
  committees, 238
  confidentiality, 252–253
  in forensic psychology, 249
  the helping relationship, 250–252
  malpractice, 257–262
  misrepresentation, 255–257
  standards, 241–242
  training, 237, 247–248
  working for an organization, 248–250

Ethical Principles of Psychologists (APA), 243, 267–275

ethics:
  committees, 238
  in counseling psychology, 239
  defined, 240
  distinguished from law, 242–243

forensic psychology, 189, 190–191
  and public policy, 239–241
  in testing, 155
  self-regulation, 241
  (*see also* ethical issues; professional ethics)

ethical standards (AACD), 277–286

evaluation (*see* assessment; tests)

evaluative tests in career development, 95

existentialism, 42

existential psychology, 38, 42, 52

expert testimony, 186–187, 188–189, 190, 191, 193, 197, 198, 203, 204, 212
  effectiveness, 194
  financial arrangements, 192

explorative stage of career development, 88, 94

eyewitness testimony, psychologist's role, 211

facilitative conditions, 51, 52, 60–62, 153, 162, 228
  concreteness, 61
  congruency, 51, 61, 62
  empathy, 51, 52, 60–61, 62
  immediacy, 61
  in testing, 150–151
  unconditional positive regard, 51, 61, 62

families, dual-career, 101

family:
  alignments, 133
  boundaries, 133, 137–138
  concepts, 132
  functioning, 133–134
  interventions (*see* interventions, family therapy)
  role in health psychology, 230–231
  sculpting, 146
  strengths, 139
  subsystems, 132–133
  triangles, 141

family law, 204–208
  best interests of the child, 204
  joint custody, 205–206
  shared parental responsibility, 206

family-life chronology, 145

family-of-origin approach, 139–143
  change, 143
  differentiation, 140
  emotional cutoff, 140–141
  family concepts, 139–141
  genograms, 142–143
  interventions, 141–143

family-of-origin approach (*continued*):
triangles, 141
family systems theory, 129–131
cybernetic model, 130
evolutionary model, 130
organization, 130–131
patterning, 130–131
wholeness, 130–131
family therapists and ethics, 247–248
family therapy:
approaches to, 131–147
counseling, 204
development, 128–129
and health psychology, 230–231
interventions (*see* interventions,
family therapy)
techniques, 135–139, 141–143,
146–147
Florida Psychological Association:
ethics and the law, 243
Florida statutes, 206
forensic psychology:
assessment, 188
consultation, 187
diagnosis, treatment and recommendations, 187
functions, 187
other, 187
free will, 38–39
frustration/aggression hypothesis, 222

gender roles/issues in therapy, 75–76
General Aptitude Test Battery, 23
genogram, 142–143
symbols, 136
goals:
group counseling, 109–110
health, 220–221
Greystone Conference, 14
group leadership:
characteristics of, 114
functions, 114–115
stages of, 115
groups, types of:
counseling, 109
encounter, 52, 108
T groups, 108–109
therapy, 109
groups/group counseling:
atmosphere, 111
characteristics, 107
cohesiveness, 111, 121–122
commitment to, 122
conflict/confrontation stage,
120–121
dynamics, 109

encounter, 52, 108
goals, 109–110
homogeneity/heterogeneity, 111
initiating, 118–119
intervention, in career development, 96–97
leadership, 113–115
membership, 111–112
norms, 110–111
preparation stage, 116–118
process, 120
productive stage, 123–124
roles, 113–115
stages, 115–125
termination stage, 124–125
types, 108–109
group stages:
cohesiveness stage, 121–122
commitment to process, 122
conflict/confrontation, 120–121
members leadership roles,
120–121
resistance, 121
initiating the group, 118–120
leadership in initiation stages,
119
process engagement, 120
the undifferentiated mass,
118–119
preparing for, 116–118
duration, 117
open versus closed, 117
preparation interview, 117–118
selection, 116–117
size, 116
productiveness, 123–124
corrective emotional experience,
123–124
termination, 124–125
growth stage of career development,
87–88
guidance, vocational, 3, 9, 19–20, 22,
92, 103, 150, 217
guidelines for body/mind health,
227–228
"guilty but mentally ill," 197

Head Start, 24
health, goals of, 220–221
health psychology:
clinical activities, 219
defined, 219
future of, 233
role of the community, 231–232
role of the family, 230–231
healthy lifestyle, achievement of, 221

helper:
  historical role, 1, 33
  motives of, 1–2
helping relationship:
  transference and counter-
    transference, 251–252
  ethical principles, 250–252
  and the law, 250–252
  organization/client conflict, 249
  (*see also* countertransference;
    transference)
helplessness, 220
history:
  assessment, 150–151
  of consultation, 171
  economic forces, 6, 21
  mental health movement, 3–4
  public policy, 20
  psychometric movement, 4
  social forces, 6
  vocational guidance movement, 2–3
Hodges' and Cooper's models of consultation, 177
holistic approach to diagnosis, 159
house-tree-person, 166
human beings, nature of, 36–38
human development, 3, 12, 43–45
human development, meta-theory
  model of consultation, 178
humanism, 37, 42, 44–45, 50–52
humankind, image of, 36–38
human services psychology, 16

ideal self, 62
identified patient, 131
immediacy, 85
individual intervention in career
  development, 95–96
individual process model, Hodges' and
  Cooper's model of consultation,
  177
industrial psychology, 13, 218
industry, career development in,
  99–100
influences on the therapeutic
  relationship:
  cross-cultural counseling, 76, 78
  expertness, 72, 73
  gender roles, 75–76
  interpersonal attractiveness, 74–75
  trustworthiness, 73–74
informed consent:
  elements of, 261
  legal safeguards, 262
initial contact stage, consultation, procedures of, 179–180

initiating stage of group counseling,
  118–120
  engagement in the process, 120
  leadership roles, 119
  undifferentiated mass, 118–119
insanity, as a defense, 196–198
  legal definitions, 196–197
  legislation, 197
institutional mental patients, 201–203
instruments in career development,
  94–95 (*see also* tests)
interest tests, in career development,
  95
internalization of the alliance process,
  58
  components, 58–59
interventions, career development,
  92–97
  assessment, 94–95
  groups, 96–97
  individual, 95–96
interventions, family therapy:
  challenging the family reality,
    138–139
  challenging the family structure,
    137–138
    boundary making, 137–138
    complementarity, 138
    unbalancing, 138
  challenging the family system,
    137–138
  communications approach, 146–147
  genogram, 142–143
  family of origin, 141–143
  paradoxes, 138–139
  reframing, 137
  role playing, 146
  sculpting, 146
  structural approach, 135–139
intervention stage, consultation, procedures of, 181–182
involuntary commitment:
  criteria for mental patients,
    202–203

Job Corps, 24
job satisfaction, 84, 86, 95, 100
Joint Commission on Mental Illness
  and Health, 171
Journal of Counseling Psychology, 12
jury selection, psychologist's role,
  210–211
juvenile justice, 200–201

leadership (*see* group leadership)
least restrictive environment, 20, 25, 201

legal rights:
  of children, 246–247
  of patients, 202
legislation, 19–27
  counseling and guidance, 22
  drugs and alcohol, 26
  insanity defense, 197
  mental health, 25
  minority groups, 26
  rehabilitation, 24
leisure, 88, 91, 93
liability, 248–250, 254–255, 258
licensing statutes:
  ethics, 243–246
  Florida, 243–245
licensure, 27–28
"litigation psychologist," 211
locus of control, 220, 221, 231

mainstreaming, 25
maintenance stage of career develop-
    ment, 88, 94
malpractice, 192, 208, 212–213,
    257–262
  increase in, 257, 259
  misuse of transference, 252
  preventing/avoiding, 259–260
  reasons for increase in legal action,
    257–258
  (see also liability)
marriage counseling, 204
maturity, career, 95
MCMI, 163, 166
mechanical mirror, 44, 47
mental health movement, 3, 4
mental measurement, 3, 10
meta-theory model of consultation:
  human development model, 178
  scientific technological model, 178
  social/political model, 179
Michigan Statutes, annotated, (1980),
    204
Millon Clinical Multiaxial Inventory
    (MCMI), 163, 166
Minnesota Employment Stabilization
    Research Institute, 22
Minnesota Multiphasic Personality In-
    ventory (MMPI), 161–162, 163,
    165, 166, 167
minority issues, 76, 77, 78, 79,
    101–103
  career development, 103
  clinical assessment, 155, 163
  in diagnosis, 156–157
  testing, 155
  (see also special populations)

Miranda rights, 198
misrepresentation, 255–257
MMPI, 161–162, 163, 165, 166, 167
M'Naghten rule, 196
Model Penal Code, 196–197
monitoring tests, use in career
    development, 95
moral growth, work and, 85–86
morality, 238–241
  criminal issues, 196
  definitions, 238–239
  (see also ethical issues)
motivation, and work, 91, 97
multicultural counseling (see cross-
    cultural counseling)

National Defense Education Act of
    1958, 13, 23, 24
National Institute of Mental Health,
    25, 129
National Occupational Conference, 22
National Register of Health Service
    Providers, 27
National Vocational Guidance Associa-
    tion, 3, 6, 8, 22
neo-Freudian (neo-psychoanalytic), 41,
    50
nondirective counseling, 5
  assessment, 151–153
"normality," 157
  differentiating from pathology,
    156–159
norms in group counseling, 110–111
"narrowed" instruments, 94

paradoxes, 138–139
parole, counseling during, 200
Parson's Meyer's models of consulta-
    tion, 176–177
pathology:
  categories, DSM III, 156
  diagnosis, 156
  patterns, 157–158
personal-injury law, 208–213
  counselor negligence, 212–213
  damages, 210
  negligence, 208, 209–210
  role of counseling psychologist,
    210–212
personality patterns, 157–158
  inventories and career development, 95
  objective tests of, 163–167
  projective tests of, 162–167
  psychology of, 3
  theories and career development,
    90–91

(*see also* assessment)
personality research form, 166
personnel selection, 84
philosophical value systems, 40–45
  culturalism, 41–42
  humanism, 42
  implications for human develop-
    ment, 43–45
    behavioral approaches, 44
    humanistic viewpoints, 44–45
    psychodynamic, 43–44
  naturalism, 41
  theism, 42–43
physical disability, 9, 11, 21, 101–103,
    211, 212 (*see also* special
    populations)
plateauing, career, 100
predictive tests, and career develop-
    ment, 95
pre-entry state, consultation, pro-
    cedures of, 179
preparation stage, group counseling,
    116–118
  duration, 117
  open versus closed, 117
  preparation interview, 117–118
  selection, 116–117
  size, 116
President's Commission on Law En-
    forcement and Administration of
    Justice, 200
privileged communication, 190–191,
    252–255
  defined, 252–253
  (*see also* confidentiality)
process engagement, group counsel-
    ing, 120
process model of consultation
    (Schein's), 175
  catalyst version, 175
  facilitator version, 175
productiveness stage, group counsel-
    ing, 123–124
  corrective emotional experience,
    123–124
professional ethics, 237–242
  confidentiality, 252–255
  ethical standards, 241–242
  law, 242–262
  morality and ethics, 238–241
  in organizations, 248–250
  public policy, 239–241
  training and research, 247–248
  (*see also,* ethical issues; ethics)
professionalism:
  defined, 237

monitoring, 238
psychoanalysis, 37, 41
psychodynamic approach, 43–44,
    48–50
Psychological Corporation, 8
psychologist as a mediator, 207–208
psychometric movement, 4, 23
psychosomatic disorders, 224, 225
psychotherapy classification systems,
    45–46
public policy, 188, 191, 198, 200, 208,
    211, 212, 231, 232
  child abuse, 247
  ethics and, 239–241
  future, 26–27
  legal rights for children, 246–247
  origins, 20–21
  societal versus client rights, 249
punishment in the legal system, 195

rationalism, 41
real self, 62
recommendations, forensic
    psychology, 187
reframing process, family therapy, 137
  enactment, 137
  focusing, 137
  intensity, 137
registry, 27
rehabilitation, 101–102
  counseling, 212
  counselors, 102
Rehabilitation Division for Disabled
    Soldiers, 24
rehabilitation psychology, 6, 10–11
Rehabilitation Services Administration,
    25
relationship, of the counseling
    psychologist:
  and the attorney, 189–191
  and the police, 199
relationship, therapeutic:
  components, 56–60
  countertransference, 57, 65–67,
    250–252
  establishing, 60–62
  internalization, 58
  and the law, 250–252
  process, 56–60
  "real," 57
  resistance, 67, 68
  skills, 60–62
  transference, 56–57, 59, 64–65
  working alliance, 56
  (*see also* therapeutic alliance)
religion, 42, 43

resistance:
    to changing unhealthy behaviors,
        221–222
    in group therapy, 121
    in therapy, 67–68
retirement, 88
right to treatment, 201
risk taking and occupational choice,
        89
role:
    conflict, 101
    overload, 101
role of counseling psychologist:
    eyewitness testimony, 211
    jury selection, 210–211
    personal injury law, 210–212
roles, group counseling, 113–115
Rorschach, 162, 164, 165, 166
"rules of evidence," 188

school:
    career development, 92, 97–99
    counselors, 97
    psychology, 218
schizophrenia, 129
scientific technological model, meta-
        theory model of consultation,
        178
SCORE formula, the, 228–229
sculpture, family, 146
self-actualization, 42, 50–51, 52, 221,
        223
self-concept, in career development,
        93
self-disclosure, 40, 63–64, 76
self-esteem, 59
self-involving statements, 64
self-theory, 38
Sentence Completion Test, 166
Sixteen Personality Factor Question-
        naire (16PF), 163
social factors in therapy:
    cross-cultural, 76–79
    expertness, 72–73
    gender roles, 75–76
    interpersonal attractiveness, 74–75
    trustworthiness, 73–74
social learning, 47, 89
    social/political model, meta theory
        model of consultation, 179
    triadic model of consultation, 177
sociological theories, and career
        development, 90
special populations:
    assessment, 155, 163
    delinquent, 21

diagnostic issues, 156–157
disabled veterans, 24–25
handicapped, 9, 21
physically impaired, 11, 101–103,
        211–212
(*see also* cross-cultural counseling;
        minority issues)
stages in group counseling:
    cohesiveness, 121–122
    conflict/confrontation, 120–121
    initiating, 118–120
    preparation, 116–118
    productive, 123–124
    termination, 124–125
"standard of care," 213, 241, 259
"statute of limitations," 209
stereotypes, and career development, 101
stress:
    dealing with, 222–227
    definition, 222, 227
    economic sources of, 223
    environmental sources of, 222–223
    physiology of, 223–224
    management, 227
    marital status and, 223
    results of, 224–227
structural approach to family therapy,
        132–139
    diagnosis, 134–135
    family alignments, 133
    family boundaries, 133
    family concepts, 132–134
    family functioning, 133–134
    interventions, 135–139
    mapping symbols, 136
    subsystems, 132–133
structure of group therapy, 110
systematic approach, to the commu-
        nity, 232
systematic desensitization, 47

techniques, counseling (*see* com-
        munication techniques;
        therapeutic skills)
techniques, family therapy, 135–139,
        141–143, 146–147
temperament inventories, in career
        development, 95
termination, group therapy, 124–125
termination stage, consultation, pro-
        cedures of, 182–183
testing (*see* assessment)
tests, use in career development,
        94–95
    ability test, 95
    achievement tests, 95

aptitude tests, 95
evaluative tests, 95
interest inventories, 95
of job satisfaction, 95
monitoring tests, 95
narrowed, 94
personality inventories, 95
predictive tests, 95
temperament inventories, 95
value inventories, 95
wide-based, 94
tests, use in counseling, 153–154,
160–161
Bender-Visual-Motor Gestalt Test,
165, 166
California Psychological Inventory
(CPI), 166
Children's Apperception Test (CAT),
166
Draw-A-Person (DAP), 166
Edward's Personal Preference
Schedule, 166
House-Tree-Person (HTP), 166
Millon Clinical Multiaxial Inventory
(MCMI), 163, 166
Minnesota Multiphasic Personality
Inventory (MMPI), 161–162, 163,
165, 166, 167
Personality Research Form, 166
Rorschach, 162, 164, 165, 166
Sentence Completion Test, 166
Sixteen Personality Factor Question-
naire (16PF), 163
Thematic Apperception Test (TAT),
164, 165, 166
Weschler Adult Intelligence Scale
(WAIS), 165
Weschler Intelligence Scale for
Children (WISC), 165
Thematic Apperception Test (TAT),
164, 165, 166
theory:
development/career, 6, 86–88, 92, 98
eclecticism, 55–56
family systems, 129–131
therapeutic alliance, 56, 57–60
bonds, 58
characteristics, 60
internalization process, 58–59
mutual goals, 57
tasks, 57
therapeutic relationship (*see* relationship, therapeutic)
therapeutic skills:
ambiguity, use of, 63
communication techniques, 69–72

confrontation, 61, 68–69
countertransference, use of, 66–67,
251–252
facilitative conditions, 60–62
self-disclosure, use of, 63–64
transference, use of, 64–66,
251–252
therapist, use of self, 146
training:
counselor, 252
ethical, 237, 247–248
multi-cultural issues, 155
specialization, 256–257
use of transference and countertransference, 251–252
trait and factor theories, and development, 88, 89
transference, 48, 50, 56–57, 59,
64–65, 250–252
treatment, forensic psychology, 187
"true reasoning," 88
type A and type B behavior patterns,
226
types of counseling groups, 108–
109

unconditional positive regard, 51, 61,
62
unconscious, 37, 44, 48, 49
United States Employment Service,
23
U.S. Public Health Service, 225
U.S. Public Law, 198–199
utility theory, 89

value inventories, use in career
development, 95
value orientations, 39–40
values, 32–33, 34, 35–36, 39–40, 43,
47
and career development, 93, 98
Veterans Administration, 6, 7, 11, 13,
21, 24, 25, 208
Vista, 24
vocational development theory, 6,
86–88, 92, 98 (*see also* career
development)
vocational guidance, 3, 9, 19–20, 22,
92, 103, 150, 217
vocational psychology, 3, 9–11, 22,
23, 84, 97, 101, 103
vocational rehabilitation, 11, 13, 22,
24–25
Vocational Rehabilitation Administration, 25

waiver of rights, 198
Weschler Adult Intelligence Scale
      (WAIS), 165
Weschler Intelligence Scale for
      Children (WISC), 165
wide-based instruments, 94–95
women, and career development, 101
work:
    ethic, 84, 85

personality, 102
role of, 84–86
Workers' Compensation Program, 208
working alliance (*see* therapeutic
      alliance)
"worried well," 224

Yale Conference on Behavioral
      Medicine, 218–219